Python for Rookies

Python for Rookies

A First Course in Programming

**Sarah Mount, James Shuttleworth and
Russel Winder**

CENGAGE
Learning·

Australia • Brazil • Japan • Korea • Mexico • Singapore • Spain • United Kingdom • United States

Python for Rookies, First Edition

Sarah Mount, James Shuttleworth
and Russel Winder

For product information and technology assistance,
contact **emea.info@cengage.com**.

For permission to use material from this text or product,
and for permission queries, email
emea.permissions@cengage.com.

British Library Cataloguing-in-Publication Data
A catalogue record for this book is available from the
British Library.

ISBN: 978-1-84480-701-7

Cengage Learning EMEA
Cheriton House, North Way, Andover, Hampshire, SP10
5BE United Kingdom

Cengage Learning products are represented in Canada by
Nelson Education Ltd.

For your lifelong learning solutions, visit
www.cengage.co.uk

Purchase your next print book, e-book or e-chapter at
www.cengagebrain.com

Printed in the UK by Lightning Source
1 2 3 4 5 6 7 8 9 10 – 13 12

Brief Contents

Contents

7 Inheriting Class   217

8 Filing Things Away   255

9 Testing, Testing   281

10 Algorithms and Data Structures   313

Preface

Why Learn to Program?

Many people ask the question "Why bother to learn to program when you can use a computer just by pointing and clicking on the desktop icons?" Well, if the software we buy and install on our computer does all that we need, then we don't need to learn to program at all. However, 'off the shelf' software doesn't always do everything that we need it to – 'off the shelf' software restricts us to the features that some programmer has decided are the ones we want. Also, often, we need to do things for which there is no ready-made software. In both of these case, we must choose one of the following options:

1. Do not actually do what we wanted or needed to do.

2. Find some way not involving a computer to do whatever we wanted or needed to do.

3. Write our own software.

Option 3 requires us to do some programming.

An example: image manipulation software, such as Photoshop or GIMP, has a vast array of effects that can be applied to an image. Effects are provided by 'plug-ins' that are just bits of software. For a given effect, the plug-in may already be installed, it may be downloadable and installable, or it may not exist. In the last case, assuming we cannot achieve the effect we want by combining effects we do have or can get, we need to write a new plug-in.

So, even if we are graphics professionals, if we are using software to do our work, then it is important to be able to program: to be *really* in control of our computer, we need to be able write our own software. Not only will we be able to extend systems such as Photoshop and GIMP, we will be able to develop new programs from scratch.

In the computing industry itself, programming is effectively an essential skill: any job in the industry involves some programming. Having a good grasp of the fundamental concepts of programming languages and systems, as well as the facilities of one or more languages, will give you a head start in terms of employability.

So the answer to the question "Why bother to learn to program when you can use a computer just by pointing and clicking on the desktop icons?" is that you cannot just point and click, there are always situations in which you need to do it yourself.

Why Python?

Why choose Python as the programming language with which to learn programming? The answer to this question has many aspects.

Python is Easy to Learn

Python is based on a programming language called ABC that was specifically developed to be easy to learn and understand. As Python has developed to become an industrial strength language, its creator, Guido van Rossum, has gone to great lengths to make sure that the language remains as easy to learn and use as possible. Programmers often describe the way Python code looks as 'clean' and 'simple', which should mean that you'll be able to pick it up quickly – we believe more quickly than other languages – and hence able to write quite sophisticated programs early in your learning.

When Python was first born, it was always hoped that it would become a language widely used in education. For that reason, Python has a lot of built-in support for learners – especially the turtle graphics module that you will meet in Chapter 1 of this book.

Python is a Real Language

Python is a language on the rise. More and more people are 'discovering' Python.

Python is Used in Different Sorts of Applications

Mustafa Thamer of Firaxis Games, talking about Civilization IV. Quoted on page 18 of the August 2005 Game Developer Magazine, http://www.gdmag.com/

"Like XML, scripting was extremely useful as both a mod tool and an internal development tool. If you don't have any need to expose code and algorithms in a simple and safe way to others, you can argue that providing a scripting language is not worth the effort. However, if you do have that need, as we did, scripting is a no brainer, and it makes complete sense to use a powerful, documented, cross-platform standard such as Python.

Python, like many good technologies, soon spreads virally throughout your development team and finds its way into all sorts of applications and tools. In other words, Python begins to feel like a big hammer and coding tasks look like nails."

Python is capable of implementing pretty much any sort of program you might wish to write. It is used in Web applications, scientific programming, business applications, image processing, games, database programming and probably anything else you can think of. The number of useful things you can do quickly with Python seems to be expanding all the time, as more and more people and companies are using the language.

Python has Fantastic Library Support and an Active User Community

> *"I have the students learn Python in our undergraduate and graduate Semantic Web courses. Why? Because basically there's nothing else with the flexibility and as many Web libraries."*

Prof. James A. Hendler, University of Maryland

Python has fantastic online support, in the form of documentation, tutorials and even books, so learners are very well supported as they learn.

Python is Increasingly Used in Industry

> *"Python has been an important part of Google since the beginning, and remains so as the system grows and evolves. Today dozens of Google engineers use Python, and we're looking for more people with skills in this language."*

Peter Norvig, Director of Search Quality at Google, Inc.

> *"NASA is using Python to implement a CAD/CAE/PDM repository and model management, integration, and transformation system which will be the core infrastructure for its next generation collaborative engineering environment. We chose Python because it provides maximum productivity, code that's clear and easy to maintain, strong and extensive (and growing!) libraries, and excellent capabilities for integration with other applications on any platform. All of these characteristics are essential for building efficient, flexible, scalable, and well-integrated systems, which is exactly what we need. Python has met or exceeded every requirement we've had."*

Steve Waterbury, Software Group Leader, NASA STEP Testbed.

A large number of jobs these days require some programming skills – even writing a spreadsheet is a form of programming. System administration, system analysis, programming (!), online content creation and games development all require programming skills of some sort. Animation also often requires some scripting and many graphics and animation packages now come with scripting capabilities built-in. Python is one of the main languages used in all these areas, so learning to program using Python is practical, not just academic.

Python Runs on Many Platforms

Python can run on (almost) any computing platform. PCs running Linux, PCs running Windows, Macs, all have the ability to run programs written in Python. Even mobile phones can run Python. Nokia, for example, supports Python on some of their phones. For most phones that do no not have Python "out of the box", it can be downloaded.

Python is Free!

Python is free in two senses. Firstly, you don't have to pay any money to get it. You can download as many copies of Python as you like from http://www.python.org/download/. Secondly, Python is *free software*, which means that anyone can get the Python source code, improve it and distribute it to anyone who wants a copy. This means that thousands of developers around the globe have been able to improve the Python language and environment, which is partly why the language is so robust, well-written and popular. You can read more about free software on the Free Software Foundation's website http://www.fsf.org.

Python, yes, but. . .

Programming languages tend to rise and fall in popularity. Python is on the way up, but at some point it will be overtaken by the Next Big Thing. So, although we think Python is a great language to work with and a great language for teaching and learning programming, in this book we deal as much with programming in general as Python in particular. In fact, most people can and should go on to study other languages, such as Java, Ruby, C++, etc. Having learnt one language, learning other languages makes you a better programmer in both languages. Indeed being able to program in four or five different types of programming language not only makes learning new languages easier, it also makes you a better programmer in all the languages. People who have, and maintain, the skill of learning new languages stay employed much longer than those people who learn a single language and have difficulty retraining.

So, Python is a great first language, but there are others, and they should be learnt.

The Coventry Perspective

In 2005 a decision was taken that Python would be the language used for introductory programming modules taught by the Creative Computing Department at Coventry University. Coventry University is not the only university to make this switch – a number of high-profile universities world wide have made the switch, and many others are actively considering it. It is becoming an increasingly popular trend.

This book evolved out of the lecture notes for the modules taught to students in 2005–6 on a wide range of degree courses, including Creative Computing, Mathematics, Business and Information Technology, and Computer Science. The different courses use the material at different speeds. For the courses in which most of the students are studying computer science (either as a major or minor) the speed can, and should be, reasonably rapid. For courses in which most of the students are simply studying programming as a tool for use in some other discipline, e.g. graphic artists working with digital media, the material usually needs to be taken more slowly and some of the computer science details skipped, or simply alluded to in passing.

Our experience of using Python in the class room has convinced us that its simplicity of style and powerful built-in modules make it ideal as an introductory language. Students are motivated by being able to write engaging and useful programs early on and our students are able to successfully construct their own arcade games by the end of the year. One module showed a 25% increase in engagement compared to it's Java-based predecessor, which we attribute to the change in language. One of the great advantages of using a language such as Python is that simple programs can be written without any of the "scaffolding" that languages such as Java require. We have found that many students are de-motivated when they find that their first "Hello world!" program is one that they will not be able to properly understand until the end of the module. With Python, not only can students write interesting programs early in their studies, they can also understand them!

No matter what the reason for studying programming, learning outcomes of the courses mean that students should, at successful completion, be able to:

1. Design and implement interactive programs using appropriate linguistic features of Python.

2. Demonstrate an understanding of both imperative and object-oriented features and know when it is appropriate to use each.

3. Write programs that make use of external libraries and APIs.

4. Specify the functionality of an algorithm (for example, formally by stating its pre- and post-conditions or informally, by describing it in English).

5. Employ various facilities for data abstraction and encapsulation.

Almost all of the introductory programming modules at Coventry are assessed by coursework only – the exception being weighted 50% examination, 50% coursework. This seems appropriate for a subject which is largely practical at introductory level. We take the view that programming is best learned by frequent practice which is regularly and formatively assessed.

Coursework for us means the creation of a portfolio of work, comprising answers to various problems and exercises set and answered during the course – the exercises we have at the end of each chapter are fairly typical of those used in our courses. Ideally, this portfolio follows the student through their course of study and becomes an impressive body of work which can be shown to potential employers. Some practical programming work is undertaken in supervised laboratory sessions ('Studios' in Coventry University parlance) and some is undertaken in the student's own time. Work is signed off weekly by the student's tutor and entered into the portfolio – this is the point at which the tutor can make checks that the work presented for the portfolio is actually the student's own work.

To give a feel for the student's capabilities at the end of a course, we expect the following:

- For a pass mark ($\geq 40\%$), a student should be able to:

  - Use appropriate Python language structures to implement a formally or informally specified algorithm.

  - Specify an algorithm both formally and informally.

  - Test a program and note where it may be deficient.

  - Appreciate that some of Python's language features can be used to create equivalent code (e.g. for loops and while loops can both be used to implement iteration). Be able to translate programs using one language feature into those using an equivalent feature (e.g. translate a for loop into an equivalent while loop and vice versa.

- For a first class mark ($\geq 70\%$), a student should be able to:

  - Consider several possible choices for the design and implementation of an algorithm.

  - Make defensible choices about which of Python's facilities for encapsulation (functions, modules, classes, etc.) to use.

– Improve a program, having tested it.

– Determine which of an API's facilities to use to perform a given task, based on the professional documentation for that API.

– Write programs that take into account the needs of users. For example, it should be clear to users of an arcade game how the game controls work.

On a twelve week module (with two hours of lectures per week) we generally start a course with the following expected schedule:

Week 1 Getting Started and Python Basics.

Week 2 Boolean Algebra and Choice.

Week 3 Repetition: Recursion.

Week 4 Repetition: Iteration and State.

Week 5 Compound Types.

Week 6 Searching and Sorting.

Week 7 Functions and Modules.

Week 8 Input / Output and Object-Oriented Programming.

Week 9 Object-Oriented Programming.

Week 10 Python Extensions (e.g.GUIs and arcade games).

Week 11 Python Extensions (continued. . .).

However, we feel it is important to devote as much time as needed to each topic so that students fully understand the material. This means we have to be prepared to rearrange the schedule as needed for a given set of students: not only is Python a dynamically bound language, our courses are dynamically bound as well.

We find that a good way of working for each part of the syllabus is for students to:

• Read from specified sections of the book before the lecture on a given part of the syllabus.

• Attend the (short) lecture associated with the material.

• Attend the practical following the lecture (which actually takes up most of the contact time) and focus on writing programs using not only the material of the current lecture but also all previous material.

• Follow up by using Self-review and other exercises to consolidate and build upon classroom learning.

New material always needs to be dealt with in the context of previous material – it is not the new material that is important in itself, but how it relates and integrates with material already covered.

Although the courses at Coventry University have a particular structure to them we have not simply copied this structure for the book. The basic flow of material is the same but the chapter structure of the book is not exactly the expected weekly structure of the Coventry University courses. There are two main reasons for this:

1. We wanted the book to be widely applicable at many universities, so we have created a book rather than a set of course notes. We believe that the structure here is strong, and applicable to a large number of courses, making it an excellent course text.

2. We wanted to ensure that the book worked independently of lectures and coursework. We wanted students to be able to work through the book either as a course text or independently as self-study.

Throughout the book, we avoid having to say "This works, but we won't tell you how or why till later" – we think this sort of thing makes programming much harder to learn. In fact, this is one of the reasons why we chose to use Python – it's much easier to understand as a beginner programmer than languages such as C, C++ and Java. We do have forward and backward references to material in the book but this is not to hide explanation, it is to create an appropriate connection of ideas: earlier coverage points forward to more detailed later coverage. The point here is to provide all the pointers and signposts for connected material. There is definitely a direction to the material in the book, so it is important that earlier chapters are read before later chapters.

The Learner Perspective

Whether or not you are studying on your own or with a teacher, you should be able to use this book to guide you through the fundamental ideas and techniques of programming. Programming is essentially a practical skill and we encourage you to spend as much time as possible reading and writing code and putting into practice the ideas you are learning.

Each chapter has self-review questions at the end to help you check that you have understood the things we believe you should have learnt by reading the chapter. Also there are exercises and challenges to give some problems that require programs to solve. What is the difference between an exercise and a challenge? The exercises should be completable based on material from the book and the online material that comes with the Python system. The challenges usually require extra research to find facts and algorithms – they are more complicated problems to solve and program.

There is a glossary at the end of the book – something we think is very important to include. Learning programming requires you to know a lot of jargon and it is important that when you meet other software developers (especially at work!) that you can talk to them in a appropriate and professional way. If you find yourself reading through a chapter and getting confused by some of the jargon, just turn to the glossary for an explanation.

Answers to a selection of the self-review questions, exercises and challenges can be found on the website for the book at http://pythonforrookies.org.

The following is a rough guide to what's in each chapter:

Getting Started Here we find out how to run Python programs and, using the Turtle module, draw some diagrams on the screen.

The Fundamentals Here we learn some of the basic concepts of programming and programming languages. In particular, we will learn about expressions, statements, commands, literals, variables and types. These will all be restudied in more detail in later chapters, but here we will learn enough to get started writing real programs.

Controlling the Flow In this chapter we focus on procedure calls, if statements and while statements, i.e. the techniques for managing flow control in a program. We start by introducing the Boolean type and how to use values, variables and expressions of Boolean type. Concepts such as recursion and iteration form the bulk this chapter. We also learn how to use recursion to draw fractal curves like this one:

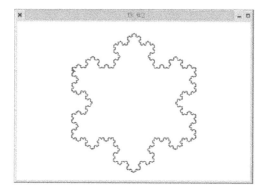

Structuring State This chapter is all about controlling the information stored in your programs. We will learn how to represent and process complex pieces of data in Python.

Functionally Modular Functions and modules are two of the basic building blocks of Python, along with objects, which are covered in the following two chapters. We have met functions in an earlier chapter: here we learn much more about them. Also we learn more about professional programming practice, including how to usefully document your programs, and how to write code for other programmers to use.

Classy Objects Object-oriented programming gained enormous popularity in the 1990s and has become a *de facto* standard in industry. In this chapter we discover how Python supports object-oriented programming. In fact, this is the first of a pair of chapters: this chapter covers classes and objects, and then there is...

Inheriting Class ...the follow-on where we learn about inheritance and how it is used to manage code.

Filing Things Away Most useful programs read data in from somewhere (a file, the keyboard, the Internet, ...) and produce some output (in a file, on the screen, etc.). In this chapter, we learn about how to do input and output to files so the data have a permanency.

Testing, Testing Here we learn about how to really test our programs and about a way of programming called Test-Driven Development (TDD) which provably cuts the number of problems in our programs, makes programming quicker, and (most importantly) even more fun.

Algorithms and Data Structures Programming is all about *algorithms* – ways of solving problems. Algorithms to search and sort data are among the most fundamental in computer science. Here, we learn about the most useful algorithms for searching and sorting, how to compare their efficiency (using 'Big O notation') and how to implement them in Python.

Threading the Code Here we find out how a program can do more than one thing at once, something that is generally far more useful than you think.

The Life of the Game An example bringing together all the strands of the book: functions, classes, methods, GUIs, events, threads.

PyGames A couple of examples of using the PyGame package to create computer games. This is again integrating material, showing how all the elements of Python programming can be brought to bear creating fun applications.

Appendices There are some appendices which present things that we thought ought to be in the book but didn't fit in the flow. One of the appendices is a glossary of terms: a place to look if you need to check the meaning of a jargon term.

Index At the end of the book there is an index to provide quick and ready access to information about a particular concept (or Python keyword) covered in the book.

Conventions used in this book

To help you find your way around this book, we have adopted a number of conventions.

Fonts

This book uses the following fonts:

- *Italic* is used to introduce new words.

- This font is used for Python code (both as displays and when items are used in the text, for example Python keywords).

Figures

Small figures that are only referred to once are placed in the text and have no caption. Larger figures, and figures that are referred to more than once in the text, appear at the bottom of the page on which they are first referenced or on the following page. These figures have a number and a caption in the margin.

Grey boxes

Grey boxes contain information which we think you should know, but which are not part of the main flow of the text.

> *An Example Aside*
> An aside looks like this.

Marginal Notes

This is a marginal note.

We use marginal notes as asides. Most of these are to reinforce a point being made in the main text or in a program. Some though are to make interesting points that arise related the text but not really anything to do with it.

Odds and Ends

Python is reputedly named after the title of the television show *Monty Python's Flying Circus*. Perhaps at some point we should ask Guido van Rossum (the originator of Python) if this is actually true.

The term 'Pythonesque' is invariably reserved for being in the way or style of Monty Python's Flying Circus. The word used to describe something being done in a way that is idiomatic in Python is 'Pythonic'.

At the ACCU 2003 conference in Oxford, Gaynor Redvers-Mutton organized a debate on whether C++ or Java is the better language for teaching programming. Francis Glassborow spoke for C++ – he was just finishing his book *You Can Do It!: A Beginners Introduction to Computer Programming* which uses C++ as a language for teaching (not computer science students, but everyone else). Russel Winder spoke for Java – he was just starting to work on the third edition of *Developing Java Software* (which is intended as a first programming text for anyone interested in programming). Actually Russel didn't speak for Java, he spoke for Python – Russel believes that Java should be learnt, but only after Python. Unplanned, Guido van Rossum was in the audience, and was most pleased at this unexpected turn of events.

Although James works at Coventry University, we have avoided any and all references to "Being sent to Coventry" and Lady Godiva in this book.

Pythons the life forms (i.e. snakes) are not poisonous, they kill prey by constricting them – pythons are related to boa constrictors. Python the programming language is definitely not poisonous, but neither does it constrict – unlike some other programming languages, which we shall not name to avoid embarrassing them.

Acknowledgements

This book was inspired from the set of lecture notes written by Sarah and James for the first cohort of Creative Computing and Multimedia students in the Creative Computing Department at Coventry University. The approach taken was a departure from the widely used objects-first, Java-based approach that had previously been adopted, and early versions of the notes benefited from discussions with colleagues in the Department and feedback from the 2005–6 students who were the first at Coventry University to be taught Python as their first programming language.

Sarah and James are particularly grateful to Professor Bob Newman for providing direction, encouragement and support for this work, especially at its inception. Sarah would also like to thank John for reading draft chapters of the early notes, generating vast quantities of coffee, putting up with late nights of writing and providing endless love and support.

James would like to thank: Steph, for constant encouragement and not minding the many evening hours spent at his desk while the first incarnation of this book was being brought into existence; Sam, for sleeping eight hours a night; and Jasmine for keeping his feet warm.

Russel would like to thank Dan Alderman, Ross Burton, Dan Tallis, Thomas Guest, Peter Dzwig and Graham Roberts for sorting out lots of stuff, some of which was trivial, and most of which was not. And, of course, Geri Winder for love, support, and general shoving to ensure that the book actually got finished.

All three authors would like to thank Gaynor Redvers-Mutton and her helpers Charlotte Loveridge (in the early days), Matthew Lane (later on), and Leonora Dawson-Bowling (during production) for actually getting the book published. Also thanks to Steve Rickaby for giving the book a good copy edit before it went to press.

Gaynor got three anonymous reviewers to provide feedback on an early draft of (a significant chunk of) the book. Actually one of them isn't anonymous to us, but to preserve a general air of mystery regarding reviewing, we won't name that person. Some of the comments made by the reviewers were spot on, some were a little unfair, as they were seeing an early draft of the material. All the comments though were constructive and very helpful in improving the book. Many thanks to all three.

Final Note

This book was produced using XEmacs (the text editor) and LaTeX (the typesetting system). Subversion, Convert (ImageMagick), GIMP, Evince, Epiphany and indeed many other tools were used, all managed using SCons, on computers running Ubuntu – though we also used computers running Gentoo, Fedora, Mac OS X, and Solaris. This just goes to prove that you don't have to be a slave to WYSIWYG authoring tools to get the job done in publishing.

Getting Started

Learning Outcomes

At the end of this chapter you will be able to:

- Use Python interactively.
- Evaluate arithmetic expressions using Python.
- Draw some simple pictures using the Python Turtle module.

- Create files containing Python programs and execute them.
- Import modules to be able to make use of facilities from the standard library.

These days, wherever electricity is available, there are computers. Although the term *computer* generally conjures up the idea of a desktop workstation or laptop, not all computers are that obvious. Almost all car engines now are controlled by one or more computers. Many household washing machines are controlled by a computer. From workstations and laptops, the Web, the Internet, televisions, set-top boxes, games consoles, cameras, washing machines, car engines, all the way down to smartcards, computers have become an integral and ubiquitous part of modern day living, at least in the first and second worlds.

Computers are not however complete systems in themselves: a computer by itself cannot actually do anything, it is just a lump of hardware that has potential. For a computer to be useful, it has to have programs to tell it what to do. The utility and usefulness of a computer depends entirely on the programs used: a computer is the hardware platform on which software directs the behavior of the complete system.

1.1 A Bit of Background

In the early days of computers (1940s–1950s) there were very few of them, they were used for academic, government or military purposes only and were programmed in *machine code* (the binary instruction language of a computer) or, if you were lucky, in a symbolic representation of machine code usually termed *assembly language*. Programming was hard and very few people did it.

As computers moved into the commercial world and the academics did research on how to program them (1950s–1970s), programming languages such as Lisp, Fortran, Cobol, Algol-60, etc., were created and used. The idea that people wrote programs and needed to understand them easily had taken hold. Time moved on, more research was done, and we got programming languages like Pascal, Ada, C, C++. Inventing new programming languages became something of an industry. Of the many hundreds of programming languages invented only some became popular and used. For example, TCL, Perl, Objective Caml, Prolog, Haskell, Java, Ruby and, of course, Python have gained widespread adoption. There are many similarities and differences between all these programming languages and the histories of them and the inter-relationships between them are very interesting. For the moment, we only want to look at two particular issues (we will address many of the other issues as we go through the book).

1. When we write programs, we use a textual representation. Computers cannot understand the programs we write directly, they have to be translated (the official term is *compiled*) into a form the computer can work with. Programming languages like C, C++, etc. require programs to be compiled to the machine code of the computer on which the program is to be executed. Programming languages like Java, and, most importantly for this book, Python, use a *virtual machine*. A virtual machine is an idealized computer for executing programs. The *statements* of programs written in virtual-machine-based programming language are compiled into the machine language of the virtual machine, and there is then a mechanism to execute these virtual machine instructions on the real computer when the program is executed.

   > *Executing* is what a program does when you double-click on its icon using a graphical user interface, or when you type a command in a command terminal – we will say more about what 'execute' means in Section 1.2, (page 3).

   You may well be asking yourself: "Why bother with virtual machines when we have real machines?" The answer has to do with being able to execute the same program on many different computers. With a language like C++, a program has to be compiled for each architecture and operating system. With languages such as Java and Python, a program compiled on one machine can be executed on another machine without recompilation. This is not a big issue for individuals working with a single machine, but it is a huge issue for organizations which have many computers, all needing to use the same programs – using virtual-machine-based languages means they do not have to ensure that all the computers are the same in order to be able to execute the program – the virtual machine mechanism does that for them.

   > An *operating system* is the software that makes all the hardware work. Examples of operating systems are: Linux, Mac OS X, Solaris, and Windows.

2. When does compilation happen from the programmer's perspective? Programs in languages like C, C++, and Java must be compiled before they can be executed: an explicitly two stage process, compile then execute. Programs in languages like Ruby and Python can be executed directly without any prior explicit compilation step, as translation of the program occurs as needed behind the scenes.

So what does this mean for us now? 'Compile as needed' virtual-machine-based languages like Python involve significantly less hassle when creating and executing programs. This means Python programs are easier to work with than C++ or Java programs, particularly when first learning programming. Python is an (almost) ideal language for learning to program. Moreover, knowing how to program in Python is a great springboard for learning other programming languages like Ruby, Java and C++, so learning Python first really is a win–win situation.

A Note on Terminology
Programmers often talk about the *source code*, or sometimes just *code*, of a program. The terms source code and code really just mean all the statements that comprise the program in the language that the programmers are using.

1.2   Executing Programs

In computing, 'executing' is used in the sense of 'perform or carry out': executing a program means getting the computer to do what the program tells it to.

It may not be immediately obvious, but to be useful a program must, as a result of executing, do something that affects the world. It doesn't have to affect it greatly, it just has to affect it in some way. If it does not then the program serves no purpose.

Perhaps the simplest program in Python is:

```
print "Hello."
```

This has the effect, when executed, of writing something to the screen of the computer. It has affected the world in that it has presented something for the user to read. Not totally earth shattering but, after all, this is only our first program.

So what has this program shown us? Well, primarily that there are ways of outputting information for the user to read and there are ways of storing data. The print statement is the basic output action in Python and the sequence of characters enclosed in double quotes (i.e. "Hello.") is called a *string literal* or more usually just a *string*. A *literal* is a value represented directly in the programming language – the value to be used is literally what we typed in.

A competitor for the simplest Python program is:

```
print 1
```

which, when executed, outputs 1. In this program we have the integer literal 1 representing the integer value one. Comparing these two programs we see that the print statement is actually being quite clever: it works out for itself how to deal with the literal in order to print sensible things to the output.

The question on your lips is, of course: "How is the program executed?" The most immediate way of executing Python programs is to use the Python system interactively. This means starting the Python system in interactive mode and then typing the statements of your program at the Python prompt. How you do this depends on which operating system you are using.

- On Linux, Mac OS X, and Unix-like systems you type the command *python* at a command prompt and this starts the Python system in interactive mode. Of course, this assumes that Python is installed, which it is by default on almost all distributions of these operating systems. If, however, the command doesn't work on your computer, you will need to download and install Python. This is probably best achieved using the package manager for your operating system – for example: synaptic, aptitude or apt-get on Ubuntu; aptitude or apt-get on Debian; yum on Fedora or Red Hat; pkg-get or pkgadd on Solaris.

- On Windows systems, there are two possibilities:

  1. Use Cygwin, which includes Python. This works very much like the Linux and Mac OS X versions of Python – mostly because it is the same as those versions!

  2. Use the Python for Windows system. Installing this (from http://www. python.org) adds a menu entry in the start menu that has two alternate ways of running Python in interactive mode:

(a) A command prompt window with Python running. This behaves identically to the Cygwin, Linux, Mac OS X, or Unix versions of Python.

(b) An IDLE (Integrated DeveLopment Environment) window – see Figure 1.1.

IDLE is available on Linux, Mac OS X, Solaris and other Unix-like systems as well as Windows systems: just type *idle* at a command prompt – assuming IDLE is installed of course!

As the name **Integrated DeveLopment Environment** implies, IDLE is more than just a Python system running in interactive mode, it is a complete environment for developing Python programs.

We are going to avoid completely any suggestion that one of the two interactive systems is better than the other. It is really down to personal taste; some people prefer one, some the other. The important thing is to use whichever you prefer and find easier to create programs with.

For the following example, we have chosen to use Python in interactive mode running on an Ubuntu system:

```
| > python
Python 2.5.1c1 (release25-maint, Apr 12 2007, 21:00:25)
[GCC 4.1.2 (Ubuntu 4.1.2-0ubuntu4)] on linux2
Type "help", "copyright", "credits" or "license" for more information.
>>> print "Hello."
Hello.
>>>
```

The >>> is the interactive Python prompt. We typed the statement, pressed the return key and the statement was executed immediately. Note that the double quotes didn't get output. The double quotes in the program tell the Python system what the string is, they are not part of the string.

Things should look (more or less) the same whichever of the interactive versions of Python you try and certainly programs will behave the same on any Python system. This is a crucial point: Python looks and behaves the same on all computers. This sameness on all computers is one of the many benefits of using a system based on a virtual machine. Programmers can create programs in the full knowledge that the virtual machine takes care of all the differences between the actual computers being used. So we have portability of programs between different computers, exactly what we, as programmers, want.

Figure 1.1

The IDLE main window on Windows.

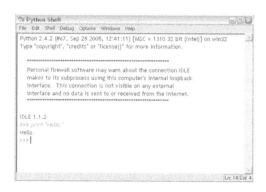

WORA Concept
Sun Microsystems use the (trademarked) phrase 'write once, run anywhere' about Java. The concept behind the phrase is as applicable to Python as it is to Java, perhaps more so.

1.3   And If Something Goes Wrong?

The two programs seen so far, being relatively simple (!), have no errors in them. Being error-free is an unusual situation for a program, but more on this later. What happens if there had been an error? The Python system would have told us so. For example, if we misspell **print** as **prin** then:

```
>>> prin 1
  File "<stdin>", line 1
    prin 1
         ^
SyntaxError: invalid syntax
>>>
```

The questions on the tip of your tongue are:

"What is *syntax*?"

and

"Why is the error at the 1 and not with the prin?"

Syntax is the way in which a statement in a language (any language, not just programming languages) is constructed.

Natural languages – languages with which humans communicate, for example English, Mandarin, Cantonese, Spanish – have syntactic rules and most speakers obey the rules. This is generally so that listeners, who assume the rules are being obeyed, can easily follow what is being said. Humans are, though, extremely good at dealing with syntactic errors in the use of language: humans use context, implicit knowledge, world knowledge and intelligence to construct a meaningful statement even in the face quite dramatic errors of syntax. It take concentration and effort, but it is done and often the meaning inferred (or guessed) is the meaning intended! Sometimes the wrong meaning is inferred and this can be the basis of much humor or the start of real, all to often violent, conflict. More usually though, visitors to a community, using a language they are not used to, can make truly awful errors in the use of the local language and yet still be able to communicate. People are good at language.

Programming languages are much, much simpler than natural languages and yet programming language compilers are usually extreme in their complete inability to deal with even the slightest divergence from the expected and allowed sequence of symbols. This is a very important point to bear in mind when programing in order to stay peaceful and sane. You have to remember that compilers are literal and, well, fundamentally stupid.

So, back to the program error. Why are we getting a syntax error in the statement:

```
prin 1
```

A nice quote, usually attributed to Richard Bornat, is: *Computers aren't stupid like an ant is stupid, computers are stupid like a brick is stupid.*

Humans who know a bit about Python will immediately say "Well **print** is spelt wrongly." However, the compiler sees the word prin but does not understand that it is a misspelling of **print**, so does not understand the word as **print** but as something else. It is only after the space when it sees the 1 that it realizes that what it is being asked to compile does not correspond with the allowed syntax of a Python statement. So it is only at the point of reading the 1 that the compiler appreciates that there is a syntax error. Compilers cannot perform any form of correction, so you get an error message and must correct the program and execute it again. This can be frustrating, but remember compilers are literal, they do not think like humans do. Actually they don't think at all!

There are two morals to this:

1. Whenever you get a syntax error, always look before as well as at the point marked to discover and understand what is wrong – it will eventually become second nature. As you get used to decoding error messages do remember that although the initial cause of the error may actually be your fault, the compiler is being very unhelpful by not deducing more about what you meant and giving sensible feedback.

2. Be patient in the face of error messages. At the risk of appearing a bit repetitive: remember, compilers are very literal and you have to do their thinking for them. Compilers are not like people when it comes to dealing with language syntax. More's the pity.

Memory

Memory in a computer is where everything gets stored during execution. It is usually measured in bytes. In the mid-1970s computers were lucky to have 16 KB of memory (16,000 bytes). In mid-2007 computers normally got delivered with at least 1 GB of memory (1,000,000,000 bytes).

1.4 Python can Calculate

Many people think of computers as just very complicated calculators, and in some sense this is true. Certainly computers know how to do their sums. For example:

> Programming languages use * rather than × for multiplication as * is on the keyboard and × is not.

```
>>> print 4 + 9
13
>>> print 4 - 9
-5
>>> print 4 * 9
36
>>> print 4 / 9
0
>>>
```

Hmmm... that last one seems a bit wrong. The first three are as expected, but that last one... definitely not expected. Having said that, Python cannot have anything so basic wrong. Perhaps then the Python view of what the *expression* 4 / 9 means is different from what we initially assume it means? This is exactly right. When humans able to do sums see this expression, they know that the result is a fraction:

$$\frac{4}{9} = 0.44\dot{4}$$

where the dot over the last digit means that that digit recurs forever. So why does Python do something different?

For various historical reasons, computers do not treat numbers quite as humans and mathematics do. For most (but not all) computers, 4 is not the same as 4.0: 4 is an *integer*, whereas 4.0 is a *floating point* number – floating point numbers are numbers with both an integer part and a fractional part, and are usually called *floats* or sometimes *reals*. In mathematics, any integer number is a real number, so 4 and 4.0 are the same value. For computers, though, integers and floats are fundamentally different: integers and floats are represented differently in the hardware. So as an *expression* in Python, 4 / 9 says divide the integer 4 by the integer 9 and return an integer result. Since the actual result is a float with only a zero in front of the point, the integer result is 0.

People sometimes use the term *decimal number* instead of floating point number, but this is not entirely useful in computing as decimal numbers can be either integer or floating point!

If instead of 4 / 9 we type 4.0 / 9.0 then we are asking Python to calculate the result of dividing the floating point number 4.0 by the floating point number 9.0, giving a floating point result:

```
>>> print 4.0 / 9.0
0.444444444444
```

This is much more like it. Well, except that there is no indication that the fraction is a recurring one. This is a consequence of computers having finite amounts of memory. Since computer floating point numbers must be finite, infinite numbers cannot be represented in the computer. This means that computer floating point numbers are not exact but are just approximations to the actual values. For now we gloss over this, but we will have to return to the issue when we start doing some serious numerical computations.

Before moving on, we should try creating some more complex expressions to see whether anything else unexpected happens, or whether our understanding of evaluating arithmetic expressions from our mathematics education is reflected in Python. So:

```
>>> print 2 + 3 * 4
14
>>> print ( 2 + 3 ) * 4
20
>>> print 2 + 3 + 4
9
>>> print 2 + ( 3 + 4 )
9
```

This seems to indicate that the operations + and * behave as we expect them to: the *precedence* (aka priority) of the operations + and * are as we expect from mathematics. Also, parentheses, (and), seem to raise the precedence of the operation, again as we expect from mathematics.

The previous expressions used only integers: what about using floating point numbers?

```
>>> print 2.0 + 3.0 * 4.0
14.0
>>> print ( 2.0 + 3.0 ) * 4.0
20.0
>>> print 2.0 + 3.0 + 4.0
9.0
>>> print 2.0 + ( 3.0 + 4.0 )
9.0
```

BODMAS

BODMAS is an acronym used by many people to describe the precedence rule of arithmetic. It stands for:

> *B*rackets
> *O*rders
> *D*ivision and *M*ultiplication
> *A*ddition and *S*ubtraction

> Some people use the acronym
> *BIDMAS* – *I*ndexes replacing
> *O*rders.

The idea behind this acronym is to help you remember that when evaluating an expression, you first evaluate things in parentheses (brackets) then things raised to powers (exponentiation or orders) then multiplication and division in left-to-right order, and finally addition and subtraction in left to right order.

So the same holds true for floating point and integer numbers. We can do further experiments but if we do we will find all the results to be very much as expected. If you are not yet convinced yourself, try some really complicated expressions and see if you can get Python to do the wrong thing. We are confident it will be very hard!

Python can be very useful as a calculator, but there is clearly more to Python than that. Computers often, and workstations and laptops always, have screens for displaying things, so let's investigate drawing pictures on the screen.

It is not actually impossible to get incorrect answers but you have to work with very large numbers to get errors. Computer numbers are of finite size so there are numbers that cannot be stored.

1.5 Turtles can Draw

1.5.1 Libraries and Modules

One of the things that makes any programming language powerful is the amount of pre-written software that comes with it. Python has an extensive *library* of software that can be used by any programmer, at any time. This means that you don't have to write every program from scratch, you can make use of things in the library to do as much as possible. This is what makes Python so powerful.

One example is databases. The Python library comes with considerable support for creating and manipulating databases. This means that if we need to write a program to manage a database we don't have to write everything: we can make use of the library to do much of the hard work for us.

Another example is the support Python offers for user interface graphics which makes building user interfaces relatively straightforward. Actually, the real complexity of user interfaces is in the design and usability of the interface rather than in its construction. Python cannot help with those issues: they are human–computer interaction (HCI) issues.

In fact, the Python library has support for a huge range of software applications, helping you in almost any programming situation: communicating over the Internet, creating webpages, drawing pictures, in fact most things you can think of.

Rather than having the whole of the library available all the time, the library is structured as a set of *modules*. Each module is self-contained and so can be used independently of other modules. This means that we can tell the Python system to use just the parts needed for a particular program. The **import** statement is the way we tell the Python system that we need to make use of a module.

Logo, The Programing Language

In 1966 Seymour Papert and Wally Feurzeig designed *Logo*, a simple language for studying some ideas in artificial intelligence. Logo was also used for programming 'turtles'. The earliest turtles were radio-controlled robots which had a pen, a bell, touch sensors and could move forward, turn right, turn left, lower the pen, raise the pen, etc. Logo evolved into a language for drawing graphics on a computer screen, in particular for moving a turtle symbol simulating the behavior of the robot turtle. This turned out to be a fun language with which to write programs. Perhaps more importantly, it was very easy for beginners, including young children, to learn to program. This was shown experimentally first by Feurzig at Hanscom Field School, Lincoln, Massachusetts, USA, and Papert at Muzzy Junior High, Lexington, Massachusetts, USA and later by Papert at various other schools and institutions – they used Logo very successfully for teaching children about algorithms and programming.

When Guido van Rossum created Python, he included a module (the Turtle module) that realized in Python the core ideas of the Logo language. People find this Python module equally simple and fun to use, so we use it in various places in this book.

1.5.2 Using the Turtle Module

In this section, we use a module called Turtle to draw simple pictures by moving a virtual robot (aka *turtle*) around the screen. Having started the Python system, we have to issue the command **import** turtle to request the Python system to do whatever is necessary to import the Turtle module:

```
Python 2.5.1c1 (release25-maint, Apr 12 2007, 21:00:25)
[GCC 4.1.2 (Ubuntu 4.1.2-0ubuntu4)] on linux2
Type "help", "copyright", "credits" or "license" for more information.
>>> import turtle
```

Now we can do something with the Turtle module. First let's try the standard demonstration to get the turtle to show us what it can do. We do this by typing turtle.demo () after the import statement:

```
>>> import turtle
>>> turtle.demo ()
```

Figure 1.2 shows the result of executing the statements. As is clear from the figure, the turtle can draw lines of different thickness, create shapes, fill those shapes and write text. What is not so obvious from the figure (given that it is monochrome) is

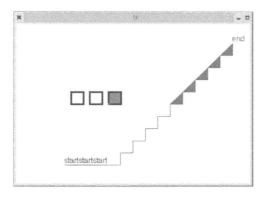

Result of running the demo function in the Turtle module. Some of this is colored red.

that various parts of the image are in different colors. If you run the demonstration yourself, you will see all the colors involved.

The statement we entered to run the turtle demo is clearly different from the **print** and **import** statements. Firstly, we used the name turtle.demo, i.e. we gave the name of the module followed by a period (aka full stop) then the name of the action. Secondly, we appended an open and close parenthesis, i.e. we typed turtle.demo ( ) rather than turtle.demo. turtle.demo is an example of a *function* and we append the parentheses to indicate that the function should be executed. If we had not put the parentheses, we get:

```
>>> turtle.demo
<function demo at 0xb7ac72cc>
>>>
```

which tells us that turtle.demo is a function that resides at some location in the memory of the computer.

"What is a function?" you are asking. A function is a way of collecting together a sequence of statements and giving it a name, so that the sequence of statements can be executed without having to type them all out. Indeed we don't even have to know what the sequence of statements is to be able to execute it, we just have to know what the name is – as with the turtle.demo function above.

Modules can have many functions: the Turtle module has many for drawing different shapes.

1.5.3   Lines and Directions

Let's now get the turtle to draw something for us. Obviously it is a good idea to clear the window first. We do this by calling the function turtle.reset, which clears the window as shown in Figure 1.3.

```
>>> import turtle
>>> turtle.demo ( )
>>> turtle.reset ( )
```

Now we have a clear screen, we can draw some shapes of our own. Let's start with something simple, a square:

```
>>> turtle.forward ( 100 )
>>> turtle.left ( 90 )
>>> turtle.forward ( 100 )
```

```
>>> turtle.left ( 90 )
>>> turtle.forward ( 100 )
>>> turtle.left ( 90 )
>>> turtle.forward ( 100 )
```

The result is shown in Figure 1.4.

To draw the square, we have used two functions, turtle.forward and turtle.left, that have integers in the parentheses of the function call. The turtle.forward and turtle.left functions require *parameters* (the numbers in the parentheses). For turtle.forward, the parameter tells the system how many units to move by – 100 in all the examples above. The units are *pixels*. Computer displays (just like televisions) are screens that are composed of a two dimensional array of pixels. Typical sizes for computer displays are 800×600, 1024×768, 1280×1024, 1600×1200, 1920×1200. High-definition television is 1368×768. (Display sizes for LCD displays are relatively simple, but things get really rather complicated for television. See, for example, http://en.wikipedia.org/wiki/Display_resolution.) For turtle.left, the parameter tells the system by how much to turn the turtle left. By default this parameter is in degrees. So turtle.left (45) means turn anticlockwise by 45°.

'pixel' is an abbreviation of 'picture element'

> **Measuring Angles**
>
> Angles can be measured in *radians* but most people learn about degrees and not radians, so the Turtle module works with degrees by default. We can work with radians if we want, we just have to call turtle.radians.

As you might already have guessed, the Turtle module also provides functions for moving backwards (turtle.backward) and turning clockwise (turtle.right), along with many other drawing functions.

1.5.4 Some Other Functions in the Turtle Module

We claimed in the caption of Figure 1.2 that parts of that diagram were drawn in red even though it does not appear so in this monochrome book. Hopefully you have run the demo to prove to yourself that this claim is actually true! So the turtle can change the color of the pen used for writing. Color changes are achieved by calling the turtle.color function. The change only applies to drawing done after the

Figure 1.4

Drawing a square.

call to the turtle.color function, so we need to draw something new to see that the change of color has happened:

```
>>> turtle.reset ( )
>>> turtle.color ( "Red" )
>>> turtle.forward ( 10 )
```

The result is shown (in monochrome) in Figure 1.5.

The turtle can also raise and lower the pen just as if we were raising and lowering a real pen on a piece of paper – this harks back to the real physical turtle controlled by Logo programs. Unsurprisingly, these functions are called turtle.up and turtle.down. Moving with a raised pen leaves no trace while, as we have already seen, moving with a lowered pen draws a line (lowered is the default position). Clearly, we can use turtle.up and turtle.down to draw a dashed line:

```
>>> turtle.up ( )
>>> turtle.forward ( 10 )
>>> turtle.down ( )
>>> turtle.forward ( 10 )
>>> turtle.up ( )
>>> turtle.forward ( 10 )
>>> turtle.down ( )
>>> turtle.forward ( 10 )
```

Figure 1.6 shows the result of executing this program.

Figure 1.5

Drawing in a new color. As the book is monochrome the line looks grey, but if you try this for yourself, you will see it is red.

Figure 1.6

Drawing a dashed line.

The Turtle module has the turtle.circle function which, unsurprisingly, draws circles. So, for example, typing:

```
>>> turtle.reset ( )
>>> turtle.circle ( 50 )
```

gives the result shown in Figure 1.7. The parameter to the turtle.circle function specifies the radius (in pixels) of the circle to be drawn. The turtle starts drawing in the direction it is facing and draws a circle of the specified radius ending in the position and direction in which it started.

The turtle.circle function can draw circular arcs as well as complete circles: we can give calls of turtle.circle a second parameter that specifies how much of a circle to draw. By typing:

```
>>> turtle.reset ( )
>>> turtle.circle ( 50 , 180 )
```

we get only a half a circle, as shown in Figure 1.8. When we call the turtle.circle function with only one parameter, the Python system assumes we are telling it to draw all 360° of the circle. Calling the function with a second parameter overrides this assumption and draws only part of the circle; in this example half a circle (180°). Circles are always drawn by traveling anti-clockwise, i.e. the center of the circle or circular arc being drawn is always to the turtle's left of its current position.

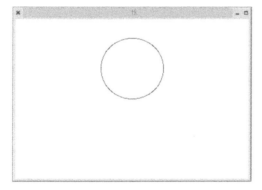

Figure 1.7

Drawing a circle.

Figure 1.8

Drawing half a circle.

Help

If at any time during an interactive session you want to find out what functions are available in a module, you can enter help mode by executing the help function:

```
>>> help ()
```

Welcome to Python 2.5! This is the online help utility.

If this is your first time using Python, you should definitely check out
the tutorial on the Internet at http://www.python.org/doc/tut/.

Enter the name of any module, keyword, or topic to get help on writing
Python programs and using Python modules. To quit this help utility and
return to the interpreter, just type "quit".

To get a list of available modules, keywords, or topics, type "modules",
"keywords", or "topics". Each module also comes with a one-line summary
of what it does; to list the modules whose summaries contain a given word
such as "spam", type "modules spam".

```
help>
```

At this prompt we can type the name of a module, for example 'turtle'. The output is quite lengthy so we will not reproduce it here. Give it a try and you will see information about the module, including what functions are available. Quite a lot of the information presented may only make sense after you have a little more experience of Python, but there is also information there that we want, such as the list of functions we can use.

The best way of finding out what each of the functions can do and what can be achieved by combining them is to experiment – although we probably ought to use the term 'play' here rather than 'experiment', since 'play' implies far more strongly that programming the turtle can be fun!

1.6 Algorithms

An *algorithm* is a sequence of instructions that can be used to carry out a task. You have already come across algorithms in your daily life: for example, if you ask someone how to get from your home to the nearest shop selling console games, the answer will be an algorithm, perhaps something such as 'go down the road, turn left at the traffic lights, take the third right and the shop is on your left'. It is important that you follow the instructions in the correct order. If you try to take the third right before you turn left at the traffic lights, you may well get very lost indeed!

Algorithm, The Word

Algorithms are named after the ninth century Persian mathematician Muhammad bin Musa al-Khwarizmi. Originally, *algorisms* were rules for performing arithmetic using Arabic numerals. By the eighteenth century, 'algorism' had become 'algorithm' and had come to mean a sequence of commands to carry out a specific task.

Augusta Ada King née Byron, Countess of Lovelace
The First Computer Programmer

The first algorithms written for a computer were Ada Byron's programs for Charles Babbage's Analytical Engine, written in 1842. Ada Byron was therefore, arguably, the first computer programmer. The language Ada was named after her as recognition of her contribution to computing.

A computer program is an algorithm expressed in a programming language so that it may be executed by a computer. As with algorithms in any context, it is important that the statements of the program are executed is the correct order. For example, if we try to call turtle.reset before we tell Python to import the Turtle module, we get this error:

```
Python 2.5.1c1 (release25-maint, Apr 12 2007, 21:00:25)
[GCC 4.1.2 (Ubuntu 4.1.2-0ubuntu4)] on linux2
Type "help", "copyright", "credits" or "license" for more information.
>>> turtle.reset ( )
Traceback (most recent call last):
  File "<stdin>", line 1, in <module>
NameError: name 'turtle' is not defined
>>>
```

The Python system is telling us that it doesn't have anything called turtle to refer to, so it can't run the turtle.reset function for us.

More often, though, getting an algorithm wrong does not result in an error message, just unexpected results. Let's take the program for drawing a square of side 100 pixels:

```
>>> turtle.forward ( 100 )
>>> turtle.left ( 90 )
>>> turtle.forward ( 100 )
>>> turtle.left ( 90 )
>>> turtle.forward ( 100 )
>>> turtle.left ( 90 )
>>> turtle.forward ( 100 )
```

and rearrange it slightly so that it is wrong (we swap the order of the last two statements):

```
>>> turtle.forward ( 100 )
>>> turtle.left ( 90 )
>>> turtle.forward ( 100 )
>>> turtle.left ( 90 )
>>> turtle.forward ( 100 )
>>> turtle.forward ( 100 )
>>> turtle.left ( 90 )
```

Figure 1.9 shows the result. Definitely not a square, but there is no error message, as there is no error as far as the Python system is concerned. The program we gave the Python system is a perfectly reasonable program and it executed it as requested. As the intention was to draw a square, the program clearly has one or more errors, but not ones the computer can detect. There is nothing wrong with the syntax of the program, it is either that the algorithm is wrong or that the correct algorithm has not been correctly implemented, so the result is not what was intended. In this case, our instructions to Python, which were intended to mean 'draw a square', resulted in an unexpected result because the code was wrong – we had the right algorithm, but wrote the statements in the wrong order. Such an error is called (obviously) an *algorithmic error* or (less obviously) a *semantic error*.

In the case of algorithms such as that for drawing a square, it is usually fairly obvious where errors are if they occur. It is then easy to correct the program. However, for anything but the smallest and simplest of algorithms this is not generally the case. Semantic errors can be hard to find and sometimes even harder to correct. It is extremely important, therefore, to plan your programs carefully and make sure you know what they *ought* to do before you write them.

Later in the book (Chapter 9) we will introduce a way of programming, Test-Driven Development, that really helps avoid semantic errors. However, we need a little more programming and Python technology before we can introduce that. So for the moment we just have to be very careful.

Always understand what the program you are writing is intended to do *before* you write it.

> **The terms bug *and* debug**
>
> Grace Murray Hopper was an early pioneer of computing. She invented the compiler in 1952 and later the programming language COBOL. She used to tell a story about a technician who fixed a 'bug' in the Harvard Mark II computer by pulling an insect out of the contacts of one of its relays. Since then, the terms *bug* meaning a mistake in a computer program and *debug* meaning to fix a bug have become widely used. For many years the logbook associated with the incident and the bug in question (a moth) were displayed at the Naval Surface Warfare Center (NSWC).
>
> However, this may not be the origin of the term. It is reported that the term bug was used in Thomas Edison's time (late nineteenth century) to mean a fault in electrical apparatus. It is even reputed to have been a term used during the development of wireless telegraphy earlier in the nineteenth century!

1.7   Designing an Algorithm: Square Spirals

Figure 1.10 shows a square spiral. To show an example of an algorithm (and of developing a Python program), we shall set ourselves the task of creating a Python program to draw such a square spiral using the Turtle module.

The first thing we have to do is fully understand the result we want to achieve. This might seem obvious, but it's amazing how many software projects fail simply because the developers writing the software never really fully understood what their client wanted.

Figure 1.9

Not a square but it was supposed to be!

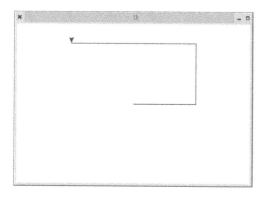

Looking at Figure 1.10, we see that a square spiral is made up of straight lines joined together at right angles, almost a square but not quite. Looking at the center of the example and tracing it out, we see that all the joins of this example are left-hand turns. So, to draw this figure, our program is going to be made up of calls to the turtle.forward and turtle.left functions. As all the joins are right-angles, the turtle will always need to turn left by 90° at the end of each straight line.

Have we mentioned what a good idea it is to understand what the program you are writing is intended to do *before* you write it?

So what distinguishes a square spiral from a square? Tracing out the square spiral from the center, we see that the straight lines get longer. In this example, we draw two lines of the same length, then increase the length of the next pair of lines, and so on. If we increase the line length too much, the shape will spiral quickly. If we increase the side length too little then we will spiral out slowly. Of course if we do not increase the length at all then there is no spiral, we end up drawing a square over and over again!

So, having thought about how to create the shape we want, we can think about creating a program. In this case thing are fairly simple: we can trace out the example and it tells us the algorithm and hence the code to write. Actually, this is often the easiest way of writing programs like this: draw the shape on a piece of paper and it tells you what the algorithm is and hence what code is needed to achieve that shape.

This:

is three sides of a square, with each side the same length. If we trace round this shape (starting from the lower left-hand corner) we see that, because the third side is the same length as the other two, the next side to be drawn will meet the first one and form a square. We don't want that, so the *third* side needs to be longer than the first two, to make a spiral. So, our square spiral algorithm will be something like this:

Move forward by some amount
Turn left 90°
Move forward by some amount
Turn left 90°
Move forward by a bit more than last time
Turn left 90°
Move forward by new amount
Turn left 90°
Move forward by a bit more than last time
Turn left 90°
Move forward by new amount
. . .

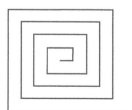

Figure 1.10

A square spiral.

This way of expressing algorithm – using 'clipped' natural language – is called *pseudocode*. Pseudocode is very much program oriented but it is not any particular programming language, nor does it have any rules. The idea is that we express the algorithm in a programming language independent way but using language that is easily translatable into any programming language.

To write our Python program we simply need to add Python-specific detail to the pseudocode expression of the algorithm. Let's say that we will start by drawing a line of length 10 and that we will increase the line length by 10 when the length to move forward by is increased. We are now in a position to write a sequence of Python statements that implements this algorithm:

```
>>> import turtle
>>> turtle.forward ( 10 )
>>> turtle.left ( 90 )
>>> turtle.forward ( 10 )
>>> turtle.left ( 90 )
>>> turtle.forward ( 20 )
>>> turtle.left ( 90 )
>>> turtle.forward ( 20 )
>>> turtle.left ( 90 )
>>> turtle.forward ( 30 )
>>> turtle.left ( 90 )
>>> turtle.forward ( 30 )
>>> turtle.left ( 90 )
>>> turtle.forward ( 40 )
>>> turtle.left ( 90 )
>>> turtle.forward ( 40 )
>>> turtle.left ( 90 )
>>> turtle.forward ( 50 )
>>> turtle.left ( 90 )
>>> turtle.forward ( 50 )
>>> turtle.left ( 90 )
>>> turtle.forward ( 60 )
>>> turtle.left ( 90 )
>>> turtle.forward ( 60 )
>>> turtle.left ( 90 )
```

which results in the drawing shown in Figure 1.11.

Figure 1.11

A square spiral drawn with the turtle.

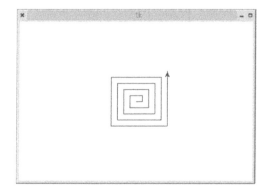

1.8 Storing and Executing Programs

You are probably thinking: "But if I want to draw the shape again, I have to type it all in again. How tedious." or even "If I want to compare two slightly different sequences, I have to type almost the same thing more than once. Irritating." So, whilst typing programs in line by line and having each statement executed as soon as we press the return key is all very instant and can be incredibly useful, it is absolutely clear that we need to be able to prepare our programs before executing them. Obviously, we need to store programs in some way independent of the Python system that we can then execute as Python programs. In fact, this is the usual way of programming: use a text editor to create a file and then get the Python system to execute that file. So for example we can use a text editor (we use XEmacs but any text editor will do) to put the statement:

> Always use a text editor for editing program code. Word processors such as OpenOffice.org and Word are not appropriate because they are intended for creating documents not programs.

> **print** "Hello."

into a file, we called our file printHello.py, and then we can then issue the command *python printHello.py* to execute the program:

```
|> python printHello.py
Hello.
|>
```

Issuing the Python command without a file name puts the system into interactive mode while giving it a file name causes the system to open the file and execute the statements in the file. Many people call this *script mode* to distinguish it from interactive mode.

The Python system is fundamentally the same whichever mode we use it in. In particular, any program executed in either way will behave the same and all errors are the same and reported in the same way. For example, the faulty Python program:

> prin 1

when executed, results in:

```
|> python helloError.py
  File "helloError.py", line 1
    prin 1
         ^
SyntaxError: invalid syntax
```

which is exactly (well almost exactly) the same message as we got in interactive mode – the difference is that the name of the file is given instead of '<stdin>'. As far as the Python system is concerned all input and output happens through files. The file could be a real file on disk or it could be a 'special' file which is actually connected to a human input device, for example the keyboard. The file associated with the keyboard is called 'stdin', hence the error message from earlier said the input was from '<stdin>' – the '<' and '>' are there to show it is a special file, and not a file on disk. The Python compilation and execution system does not distinguish the two cases, a file is a file as far as it is concerned. So using the Python system in either script mode or interactive mode really is the same.

In this chapter we have found that:

- Python programs are sequences of statements.
- Python handles arithmetic and arithmetic expressions very much as expected, except for the issue of integer and floating point numbers.
- Python has a large library, structured as a set of modules.
- Python modules contain functions which we can call to do various things.
- The Python system has an interactive mode and a script mode.
- Python programs are usually constructed using a text editor as files on disk, and then executed in script mode.

Self-Review Questions

Self-review 1.1 Why is the following the case?

```
>>> print 4 + 9
13
>>>
```

Self-review 1.2 Why is the following the case – rather than the result being 13?

```
>>> print "4 + 9"
4 + 9
>>>
```

Self-review 1.3 Why does the expression 2 + 3 * 4 result in the value 14 and not the value 24?

Self-review 1.4 What is a module and why do we have them?

Self-review 1.5 What is a library and why do we have them?

Self-review 1.6 What does the statement turtle.demo ( ) mean?

Self-review 1.7 What is an algorithm?

Self-review 1.8 Why are algorithms important in programming?

Self-review 1.9 What shape does the following program draw?

```
turtle.forward ( 100 )
turtle.right ( 90 )
turtle.forward ( 50 )
turtle.right ( 90 )
turtle.forward ( 100 )
turtle.right ( 90 )
turtle.forward ( 50 )
```

Self-review 1.10 The Turtle module provides a function to draw circles. If this function was not available, what algorithm would you use to draw a circle?

Self-review 1.11 What does the function turtle.goto do?

> *Hint: Use the Python help system to help you!*

Self-review 1.12 What is stdin?

Self-review 1.13 What is 'script mode'?

Programming Exercises

Exercise 1.1 Estimate the size of your computer screen by importing the Turtle module and causing the turtle to move 1 pixel (though you may want to try 10 pixels!).

Exercise 1.2 Experiment with the 'square spiral' program, varying the lengths of various lines. Which values make spirals and which do not? Which values make the nicest-looking spiral?

Exercise 1.3 Write a program to draw a right-angled triangle looking something like:

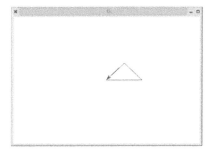

Exercise 1.4 Write a program to draw a red circle, then a yellow circle underneath it and a green circle underneath that. The result should look something like:

It is true that in this monochrome rendition, the colors just appears in various shades of grey, but the colors will work on your computer – unless you have a monochrome screen!

> *Hint: We used the function turtle.goto as well as the functions turtle.up, turtle.down, turtle.color and turtle.circle in our solution.*

Exercise 1.5 Amend your program from the previous question so that the circles are filled and hence the result looks something like:

These circles are definitely filled with the right color when we run the program on our computers even though they just look greyish in this book.

Hint: We used the function turtle.fill in our solution.

Exercise 1.6 Write a program to draw a regular hexagon. The result should look something like:

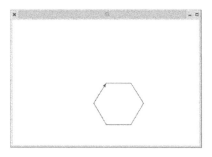

Hint: Regular hexagons have six sides, of equal length, which meet at an internal angle of 120°.

Exercise 1.7 Write a program to draw the first letter of your name.

Challenges

Challenge 1.1 Write a program to create a triangular spiral, as in:

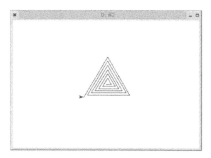

Hint: This is easiest if you work with equilateral triangles – it gets very complex otherwise.

Challenge 1.2 Write a program to draw this 'envelope' figure:

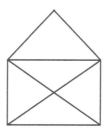

> Hint: *You may want to start by doing some trigonometry to sort out all the angles and lengths. Pythagoras' Theorem will almost certainly come in useful: Pythagoras' Theorem states that for a right-angled triangle:*
>
> $$hypotenuse = \sqrt{x^2 + y^2}$$
>
> *where* hypotenuse *is the longest side of the triangle and x and y are the lengths of the other two sides.*
>
> Hint: *To find the square root of a number in Python, you need to import the module* math *and call the function* math.sqrt: *to find the square root of 2, you import the* math *module, then write* math.sqrt(2).

Challenge 1.3 Draw the following figure:

The Fundamentals

Learning Outcomes

At the end of this chapter you will be able to:

- Describe the fundamental structures of a program: sequence, selection, iteration and function call.
- Describe how Python expressions are evaluated.

- Describe the idea of type and determine the type of a value or variable using the Python interpreter.
- Implement simple algorithms using selection, iteration and functions.

2.1 Types

In the turtle drawing programs of the previous chapter we had *literals* such as 10, 20, etc., all of which are integers. In Section 1.4 we introduced the fact that computers generally distinguish integers (e.g. 10) and floats (e.g. 10.0) as being different and treated differently. To use the jargon, integers and floats are two *types* of number. Even before using 10 and 10.0, in Section 1.2, we introduced the fact that "Hello." was a *string*. String is another type.

Modern programming languages are 'typed' languages, which means that the type of a thing in a program is an important property of that thing – being a typed language doesn't refer to a program being typed in at a keyboard! In typed programming languages, all data, indeed every part of a program, including functions, have a type.

Python has a function (called type) in its library for determining the type of something. So for example:

```
>>> print type ( 10 )
<type 'int'>
>>>
```

the <type 'int'> says that the type of 10 is 'int', which is the Python way of saying integer.

If we try type (10.0), we get the result <type 'float'>. Indicating that 10.0 is of type 'float'. As noted in the previous chapter (page 7), floating point numbers are numbers that have a fractional part, i.e. decimal digits after the decimal point, as well as an integer part (the numbers before the decimal point). The reason for distinguishing integer and floating point numbers is to do with the way computer hardware works: integers and floats are represented differently in the memory of (most) computers. The details of this need not worry us as long as we bear in mind that they are different types as far as Python is concerned.

Entering type ("abcde") results in <type 'str'> indicating that "abcde" is a 'str', which is the Python way of saying string. If we try type ('abcde') the result is also <type 'str'>, so it seems that we can use either single quotes or double quotes to indicate that a literal is a string. This implies that the statements:

```
print "Hello."
print 'Hello.'
```

are both the same. Actually, this is not strictly true, but the differences between them won't affect us for the moment.

On page 10 we showed what happens when the parentheses are omitted from a function call – the Python system simply reports that 'demo' is a function residing at some address in memory. So what happens if we apply the function type to the name of a function?

```
>>> import turtle
>>> print type ( turtle.demo )
<type 'function'>
>>>
```

So 'function' is a type and, indeed, is the type of all functions.

Are you perhaps asking what happens if we enter things like type (type (10)) and type (type ("abcde"))? Let's try it:

```
>>> print type ( type ( 10 ) )
<type 'type'>
>>> print type ( type ( 10.0 ) )
<type 'type'>
>>> print type ( type ( 'abcde' ) )
<type 'type'>
>>> print type ( type ( turtle.demo ) )
<type 'type'>
>>>
```

So in all cases the result is the type 'type'.

In case you were wondering, the result of type (type (type (12))) is <type 'type'>. So types are types too. Although this is an important point for certain aspects of Python programming, it is not an issue for the first stages of learning to program, and so not an issue for this book. Once you have experience of Python programming, and are looking at intermediate and advanced books, then it will be an important issue.

2.2   Expressions, Operators and Operands

As we saw in Section 1.4, Python allows us to do all sorts of arithmetic. So, for example, we saw statements such as:

```
print 2 + 3 * 4
print ( 2 + 3 ) * 4
print 2 + 3 + 4
print 2 + ( 3 + 4 )
```

The:

        2 + 3 * 4
        (2 + 3) * 4
        2 + 3 + 4
        2 + (3 + 4)

are all examples of *expressions*. An expression is something that can be *evaluated*, resulting in a single value. We can have expressions involving integers and floats, as we have seen previously:

Expression	Value
12 + 9	21
91.5 + 8.5	100.0
1 * 10 + 3	13
1 + 10 * 3	31

These expressions are evaluated in a way that leads to the same results that we are used to from arithmetic. Python also allows expressions involving strings. So for example:

Expression	Value
"Leaping" + "Lizards"	"LeapingLizards"
"43" + "7"	"437"
"43 + 7"	"43 + 7"

Using + between two strings means create a new string that consists of the two strings concatenated, i.e. joined together.

Symbols such as + and * are called *operators* and the values they operate on are called *operands*. Operators are classified according to the number of operands. So + is a *binary operator*, since it requires two operands. It is also an *infix operator*, since the operator sits between the two operands. Expressions are combinations of operators and operands.

The format or *syntax* of a print statement is:

        print < *expression* >

You may be asking yourself how is it then that we can have statements such as:

        print 'Hello.'

The answer is that a literal is an expression with no operators: the literal 'Hello.' is an expression with no operators that results in the string value 'Hello.'.

Print is not a Function

In Python **print** is not a function:

```
>>> print type ( print )
  File "<stdin>", line 1
    type ( print )
                ^
SyntaxError: invalid syntax
>>>
```

In Python a print statement is a special statement, a command, not a call of a function.

2.3 Expressions and Type

We said earlier that everything in a Python program has a type. So you might well ask: what is the type of an expression? In fact, expressions themselves don't have a type, but the values that results from the evaluation of expressions certainly do. People often talk about the type of an expression when what they mean to talk about is the type of the result. So, for example:

21 + 9

is the addition of two integer operands, resulting in an integer. The expression:

91.5 + 8.5

is the addition of two floats, resulting in a float. We can show this using the Python system interactively:

The expression that is the parameter to a function is always evaluated before the function is called.

```
>>> print type ( 12 + 9 )
<type 'int'>
>>> print type ( 91.5 + 8.5 )
<type 'float'>
>>>
```

So what about the expression:

21 + 9.0

In human arithmetic terms such an expression is fine since, in mathematics, numbers are all just numbers. We know the answer is 30. Or is it 30.0? Mathematically there is actually a difference between 30 and 30.0, but it has less to do with type and more to do with accuracy. So whilst humans don't generally worry about type, computers do. Computers cannot add integers and floats directly as we can. Computers distinguish integer and float numbers because the way in which the hardware deals with these types of value is totally different: computers can add an integer to an integer and they can add a float to a float, but they cannot add an integer to a float or a float to an integer. Yet programming languages generally allow *mixed type expressions* such as:

21 + 9.0

and indeed this expression is fine in Python. This is very sensible: why should programmers have to deal with the bizarre features of the computer? The whole point of having *high-level languages* like Python is exactly so that we can express algorithms in ways that are easy for us, the programmers, using our real-world knowledge of numbers and arithmetic.

So what does the Python system do to evaluate:

21 + 9.0

You may well have guessed already – it converts this expression to:

21.0 + 9.0

i.e. it converts the integer value 21 into the float value 21.0 so that the addition can happen. The result of the evaluation is the float value 30.0. We can confirm this:

```
>>> print 21 + 9.0
30.0
>>> print type ( 21 + 9.0 )
<type 'float'>
>>>
```

This behind-the-scenes conversion of values from one type to another is called *coercion*. The implication of being forced is most apposite!

Implicit coercion, i.e. coercion that is undertaken by the system automatically, is what allows programming languages to support mixed-type expressions. Python is hiding the fact that computers must deal with integers and floats differently, giving us the appearance that it just deals in numbers as humans do in arithmetic. This is good – mostly. There is a downside: even though we are writing what look like expressions as we would write in arithmetic, they are not quite the same. The coercion is an integral part of the evaluation and readers of the program need to be aware that this is the case, as it can affect the value generated: in a program, the type structure of the expression is an important thing, and something we as programmers must take into account – the computer's separation of integers and floats is not removed, it is just hidden.

This use of implicit coercion to allow us to write mixed type expressions is the first hint of *abstraction*, the absolute cornerstone of what programming is about. We will come back regularly to issues of abstraction throughout the book.

2.4   Operators and Precedence

Basic arithmetic has only four operators (+ , − , × , ÷) but Python supports nine arithmetic operators: + , - , * , / , ** , % , // , + , - . Did you spot that we have both + and - in the list twice? This is not a typographical error. The symbols + and - have two distinct meanings as operators depending on the number of operands – this is called the *arity* of the operator. Used with two operands the + and - operators are, respectively, the familiar addition and subtraction infix binary operators:

```
>>> print 4 + 3
7
>>> print 4 - 3
1
>>>
```

So what is the other use of + and - ? These symbols can be used as operators with only one operand, for example:

```
>>> print + 2
2
>>> print - 2
-2
>>>
```

Here + and - are being used as *unary operators*, i.e. operators with only one operand. Moreover, they are *prefix* unary operators, as the operator appears before the operand.

So what are the other Python arithmetic operators? The binary arithmetic operators are:

+	Addition	**	Power
-	Subtraction	%	Remainder
*	Multiplication	//	Floor
/	Division		

The four on the left are the familiar arithmetic operators – except that Python (along with most other programming languages) uses * for multiplication and /

for division, rather than × and ÷. The reason for this is actually very simple: the symbols × and ÷ do not appear on a keyboard. There is a huge history to why keyboards are the way they are, but that isn't really of importance for us here, so we will not delve deeply into the details.

> ### QWERTY is Queer
>
> The QWERTY keyboard most of us use in the English-speaking world is based on the Victorian typewriter key layout. The layout was determined by the frequency of use of the keys and the mechanics of the physical system. Victorian typewriters were totally mechanical and involved keystrokes causing hammer heads to strike paper on a roller. The layout of the keys was devised to try and minimize the number of hammer head clashes for the fast typing Victorian typists.

In mathematics, we often see equations such as:

$$E = mc^2$$

where E is the energy associated with something, m is the mass of that something and c is the speed of light in a vacuum – this equation is perhaps Einstein's most famous piece of work, though it is arguably not his most important contribution to physics. To understand the equation, we have to know that, in mathematics, juxtaposition (two things next to each other) means multiplication, and superscript means 'raise to the power of'. So mc^2 is a more compact way of writing $m \times c \times c$. If we needed to write this in a program, we could write the expression:

    m * c * c

but in Python we can use the power operator (**) to write:

    m * c ** 2

reflecting much more directly the original equation: the ** operator is an infix binary operator that calculates the value of the first operand raised to the power of the second operand. But there is a potential problem: is the * evaluated before or after the **?

Expression	Possible meanings
m * c ** 2	m * c * m * c
	m * c * c

From basic arithmetic we are used to the fact that:

    print 1 + 2 * 3

evaluates to the value 7. Python evaluates this expression in exactly the same way, resulting in the value 7. The point here is that just as in arithmetic, Python evaluates multiplication before evaluating addition, so the 2 * 3 is evaluated, then 1 + 6 is evaluated, resulting in the value 7. As we noted in the previous chapter (page 7), multiplication has a higher *precedence* than addition and expression evaluation always occurs in precedence order. The term *priority* is sometimes used instead of the term precedence, but they are just two different words for the same concept (in this context anyway). We will use the term precedence throughout this book.

If operators did not have precedence and expressions were evaluated from left to right then 1 + 2 * 3 would be evaluated by first evaluating 1 + 2 and then 3 * 3 to give us the value 9. Definitely not what is expected from normal arithmetic! It is good that Python follows arithmetic – Python follows the Principle of Least Surprise.

The Principle of Least Surprise

The Principle of Least Surprise is a very useful principle for guiding the building of programs as well as creating a programming language. If a system acts in the way a user expects it to, and gives no surprises, then the system works the way the user thinks it works – and that is exactly how it should be.

From our knowledge of arithmetic we know that we can use parentheses to create a higher precedence *sub-expression* – a sub-expression is just an expression that is part of a bigger expression. Python supports this way of changing the precedence of sub-expressions. So if we really do want to get the value 9 and not 7 from 1 + 2 * 3, then we can use parenthesis to raise the precedence of the sub-expression:

print (1 + 2) * 3

Returning to the problem of what the expression m * c ** 2 means, simply by knowing that the power operator has higher precedence than multiplication, there is immediately no problem and only one meaning:

m * c ** 2

is equivalent to:

m * c * c

To summarize, Python enforces the following operator precedence:

highest	+ (unary) - (unary)
	**
	* / % //
lowest	+ -

Operators of a higher precedence are evaluated before operators of lower precedence, with operators at the same level being evaluated left-to-right. These precedence rules ensure that Python expressions are evaluated as closely as possible to how we expect from arithmetic. Python actually has a few more operators that can be used in expressions, so this is not a complete table of precedence. The full table for Python can be seen in the reference manual, which is available online at http://www.python.org/doc/current/ref/summary.html.

2.5 Variables

2.5.1 Creating and Using Variables

Did you spot that in the previous section we started using expressions with things like m and c in them? Until then we had only ever used literals in our expressions. Programming only with literals can get very frustrating, because it severely limits the programs we can write. What we have slipped in by using names rather than literals in expressions is the idea of a *variable*. A variable is a name that we can associate with a value. An association is created using an *assignment* statement. For example, the statements:

c = 299792458
m = 1

create a variable m associated with the value 1 and a variable c associated with the value 299792458. Once such associations have been set up, we can use the variable names in expressions and, when the expressions are evaluated, the value with which a variable is associated is used in the evaluation. So the program:

```
c = 299792458
m = 1
print m * c ** 2
```

when executed, results in:

```
89875517873681764
```

which tells us that 1Kg of matter is equivalent to 89,875,517,873,681,764 Joules of energy – that is an awful lot of energy!

Why are variables so important in programming? Because they allow us to store the results of expression evaluations. The syntax of the assignment statement is:

$$<variable\ name> = <expression>$$

so as well as being able to assign literal values to variables, we can assign the results of expression evaluations to variables. So, for example:

```
c = 299792458
m = 1
e = m * c ** 2
print e
m = 2
e = m * c ** 2
print e
```

When this program is executed, it results in the output:

```
89875517873681764
179751035747363528
```

Printing out just the value is not very good interaction with the user: our program should do better. One way of writing out a more comprehensible message is to use the fact that the print statement can print out a list of things separated by commas:

```
c = 299792458
m = 1
e = m * c ** 2
print m , 'Kg of mass is equivalent to' , e , 'Joules of energy.'
```

We output many things with a single print statement by separating the items with a comma.

When executed, this displays:

```
1 Kg of mass is equivalent to 89875517873681764 Joules of energy.
```

Each of the items in the list following the **print** is an expression. So, instead of the above, we can write:

```
c = 299792458
m = 1
print m , 'Kg of mass is equivalent to' , m * c ** 2 , 'Joules of energy.'
```

and the output, when the program is executed, is the same as the previous version.

Variables may not seem exactly earth shattering presented like this, but when we use them with other features that we will introduce shortly, they really do allow some very nice ways of writing programs.

2.5.2 Types of Variables

As we noted earlier, everything in Python has a type associated with it. So what are the types of m, c and e? The type of a variable is the type of the value with which it is associated. So after:

```
m = 1
```

the variable m has type int because 1 has type int. We can show this by using the type function:

```
>>> m = 1
>>> print type ( m )
<type 'int'>
>>>
```

Even if the variable is assigned using an expression, it still has a type: the type of the result of the expression evaluation. So:

```
>>> m = 1
>>> c = 299792458
>>> m = 1
>>> e = m * c ** 2
>>> print type ( e )
<type 'long'>
>>>
```

Hmmm... type long, what the...is that? Well, it is a sort of integer. Computer hardware generally has a number of different sorts if integer (and a number of different sorts of float as well). Hardware stores values differently to try and make operations as fast and efficient as possible. Hence int and long: an int is a 'normal' size integer, while a long is bigger, can store more different values, but is slower to work with, and so is not used where an int will do. Sensibly, Python hides all these issues so that we don't need to worry about them. We aren't trying to avoid explaining it, it is just not an issue in Python – Python is a high-level language and so can and should make things easy for us by dealing with the hardware issues. Which it does.

2.5.3 Variables are Indeed, Variable...

In our previous programs we generally created new variables to store the result of each expression evaluation. It was quite natural to do this for the calculations we were undertaking, and so not at all wrong. However, we did slip in a couple of 'reassignments', i.e. we assigned a new value to a variable we had previously assigned. The value associated with the variable can be changed. This seems quite natural given that the term used for these things is *variable*!

For example, we could have written the above program as:

```
c = 299792458
c = c ** 2
print '1Kg of mass is equivalent to' , c , 'Joules of energy.'
```

but, although this shows that we can change the value with which a variable is associated, we suggest it would be a bad program for two reasons:

1. The speed of light is a constant – in current theories anyway – so changing the value with which the variable is associated means the variable doesn't properly represent the concept of the value of the speed of light.

2. The program doesn't really express the intention of calculating the amount of energy associated with a given amount of mass.

It is true that the result of running the program is the same as for the previous version of this program, but in programming getting the right result is not the only issue. Certainly getting the right result is crucial, but the comprehensibility of the code, and hence how easy it is to evolve as needed, are also important issues. It is therefore a wise move for our programs to express clearly the algorithms and intention, even if that means a few more variables or lines of code.

Unfortunately Python doesn't have a way of saying "Once I have set the value associated with this variable, it cannot be changed." It is therefore a matter of programmer responsibility not to use a variable for an inappropriate purpose. It is true that other languages have the capability of controlling access to variables, but sadly Python does not. Perhaps in the future it will.

So when might it be sensible and appropriate to change the value associated with a variable? Well, whenever it is appropriate! We will see some naturally sensible uses of changing the value associated with a variable in the next section.

2.5.4 ... And So are Their Types

Remember we said that the type of a variable is the type of the last assigned value? This means that if we change the value associated with a variable, we might be changing its type. Of course this is not surprising: Python is a dynamic programming language, which means that nothing is static.

We can see this in action by trying it:

```
>>> m = 1
>>> print type ( m )
<type 'int'>
>>> m = 2.0
>>> print type ( m )
<type 'float'>
>>>
```

This could make you think "So what?" or it might make you think "That is really interesting, it opens up a whole new way of thinking about computers and programming." The reality is the latter, but if you currently think the former, hopefully we can change your view.

2.6 Sequence and Iteration

So far we have written all our programs as a single *sequence* of statements. The statements of the sequence have been executed in the order they appear from the beginning to the end. Effective for some algorithms, but limiting.

In Section 1.7 (page 16) we created a 'square spiral' algorithm and program. There we described and implemented a simple sequence, yet the algorithm (see page 17) actually exhibits great repetitiveness. We can express this repetitiveness quite concisely using the concept of *iteration*:

Iteration structures like this are generally called *loops*.

```
Initialize n to 10
Repeat
    Move forward by n pixels
    Turn left 90°
    Move forward by n pixels
    Turn left 90°
    Increment n by 10
```

There are three parts to this algorithm:

1. The initialization of the variable n.

2. The repetition specification. In this case, just repeat forever.

3. The sequence that is repeated, including changing the value of n.

All programming languages support sequence and iteration in one way or another. Python has a construct that expresses the sort of iteration of this algorithm directly, the *while statement* (also known as a *while loop*):

```python
import turtle

n = 10
while True :
    turtle.forward ( n )
    turtle.left ( 90 )
    turtle.forward ( n )
    turtle.left ( 90 )
    n += 10
```

while True is Python-speak for 'always do'.

The program starts with the necessary import statement so that we have the turtle module loaded. The program then has the statement n = 10, which creates an integer variable n associated with the value 10. There is then a while statement construct which indicates that the following (indented) sequence is to be repeated forever – the **True** says always do the loop. Note the colon; a very important bit of syntax that colon, it marks the end of the while statement itself and the beginning of the sequence that is the body of the loop.

In general, loops like this that go on forever are a bad idea.

The body of the while loop is a sequence of statements that is indented with respect to the while statement itself. The first four statements of this while loop body are function calls to the turtle module, just as in our turtle programs of the previous chapter. Note though that whilst the amount by which we turn is a constant, the amount by which we move forward is determined by the variable n. At the end of the while loop we change the value associated with n: n += 10 is a form of assignment that means set the value associated with n to whatever it was plus 10. This means that the next time the sequence is executed, the amount moved forward will be larger than it was before. This program draws the same square spiral as the previous program, but expressed using an iteration construct rather than just a long sequence.

The indentation of the statements comprising the body of the while loop is critical. Python depends on indentation to determine what is and is not part of the loop body. Other programming languages such as C, C++, Java, Ruby, Groovy, do not use indentation in this way. Using indentation in this way cuts down the number of punctuation symbols and forces us to make our code readable! Easy readability of source code is very important to everyone involved in programming, and Python is one of the few languages that really enforces it. In most programming languages, indentation is used for readability, but it is ignored by the tools used for compiling. An extra tick for Python!

Although this program directly expresses the algorithm, there is a problem. The while statement goes on forever. In the jargon, this is an *infinite loop*. Except for some special situations, infinite loops are bad. So even though this program is a significant improvement over the previous ones – which represented the iterative algorithm with a long sequence of statements – it still isn't a good program.

Infinite Loops

So why are infinite loops considered bad? When are infinite loops a good thing?

In the square spiral program, drawing continues for ever, drawing longer and longer lines. After about fifteen complete 'squares', all the drawing happens outside the default-sized drawing area. If the window is resized, we see that the program still going. Eventually, the program will outgrow the resources available on the computer: after a while the program will require more memory than the computer has. It may take many years, but it will happen. In the meantime, the program is using the processor to very little useful effect.

An example of a program we want to run for ever and not go wrong or run out of computing resources is an automatic teller machine (ATM) – we expect the machine to be available at all times, and in a state to allow us to get cash out of it. Systems such as DVD players, iPods, etc. all have a need to run for as long as they are required to.

Infinite loops should only be used when a program really does have to continue for ever in order to be deemed to be functioning correctly .

2.7 Comparisons

If we are supposed to avoid infinite loops except where they are really needed, how do we *not* have infinite loops? The general form of the while loop is:

```
while <Boolean expression> :
    <statement sequence>
```

You are immediately asking: "What is a 'Boolean expression' as opposed to an 'expression'?". We are introducing a new type here, Boolean. The Boolean type has just two values, represented by the literals **True** and **False**. A Boolean expression is an expression that results in a Boolean value.

So what are the semantics of the while statement? If the Boolean expression evaluates to **True** then the loop body is executed, if it evaluates to **False** the loop terminates – termination means that the sequence comprising the loop body is not executed and execution proceeds with the statements following the loop.

The Boolean Type

George Boole (1815–1864) invented the mathematics of systems that can have only the values 0 or 1 (false or true) which was named after him: Boolean Algebra. This algebra is the foundation on which all computers are based. In recognition of the importance of Boolean Algebra to computing, the data type that can only the values **True** or **False** is called Boolean.

In the square spiral program of the previous section we used the literal **True** for the Boolean expression, which results in an infinite loop – the loop body is always executed, there is no escape. A literal is an expression that evaluates to the value of the literal, so **True** is a valid Boolean expression, just as 10.5 is a valid float expression. The issue here is that the square spiral program isn't really the right circumstance to be using an infinite loop. What we really want to do is to write a certain number of lines, or continue until the line length reaches a certain value. What we need is to have Boolean expressions that can express this sort of requirement.

So this leads us to ask the question: what operators are there that we can use to create Boolean expressions? Python actually has many operators that can be used, some of which we are going to leave until later (Section 3.1, page 61). For now we are just going to look at comparison operators.

In mathematics, there are six operators that compare values: $<, \leq, =, \neq, \geq, >$. All of them are binary operators that result in a Boolean value (either 'true' or 'false'). Programming languages, including Python, also have these comparison operators, but they cannot use the $\leq, \neq,$ and $\geq$ symbols as they do not appear on standard keyboards. Instead, like the power operator, we have symbols for the operators that are composed of two consecutive characters with no space between them. So Python has the comparison operators:

<	less than	>	greater than
<=	less than or equal to	>=	greater than or equal to
==	equal to	!=	not equal to

The operator <> can also be used for 'not equal to', i.e. it means the same as !=.

You might think that using == for 'equal to' is silly since we could just use = as in mathematics. However, = is used in Python (and other programming languages) for the assignment statement, and it is not good to use the same symbol for two different things.

So we are now in a position to write a better version of the square spiral program (i.e. no infinite loops):

```
import turtle

n = 10
while n < 140 :
    turtle.forward ( n )
    turtle.left ( 90 )
    turtle.forward ( n )
    turtle.left ( 90 )
    n += 10
```

By using the expression n < 140 as the Boolean expression in the while statement, we have a loop that terminates: n starts with the value 10, and on each run through the loop we add 10, so the value of n will eventually become equal to 140 and the loop will *terminate*.

Reasoning about the termination of loops is very important. Whenever we write a loop, we must always check to make sure that:

- The loop has a *termination condition*, i.e. there is a situation in which the loop is actually going to terminate. In this example, the termination conditions is n < 140, so the loop terminates if the variable n is associated with any value larger than 140.

- The termination condition can be achieved. The Boolean expression involves variables and values that are associated with the loop. In this case the termination condition involves the control variable of the loop and so can be achieved.

- The termination condition will be achieved. The variables involved in the termination condition and manipulated in the loop are altered so that, at some point, the termination condition will be met. In this case n is initially associated with the value 10 and is incremented by 10 in each loop. So after fourteen times around the loop, it will terminate.

We have labored the point a bit here, but the idea is to show how easy it can be to determine if and when a loop terminates by analyzing the code. Being careful to do this can avoid a lot of pain by avoiding having things go wrong.

Explicitly infinite loops used in appropriate circumstances are fine. Unexpected infinite loops are, generally, anathema, as it can be hard to discover why the program is in an infinite loop when it shouldn't be – there is nothing quite as bad as having a loop that you think is going to terminate but which is, in fact, an infinite loop. So we must always check the termination condition and bodies of non-infinite loops to make sure that they will, in fact, terminate.

2.8 Selection

Comparison operators allow programs to make decisions. In the square spiral program the decision is when to terminate the loop. Comparisons also allow for more general decision making. In particular, all programming language support selecting between two courses of action: the if statement.

The earlier square spiral programs all drew anti-clockwise spirals. What if we want to have a clockwise spiral? We could just write a separate program:

```
import turtle

n = 10
while n < 140 :
    turtle.forward ( n )
    turtle.right ( 90 )
    turtle.forward ( n )
    turtle.right ( 90 )
    n += 10
```

but this feels very unsatisfactory to us as we feel we really ought to be able to make the same program draw either form of spiral. The core algorithm is the same in both case, so having to write a different program must be considered as inadequate. What can we do? By observation of the two programs, we see that the only difference between them is that an anti-clockwise spiral requires us to turn left, while a clockwise spiral requires us to turn right. So being able to select between two different choices of turning direction seems exactly what we need. The if statement provides a way to do this:

```
import turtle
```

Lines starting with a # are comment lines: comments are notes for the reader of the program – they are ignored by the Python system.

```
# For an anti-clockwise spiral, set this to False.
isClockwise = True
n = 10
while n < 140 :
    turtle.forward ( n )
    if isClockwise :
        turtle.right ( 90 )
    else :
        turtle.left ( 90 )
    turtle.forward ( n )
    if isClockwise :
        turtle.right ( 90 )
    else :
        turtle.left ( 90 )
    n += 10
```

There are two if statements in the code, one for each of the turns to be made:

```
if isClockwise :
    turtle.right ( 90 )
else :
    turtle.left ( 90 )
```

Each if statement starts with the word **if**, then has a Boolean expression and a colon. The first indented part is the statement sequence that is executed if the Boolean expression evaluates to true. Then there is an **else**, also followed by a colon, which is at the same indentation level as the **if** word. The **else** part also has an indented statement sequence that is executed if the Boolean expression evaluates to false.

Using a Boolean variable as a Boolean expression is perfectly reasonable, all that is needed is a Boolean value – and it looks so much neater than isClockwise == **True**!

Before progressing further with the square spiral program, we should note that the if statement doesn't have to have an else part. If statements can look like:

```
if isClockwise :
    turtle.right ( 90 )
```

This means that the indented code is executed if the Boolean expression is true and skipped if it is false. So the syntax of the if statement is one of:

```
if <Boolean expression > :          if <Boolean expression> :
    <statement sequence>                <statement sequence>
                                    else :
                                        <statement sequence>
```

Returning to the square spiral program, we should ask two questions:

1. Why do we have to edit the program to choose between clockwise and anti-clockwise spirals?

2. Why do we have to use the same statement sequence twice? Why are we having to replicate code – the forward action and if statement are replicated, and replication of code is something we really should be avoiding.

We solve Question 1 by introducing input, which we will do in the next section. To solve Question 2 we need to write our own functions, which we will introduce in the following section.

2.9   Getting Input from the User

Question 1 in the previous section raised the point that it is all very well having decision-making capabilities in a program, but if the program itself has to be edited simply to set the data needed to create the right output, then something is really wrong. Providing the data to select between clockwise and anti-clockwise spiral drawing is definitely something the user of the program should be able to provide without editing the program. Obviously there needs to be a way for the user to provide data when the program is run, i.e. we need a way of getting input from the user.

Python has a couple of statements that write a prompt on the screen and then get whatever the user types at the keyboard:

- raw_input returns whatever is typed, as a string.

- input processes the input as a Python expression to create values of a type appropriate for the input entered by the user.

An example of using raw_input is:

We put this code in a file called echo_raw_input.py…

```
s = raw_input ('Input a string : ')
print 'You entered : "' , s , '" which is of type' , type (s)
```

which just echoes back whatever we type:

…so we can execute it in script mode.

```
|> python echo_raw_input.py
Input a string : blah blah
You entered : " blah blah " which is of type <type 'str'>
```

This form of input can be very useful, but the value returned by the raw_input function is always a string. If we want to get values of other types using raw_input, we have to call raw_input and then process the string that gets returned ourselves. Such processing is called *parsing*, and it can be a very complex activity. Fortunately, we don't have to worry about parsing things ourselves for most simple cases, as there is the input function which processes input to create values of types other than string. So, for example, the program:

We put this code in a file called echo_input.py…

```
s = input ('Input : ')
print 'You entered : "' , s , '" which is of type' , type (s)
```

parses the input for us:

…so we can execute it in script mode.

```
|> python echo_input.py
Input  : 1
You entered :  " 1 " which is of type <type 'int'>
|> python echo_input.py
Input : True
You entered : " True " which is of type <type 'bool'>
```

The input function parses the input and delivers a value with an appropriate type. In this example, we input an integer number, and instead of just returning a string as raw_input would, input parses the input and delivers the value 1 of type int. This is just what we need for the square spirals program.

Using input can sometimes lead to problems:

```
|> python echo_input.py
Input  : blah blah
Traceback (most recent call last):
  File "./echoInput_2.py", line 3, in ?
    s = input ('Input  : ')
  File "<string>", line 1
    blah blah
            ^
SyntaxError: unexpected EOF while parsing
```

What is happening here? Because we are using the input statement, the characters we type are treated as a Python expression to be evaluated, and blah blah is not legal Python. Using input, if we want to input a string, we must surround it in single or double quotes to make it a valid Python expression. So:

```
|> python echo_input.py
Input  : 'blah blah'
You entered :  " blah blah " which is of type <type 'str'>
```

2.10 Functions

2.10.1 Defining and Using Functions

Functions are a mechanism for creating chunks of code that can be used again and again. We have already used functions in our programs. For example:

```
turtle.left ( 90 )
turtle.forward ( n )
```

are function calls – we are calling a function and providing a *parameter value* (the value between the parentheses) that the called function can use during its execution. Someone wrote the code to perform the actions of moving forward, turning left, and turning right, and we just use them as and when we want. This avoids us having to write the code, and avoids replication of code. So how can we create a function to solve our code replication problem in the square spiral program? Here is a program in which we create a function and then use it as part of our square spiral program:

```
import turtle

isClockwise = input ( 'Type False or 0 for anti-clockwise, True or 1 for clockwise: ' )

def drawSideAndTurn ( amount ) :
    turtle.forward ( amount )
    if isClockwise :
        turtle.right ( 90 )
    else :
        turtle.left ( 90 )

n = 10
while n < 140 :
    drawSideAndTurn ( n )
    drawSideAndTurn ( n )
    n += 10
```

NB We have changed to using input for this version of the program as well as introducing a function.

We have created a function drawSideAndTurn that draws a side and performs a turn – note how we named the function so that it describes what it does. *Self-documenting code* is code that is written in such a way that it explains its own function and behavior – when you read the code, you immediately understand what it is doing. In this case choosing a descriptive name for the function is part of the principle of writing self-documenting code, and writing self-documenting code is 'A Good Thing'. Of course, you may well be asking yourself what the:

```
def drawSideAndTurn ( amount ) :
```

syntax is all about. The word **def** says we are defining a function, drawSideAndTurn is the name of the function. The parentheses surround the list of *parameter variables*, of which there is one, amount. The colon says that the following statements that are indented, up to, but not including, the first statement that is not indented, is the function body – in this case the call to turtle.forward and the if statement.

drawSideAndTurn is a one-parameter function, so, when we call it, we give it a single value. In the while loop of the program above, the variable n is given as the parameter value. The value associated with n at the time of the call is used to initialize the function's parameter variable for this call of the function.

Functions can have as many parameters as needed, although it is usual to have less than six parameters – but this is only a general guideline.

Parameters are the way of passing values into a function when the function executes, so that the function's behavior can depend on the value passed.

2.10.2 Functions and Abstraction

Using function calls in the spiral program means that we do not have to replicate the code for drawing a side and turning twice. The reason why this is good is twofold:

1. The various parts of the code are easier to comprehend: they are small and *cohesive*.

2. Each part of the algorithm only ever appears once, which makes it easier to change things in the future.

This is an example of *abstraction*: we have put the detail in the function so that the main code sequence is smaller and more comprehensible.

We use abstractions all the time in our daily lives. For example, we can talk about 'a table'. This is a very abstract concept and yet it means something to (almost) everyone who speaks English. Generally people will think of four vertical legs and a horizontal surface and think of it as something to put things on. There are an infinite number of things that count as tables, but by abstracting we can talk about any or all of them without describing all the details. Abstractions enable human beings to communicate.

In programming, creating functions is one of the fundamental abstractions that enable us to communicate the implementations of algorithms to ourselves, to other people, and, of course, to the computer. Abstraction is the cornerstone of programming.

2.10.3 Functions as Actions and Functions as Values

Functions like drawSideAndTurn, turtle.forward, turtle.left and turtle.right just do something; functions such as these collect together a sequence of action statements, they do not calculate a value. These functions are abstractions over actions.

From mathematics, we are familiar with functions. For example:

$$y = f(x)$$

The function f is a relationship between the variable x and the variable y. Instead of being an abstraction over actions, a mathematical function is about relationships between values – mathematical functions calculate values. So the obvious question is: do programming languages, and Python in particular, allow functions to be used to calculate values rather than performing actions? The answer is a resounding "yes".

As well as having parameters to allow the caller of a function to pass some values, a function can return a value. Functions that have return values can be used in expressions, and herein lies the real power of functions in programming languages.

> *Side Effects*
> The term *side effect* is used to describe the actions that happen in a function that are not directly associated with calculating a return value. Functions in mathematics never have side effects, since they are only about values. Functions in Python may or may not have side effects. It is generally agreed that side effects should be minimized to those that are absolutely essential for the correct execution of the program – some people think side effects should be eradicated completely, but that is another story.

The Python system comes with a number of functions that calculate values, all of which are free from side effects. One example is **abs**: 'abs' stands for 'absolute value'. it is a function that can be applied to numbers (either integers or floats) and, if the number is positive, it returns that value. If however the parameter is a negative value, then the function returns the negation of that value, i.e. it returns the positive number of the same magnitude. Not an earth-shatteringly interesting function, agreed, but it can nonetheless be immensely useful. Say we are given the coordinates of two corners of a rectangle, for example:

we can write a function that calculates and returns the area of the rectangle:

```
def areaOfRectangle ( x1 , y1 , x2 , y2 ) :
    return ( x2 - x1 ) * ( y2 - y1 )
```

We use a *return statement* to let the Python system know that the function returns a value and that the following expression evaluates to the value that should be returned. So let's try it:

```
>>> def areaOfRectangle ( x1 , y1 , x2 , y2 ) :
...    return ( x2 - x1 ) * ( y2 - y1 )
...
>>> print areaOfRectangle ( 0 , 0 , 10 , 10 )
100
>>>
```

In interactive mode, we have to type in a blank line at the end of the function to tell the Python system the function has ended.

That seems to do the right thing. We must, though, try a few more data points to give us some confidence that the function is actually giving the right area values:

```
>>> print areaOfRectangle ( 10 , 5 , 40 , 25 )
600
>>> print areaOfRectangle ( -10 , -10 , 10 , 10 )
400
>>> print areaOfRectangle ( 10 , 10 , 0 , 0 )
100
>>> print areaOfRectangle ( 0.5 , 0.5 , 10.5 , 10.5 )
100.0
>>> print areaOfRectangle ( 10.5 , 10.5 , 0.5 , 0.5 )
100.0
>>> print areaOfRectangle ( 0.5 , 0.5 , 10 , 10 )
90.25
>>>
```

OK, this seems most satisfactory. We can use integers or floats and our function does the right thing. The function appears to be correct. Well maybe not. All the examples give the coordinates of the bottom-left corner and top-right corner. What happens if we give the top-left corner and bottom-right corner coordinates?

```
>>> print areaOfRectangle ( 0 , 10 , 10 , 0 )
-100
>>>
```

Uuurrrggghhh... the result appears to be a negative area, but this cannot be: areas are always positive. We can deal with this behavior of the function by always ensuring that the values given as parameters are the bottom-left and top-right coordinates, or we can do the right thing and fix the definition of the function by using abs:

```
def areaOfRectangle ( x1 , y1 , x2 , y2 ) :
    return abs ( ( x2 - x1 ) * ( y2 - y1 ) )
```

Now we have removed the assumption that was in the earlier version and the function now gives the correct (positive) result:

```
>>> def areaOfRectangle ( x1 , y1 , x2 , y2 ) :
...    return  abs ( ( x2 - x1 ) * ( y2 - y1 ) )
...
>>> print areaOfRectangle ( 0 , 10 , 10 , 0 )
100
>>> print areaOfRectangle ( 0 , 0 , 10 , 10 )
100
>>> print areaOfRectangle ( 10 , 10 , 0 , 0 )
100
>>> print areaOfRectangle ( 0.5 , 0.5 , 10 , 10 )
90.25
>>> print areaOfRectangle ( 0.5 , 10 , 0.5 , 10 )
0.0
>>> print areaOfRectangle ( 0.5 , 10 , 10 , 0.5 )
90.25
>>>
```

This is better. So the abs function does have a use.

Did you spot that not only is abs a value-returning function with no side effects, so is areaOfRectangle. We have written our first value-returning function. All we needed to do was use a return statement with an expression. Easy.

> ### Referential Transparency
> If a function has no side effects and always has the same return value for any given parameter(s), then it is said to be *referentially transparent*. Many people believe that referential transparency is not only good but is essential in all functions.

The abs and areaOfRectangle functions are examples of referentially transparent functions: no matter how many times you call the function with the same parameters, the function will always return the same value.

2.10.4   The Type of a Function

Although functions such as areaOfRectangle and abs are of type function:

```
>>> print type ( areaOfRectangle )
<type 'function'>
>>> print type ( abs )
<type 'builtin_function_or_method'>
>>>
```

the value returned by the function definitely is not. When programmers talk about the 'type of a function', they are not referring to the type function but are talking about the type of the return value of a function. So what is the type of the return value from the abs function?

```
>>> print type ( abs ( -4 ) )
<type 'int'>
>>> print type ( abs ( 20.56 ) )
<type 'float'>
>>>
```

The abs function is returning a value of the type we expect it to. This is very reasonable. But what are the values being returned?

```
>>> print abs ( -4 )
4
>>> print abs ( 20.56 )
20.56
>>>
```

Expecting the Unexpected

If you try using the Python system in interpreter mode to output the value of an object just by naming it, sometimes you see things that might initially surprise you:

```
>>> print abs ( 20.56 )
20.56
>>> abs ( 20.56 )
20.559999999999999
>>>
```

Not quite what we were expecting. The values are nearly the same but not exactly so. And therein lies the issue: integer numbers are always held exactly in a computer, but float numbers are not. Computer hardware cannot, in general, represent floats exactly, so float values may have tiny amounts of variation during expression evaluation. This means we can sometimes get what appear to be surprising effects. The Python system is very careful to try and avoid any of these 'surprises' from being really surprising, so, despite the above:

```
>>> print 20.56 == abs ( 20.56 )
True
>>>
```

Although the abs function is a built-in function of the Python system, how might we implement this as an explicitly declared function? The function:

```
def abs ( x ) :
    if x < 0 :
        return -x
    else :
        return x
```

seems to do the job:

```
>>> print abs ( 2 )
2
>>> print abs ( -2 )
2
>>> print abs ( 2.0 )
2.0
>>> print abs ( -2.0 )
2.0
>>> print abs ( 'c' )
c
>>>
```

Did you spot that last statement we tried? The function appears to do the right thing even for parameter values that are not numbers! This abs functions works no matter what the type of x as long as the expression x < 0 can be evaluated. So we can use integers or floats as parameters and it all works: the type of the function is the type of whichever value was returned. But how is it that abs ('c') worked? Characters are stored as integer values in the computer, so there is a way of interpreting the expression 'c'< 0 and hence the expression is not an error. But does it make sense? Well, not really, since there is no concept of a negative character value.

So, because abs ('c') is not really a sensible use of the abs function, the built-in abs function checks to ensure that the parameter value is a number and does not work for other types:

```
>>> print abs ( 'c' )
Traceback (most recent call last):
  File "<stdin>", line 1, in ?
TypeError: bad operand type for abs()
>>>
```

This is entirely by design and is reasonable: the concept of absolute value only applies to numbers, so Python reinforces this by ensuring that the function is only applied to values of the right type.

Missing out the End-of-line

Python allows the end-of-line to be omitted after a : in a statement. So for example, we can write our abs function:

```
def abs ( x ) :
    if x < 0 : return -x
    else : return x
```

This feature is generally only used in a few very specific situations – the above is just such a situation. There is only a single statement following the : and the code seems more readable without the additional end-of-lines. Ease of reading the code is always the primary criteria, but this is very much an individual and subjective thing.
   If in any doubt, use an end-of-line.

What about other varieties of function where there is less restriction? The Python system has min and max functions that return the lesser or greater of two values respectively. Such functions can be applied to any values that have an ordering so that comparisons are possible. Trying min:

```
>>> print min ( 2 , 3 )
2
>>> print min ( 3.0 , 2 )
2
>>> print min ( 3 , 2.0 )
2.0
>>> print min ( 'c' , 'a' )
a
>>>
```

Clearly no surprises, the functions works no matter what types x and y are as long as the expression x < y can be evaluated. Python does what we expect it to! Python is again showing adherence to the Principle of Least Surprise.

A function that is able to take parameters of any type is usually called a *generic function*, and the parameter variable that is able to work with values of any type is called a *polymorphic variable*. So here min is a generic function and the parameter variables x and y are acting as polymorphic variables.

Generic functions are generally good things since they can usually do more that you intended originally. In this case, the min function, which we originally intended for dealing with integers and floats, can be used with characters. Is min an earth-shatteringly important function? Clearly not. Is polymorphism an exceedingly important feature of Python? Oh, yes, yes, yes, yes, yes.

2.11 Functions Are Data

In the earlier version of the drawSideAndTurn function, the decision about whether we are doing an anti-clockwise or clockwise square spiral is made every time the function is called. Yet the decision need only be made once, at the point we do the input. So how can we do this? We can use a variable of type function!

```
import turtle

turn = turtle.left
if input ( 'Type False or 0 for anti-clockwise, True or 1 for clockwise: ' ) :
    turn = turtle.right

def drawSideAndTurn ( amount ) :
    turtle.forward ( amount )
    turn ( 90 )

n = 10
while n < 140 :
    drawSideAndTurn ( n )
    drawSideAndTurn ( n )
    n += 10
```

The variable turn is associated with a function, turtle.left. Depending on the result of the user input, we may change the function that turn is associated with to turtle.right. Thus the decision about whether to create a clockwise or anti-clockwise spiral is made at the point of user input, with the choice stored using the variable turn. When it comes to actually making the turn (in the function drawSideAndTurn), there is no longer any selection, only a call to the function with which turn is associated.

2.12 An Example Development: Drawing Circles

As an example of developing a program, let's create a program to draw the image:

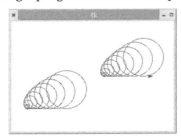

2.12.1 Thinking about the Problem

Before trying to write any code, we must think about the problem and what is needed. The following spring to mind immediately:

- Drawing this image seems to imply making use of the Turtle module. There are other ways of drawing images with Python, but this looks like a job for Turtle.

- There are two major parts to the image, so this looks like a job for a function called twice, with some positioning between the two calls. We can describe this in pseudocode as:

    Move to first position
    Draw circles
    Move to second position
    Draw circles

- The parts themselves look like a sequence of larger and larger circles with a move to the right before drawing the next. This seems like a job for some iteration. We can describe the *Draw circles* pseudocode line using pseudocode, as:

    Set radius of first circle
    Repeat 10 times
      Draw circle of given radius
      Move right a bit
      Increase radius for next circle

- The Turtle module has a function for drawing a circle, so we need to find out how to use that.

So the overall image is a couple of calls of a function that draws a sequence of circles, probably using iteration. Now, having thought about what is needed, we need to do some experimenting and evolving of code.

2.12.2 Drawing a Sequence of Circles

The start point seems to be to try and get the sequence of circles, so let's write a program to draw the circles. As we know we are going to need to draw the sequence of circles more than once, let's create a function for doing the drawing. To start, we draw just one circle:

```
import turtle

def drawCircles ( ) :
    turtle.circle ( 10 )

drawCircles ( )
```

This gives us a framework in which to evolve things – except that when we run the code, the frame with the image disappears immediately. We need to put something at the end of our program to stop that happening. A bit of input will do that. We'll add it in the next version of the program.

The next step is to get the sequence of circles. Let's try putting some iteration in the function:

```
import turtle

def drawCircles ( ) :
    i = 0
    while i < 10 :
        turtle.circle ( i * 4 )
        i += 1

drawCircles ( )

raw_input ( 'Press any key to terminate: ' )
```

2.12.3   Counted Iteration – the For Loop

When we first wrote the program above, we accidentally wrote the function incorrectly as:

```
def drawCircles ( ) :
    i = 0
    while i < 10 :
        turtle.circle ( i * 4 )
```

which resulted in an infinite loop. The problem was obvious in this case, as the turtle just kept on redrawing the one and only circle: we had failed to check the loop termination condition properly. Errors like this are unfortunately quite common and this just shouldn't have to be the case. In fact, this sort of iteration structure – where we count through numbers from 0 up to, but not including, a given number – is so common that Python has some syntax for it, the *for loop*. So, whilst we can always write counted iteration along the lines of:

```
i = 0
while i < 10
    . . .
    i += 1
```

Ellipsis (three dots) is used to indicate that there is some code present but it does not need to be specified for the point being made.

we can write the same iteration as:

```
for i in range ( 10 ) :
    . . .
```

The Python system takes care of all the things needed to initialize, check and increment the counter that is used for the iteration. How does it work? The range (10) function call creates a list of the values from 0 to the number one less that the parameter, so in this case, this means the list 0, 1, 2, 3, 4, 5, 6, 7, 8, 9. The **for** then causes the body of the loop to be executed 10 times setting the variable (i in this case) to 0 the first time round, to 1 the next time round, and so on. Thus the effect is exactly the same as the **while** loop, but with much less clutter – and hence less to go wrong!

The idea of *counted iteration* is common is programming, so it is right to have a construct for it to minimize the hassle and maximize the ease of programming.

In fact, the **for** statement can be used for more than counted iteration, but more on that in the next chapter.

2.12.4 Finishing the Circles

Returning to the problem at hand, to create the sequence of circles, we need to introduce an offset between each of the circles we draw:

```
import turtle

def drawCircles ( ) :
    for i in range ( 10 ) :
        turtle.circle ( i * 4 )
        turtle.up ( )
        turtle.forward ( i * 2 )
        turtle.down ( )

drawCircles ( )

raw_input ( 'Press any key to terminate: ' )
```

The turtle.up and turtle.down functions are used so that the move forward does not draw a line.

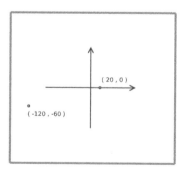

OK, this looks very like one of the circle sequences. Now all we need to do is to extend the program to draw both instances of the offset circles in roughly the right place. We could use the features of the turtle module we have met already to raise the pen, turn in an appropriate direction, move an appropriate distance, turn to face the right direction, and put the pen down. However, this would require a lot of fiddling and experimentation when there is an easier way: we can use the turtle.goto function.

The turtle module drawing area is a bit like graph paper: each point of the drawing area has an (x, y) coordinate – x is the left–right position and y is the up–down position. The center of the drawing area is coordinate $(0, 0)$, and is called the *origin*. Positive values of x are to the right of the origin, and positive values of y are up from the origin. So we could mark two locations, (-120, -60) and (20, 0) thus:

The turtle.goto function is used to reposition the turtle to a given coordinate without changing the orientation or pen state of the turtle. Since this is a move of the turtle, if the pen is down, we will draw a line. This is not what we want: we want to do a repositioning with the pen up so as not to draw a line. This clearly indicates that we should create a function to package this to create a "move to a given location without drawing anything" action. We'll call the function setPostion. Using this new function and the drawCircles function we have already, we can create the program that draws the complete diagram:

```
import turtle

def setPosition ( x , y ) :
    turtle.up ( )
    turtle.goto ( x , y )
    turtle.down ( )

def drawCircles ( ) :
    for i in range ( 10 ) :
        turtle.circle ( i * 4 )
        turtle.up ( )
        turtle.forward ( i * 2 )
        turtle.down ( )

setPosition ( -120 , -60 )
drawCircles ( )
setPosition ( 20 , 0 )
drawCircles ( )

raw_input ( 'Press any key to terminate: ' )
```

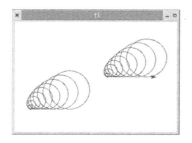

setPosition wraps a call to turtle.goto so that the turtle.up and turtle.down functions can be used to ensure that the move does not draw a line.

This in an important point about the Turtle module – it doesn't have separate 'move and draw' and 'move but don't draw' operations: it has move operations, and, if the pen is up, there is no drawing, whereas if the pen is down, there is. So we encapsulate our desire to have a 'just move don't write' operation by creating a function. This is abstraction at work again. We build the functions we need to express easily the solution to our problem out of the bits we have.

2.13   An Example Development: Currency Conversion

As another example of developing a program, let's consider creating a program to convert from one currency to another.

2.13.1   US Dollars to UK Sterling

To start, we consider conversion from US Dollars to UK Sterling. Clearly we need to know how much to change and what the exchange rate is. Let's assume we are going to change $10 and that the exchange rate is 0.541272. We can then write the program:

```
dollars = 10
exchangeRate = 0.541272
pounds = dollars * exchangeRate
print dollars , 'USD is' , pounds , 'GBP'
```

On executing this program we get:

```
10 USD is 5.41272 GBP
```

which is as expected. However this program solves only one problem and doesn't really do anything more that a few taps on a calculator could achieve. We can do better by obtaining the value from the user when they run the program:

```
dollars = input ( '$ to exchange : ' )
exchangeRate = 0.541272
pounds = dollars * exchangeRate
print dollars , 'USD is' , pounds , 'GBP'
```

2.13.2 Adding UK Sterling to US Dollars

Now how about going the other way, from UK Sterling to US Dollars? The temptation might be just to write a new program, but let's avoid that temptation. The main reason for this is that the algorithm and indeed the exchange rate are the same and we want to avoid replication. So, using some if statements to introduce selection:

```
import sys

currency = raw_input ( 'GPB or USD being tendered to exchange : ' )
amount = input ( 'Amount to exchange : ' )
exchangeRate = 0.541272
convertedAmount = 0
convertedCurrency = ""
if currency == 'GBP' :
    convertedAmount = amount / exchangeRate
    convertedCurrency = 'USD'
else :
    if currency == 'USD' :
        convertedAmount = amount * exchangeRate
        convertedCurrency = 'GBP'
    else :
        print currency, 'is not a currency this program can currently deal with.'
        sys.exit ( )
print amount, currency, "is", convertedAmount, convertedCurrency
```

Hmmm...This looks a little bit less neat than we would like it to: we want to select between three options ('USD', 'GBP', or something else) and having to use the if-else construct (which is selecting between two choices) makes the code a bit ungainly. Is there anything we can do about it? Yes – but then you probably guessed that was going to be the answer from the way we led up to it.

2.13.3 The If Statement Revisited

When we described the if statement earlier (Section 2.8, page 38), we didn't include a variation of the if statement that is exactly what we need in this situation. As well as the if and if-else forms shown earlier, there are if-elif and if-elif-else forms:

elif is a short form of **else if**. Some people use one, some the other, both are valid – but always be consistent, we use **elif**.

```
if <Boolean expression> :
    <statement sequence>
{
elif <Boolean expression> :
    <statement sequence>
} *
{
else :
    <statement sequence>
} ?
```

The braces ({ and }) are used here to enclose bits of the syntax, they are not themselves part of the Python syntax. The asterisk (*) and question mark (?) are also saying something about syntax rather than being part of the language. The asterisk means any number of times and the question mark means it is optional. So an if statement has an if clause, then some number of elif clauses and there may or may not be an else clause.

Let's rewrite the program using this variant of the if statement:

```
import sys

currency = raw_input ( 'GPB or USD being tendered to exchange : ' )
amount = input ( 'Amount to exchange : ' )
exchangeRate = 0.541272
convertedAmount = 0
convertedCurrency = ""
if currency == 'GBP' :
    convertedAmount = amount / exchangeRate
    convertedCurrency = 'USD'
elif currency == 'USD' :
    convertedAmount = amount * exchangeRate
    convertedCurrency = 'GBP'
else :
    print currency, 'is not a currency this program can currently deal with.'
    sys.exit ()
print amount, currency, "is", convertedAmount, convertedCurrency
```

This looks much more like our intention, and is therefore a better program: using the full syntax capabilities of Python enables us to express what we mean more easily, making for simpler and more comprehensible programs.

2.13.4 Adding Australian Dollars

Now how about adding Australian Dollars to the conversion capabilities of this program? We could extend the structure and idea of the previous program:

```
import sys

fromCurrency = raw_input ( 'Currency being tendered to exchange : ' )
toCurrency = raw_input ( 'Currency requested : ' )
amount = input ( 'Amount to exchange : ' )

USD_GBP_rate = 0.541272
USD_AUD_rate = 1.34958
GBP_AUD_rate = 2.5060

def notImplemented () :
    print 'The requested currency conversion is not yet implemented.'
    sys.exit ()

convertedAmount = 0
convertedCurrency = ""
if fromCurrency == 'GBP' :
    if toCurrency == 'USD' :
        convertedAmount = amount / USD_GBP_rate
    elif toCurrency == 'AUD' :
        convertedAmount = amount * GBP_AUD_rate
    else :
        notImplemented ()
elif fromCurrency == 'AUD' :
    if toCurrency == 'USD' :
        convertedAmount = amount / USD_AUD_rate
    elif toCurrency == 'GBP' :
```

```
                    convertedAmount = amount / GBP_AUD_rate
            else :
                    notImplemented ( )
    elif fromCurrency == 'USD' :
        if toCurrency == 'GBP' :
                convertedAmount = amount * USD_GBP_rate
        elif toCurrency == 'AUD' :
                convertedAmount = amount * USD_AUD_rate
        else :
                notImplemented ( )
    else :
        notImplemented ( )

    print amount , fromCurrency , 'is' , convertedAmount, toCurrency
```

This program certainly works as intended, but if you are thinking that it is beginning to look a bit ugly as an algorithm, and as a program, then congratulate yourself – we certainly think this is the case. The point here is that we have probably reached the limit of this algorithmic approach – if we try to add another currency to this program, everything gets very messy indeed. To take this program further we need to have a completely new approach, one that is data oriented as opposed to the purely decision-oriented approach of the above programs. We will revisit this problem in Section 4.8.3 (page 143).

> ### Chapter Summary
>
> In this chapter we have found that:
>
> - Everything in Python has a *type*.
> - Operators and operands are combined to create expressions.
> - Variables are names that associate with values, and the association can be changed.
> - Using variables helps us to create programs that are easy to read and understand.
> - There are a number of important programming constructs:
>   - Sequence.
>   - Iteration – the **while** and **for** statements.
>   - Selection – the **if** statement.
> - Boolean expressions are important for controlling iteration and selection.
> - Doing simple input is simple using input and raw_input.
> - Functions are used to create abstractions. Cohesion, encapsulation, side effects and referential transparency are important issues when creating functions.

Self-Review Questions

Self-review 2.1 What are the types of the following literals? 1, 1., 1.0, "1", "1.", "1.0", '1', '1.', 100000000000000000, 100000000000000000., 100000000000000000.0.

Self-review 2.2 Explain the difference between the following two statements:

```
print 12
print "12"
```

Self-review 2.3 Highlight the literals in the following program:

```
a=3
b='1'
c=a-2
d=a-c
e="dog"
f=', went to mow a meadow.'
g='man'
print a,g,"and his",e,f,a,g,",",d,g,",",c,g,"and his",e,f
```

Self-review 2.4 What is the output of the above program?

Self-review 2.5 What are the types of the variables a, b, c, d, e, f, g in the above program?

Self-review 2.6 Is there a difference between the *type* of the expressions "python" and 'python'?

Self-review 2.7 What is the result of 4+4/2+2?

Self-review 2.8 Add brackets as needed to the above expression to make the answer:

a. 2

b. 5

c. 6

Self-review 2.9 What is iteration?

Self-review 2.10 What is the difference between the expressions c = 299792458 and c = 2.99792458 * 10 ** 8?

Self-review 2.11 What does this expression n < 140 mean? I.e. what test is undertaken and what is the value and type of the result?

Self-review 2.12 What is the value of the variable val after the executing the expression val = 1 / 2? What is the type of val?

Self-review 2.13 What is the value of the variable val after the executing the expression val = 1 / 2.0? What is the type of val?

Self-review 2.14 What are the possible values contained in a variable of type bool?

Programming Exercises

Exercise 2.1 The program:

```
import turtle

scale = 4

## Letter A
turtle.down ( )
# Point upwards to begin
turtle.left ( turtle.heading ( ) + 90 )
turtle.right ( 20 )
turtle.forward ( 10 * scale )
turtle.right ( 70 )
turtle.forward ( 1 * scale )
turtle.right ( 70 )
turtle.forward ( 10 * scale )
turtle.backward ( 5 * scale )
turtle.right ( 90 + 20 )
turtle.forward ( 5 * scale )
#Move to right of letter and over 1 * scale
turtle.up ( )
turtle.backward ( 5 * scale )
turtle.left ( 110 )
turtle.forward ( 5 * scale )
turtle.left ( 70 )
turtle.forward ( 1 * scale )

## Letter B
turtle.down ( )
# Point upwards to begin
turtle.left ( turtle.heading ( ) + 90 )
turtle.forward ( 10 * scale )
turtle.right ( 90 )
turtle.forward ( 4 * scale )
turtle.right ( 90 )
turtle.forward ( 4 * scale )
turtle.left ( 90 )
turtle.backward ( 1 * scale )
turtle.forward ( 2 * scale )
turtle.right ( 90 )
turtle.forward ( 6 * scale )
turtle.right ( 90 )
turtle.forward ( 5 * scale )
# Move to right of letter
turtle.up ( )
turtle.right ( 180 )
turtle.forward ( 6 * scale )

## Letter C
turtle.down ( )
# Point upwards to begin
turtle.left ( turtle.heading ( ) + 90 )
turtle.forward ( 10 * scale )
```

```
turtle.right ( 90 )
turtle.forward ( 4 * scale )
turtle.backward ( 4 * scale )
turtle.left ( 90 )
turtle.backward ( 10 * scale )
turtle.right ( 90 )
turtle.forward ( 4 * scale )
# Move to right of letter
turtle.up ( )
turtle.forward ( 1 * scale )

# Pause
raw_input ( "Press any key to end." )
```

causes the following when executed:

The code for writing each individual letter is fairly easy to spot, because of the comments. There's a much easier way to divide this code up though: functions. The exercise then is to:

1. Modify the code so that each letter is drawn by a function: drawA ( ) for the letter A, for example.

2. Add the letters "D" and "E" as functions.

3. Amend the code to display the word "DECADE" rather than "ABCDE".

Exercise 2.2 Rewrite your answer to Exercise 1.4 (three colored circles one above the other) using a function.

Hint: The function should probably have three parameters.

Exercise 2.3 Rewrite your answer to Exercise 1.5 (three colored, filled circles one above the other) using a function.

Hint: The answer should be a trivial extension to the answer of the previous question.

Exercise 2.4 Rewrite your answer to question Exercise 1.6 (drawing a hexagon) using iteration.

Exercise 2.5 Extend your answer to the previous question so that the number of sides to draw is a parameter – this is a programming solution for Self-review 1.10. How many sides do you need before it looks like a circle?

Exercise 2.6 Rewrite your answer to Challenge 1.1 using a function.

Exercise 2.7 Write a program to draw the following image:

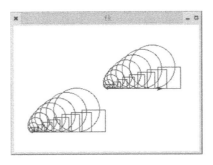

Exercise 2.8 When the code:

```
import turtle

sides = 3
length = 5

for i in range ( sides ) :
    for j in range ( length ) :
        turtle.forward ( 10 )
        turtle.circle ( 10 )
    turtle.right ( 120 )

raw_input ( 'Press any key to end' )
```

is executed the result is:

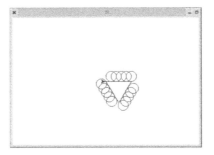

i.e. it draws a triangle with circles along its edges. The *intention* was that modifying the variable sides would allow you to draw a square (by setting it to 4), a pentagon (setting it to 5) and so on. This doesn't currently work, however. The programmer clearly became distracted and left the program half finished. Your job is to make the code work as intended.

Hint: Remember that for any regular polygon, the external angles always add up to 360. If they didn't, it would either not be closed or it would overlap, or it would not be regular!

Challenges

Challenge 2.1 Go back and make sure you finish the programming exercise on creating polygons surrounded by circles. If necessary modify the program so that the drawing is undertaken by a function with parameters for side length and number of sides. Then add a further parameter to your function that allows the size of the circles to be adjusted. Finally, write a program that asks the user to enter values for side length, number of sides and size of circles – this is now a general purpose regular-polygon-surrounded-by-circles generator. Not entirely useful per se, but fun!

Challenge 2.2 Can you spot a way of making money given the exchange rates in the last version of the currency conversion program? The trick is to write a program to show how much you could lose or make by exchanging between these currencies.

What stops people (as opposed to banks) exploiting this for profit?

(If you are a bank, the opportunities here are called *currency arbitrage*, but it is a high-risk activity.)

Controlling the Flow

Learning Outcomes

At the end of this chapter you will be able to:

- Construct Boolean expressions.
- Use if statements with **if**, **elif** and **else** clauses to execute blocks of code based on Boolean expressions.
- Implement recursive functions that terminate correctly.
- Identify the *base case* and *recursive case* of a recursive function.
- Implement recursive and iterative algorithms in Python.
- Determine how many times the body of a loop will be executed and whether a loop will terminate.

- Use the keywords **break** and **continue** for fine-grained control over iteration.
- Implement nested loops.
- Convert a **for** loop into an equivalent **while** loop and vice versa.
- Choose appropriately when to use **while** rather than **for** loops.
- Draw fractal curves (such as the von Koch Snowflake) using the Turtle module.

In this chapter we are going to take a more detailed look at various aspects of the control flow mechanisms we introduced in the last chapter – sequence, selection, iteration, and function call – and introduce a special form of function call – recursion. The first step is to look in more detail at Boolean expressions, answering some of the questions left over from the last chapter.

3.1 Boolean Expressions

In Section 2.7 (page 36) we introduced the Boolean type and Boolean expressions that involved just a single comparison. We said that there were other operators that could be used in Boolean expressions, but didn't say what they were. This is the section where we introduce them. The point is, of course, that having single comparison expressions is useful, but we really need to be able to express more complicated conditions for our selection and iteration constructs.

3.1.1 And, Or, and Not

In the last chapter we introduced **False** and **True** as the literals of the Boolean type. We also saw that variables can be of Boolean type and that we can use assignment with such variables. So, for example:

```
over18 = True
isMale = False
```

Clearly, there is an assumption here that all people are either male or female.

assigns the value **True** to the Boolean variable over18 and the value **False** to the Boolean variable isMale. We can use Python in interactive mode to try this out and prove it to ourselves:

```
>>> over18 = True
>>> print type ( over18 )
<type 'bool'>
>>> print over18
True
>>>
```

'bool' is Python's internal way of saying Boolean.

In the last chapter (page 37) we introduced the comparison operators, which are binary operators that compare two values of the same type and return a Boolean value. So, for example, we can determine whether someone's age is over 21, or if they have a shoe size greater than 10, using expressions like:

```
age > 21
shoeSize < 10
```

but how can we express the condition 'adult female'? On the assumption that adult means being at least 18 and that being female means not being male, we need to express that both age >= 18 and isMale != **True** are true at the same time. In the spirit of extensive experimentation, let's try something to see if we can express that one condition *and* another condition are both true:

```
>>> age = 21
>>> over18 = age > 18
>>> isMale = False
>>> isFemale = isMale != True
>>> print over18 and isFemale
True
>>>
```

It seems that Python understands the word **and** between two Boolean values. This is promising. In fact, the keyword **and** is an operator that creates a Boolean expression from two Boolean expressions: it is a binary, infix operator. The result of the **and** operator is **True** if, and only if, both operands are **True**, otherwise it is **False**.

A *binary operator* is one that has two operands. An *infix operator* is one that appears between the operands.

Did the statement:

```
isFemale = isMale != True
```

seem awkward to you? Using the expression:

```
isMale != True
```

or alternatively:

```
isMale == False
```

strikes us as a clumsy way of changing a Boolean value into the other Boolean value – after all, we never have to use:

```
isMale == True
```

or:

```
isMale != False
```

we can just use isMale. The **not** operator is what we need to make things simpler. The **not** operator is a prefix, unary operator that returns **True** if the operand is **False** and **False** if the operand is **True**: **not** returns the reverse of the Boolean value of its operand:

```
>>> isMale = True
>>> print isMale
True
>>> print not isMale
False
>>>
```

A *unary operator* is one that has a single operand. A *prefix operator* is one that appears before the operand.

So, we can express the idea of 'adult female' as over18 **and not** isMale:

```
age = 21
over18 = age >= 18
isMale = False
isAdultFemale = over18 and not isMale
```

This code sets the integer variable age to 21, then uses it in a comparison expression to set the Boolean variable over18 to **True** (age >= 18 evaluates to **True**), then the variable isMale is set to **False**, and lastly a Boolean expression is evaluated to set the variable isAdultFemale. The expression over18 **and not** isMale evaluates **True** if over18 is true and isMale is false – so in this case isAdultFemale is set to **True**.

Boolean expressions can be composed of expressions, so we could have written the above sequence as:

```
age = 21
isMale = False
isAdultFemale = age >= 18 and not isMale
```

avoiding the need for the variable over18. To understand how the expression in this last statement is evaluated, we have to know that the >= operator has higher precedence than **and**. So the sub-expressions age >= 18 and **not** isMale get evaluated and then the operator **and** is evaluated using the results of the evaluations of the sub-expressions. It is as though we had written:

```
isAdultFemale = ( age >= 18 ) and ( not isMale )
```

but we didn't need to have the parentheses because the precedence of the operators means that this is how it is evaluated anyway without them.

The approach of avoiding using parentheses except where they are definitely needed is very prevalent in programming. In the main this is a sensible approach, but we feel that if there is any doubt, or it makes it easier to read the code, then parentheses should be used. Correct and readable code is far, far more important than typing fewer characters.

Use parentheses in expressions if it makes the code easier to read.

In the following example we have used parentheses precisely because it helps make the code more easily readable:

```
BAD_DEBT_CODE = 100
income = 20000
age = 23
code = 0
offerMortgage = ( age >= 21 ) and ( income >= 18000 ) and ( code != BAD_DEBT_CODE )
```

In the Boolean expression of the last line, offerMortgage will be **True** only if all three sub-expressions evaluate to **True**, i.e. age is greater than or equal to 21, income is greater than or equal to 18,000 and code is not equal to the value of BAD_DEBT_CODE – in this sequence offerMortgage will be **True**.

As a general rule it is good to keep Boolean expressions simple and short. However, there are occasions when well-written code requires quite lengthy expressions. In these (infrequent) situations, it can be very helpful to split a statement across multiple lines in the file: long expressions can be more easily read if they are split across multiple lines of the file. In Python, this is achieved by placing a \ (backslash) character at the end of the line that is not the end of a statement and continuing the statement on the next line. Lines split this way will be interpreted as a single statement. So, as an extreme example:

```
BAD_DEBT_CODE=100
income = 20000
age = 23
code = 0
depositPercent = 0.8
offerMortgage = \
            ( code != BAD_DEBT_CODE ) and \
            ((( depositPercent >= 0.1 ) and ( age >= 21 ) and ( income >= 18000 )) or \
             ( income / 5000 >= age ))
```

The \ must be the last character on the line. Be careful there are no spaces or tabs after the \.

Did you spot the fact that we slipped in a new operator? The **or** operator is a binary, infix operator as is the **and** operator. The result of an **or** operation is **True** if either or both of the operands are **True** and **False** if, and only if, both operands are **False**. **or** has the same precedence as **and**, so parentheses are often essential!

So under what circumstances does this code indicate that someone can be offered a mortgage? To understand the expression we need to break it down and examine the sub-expressions separately. The rules of precedence require that sub-expressions within brackets are evaluated before (sub-)expressions involving the parenthesized sub-expressions. So we immediately separate out:

A. code != BAD_DEBT_CODE

B. ((depositPercent >= 0.1) **and** (age >= 21) **and** (income >= 18000)) **or** (income / 5000 >= age)

A is straightforward since it is a single comparison. B is a little more complex so we need to deconstruct it further. Hopefully, it is clear that the overall expression is simply A **and** B. Deconstructing B, we have the sub-expressions:

C. (depositPercent >= 0.1) **and** (age >= 21) **and** (income >= 18000)

D. income / 5000 >= age

B can now be written as C **or** D and the whole expression is A **and** (C **or** D). We can also deconstruct C into:

E. depositPercent >= 0.1

F. age >= 21

G. income >= 18000

if we want, so that we think of the whole expression as A **and** ((E **and** F **and** G) **or** D).

To qualify for a mortgage therefore, A must evaluate to **True** (code is not equal to BAD_DEBT_CODE) and either C or D must be true. C is true for people over 21 that have a 10% or greater deposit and an income of over 18,000. D is true for people who earn at least 5 times their age, in thousands. That is, a nineteen-year-old must earn at least 95,000.

We suspect that no bank anywhere will ever actually give loans on the basis of the expression here, mostly because the total value of the loan requested is not part of the calculation! It is a good example of a Python Boolean expression though.

Truth Tables

A *truth table* is an enumeration of all the possibilities of input and result of the evaluation of an expression. So if we have two Boolean variables x and y, we can enumerate all the possibilities for the **and** and **or** operators:

x	y	x **and** y	x **or** y
False	False	False	False
False	True	False	True
True	False	False	True
True	True	True	True

For the **not** operator, we only need a single input:

x	**not** x
False	True
True	False

Boolean Operations

Boolean operations will be familiar to anyone who has studied logic, propositional calculus, or digital electronics. Here is a table showing the equivalence:

x **and** y	x **or** y	**not** x
$x \wedge y$	$x \vee y$	$\neg x$
$x \cdot y$	$x + y$	$\bar{x}$

The notations may be different but it is the same set of Boolean operations. More detail can be found in Appendix B.

3.1.2 Being In Between

When writing relationships between variables in mathematics it is common to see expressions like $a < b < c$ – which says that a is less than b, and b is less than c, and (consequently) that a is less than c. Many programming languages (C and C++, for example) do not allow expressions of this sort. The argument goes as follows: *In which order do we evaluate the subexpressions – do we evaluate $a < b$ or $b < c$ first? In fact, does it matter? The result of the evaluation is a Boolean value, and we cannot compare a Boolean value with a number. The expression is therefore not meaningful and so is not allowed.* In languages that take this position over comparison expressions we have to write such expressions explicitly using Boolean operators. So, for example:

    a < b **and** b < c

The problem here is that the language is only offering operators that can be executed by the computer directly and so the expressions that are possible are strongly constrained by the underlying hardware.

Python takes a different stance on this. It is a high-level language and does not feel bound to offer only the operations directly executable by the underlying computer. Why should a high-level language be constrained by the restrictions of the underlying computer – it is a high-level language! So, in Python, we can write:

```
a < b < c
```

and the Python system sorts out all the necessary evaluations for us.

So, for example, if we needed to check that a person was a minor in one of our programs, we might, perhaps, use a Boolean expression such as:

```
age > 0 and age < 21
```

but, in Python, we can write this as:

```
0 < age < 21
```

which expresses more directly the relationship between a, b, and c.

Why check to ensure age is greater than zero? Perhaps the program uses negative numbers to represent the age of fetuses and unborn babies, or for some other meaning. Testing that a value is in a reasonable range for the algorithm is important. The correctness and sense of any expression are not just a question of whether it has the right syntax for the language, it also depend on the context and purpose.

Having Attitude

Many people will say "This point about comparison expressions is a small point, why make a big deal of it?" It is really about attitude. Languages that focus on what the computer can do are useful and important (for writing operating systems, for example) but languages that focus on being able to express solutions to problems in the real world are much more useful for the average programmer.

We are not restricted to using the less than operator. All the following are valid expressions:

a <= b < c	a < b == c	a >= b > c	a > b == c
a < b <= c	a <= b == c	a > b >= c	a >= b == c
a <= b <= c	a == b < c	a >= b >= c	a == b > c
	a == b <= c		a == b >= c

We can even do things like:

```
a < b < c < d < e
```

and this means exactly what you might expect from mathematics: the expression evaluates to **True** only if a is less than b and b is less than c and c is less than d and d is less than e. Some care using this feature of Python is in order however. Python allows any arbitrarily complex combination of these comparison operators, many of which will be extremely incomprehensible. So this feature of Python is extremely useful – but only when used carefully so that the expressions are clear, readable and comprehensible. For example, the expression:

```
a < b > c == d
```

is almost certainly beyond the boundary of easy comprehensibility. Clarity is everything.

3.2 Blocks

In previous examples of if statements, while statements and functions, we emphasized very strongly that structured indentation of the code is very important. In this section, we amplify this further.

If statements, while statements and function definitions are all examples of *compound statement*. Compound statements are ways of managing statement sequences, which in this context are called *blocks*.

3.2.1 Indentation

Using an if statement as an example, here is a sequence that includes a compound statement that uses a block:

```
age = 21
drinksTab = 0
if age >= 18 :
    print 'Welcome to the club.'
    print 'Please accept a complementary drink worth 10 points.'
    drinksTab = -10
```

So why is the indentation so critical? Let's investigate the point by trying something that is an error. If we forget to do the indentation then we have:

```
age = 21
drinksTab = 0
if age >= 18 :
print 'Welcome to the club.'
print 'Please accept a complementary drink worth 10 points.'
drinksTab = -10
```

When we try to run this we get the error message:

```
    print "Welcome to the club."
        ^
IndentationError: expected an indented block
```

It is the indentation of the statement sequence after the if keyword, Boolean expression and colon that defines the block of code that is part of the if statement: if we have no such statements then it is an error. Say, though, that we had written:

```
age = 21
drinksTab = 0
if age >= 18 :
    print 'Welcome to the club.'
print 'Please accept a complementary drink worth 10 points.'
drinksTab = -10
```

This code is not an error as far as the Python language is concerned, it will run: the indented statement is part of the block controlled by the if statement, whilst the non-indented statements are part of the block that is the main sequence. It is highly unlikely, however, that this code is correct – it is giving everyone a complementary drink, which probably means an alcoholic drink, and it is almost certainly illegal to offer minors alcoholic drinks. Here then, we have another example of an *algorithmic error* (also known as *semantic error* or sometimes *logic error*). The indentation defines the structure of the code, so not indenting correctly is an error.

The Python grammar uses the term *suite* rather than the term *block*, but we use the term *block* since that is more widely used and understood.

> **Indentation and Blocks**
>
> Python is unique among popular programming languages in using indentation to define blocks of code. Other programming languages use a bracketing system – there is an open block symbol and a close block symbol. For example, C, C++ and Java use { to open a block and } to close a block. Python has no such mechanism.

Actually, if we were to claim that indentation is the only mechanism of defining a block in Python, it would be a untrue. However, let's not worry about the other mechanisms just now.

> **Editors and Indentation**
>
> Most people find that two spaces, four spaces or a single tab is the best way of indenting statements. Many editors used for editing programs (Emacs and XEmacs among them) have special modes for editing Python programs that understand the indentation rules and do lots of things for you when editing Python source code. Of course, there is also IDLE, which is Python's own development environment. It defaults to an indent of four spaces, but this is customizable.

3.2.2 Nesting

Compound statements can be statements within a block. This should really be no surprise, as we have already used compound statements in a block: our programs, being a single sequence of statements, are themselves blocks. In the following example we show a compound statement within a compound statement:

```
age = 21
isMale = True
drinksTab = 0
if age >= 18 :
    print 'Welcome to the club.'
    if isMale :
        print 'Please accept a complementary drink worth 10 points.'
        drinksTab = -10
    else :
        print 'Free drinks for ladies all night!'
```

The main block contains an if statement that contains another if statement. We now have levels of indentation: the second if statement is indented relative to the first.

It is true that we can write the above as:

```
age = 21
isMale = True
drinksTab = 0
if age >= 18 and isMale :
    print 'Welcome to the club.'
    print 'Please accept a complementary drink worth 10 points.'
    drinksTab = -10
if age >= 18 and not isMale :
    print 'Welcome to the club.'
    print 'Free drinks for ladies all night!'
```

This is a poorer program, though, for two reasons:

1. We are repeating the test for being over 18.

2. We are repeating the printing of the welcome message.

The previous version had no such replication. The use of nesting expresses the algorithm more clearly and, moreover, the indentation makes it easier to read and comprehend the code, and, thus, infer the algorithm correctly. As we hope is obvious, being able to easily read code so as to understand what it is doing and trying to do is crucial for programming. This clearly means that we should *always* write our code to express our algorithms and intentions clearly, making it easily readable and comprehensible by other programmers – and ourselves!

Simplicity of expression and ease of understanding must always be the primary drivers for how we write our code.

3.2.3   Algorithmic and Development Issues

So far in the 'club bouncer' program we have been concerned only with issues of people being over 18. This is not a good approach to developing a program, as we are ignoring likely possibilities. What happens if a fifteen-year-old tries to get into the club. Currently our program ignores this possibility and so does nothing. Not good. As ever, though, programming is an iterative (!) process, so having discovered the problem, we just get on and evolve the program to remove the bug. Here is a new version:

```
age = 21
isMale = True
drinksTab = 0
if age >= 18 :
    print 'Welcome to the club.'
    if isMale :
        print 'Please accept a complementary drink worth 10 points.'
        drinksTab = -10
    else :
        print 'Free drinks for ladies all night!'
elif age < 16 :
    print 'No way, this is an over 18\'s club.'
else :
    print 'The club is for over 18\'s only, sorry you cannot be admitted.'
```

> **Mixing Quotes**
>
> In the above code we had to use \' to get a single quote in a string delimited by single quotes. Instead of doing this, we could have used double quote delimiters for the string, so that the single quote does not need to be *escaped* with a backslash:
>
> ```
> print "No way, this is an over 18's club."
> ```

The above program works, but we can do better. For example, we have 'hard wired' the literal 18 into the code. So what do we do if the minimum age is 21? We have to edit the 18 and although there is only one instance in the above code, there might have been lots of them in the code. Clearly we should replace use of literals with use of variables in these sorts of situation. So we introduce a variable minimumAge to deal with the minimum admittance age. We also introduce a variable to deal with the obviously too young age, let's call that farTooYoungAge:

```
minimumAge = 18
farTooYoungAge = 16

drinksTab = 0
if age >= minimumAge :
    print 'Welcome to the club.'
    if isMale :
        print 'Please accept a complementary drink worth 10 points.'
        drinksTab = -10
    else :
        print 'Free drinks for ladies all night!'
elif age < farTooYoungAge :
    print 'No way, this is an over 18\'s club.'
else :
    print 'The club is for over 18\'s only, sorry you cannot be admitted.'
```

This way of doing things is good because if we ever need to change the minimum age (from 18 to 21, for example), we only have to change one value. This minimizes our chances of getting it wrong; we know that all comparison expressions use the same value. It also means that we can have the age set somewhere near the top of our program, while the comparison expressions may be buried anywhere in the code.

Whilst this example may seem a little trivial, do not underestimate the positive effect of using variables instead of literals in the main code. This way of using variables really does decrease the number of bugs (errors) we get in our code.

3.3 Functions and Recursion

3.3.1 Recursive Functions

In mathematics, you often see functions defined in terms of themselves – such functions define a sequence of values and are termed *recurrence relations*. The classic example used in most programming books is factorial – in fact, factorial is used widely in combinatorics and statistics, so it is an important function.

The definition of factorial is the recurrence relation:

A recurrence relation is a sequence or function that is defined in terms of itself.

$$\text{factorial}(x) = \begin{cases} 1 & x = 0 \\ x \times \text{factorial}(x-1) & x > 0 \end{cases}$$

What the equation says is that factorial(x) has the value 1 if x has the value 0, and the value $x \times$ factorial($x-1$) for all other values of x.

To understand what this really means, let's work through an example. Let's evaluate factorial(4). We expand the expression using the $x > 0$ case while the parameter is not 0 and then use the $x = 0$ case. Thus, we get:

$$\begin{aligned} \text{factorial}(4) &= 4 \times \text{factorial}(3) \\ &= 4 \times 3 \times \text{factorial}(2) \\ &= 4 \times 3 \times 2 \times \text{factorial}(1) \\ &= 4 \times 3 \times 2 \times 1 \times \text{factorial}(0) \\ &= 4 \times 3 \times 2 \times 1 \times 1 \\ &= 24 \end{aligned}$$

Most programming languages, including Python, do not have a built-in factorial function, so we must define our own. Working directly from the mathematical definition, we can try the following Python definition:

```
def factorial ( x ) :
    if x == 0 :
        return 1
    else :
        return x * factorial ( x - 1 )
```

which is a *recursive function* and, guess what, it works! We can show this by trying it:

```
>>> def factorial ( x ) :
...     if x == 0 :
...         return 1
...     else :
...         return x * factorial ( x - 1 )
...
>>> print factorial ( 4 )
24
>>> print factorial ( 6 )
720
>>>
```

and clearly it does work as expected. Which is good.

3.3.2 Base Cases, Recursive Cases and Termination

In the definition of the factorial function (both in mathematics and in Python), there are two cases:

Base case. The case for a given value of the parameter, $x = 0$ in this example.

Recursive case. The case used whenever the base case is not applicable. This case involves a recursive call of the function with an altered parameter.

The base case is so called because it is the case that acts as a base; it is the case that stops the recursion going on forever. Looking back at the example of evaluating factorial(4) in the previous subsection, we used the recursive case until the base case was appropriate, then we used the base case, which stopped the recursion. This idea of recursion, base case and termination are extremely crucial for successful use of recursive functions.

The base case and the change to the value used in the recursive case are very much related. The very worst case scenario is not having a base case at all. What happens if we had defined our factorial function as:

```
def factorial ( x ) :
    return x * factorial ( x - 1 )
```

i.e. we only have the recursive case? Let's investigate this by doing an evaluation by hand:

$$
\begin{array}{rcl}
\text{factorial (4)} & \longrightarrow & \text{4 * factorial (3)} \\
& & \text{4 * 3 * factorial (2)} \\
& & \text{4 * 3 * 2 * factorial (1)} \\
& & \text{4 * 3 * 2 * 1 * factorial (0)} \\
& & \text{4 * 3 * 2 * 1 * 0 * factorial (-1)} \\
& & \text{4 * 3 * 2 * 1 * 0 * -1 * factorial (-2)} \\
& & \text{4 * 3 * 2 * 1 * 0 * -1 * -2 * factorial (-3)}
\end{array}
$$

Hmmm... this never ends – evaluation goes on, and on, and on, forever. This situation is called *infinite recursion* and it is not good.

Although the recursion is infinite, the Python program will not execute forever. The Python system has a limit to the number of recursive calls a function can make to protect against infinite recursion. When executing a program that involves seemingly infinite recursion, you get the error message:

RuntimeError: maximum recursion depth exceeded

The *recursion depth* is the number of times a function calls itself. The Python system sets the recursion depth to a number such that it is highly unlikely that any recursive function will ever reach the maximum recursion depth unless it describes an infinite recursion.

The main point here is that the base case is required for recursion to terminate, and termination is essential. However, simply having a base case is not the only component of termination. It is also important that, in the recursive case, the parameter value of the recursive call is different from the current call so that the base case will eventually be reached. In our definition of factorial, the recursive call uses the expression x - 1, which means that it is absolutely certain that the parameter value will at some point have the value 0 and so the base case will be used instead of the recursive case – termination is guaranteed.

Actually, there are cases in which the definition of factorial (the one from the previous subsection that is) leads to infinite recursion. Have you worked out what these cases are? If you have, well done. If you haven't, then you are probably not thinking negatively or fractionally enough (hint, hint!).

Infinite recursion is definitely bad!

3.4 Exceptional Behavior

In mathematics, factorial is only defined for non-negative integers. Mathematically it makes no sense to ask what the factorial of a negative number is. Nor does it make sense to ask what the factorial of a floating point number is because factorial is only defined for integers. Python distinguishes integers and floating points but it does not separate negative integers, positive integers and the integer 0. In fact, when we define a Python function, we don't specify a type at all for the parameter variable, which means that functions can be called with a parameter value of any type, even ones that are not permitted mathematically. As the programmers of the function, we have a responsibility to deal with these 'un-mathematical' situations in a sensible way so that people using our function do not get unexpected, incorrect behavior – remember the Principle of Least Surprise (page 31). With the factorial definition of the previous subsection, if we make a call with a negative integer value or any floating point value, we get infinite recursion and execution halts when the maximum recursion depth is reached.

One approach to dealing with this problem is to abdicate all responsibility and rather than finding a sensible value to return, just terminate the program with an error message:

```
import sys

def factorial ( x ) :
    if x < 0 :
        print 'factorial not defined for negative numbers'
        sys.exit ( )
    elif x == 0 :
        return 1
    else :
        return x * factorial ( x - 1 )
```

This is the wrong thing to do for two reasons:

1. It is unacceptable for the factorial function to terminate execution. It is the responsibility of the program using the function to decide what to do in the case of error.

2. It is unacceptable for the factorial function to perform any output. It is the job of the program using the function to handle all input/output. If you think about a Python program that presents a graphical user interface, how does the factorial function know what to output and where? It doesn't, and it makes no sense to allow it to happen.

What can we do then? The factorial function needs a way to communicate with the program that called it in a way that is not just returning a value. The correct way of dealing with this situation is to raise an *exception*. An exception is a way of saying "there is a problem that it is not my responsibility to deal with." The idea is that responsibility for dealing with the problem is somewhere else, and that that code must deal with the exception if it is raised. Here is the factorial function coded so that it raises an exception if the parameter is a negative value:

```
def factorial ( x ) :
    if x < 0 :
        raise ValueError , 'Factorial not applicable to negative values.'
    elif x == 0 :
        return 1
    else :
        return x * factorial ( x - 1 )
```

ValueError is the name of an exception type that comes as standard with the Python system.

When a situation occurs which is wrong and exceptional, we raise an exception. Here, if the parameter is negative, we raise an exception using a raise statement:

```
raise ValueError , 'Factorial not applicable to negative values.'
```

After the **raise** keyword we have two 'parameters': the type of an exception type, in this case ValueError, and a string that gives some explanation of the problem. The string will be output if the exception is raised. Let's investigate what happens using interactive mode:

```
>>> def factorial ( x ) :
...     if x < 0 :
...         raise ValueError , "Factorial not applicable to negative values."
...     elif x == 0 :
```

```
...        return 1
...     else :
...        return x * factorial ( x - 1 )
...
>>> print factorial ( 4 )
24
>>> print factorial ( -4 )
Traceback (most recent call last):
  File "<stdin>", line 1, in ?
  File "<stdin>", line 3, in factorial
ValueError: Factorial not applicable to negative values.
>>> print factorial ( 6 )
720
>>>
```

The type of the exception and the explanation string are output.

We haven't had to do anything special for the exception to do its job: the Python system, in interactive mode, has ways of dealing with exceptions if we have not done something ourselves.

In script mode, if an exception is raised that our code does not deal with, then execution terminates:

```
Traceback (most recent call last):
  File "factorial_recursive_exception.py", line 12, in ?
    print factorial ( -4 )
  File "factorial_recursive_exception.py", line 3, in factorial
    raise ValueError , 'Factorial not applicable to negative values.'
ValueError: Factorial not applicable to negative values.
```

which for now is entirely acceptable. We will look at how to deal with exceptions in our code shortly – Section 3.9 (page 95).

3.5   Asserting the Truth

We now seem to have a factorial function that appears to do the right thing. The obvious question is clear from the previous sentence: how can we be more sure that the function does what we say it does? We have tried a few values interactively and ensured that the result is as it should be, but can we do better? The answer is clearly "yes".

Python has a feature called the assert statement that allows us to require that a Boolean expression be true for execution of the program to continue. So we can have statements like:

```
assert x ==1
```

in our code and if x == 1 is *not* true when the statement is executed then an exception called AssertionError is raised. If the expression is true, execution just continues. So an assertion allows us to require that things we expect to be true in our program actually are. This sounds *very* useful for ensuring that our functions do what they say they do. Instead of using print statements and checking them ourselves, we can use assert statements and let the Python system do the hard work.

So for the factorial function we can have the statements:

```
assert factorial ( 4 ) == 24
assert factorial ( 6 ) == 720
```

in the same file as the function. Then, we can execute the file:

```
| > python factorial_recursive_tested.py
| >
```

Nothing seemed to happen. Well actually none of the assertions failed to be true. So for the tests that we have assertions for, the function does what it is supposed to. This doesn't mean that the function is correct, it means that it works for those cases we test. There is an important issue here: we have to choose our tests carefully so that we can have confidence that the cases we don't test for will also work.

This is leading us inexorably towards a way of working with our code. When we write a function we should write some assert statements in the file that provide a test that the function does actually do what we think it should do. Then if we make any changes to the function we can run the file and the asserts will check to ensure that the function still does the right thing.

What happens if an assertion fails? Say we add an assertion that we know should fail:

```
assert factorial ( 2 ) == 1
```

then, when we execute the file, an exception is raised:

```
Traceback (most recent call last):
 File "factorial_recursive_tested.py", line 12, in ?
  assert factorial ( 2 ) == 1
AssertionError
```

and the program terminates. This is exactly the right thing to happen, of course. If we put a correct assertion in the program and it causes an exception, then the function has an error in it. We must fix the code immediately so that we can run the program and not have an assertion failure.

In this case we added an assert statement that did not represent a correct assertion: it was a known error to show the result of an assertion failure. Obviously we now remove this assert statement, as it is not correctly representing what should happen. Of course, we will leave all the assert statements that represent true 'facts'. Indeed we could, perhaps should, add some more.

3.6 The __name__ Technique

The complete file for the factorial function actually looks like:

```
def factorial ( x ) :
    if x < 0 :
        raise ValueError , 'Factorial not applicable to negative values.'
    elif x == 0 :
        return 1
    else :
        return x * factorial ( x - 1 )

if __name__ == '__main__' :
    assert factorial ( 4 ) == 24
    assert factorial ( 6 ) == 720
```

The assert statements are part of an if statement. Why is this?

The way the Python system works, the way it does compilation before execution, and the way that documentation is generated, all require that a program can be read and executed multiple times. Things like function definitions are fine, as they do not actually do anything until they are called. Putting statements at the top level of a program is, however, problematic. Python therefore has a special built-in variable called __name__ which takes on the value '__main__' when the code is expected to actually execute rather than just be read. By using an if statement in the way shown above, we ensure that things work the way we expect them to in all circumstances.

You may well be asking: "Why bother, in this case it doesn't matter." Yes, it is true that in this case it doesn't matter, but it is better to get into the habit now so that there are no unexpected problems later.

3.7 Some Example Recursive Functions

3.7.1 Searching for Sub-Sequences

A problem that is surprisingly common is needing to know whether a sequence contains a specific sub-sequence. One example is searching for genes in chromosomes. A chromosome is a very long DNA molecule that comprises a sequence of genes, which are themselves sequences of bases. The four bases are Adenine, Guanine, Cytosine, and Thymine, but they are usually denoted by their initial letter: A, C, G, and T. This means that a chromosome can be represented as a string, with genes being sub-strings. Finding and identifying genes becomes a question of finding sub-strings in strings. This is obviously a highly over-simplistic view of things, but we are only trying to indicate that searching for sub-sequences is actually important!

So, if we have a sequence, how can we check whether it contains a given sub-sequence? There are many ways – this turns out to be a surprisingly complex problem with some very elegant, but complex, solutions. For the moment, let's keep things simple. Thinking 'recursive function', we could say something along the lines of:

> *if sub–sequence is at the start of the sequence return true*
> *recursively call the function with sequence parameter not including the first item*

So the algorithm is to check whether the sub-sequence is present at the start of the sequence, and if it isn't, we make a recursive call but with a sequence parameter that is the old sequence parameter without the first item.

Since we are creating a recursive function, we must check the base case, recursive case and termination. When making a recursive call, the sequence used in the call is shorter than the current sequence. This means that, at some point, a call is made with an empty sequence. This means we have a definite base case and termination condition. Actually though, we don't need to go that far. At some point the sequence we are calling with is shorter than the sequence we are looking for and so it is certain that a match cannot be found – a sub-sequence of length five cannot be present in a sequence of length four. This makes for a better base case and termination condition. So we can refine the algorithm:

> *if sequence is shorter than sub–sequence return false*
> *if the sub–sequence is at the start of the sequence return true*
> *recursively call the function with sequence parameter not including the first item*

That seems 'codable' in that the algorithm seems straightforward enough to write a Python version:

```
def contains ( sequence , subsequence ) :
    if len ( sequence ) < len ( subsequence ) :
        return False
    if sequence [ : len ( subsequence ) ] == subsequence :
        return True
    return contains ( sequence[1:] , subsequence )
```

This is an example of Linear Search. More detail about searching for things is presented in Section 10.2.1 (page 315).

We can check that this does what we expect it to by executing it with some trial values:

```
>>> print contains ( 'hello' , 'hello' )
True
>>> print contains ( 'hellohello' , 'lloh' )
True
>>> print contains ( 'hello' , 'goodbye' )
False
>>> print contains ( 'hello' , 'good' )
False
>>>
```

which seems to be correct. Of course, now that we know about the assert statement, we can put these 'facts' into our program, so that the file contains:

```
def contains ( sequence , subsequence ) :
    if len ( sequence ) < len ( subsequence ) :
        return False
    if sequence [ : len ( subsequence ) ] == subsequence :
        return True
    return contains ( sequence[1:] , subsequence )


if __name__ == '__main__' :
    assert contains ( 'hello' , 'hello' )
    assert contains ( 'hellohello' , 'lloh' )
    assert not contains ( 'hello' , 'goodbye' )
    assert not contains ( 'hello' , 'good' )
```

which when executed results in:

```
|> python contains_recursive.py
|>
```

Exactly what we need.

3.7.2 Power

As another example of a recursive function that implements a mathematical function let's look at a function to calculate a value to the power of another value, i.e. a function to calculate *exponentiation*, x^y – x is called the *base* and y the *exponent*.

```
def power ( base , exponent ) :
    if exponent == 0 :
        return 1
    else :
        return base * power ( base , exponent - 1 )
```

It is true that Python has the ** operator built in to the system so we don't actually need this function in 'real programs'. But it does make a nice example of a recursive function.

This is the first example of a function with more than one parameter. Here we have two parameters: the value being raised (base); and the value to be raised to (exponent).

As with factorial in the previous section, we can use an example evaluation to show what happens in a given case. Let's try 2^4, which we know is $2 * 2 * 2 * 2$, which is 16. Hand-evaluating the Python code, we get:

$$
\begin{aligned}
\text{power}(2,4) \quad \longrightarrow \quad & 2 * \text{power}(2,3) \\
& 2 * 2 * \text{power}(2,2) \\
& 2 * 2 * 2 * \text{power}(2,1) \\
& 2 * 2 * 2 * 2 * \text{power}(2,0) \\
& 2 * 2 * 2 * 2 * 1 \\
& 16
\end{aligned}
$$

The recursion is on the exponent and at each step we multiply by the base, which is a direct reflection of the definition of exponentiation.

We can show that this function behaves as expected by trying it out interactively:

```
>>> def power ( base , exponent ) :
...    if exponent == 0 :
...        return 1
...    else :
...        return base * power ( base , exponent - 1 )
...
>>> print power ( 2 , 5 )
32
>>> print power ( 100 , 0 )
1
>>> print power ( 3 , 4 )
81
>>> print power ( 9 , 2 )
81
>>>
```

or, of course, better by putting assertions in the file and executing the file:

```
def power ( base , exponent ) :
    if exponent == 0 :
        return 1
    else :
        return base * power ( base , exponent - 1 )

if __name__ == '__main__' :
    assert power ( 2 , 5 ) == 32
    assert power ( 100 , 0 ) == 1
    assert power ( 3 , 4 ) == 81
    assert power ( 9 , 2 ) == 81
```

which when executed gives us:

```
|> python power_recursive_1.py
|>
```

as expected. As we should with all recursive functions, we check that termination is guaranteed:

- We have a base case which is used when y has the value 0 – raising any number to the power 0 always results in 1.

- In the recursive case, the variable y is decremented by one, so, if the initial value of y is positive, then the recursion will terminate.

We have a problem: what happens if a negative exponent is given? We get an infinite recursion. We can see that this is the case by hand-evaluating a call with a negative parameter:

$$\text{power}(2,-4) \quad \longrightarrow \quad \begin{aligned} &2 * \text{power}(2,-5) \\ &2 * 2 * \text{power}(2,-6) \\ &2 * 2 * 2 * \text{power}(2,-7) \\ &\quad\ldots \end{aligned}$$

Clearly the base case and recursive case do not combine to lead to a sensible termination condition when the parameter is negative. This situation is, though, very different to the one we saw with the factorial function in the previous section. For power, we know that it is sensible to work with a negative exponent. The equation:

$$x^{-y} = \frac{1}{x^y}$$

tells us what the meaning is. So rather than a negative parameter being an error that requires raising an exception, we simply need to amend our function to extend its applicability:

```python
def power ( base , exponent ) :
    if exponent < 0 :
        return 1.0 / power ( base , -exponent )
    elif exponent == 0 :
        return 1
    else :
        return base * power ( base , exponent - 1 )

if __name__ == '__main__' :
    assert power ( 2 , 5 ) == 32
    assert power ( 100 , 0 ) == 1
    assert power ( 3 , 4 ) == 81
    assert power ( 9 , 2 ) == 81
    assert power ( 2 , -5 ) == 1.0 / 32
    assert power ( 100 , -0 ) == 1
    assert power ( 3 , -4 ) == 1.0 / 81
    assert power ( 9 , -2 ) == 1.0 / 81
```

Note how we extend the tests by adding new assert statements to test for negative exponents. We do not remove any of the previous tests, we just add more.

With this definition of power, all recursion happens with a positive value for the exponent, so now termination is guaranteed. We still have a problem if the exponent is a floating point number. Although mathematically this is possible, the algorithm we have (of repeated multiplications) only works for integer exponents. We are going to leave this as an unsolved problem, since we know that the Python ** operator (which we would use for real programs) gets it right.

3.7.3 Powering Efficiency

Recursive functions often get 'bad press' from some quarters because they are said to be slow or use too much memory. The arguments used are generally specious, i.e. wrong. We haven't talked yet about issues of *efficiency* (how fast or slow your programs are or how much memory they need to run), because now is not the time to worry about these issues. In fact, for most programs, efficiency isn't really that important at all. Python programs generally run fairly quickly and it's generally more important to write readable, comprehensible and *correct* programs than it is to write efficient ones – it is trivially easy to write a program that runs incredibly quickly, as long as it does not have to be correct! Having said this, there are a number situations in which efficiency really is very important. Animations and arcade games immediately spring to mind. Also, low-power, embedded systems always have an efficiency issue – for example, watches, mobile phones, fly-by-wire aircraft systems.

There is actually one form of efficiency that is worth discussing now and that is *algorithmic efficiency*. This is generally the most important form of efficiency, and it is very little to do with how fast the Python system runs code, it is much more to do with selecting the right algorithm to solve the problem.

Thinking about our **power** function, if we rewrite it:

```
def power ( base , exponent ) :
    if exponent < 0 :
        return 1.0 / power ( base , -exponent )
    elif exponent == 0 :
        return 1
    else :
        if exponent % 2 == 0 :
            return power ( base * base , exponent / 2 )
        else :
            return base * power ( base , exponent - 1 )
```

it will execute far faster that the previous version. Why? Because we have used a far more efficient algorithm. What we have done here is to note that:

$$x^{2n} = (x^2)^n$$

so that we dramatically cut the the number of times we make a recursive call, and also dramatically cut the number of multiplications – at the expense of adding one multiplication. For example, with $x = 3$ and $n = 5$:

$$
\begin{aligned}
3^{10} &= 3 \times 3 \times 3 \times 3 \times 3 \times 3 \times 3 \times 3 \times 3 \times 3 \\
&= (3 \times 3) \times (3 \times 3) \times (3 \times 3) \times (3 \times 3) \times (3 \times 3) \\
&= 9 \times 9 \times 9 \times 9 \times 9 \\
&= (3^2)^5
\end{aligned}
$$

To evaluate the expression on the right side of the first line requires nine multiplications. To evaluate the expression on the right side of the third line (which gives the same result) only requires six multiplications, and so is algorithmically more efficient.

In the earlier implementation of **power**, each recursive case required n multiplications. In the revised implementation, at most $2 \log_2 n$ multiplications are needed (where $\log_2 n$ is the logarithm of n to the base 2). This is a good example of how a basic understanding of mathematics can help to improve code enormously by improving algorithms. In Chapter 10 we will take a more detailed look at efficiency, how to tell roughly how fast your algorithms are, and how to compare different algorithms.

For the moment, the moral of this story is that studying algorithms is important and choosing a good one is a real programming skill.

3.7.4 Fibonacci Numbers

Both the examples we have seen so far have had a fairly simple structure, one base case and one recursive case. For this example, we look at the Fibonacci Sequence, which is defined by the recurrence relation:

$$F_n = \begin{cases} 0 & n = 0 \\ 1 & n = 1 \\ F_{n-1} + F_{n-2} & n > 1 \end{cases}$$

Note that there are two base cases. This is essential because the recursive case involves references to two distinct previous values in the sequence. By hand-evaluating the recurrence relation, we find that the first few numbers in the sequence are:

$$0, 1, 1, 2, 3, 5, 8, 13, 21, 34, 55, 89, \ldots$$

The implementation of a function for calculating the nth Fibonacci number is fairly straightforward since it echoes directly the recurrence relation definition:

```
def fibonacci ( n ) :
    if n < 0 :
        raise ValueError , 'Fibonacci cannot be applied to a negative parameter.'
    elif n == 0 :
        return 0
    elif n == 1 :
        return 1
    else :
        return fibonacci ( n - 1 ) + fibonacci ( n - 2 )
```

We can show that this appears to give the right result interactively:

```
>>> def fibonacci ( n ) :
...     if n < 0 :
...         raise ValueError , 'Fibonacci cannot be applied to a negative parameter.'
...     if n == 0 :
...         return 0
...     if n == 1 :
...         return 1
...     else :
...         return fibonacci ( n - 1 ) + fibonacci ( n - 2 )
...
>>> print fibonacci ( 0 )
0
>>> print fibonacci ( 1 )
1
>>> print fibonacci ( 2 )
1
>>> print fibonacci ( 3 )
2
>>> print fibonacci ( 4 )
3
>>> print fibonacci ( 5 )
5
>>> print fibonacci ( 6 )
8
```

```
>>> print fibonacci ( 7 )
13
>>> print fibonacci ( 8 )
21
>>> print fibonacci ( 9 )
34
>>>
```

or we can put assertions into the file (we skip showing the code of the function) and execute it:

```
if __name__ == '__main' :
    assert fibonacci ( 0 ) == 0
    assert fibonacci ( 1 ) == 1
    assert fibonacci ( 2 ) == 1
    assert fibonacci ( 3 ) == 2
    assert fibonacci ( 4 ) == 3
    assert fibonacci ( 5 ) == 5
    assert fibonacci ( 6 ) == 8
    assert fibonacci ( 7 ) == 13
    assert fibonacci ( 8 ) == 21
    assert fibonacci ( 9 ) == 34
```

Did you notice that we said "appears to give the correct result"? The doubt here is entirely intentional: to show that the code is correct we would need to try it with every possible value of the parameter and that is impossible – there are an infinite number of integers, so it would take an infinite amount of time to try all possible numbers. We shall return to the issue of proper testing of code in Chapter 9. For now we continue using assertions to show that the code does what it is supposed to in some representative cases. This gives us some confidence that the code is reasonably correct.

As ever with recursive functions, we must consider the issue of termination. Showing that the termination condition is valid and holds in this case is relatively straightforward:

It is important to remember that there are two base cases for this recurrence relation.

- The recursive case relies on the two previous values and so at each recursion we do get closer to the base cases.

- There are two base cases, so that when either $n = 0$ or $n = 1$ the recursion terminates.

- Negative indexes cause an exception to be raised and so do not cause infinite recursion.

So, it appears that this is a good implementation of the Fibonacci numbers as a recursive function.

Enough of the mathematical functions, let's do some graphics. Recursively, of course.

3.7.5 Visual Recursion: Fractals

Figure 3.1 shows a von Koch Snowflake – some people ignore the "von" and call it a Koch Snowflake, but this is not correct as the mathematician who 'discovered' this curve was Niels Fabian Helge von Koch. A von Koch Snowflake is an example of a *fractal curve* – mathematicians often use the alternative term *self-similar*. If you look at the overall shape of one of the sides, it looks like a line with a triangle in the middle (something like _/_). If you look closer at each part of the line, it looks just the same. The property of fractals is that, however closely you 'zoom' in on them, they look the same – hence the term 'self-similar'. Any particular drawing of the fractal will have a limit to how far you can zoom in and see self-similarity – this is a feature of the drawing, not of the fractal curve.

In this section, we're going to develop a program to draw a von Koch Snowflake using Python's Turtle module.

A First Version

Our starting point is that we want to create a function that we can call to do the whole drawing:

> vonKochSnowflake ( )

We probably want to be able to specify whatever sizes control the drawing of the von Koch Snowflake. Clearly the main size is the overall length of the figure. However, there is another size that is important – we need to specify the smallest line length that is to be drawn. Fractal curves are mathematically infinite: you can always zoom in and see the same structure. However, computer equipment has restrictions. In particular, screens are composed of pixels. To try to draw anything smaller than 1 pixel in length means drawing something 1 pixel in length or nothing at all – drawing to a computer screen always means drawing an integer number of pixels. Pixels are actually quite small, so you generally need to draw something bigger than 1 pixel to be able to see whatever is drawn. Putting all this together, we actually need a two parameter function:

> vonKochSnowflake (overallLength , smallestLineLength)

Next we need to think about what the function should do. Looking at the shape of the curve it may not be totally obvious, but the starting shape is a triangle. From this insight, an abstract idea of what's going on is reasonably clear. To draw a von Koch Snowflake we need to draw an equilateral triangle (i.e. a triangle with all sides of the same length) of which each side is not a line but a 'von Koch curve'. This means draw a 'von Koch curve', then turn right by 120°, draw a second 'von Koch curve', turn right by 120°, then draw the third 'von Koch curve'. In Python this is going to look like:

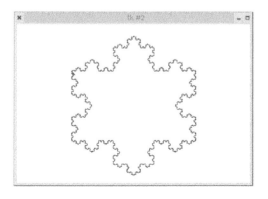

A von Koch Snowflake.

```
def vonKochSnowflake ( overallLength , smallestLineLength ) :
    '''Generate a von Koch Snowflake (which is a triangle of von Koch Curves).'''
    initialize ( )
    vonKochCurve ( overallLength , smallestLineLength )
    turtle.right ( 120 )
    vonKochCurve ( overallLength , smallestLineLength )
    turtle.right ( 120 )
    vonKochCurve ( overallLength , smallestLineLength )
```

Have you spotted the rather weird string that is the first line of the block? It has two weirdnesses:

1. This is a string with three singles quotes at the beginning and end.
2. The string is not assigned to a variable and not used.

Point 1 introduces the fact that there are a couple more forms of string in Python than we have seen so far. We have seen strings delimited by single quotes and double quotes. Strings in Python can also be delimited by triple single quotes or triple double quotes. The difference between using single delimiters or triple delimiters is that newlines can appear in triple-delimited strings but not single-delimited strings. So:

```
'''This is an example of a string
that includes end-of-lines
as data in the string.'''
```

is a valid string. For what are probably obvious reasons, strings delimited with single delimiters are called *short strings* and those with triple delimiters are called *long strings*.

To explain Point 2, Python has a rule that if a long string is the first item in the block of a function definition, it is treated as a documentation string for the function. Not only is a documentation string in the source code, but the Python system can process these comments to make both printed and online documentation. Here is not the time or place to go into the details of this, but the whole idea and mechanism of documentation will become very important in later chapters. It is probably worth getting into the habit of providing these documentation strings, even for small programs, as it is very useful when programs become larger.

You can get a hint of the documentation capabilities of the Python system using interactive mode: if you type the function into the Python system in interactive mode, you can ask to be given the documentation on the function by typing help (vonKochSnowflake). In this case you get:

```
>>> def vonKochSnowflake ( overallLength , smallestLineLength ) :
...     '''Generate a von Koch Snowflake of overall size given by the first parameter.'''
...     initialize ( )
...     vonKochLine ( overallLength , smallestLineLength )
...     turtle.right ( 120 )
...     vonKochLine ( overallLength , smallestLineLength )
...     turtle.right ( 120 )
...     vonKochLine ( overallLength , smallestLineLength )
...
>>> help ( vonKochSnowflake )
Help on function vonKochSnowflake in module __main__:

vonKochSnowflake(overallLength, smallestLineLength)
    Generate a von Koch Snowflake of overall size given by the first parameter.
>>>
```

We have done quite a lot work on this program but haven't mentioned recursion yet, nor have we mentioned how to actually draw anything. In fact, all the complexity of drawing von Koch Snowflakes is in drawing the 'von Koch curve', and this is where the recursion comes in. A 'von Koch curve' is a shape like _/_ in which each of the four segments is either itself a 'von Koch line' or, if the length of the line is less than the smallest line to be drawn, is just a straight line. So here is the recursion – we are drawing four line segments in a specific relationship where for each of the segments we either:

- move forward a certain amount to draw a straight line – the base case; or

- draw a 'von Koch curve' that is appropriately smaller than the one we're currently drawing – the recursive case.

As all the 'triangles' involved are equilateral, all angles are multiples of 60° and all line segments are one third of the overall length of a line. Thus, it is actually quite straightforward to write this function, precisely because we are using recursion:

```
def vonKochCurve ( overallLength , smallestLineLength ) :
    '''Draw a von Koch curve of length given by the first parameter.'''
    oneThirdLength = overallLength / 3.0
    if oneThirdLength <= smallestLineLength :
        turtle.forward ( oneThirdLength )
    else :
        vonKochCurve ( oneThirdLength , smallestLineLength )
    turtle.left ( 60 )
    if oneThirdLength <= smallestLineLength :
        turtle.forward ( oneThirdLength )
    else :
        vonKochCurve ( oneThirdLength , smallestLineLength )
    turtle.right ( 120 )
    if oneThirdLength <= smallestLineLength :
        turtle.forward ( oneThirdLength )
    else :
        vonKochCurve ( oneThirdLength , smallestLineLength )
    turtle.left ( 60 )
    if oneThirdLength <= smallestLineLength :
        turtle.forward ( oneThirdLength )
    else :
        vonKochCurve ( oneThirdLength , smallestLineLength )
```

So what about that function initialize that hasn't been mentioned yet? Here it is:

```
def initialize ( color = 'blue' ) :
    '''Prepare to draw a von Koch Snowflake.'''
    turtle.clear ()
    turtle.up ()
    turtle.goto ( -100.0 , 55.0 )
    turtle.setheading ( 0 )
    turtle.color ( color )
    turtle.down ()
```

This function just initializes the turtle in various ways: it clears the screen, raises the pen so there is no drawing when the turtle goes to a given position, points the turtle east (0° means point eastward), changes the line color and finally ensures that the pen is down so that any future movement draws on the screen.

There is clearly some 'magic' going on with this function. We called it with no parameters yet the function appears to take a parameter:

```
def initialize ( color = 'blue' ) :
```

Not to mention the fact that the parameter appears to have a value assigned to it. Having an assignment to a parameter variable in this way means that the parameter value has a default value, in this case 'blue'. This means that we can call the function with a parameter value:

```
initialize ( 'red' )
```

in which case the parameter variable (color) associates with the value 'red' and the assignment of the default parameter value is ignored. Alternatively, if we call the function with no parameters:

```
initialize ( )
```

the default parameter value assignment is used (instead of the Python system complaining that a parameter value was not given) and the parameter variable (color) is associated with the value 'blue'.

This 'default parameter value' feature is present in languages like C++ as well as Python and can prove very useful. It means that we can easily write functions that can be used in multiple ways without having to replicate code. In this example we have, in a single function, effectively written two functions, one that sets the color to 'blue' and one that sets it to whatever the call specifies.

Review and Second Version

Reviewing a program after it is 'finished' is *always* a good idea.

Although the program we have created above does the job, it feels incomplete, and not just because we haven't presented it as a whole. In particular, having to replicate the test in the vonKochCurve function feels very wrong. We had to do this because we weren't able to use a variable of type function – the turtle.forward function takes one parameter and the vonKochCurve function takes two, and this effectively stops us using a parameter of type function. What can we do about this? Let's look at the complete second version program and then discuss it.

```
import turtle

def initialize ( color = 'blue' , smallest = 1.0 ) :
    '''Prepare to draw a von Koch Snowflake.'''
    turtle.clear ( )
    turtle.up ( )
    turtle.goto ( -100.0 , 55.0 )
    turtle.setheading ( 0 )
    turtle.color ( color )
    turtle.down ( )
    global smallestLineLength
    smallestLineLength = smallest

def vonKochCurve ( overallLength ) :
    '''Draw a von Koch Curve of a given length. The global variable smallestLineLength is assumed to be set.'''
    oneThirdLength = overallLength / 3.0
    if oneThirdLength <= smallestLineLength :
        moveFunction = turtle.forward
    else :
        moveFunction = vonKochCurve
```

```
            moveFunction ( oneThirdLength )
            turtle.left ( 60 )
            moveFunction ( oneThirdLength )
            turtle.right ( 120 )
            moveFunction ( oneThirdLength )
            turtle.left ( 60 )
            moveFunction ( oneThirdLength )

    def vonKochSnowflake ( overall , smallest = 1.0 , color = 'blue' ) :
            '''Generate a von Koch Snowflake (which is a triangle of von Koch Curves).'''
            initialize ( color , smallest )
            vonKochCurve ( overall )
            turtle.right ( 120 )
            vonKochCurve ( overall )
            turtle.right ( 120 )
            vonKochCurve ( overall )

    if __name__ == '__main__' :
            vonKochSnowflake ( 200.0 , 2.0 , 'brown' )
            raw_input ( 'Press any key to terminate' )
```

Looking at the vonKochCurve function, we have made this a one parameter function so that the *signature* of the vonKochCurve function and the turtle.forward function are the same. This means we can use a variable to deal with the decision about whether to draw a line or a von Koch curve, and the function looks a lot neater and tidier. However, this means that we have to get the smallestLineLength variable from somewhere – it is not a parameter to the function.

To deal with the issue of smallestLineLength, we have changed initialize to become a two-parameter function. Not only does it set the color of the drawing, it sets a *global variable* – a global variable is one that is in *scope*, i.e. usable, everywhere. Many people consider global variables to be anathema. The problem is that a global variable can be assigned to in any part of the code, so it can become extremely difficult to reason about the code. We get away with it here as the program is small and our use is clear. For larger programs we do not use global variables but instead use classes or modules, but that is a topic for a later chapter (Chapter 6).

This second version looks cleaner and more elegant than the first, the only downside being the use of a global variable, but then programming is always about trade-offs.

3.8   Iteration Revisited

Recursion is clearly a control flow mechanism: it is a way of repeating things. In the last chapter we introduced iteration as a way of repeating things. Obviously there must be a relationship between these two. Generally, any algorithm that can be implemented using recursion can be implemented using iteration and vice versa. However, some algorithms are best expressed using recursion and some are best expressed using iteration. A skill of programming is knowing how to decide when an algorithm leads to a given implementation strategy.

To investigate the various relationships between algorithm, recursion and iteration, we will rewrite some of the recursion examples from the previous section using iteration. By seeing comparative examples, you will be able to develop the skill and intuition needed to decide when recursion might be more appropriate than iteration and vice versa.

3.8.1 Counted Iteration – For Loops

Iteration often (but not always) implies counted iteration, which means using some sort of counter. A condition involving the counter is tested, the loop performs some action, a value is added to a counter and the whole loop repeated. At any give time, the counter tells us how many times we have performed the repetition. In the last chapter (Section 2.12.3, page 49) we saw the while loop used for doing this explicitly but introduced the for loop to avoid having to do all the fiddly bits. We introduced code like:

```
for i in range ( 10 ) :
    . . .
```

The function call range (10) generates the list of integers 0, 1, 2, 3, 4, 5, 6, 7, 8, 9, which are then used as the values of i. This is fine if we always want to start counting from 0, but this is not always the case. What happens if we want to start from 1? There is another version of the range function that we can use:

```
for i in range ( 1 , 10 ) :
    . . .
```

This generates the list 1, 2, 3, 4, 5, 6, 7, 8, 9. We can show this by trying it:

```
>>> for i in range ( 1 , 10 ) :
...     print i
...
1
2
3
4
5
6
7
8
9
>>>
```

What's going on here? The **for** statement tells the Python system to do something repeatedly. i **in** range (1 , 10) tells the Python system for which values we want to perform the repeated actions. Here, i is a variable name that acts as our counter. There is nothing special about the name i here, we could have used any variable name at all – a, counter or _counter would all have worked just as well. The **in** range (1 , 10) part tells the Python system what values to give to i (our counter) each time we do the repetition. **in** is a Python keyword (and is compulsory here) but range is just a function call. range is a built-in function that generates a sequence of numbers. range (a , b) creates a sequence of numbers from a to b - 1 (inclusive). We can call range any time we want to, just like any other function:

```
>>> print range ( 10 )
[0, 1, 2, 3, 4, 5, 6, 7, 8, 9]
>>> print range ( 1 , 5 )
[1, 2, 3, 4]
>>>
```

Another variation in the use of the range function is that we can give it three parameters. In this guise, range changes the step between each value, i.e. we can tell range that we want to count up in numbers other than 1. So, for example, if we just want odd numbers from 1 to 9, we can say:

```
>>> print range ( 1 , 10 , 2 )
[1, 3, 5, 7, 9]
>>>
```

This feature of a function name being able to take a different number of parameters is called *overloading*. We will see quite a lot of this as we progress in our learning of Python.

The last part of the **for** loop, following the colon (:), is the *body* of the loop – this is the block that should execute repeatedly. Remember that statements in the body must be indented to show that they belong to the block that is the loop body.

So, in general, a **for** loop looks like this:

```
for <variable> in <sequence> :
    <body>
```

We'll say more about sequences and lists in the next chapter.

We said the counter is a new variable name. Its *scope* (where it's visible and accessible in code) is the body of the loop and the code that follows it. The following highlights some of the major issues of scope in this context:

```
>>> i = 1
>>> print i
1
>>> for i in range ( 5 ,11 ) :
...     print i
...
5
6
7
8
9
10
>>> print i
10
>>> for j in range ( 6 , 12 ) :
...     print j
...
6
7
8
9
10
11
>>> print j
11
>>>
```

To summarize this example, we create a variable called i, print it, use it in a **for** loop as a counter, then print it again. Even after the loop the variable remains associated with the last value it was associated with in the loop. Following this, we have a loop with a counter j, and, even though j is newly created in the for statement, we can still use it after the loop.

Allowing for loop variables to continue to be in scope after the for loop is a moot point. Many languages (e.g. C++) that used to behave like this have changed so that the for loop variable is only in scope within the loop body. So even though Python allows this, it is not clear that it is a good thing.

3.8.2 Factorial Revisited

We used the factorial function as the initial introduction to recursive functions, so it seems entirely appropriate to use this as the first example of rewriting a recursive function as an iterative function. To progress this, we have to observe that factorial can be expressed not only as a recurrence relation, but also as a simple product equation:

$$\text{factorial}(x) = \begin{cases} 1 & x = 0 \\ 1 \times 2 \times 3 \times \ldots \times (x-1) \times x & x > 0 \end{cases}$$

> **Factorial Specified using Product Notation**
>
> For those people with a more mathematical background, you may prefer the 'product of values' definition of factorial using formal product notation:
>
> $$\text{factorial}(x) = \begin{cases} 1 & x = 0 \\ \prod_{i=1}^{x} i & x > 0 \end{cases}$$

Describing factorial as a product of values makes it explicit that factorial is evaluated using multiple multiplications. We can code this directly:

```python
def factorial ( x ) :
    if x < 0 :
        raise ValueError , 'Factorial not applicable to negative values.'
    elif x == 0 :
        return 1
    else :
        value = 1
        for i in range ( 1 , x + 1 ) :
            value *= i
        return value

if __name__ == '__main__' :
    assert factorial ( 4 ) == 24
    assert factorial ( 6 ) == 720
    assert factorial ( 21 ) == 51090942171709440000
```

Remember that range (1 , x) does not include an iteration with the value x. Hence the x + 1 here.

This version of factorial still has a problem with float parameters.

We have used counted iteration counting from 1 to x (including x, hence the x + 1), and used a temporary variable (value) to hold the value that we are building. We return the final value value as the result.

The assert statements in the program check that the function does the right thing, as far as we test it, simply by running the program. However, we cannot test more than one exception case by running a script since, as soon as an exception occurs, execution terminates. It seems then that we can only investigate the behavior in error situations by working interactively:

```python
>>> def factorial ( x ) :
...     if x < 0 :
...         raise ValueError , 'Factorial not applicable to negative values.'
...     elif x == 0 :
...         return 1
...     else :
...         value = 1
...         for i in range ( 1 , x + 1 ) :
```

```
...        value *= i
...      return value
...
>>> print factorial ( 4 )
24
>>> print factorial ( 6 )
720
>>> print factorial ( 21 )
51090942171709440000L
>>> print factorial ( -4 )
Traceback (most recent call last):
  File "<stdin>", line 1, in ?
  File "<stdin>", line 3, in factorial
ValueError: Factorial not applicable to negative values.
>>> print factorial ( 6 )
720
>>>
```

We will see in Section 3.9 how to deal with this problem and hence how to automate the testing of exceptional behavior.

Did you spot that the result of factorial (21) had an L at the end? This indicates that the result is not of type int but is of type long:

```
>>> type ( 1 )
<type 'int'>
>>> type ( 51090942171709440000 )
<type 'long'>
>>> type ( 51090942171709440000L )
<type 'long'>
>>>
```

int and long values are all integers, the difference between them is an internal Python system issue that we do not have to worry about, because the Python system takes care of all the hidden computer-related issues like this. We just have to be aware that it is the case.

3.8.3 Sequence Searching Revisited

In Section 3.7.1 (page 76) we created a recursive function for searching for a specific sub-sequence of a sequence. It is probably obvious that there is a straightforward iterative version of the algorithm:

```
def contains ( sequence , subsequence ) :
    for i in range ( len ( sequence ) - len ( subsequence ) + 1 ) :
        if sequence [ i : i + len ( subsequence ) ] == subsequence :
            return True
    return False


if __name__ == '__main__' :
    assert contains ( 'hello' , 'hello' )
    assert contains ( 'hellohello' , 'lloh' )
    assert not contains ( 'hello' , 'goodbye' )
    assert not contains ( 'hello' , 'good' )
```

3.8.4 Power Revisited

Continuing the idea of showing an iterative version of the recursive functions we created earlier, here is an implementation of the power function using iteration:

```
def power_evaluate ( base , exponent ) :
    '''Calculate base to the power of exponent assuming exponent is an integer and positive.'''
    value = 1
    for i in range ( 0 , exponent ) :
        value *= base
    return value

def power ( base , exponent ) :
    '''Calculate base to the power of exponent assuming exponent is an integer.'''
    if exponent < 0 :
        return 1.0 / power_evaluate ( base , -exponent )
    elif exponent == 0 :
        return 1
    else :
        if exponent % 2 == 0 :
            return power_evaluate ( base * base , exponent / 2 )
        else :
            return power_evaluate ( base , exponent )

if __name__ == '__main__' :
    assert power ( 2 , 5 ) == 32
    assert power ( 100 , 0 ) == 1
    assert power ( 3 , 4 ) == 81
    assert power ( 9 , 2 ) == 81
    assert power ( 2 , -5 ) == 1.0 / 32
    assert power ( 100 , -0 ) == 1
    assert power ( 3 , -4 ) == 1.0 / 81
    assert power ( 9 , -2 ) == 1.0 / 81
```

Here we have created two functions as part of the implementation. The power function is very similar to the recursive implementation: it is responsible for dealing with negative exponents and the optimization. The *support function*, power_evaluate is the function that actually does the calculation using an iterative algorithm.

In power_evaluate we have two variables: value, which is a temporary variable to hold the intermediate values while we're still working out what value we want to return, and i which is the loop counter. To calculate what base to the power exponent is, we need to go round a loop exponent times, multiplying value by base each time.

3.8.5 General Iteration – While Loops

Counted iteration is fine if you know how many times you want the loop to execute, but this is not always the case. There are times when the iteration is *data driven*, i.e. the iteration continues until some condition is true. This is really what the while loop is for.

```
while <Boolean condition> :
    <body>
```

Here is a (relatively trivial) example:

```
>>> while not raw_input ( ) == '9' :
...     print 'Enter 9 to exit.'
...
1
Enter 9 to exit.
2
Enter 9 to exit.
3
Enter 9 to exit.
4
Enter 9 to exit.
9
>>>
```

The function raw_input reads a value from the keyboard and returns that value as a string. Our while loop starts off by calling raw_input and checking if the value it returns is '9'. If it isn't, we print out 'Enter 9 to exit.'. Next, we jump back to the top of the loop and test the condition **not** raw_input ( ) == '9' again. We keep doing this until the condition is false, when we jump out of the loop. The point here is that it is the data that is driving the iteration, not counting.

3.8.6   Adding Complexity to Loops – Break and Continue

There are times when counted iteration or data-driven iteration are not up to the task of easily expressing the necessary algorithm. This situation often occurs when you have an algorithm that requires both counted and data-driven iteration.

To support this sort of situation, Python, like other programming languages, has a break statement and a continue statement that can be used to create extra complexities in an iteration. We are using the term 'complexity' here intentionally to indicate that an iteration that uses break or continue statements is more complex than one that doesn't and so is harder to understand. They should, therefore, only be used when necessary.

So what do these statements do?

- The break statement exits immediately from the innermost enclosing loop.

- The continue statement causes the rest of the current innermost enclosing loop body not to be executed and for the next iteration of the loop to be started immediately.

This may sound a little complicated. Let's look at an example of the break statement. Here we have a counted iteration that we wish to terminate if the input has a specific value – a mix of counted and data-driven iteration:

```
>>> for i in range ( 1 , 100 ) :
...     if raw_input ( ) == '9' :
...         break
...     else :
...         print 'Iteration ' + str ( i )
...
a
Iteration 1
s
Iteration 2
d
```

```
Iteration 3
f
Iteration 4
9
>>>
```

Here, if the user enters 9 at the keyboard, we break out of the loop. Otherwise we print the count of iterations that have already occurred and keep going.

3.8.7   Loop Else Clauses

A feature of for and while loops that can occasionally be immensely useful is that while and for statements may end with an **else** clause. If the loop construct does have an else clause then it is only executed if the loop terminates *without* a break statement being executed.

Here's a simple example:

```
>>> for i in range ( 1 , 5 ) :
...     if raw_input ( ) == '9' :
...         break
...     else :
...         print 'Iteration ' + str ( i )
... else :
...     print 'Completed the sequence without a 9 being pressed.'
...
a
Iteration 1
s
Iteration 2
d
Iteration 3
f
Iteration 4
Completed the sequence without a 9 being pressed.
>>>
```

3.8.8   An Example of Loop Else: Prime Numbers

As an example of using nested loops, the break statement and the loop else clause, we present a program that prints out the first few prime numbers. A prime number is one that can be divided only by itself or 1 without leaving a remainder. 2, 3, 5, 7, 11, 13 are all prime numbers.

All prime numbers other than 2 are odd.

As we are printing out the first few of anything, it sounds like iteration, so we need a loop. Within this loop we have to see if a number is divisible by any other number, which seems like another iteration, a nested loop. As a first attempt, we came up with the following program:

```
def primes ( n ) :
    '''Print out all the prime numbers less than n.'''
    for i in range ( 2 , n ) :
        for j in range ( 2 , i ) :
            if i % j == 0 :
                break ;
        else :
            print str ( i ) + ' ' ,
```

The algorithm here is to look through the integers from 2 to n (not including n) and if there are no *factors* (i.e. numbers that divide the number without remainder), then we print it (as it is prime), otherwise we don't (as it is not prime). This is the outer loop. On each iteration of this loop we iterate through all the numbers from 2 to i (the number being tested, but not including it) to see if the number has any factors. To do this we use the remainder operator (%) to see if a number divides another without a remainder. If a number other than 1 and itself divides with no remainder, i.e. the number has factors, then the number is not prime and we break out of the inner loop. If this happens the loop else clause is not executed. If on the other hand all divisions result in a remainder, then the number is prime, we complete the inner loop without executing a break statement, and so the loop else clause is executed and we print out the value of the prime number.

Here is an example execution, to show the result:

```
>>> def primes ( n ) :
...     '''Print out all the prime numbers less than n.'''
...     for i in range ( 2 , n ) :
...         for j in range ( 2 , i ) :
...             if i % j == 0 :
...                 break ;
...         else :
...             print str ( i ) + ' ' ,
...
>>> print primes ( 50 )
2 3 5 7 11 13 17 19 23 29 31 37 41 43 47
>>>
```

This is, algorithmically, a very inefficient algorithm for finding prime numbers. For one thing, it keeps repeating tests for factors that have already been done. Also, from Number Theory, we know that all factors of a number must have a value of less than the square root of the number, so we only actually need to test up to $\sqrt{i}$ and not i in the inner loop. However calculating square roots is expensive, and so it may be more efficient just to do all the tests anyway. Let's not worry about this just now. We will return to it in Section 4.1.2.

3.9 Handling Exceptions

When we implemented the factorial and fibonacci functions earlier in this chapter, we used raise statements to raise exceptions, but we didn't show how you might deal with them. Instead we just made use of the default Python behavior of terminating the program. This will not always be useful – we need to be able to intervene when an exception occurs. Python has a tool for providing this capability, the try–except statement.

As an example, here is the recursive fibonacci function with an interactive program that uses a try–except statement to deal with any exceptions:

```
def fibonacci ( n ) :
    if n < 0 :
        raise ValueError , 'Fibonacci cannot be applied to a negative parameter.'
    elif n == 0 :
        return 0
    elif n == 1 :
        return 1
```

```
        else :
            return fibonacci ( n - 1 ) + fibonacci ( n - 2 )

if __name__ == '__main__' :
    while True :
        value = input ( 'Input value of x : ' )
        try :
            print 'F (' + str ( value ) + ') = ' + str ( fibonacci ( value ))
        except :
            print 'Fibonacci raised an exception.'
```

The block that contains the function call that may cause an exception is in the block associated with the **try** (the try block) which has an associated **except** block. The try block is executed and if there is an exception the except block is executed. If there is no exception the except block is not executed.

What happens when we run this program?

```
| > python fibonacci_handledException.py
Input value of x : 5
F ( 5 ) = 5
Input value of x : 20
F ( 20 ) = 6765
Input value of x : -5
Fibonacci raised an exception.
Input value of x : 8
F ( 8 ) = 21
. . .
```

That seems satisfactory. We haven't shown our program correct, but at least it has no obvious errors, and we have taken control of exception handling.

On page 90 we said we there was a way of handling exceptions that would allow us to test the exception behavior of the factorial function without the program terminating. The try–except statement is what we need. For assertions that test correct results, we want the program to terminate if there is an exception because all the assertions are supposed to pass. To test that the function correctly throws an exception when it should, we need to use a try–except statement to trap the expected exception and do nothing when it happens, and generate an exception if it doesn't. The point here is that the test should generate an exception and so if it doesn't this is an error and requires that an exception be generated. The following version of the factorial program shows what we have to do:

```
def factorial ( x ) :
    if x < 0 :
        raise ValueError , 'Factorial not applicable to negative values.'
    elif x == 0 :
        return 1
    else :
        value = 1
        for i in range ( 1 , x + 1 ) :
            value *= i
        return value

if __name__ == '__main__' :
    assert factorial ( 4 ) == 24
    assert factorial ( 6 ) == 720
    assert factorial ( 21 ) == 51090942171709440000
```

```
try :
    factorial ( -5 )
    raise AssertionError , 'Factorial failed to throw exception on negative parameter.'
except ValueError :
    pass
```

There are three things to note here:

1. We have two statements in the try block. The call to factorial that is supposed to generate a ValueError exception, followed by a statement explicitly raising an AssertionError exception. Since the function call should generate an exception, the raise statement should never be executed. If the functional call fails to generate an exception then the raise statement is executed, generating a AssertionError exception.

2. After the **except** keyword we specify the name of the exception we are going to handle in this except block. Here, we handle only exceptions of type ValueError. All other exceptions are ignored and not handled. This means that if the factorial function generates any exception other than ValueError, or fails to generate an exception, resulting in an AssertionError being raised, the exception will not be handled and the program will terminate with the exception that was raised.

3. We have used the *pass statement* in the except block. We have to have at least one statement in the except block, but we don't actually want to do anything. So rather than invent some specious action that does nothing, Python has the pass statement, which does absolutely nothing. The pass statement is used whenever we need to have a statement because the language requires it but we don't actually want to do anything. This is surprisingly useful.

If we execute the program, we should get:

```
| > python factorial_iterative_handledExceptions.py
| >
```

and know that not only have we tested some correct calculations, we have also tested that the function behaves correctly in error situations.

Chapter Summary

In this chapter we have found that:

- The **and**, **or**, and **not** operators allow us to create complex Boolean expressions.
- Compound statements and code blocks can be nested.
- Recursion and recursive functions are a useful technique for easily expressing algorithm that are recursive, for example recurrence relations.
- Recursion must be carefully controlled: base case and recursive case must cooperate to ensure termination of the recursion.
- Recursion can be useful for drawing shapes such as the von Koch Snowflake.
- Python's iteration constructs are many and varied, involving for loops, while loops, break statements, continue statements, and else clauses.
- Loops can be nested to create complex iterations.
- Exception are used for dealing with error situations and unusual cases.

Self-Review Questions

Self-review 3.1 The following expression is true when age is 21 and height is 120, or age is 21 and height is 140:

$$(\text{age} == 21 \text{ and height} == 120) \text{ or } (\text{age} == 21 \text{ and height} == 140)$$

Can you write the expression with fewer terms?

Self-review 3.2 Simplify the following Boolean expressions:

1. a **or** (b **and** c) **not** a
2. b **and** c **or False**
3. a **and** b **or** c **or** (b **and** a)
4. a == **True or** b == **False**

Self-review 3.3 'Nand' is an operator that is false only when both of its operands are true. Python doesn't have a nand operator, so how can we write an expression that is equivalent to A nand B?

Self-review 3.4 Under what conditions would the following code sequences print 'B'?

1.
```
if thing1 > 10 :
    print 'A'
else:
    print 'B'
```

2.
```
if thing1 > 10 :
    print 'A'
elif thing1 > 200 :
    print 'B'
```

3.
```
if thing1 > 10 :
    print 'A'
if thing1 > 200 :
    print 'B'
```

4.
```
if thing1 > 10 and thing1 < 10 :
    print 'A'
else:
    print 'B'
```

Self-review 3.5 How many times will Python execute the code inside the following while loops? You should answer the question *without* using the interpreter! Justify your answers.

1.
```
i = 0
while i < 0 and i > 2 :
    print "still going ..."
    i = i+1
```

2.
```
i = 25
while i < 100 :
    print "still going ..."
    i = i - 1
```

```
3.      i = 1
        while i < 10000 and i > 0 and 1 :
            print "still going ..."
            i = 2 * i

4.      i = 1
        while i < 10000 and i > 0 and 0 :
            print "still going ..."
            i = 2 * i

5.      while i < 2048 and i > 0 :
            print "still going ..."
            i = 2 * i

6.      i = 1
        while i < 2048 and i > 0 :
            print "still going ..."
            i = 2 * i

7.      for i in [] :
            print "foobar!"
```

Self-review 3.6 What extra assert statement would be worth adding to the set of assertions that test the contains function on page 77 and page 91?

Self-review 3.7 Explain the difference between the iterative version of factorial on page 90 and the following:

```
def factorial ( x ) :
    if x < 0 :
        raise ValueError , 'Factorial not applicable to negative values.'
    elif x == 0 :
        return 1
    else :
        value = 1
        for i in range ( x , 1 , -1 ) :
            value *= i
        return value
```

Self-review 3.8 Compare the first power function (in Section 3.7.2) to the more efficient one in Section 3.8.4. How many multiplications does each implementation make to evaluate power (3 , 5)? Make sure you show your reasoning.

Self-review 3.9 Referring to the recursive function for generating numbers in the Fibonacci Sequence (page 81), how many calls to fibonacci are made to evaluate fibonacci (5)? Can you write down a general rule for how many calls must be made to evaluate fibonacci (n)?

Self-review 3.10 What lists do the following expressions evaluate to?

1. range (1 ,100)
2. range (1 , 50 , 2)
3. range (1 , 25 , 3)
4. range (10 , -10 , -2)

Self-review 3.11 The following code contains the names a, b and c. What is the scope of each of the them?

```
a = 10
for b in range ( 1 , 10 ) :
    c = b + 10
    print c
```

Self-review 3.12 What does the following code do? How might it be used in a larger program?

```
print 'Menu:'
print '1. Play game'
print '2. See high score table'
print '3. Exit'
i = -1
while i < 1 or i > 3:
    j = raw_input ( 'Enter choice: ' )
    try :
        i = int ( j )
    except :
        continue
```

Self-review 3.13 For the following recursive function, label the base cases and recursive cases. What do these functions do?

```
def m ( a , b ) :
    def mm ( a , b , c ) :
        if a == 0 : return c
        else : return mm ( a - 1 , b , c + b )
    return mm ( a , b , 0 )

def d ( a , b ) :
    def dd ( a , b , c ) :
        if a < b : return c
        else : return dd ( a - b , b , c + 1 )
    return dd ( a , b , 0 )
```

Hint: You are almost certainly already familiar with these algorithms, just not in this form! You might want to try working out what these functions would return for some simple input values.

Self-review 3.14 We are to write some assert statements of the form:

```
assert ( m ( ? , ? ) == ? )
```

and

```
assert ( d ( ? , ? ) == ? )
```

to create tests for the two functions from Self-review 3.13. What assert statements would it be useful to put into a test? What parameter values might cause problems for m and d?

Self-review 3.15 What do the Python keywords **break** and **continue** do?

Self-review 3.16 What does the following print out?

```
for i in range ( 1 , 10 ) :
    for j in range ( 1 , 10 ) :
        print i * j ,
    print
```

Self-review 3.17 What do they keywords **raise**, **try** and **except** mean?

Programming Exercises

Exercise 3.1 Implement a recursive Python function that returns the sum of the first *n* integers.

Exercise 3.2 Implement an iterative Python function that returns the sum of the first *n* integers.

Exercise 3.3 Implement an iterative Python function to generate numbers in the Fibonacci Sequence.

Exercise 3.4 While and for loops are equivalent: whatever you can do with one you can do with the other. In the following programs, convert the following while loops into for loops and the for loops into while loops. Of course, your new loops should give the same results as the old ones!

1.
```
for i in range ( 1 ,100 ) :
    if i % 3 == 2 :
        print i , "mod" , 3 , "= 2"
```

2.
```
for i in range(10):
    for j in range(i):
        print '*',
    print "
```

3.
```
i = 0
while i < 100 :
    if i % 2 == 0 :
        print i , "is even"
    else :
        print i , "is odd"
    i = i + 1
```

4.
```
char = ""
print "Press Tab Enter to stop and Enter to keep going ..."
iteration = 0
while not char == "\t" and not iteration > 99:
    print "Keep going?"
    char = raw_input()
    iteration += 1
```

Exercise 3.5 Using books, the Web, or any other resource, find out what a logic gate is, and, in particular, what a half adder is. An output of the work should be a table showing the inputs and outputs for a half adder.

Implement a half adder as a few lines of Python code. Write a test program that shows that your implementation works as expected. You should be able to test that your code works for *all* possible input values.

Exercise 3.6 The following shows a Cesàro Fractal (also known as a Torn Square fractal). Write a program to draw this figure.

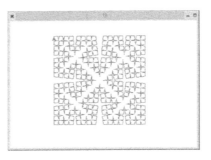

Hint: *The Cesàro Fractal is based on a square. Each line, if it is longer than the minimum line length, is a line with an extra triangular section:*

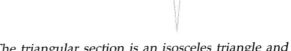

The triangular section is an isosceles triangle and is always on the 'inside' of the square.

Exercise 3.7 Self-review 3.13 contained recursive implementations of functions m and d. Write equivalent functions that use iteration rather than recursion to produce the same results

Exercise 3.8 Write a function that capitalizes all the vowels in a string.

Hint: *We have generally used indexing and the range function when using for loops. We can also use for loops for iterating over the characters in a string. For example:*

> **for** *char* **in** *'foobar' :*
> **print** *char*

Hint: *Look at the documentation on strings: it has functions one or more of which are useful for this exercise. You might try using Python in interactive mode, importing the string module, and asking for help:*

> >>> *import string*
> >>> *help(string)*
> . . .

or look up the string module in the Python documentation.

Exercise 3.9 Use the Turtle module and nested loops to draw the following shape:

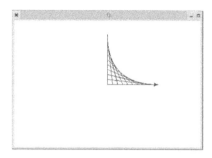

Exercise 3.10 Linux, Mac OS X, Solaris and other Unix-like systems have a command cal that, when run without a parameter, prints out the calendar for the current month. For example:

```
|> cal
      May 2007
Mo Tu We Th Fr Sa Su
    1  2  3  4  5  6
 7  8  9 10 11 12 13
14 15 16 17 18 19 20
21 22 23 24 25 26 27
28 29 30 31

|>
```

Use loops and nested loops to print out a similar table for this month. Try to make sure that your columns line up correctly, like the example above!

Challenges

Challenge 3.1 The following shows a Dragon Curve.

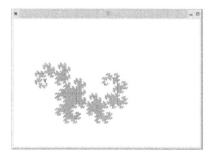

Find an algorithm for drawing a Dragon Curve and write a program to draw a figure such as the one shown.

Hint: The starting point for a Dragon Curve is a straight line, but you always have to deal with two lines at a time. So this is not a simple recursion – more than one recursive function is needed.

Challenge 3.2 One application area in which iteration and recursion are particularly useful is user interfaces – programs that directly interact with people. These include websites, games, spreadsheets, and so on. For this challenge, you will create a text-based user interface to the Python turtle. The idea behind this is to let people use the turtle without having to learn Python first.

As a start, here is some code that allows you to move the turtle around using the keys a, s, w, and d on the keyboard:

```python
import turtle

def turtle_interface ( ) :
    """Allow the user to control the turtle via the keyboard."""
    steps = 10
    angle = 5
    while True :
        i = raw_input ( )
        if i == 'w' : turtle.forward ( steps )
        elif i == 's' : turtle.backward ( steps )
        elif i == 'a' : turtle.left ( angle )
        elif i == 'd' : turtle.right ( angle )
        elif i == 'q' : break
        else : continue

print 'Control the turtle!'
turtle_interface()
```

Improve this code by adding:

1. A function to print out a menu before the user starts. This should explain which keys are used to control the turtle. (Make sure that you keep the key map up to date as you add new functionality to the program.)

2. User options to perform the following functions:
   (a) Clear the screen.
   (b) Lift the 'pen' of the turtle off the page.
   (c) Put the pen back down on the page.
   (d) Change the width of the line that the turtle draws.
   (e) Draw a circle. Better still, let the user decide how big a radius the circle should have.
   (f) Change the color of the turtle. Allow the user to choose from a small number of colors (say, red, blue, green and black).

   (You may well need to read through the documentation for the Turtle module to implement these.)

3. Undo capability. You will need to store the last key the user pressed and write some code (maybe in a separate function) to map keys onto their opposite actions. This might not be possible for some user options (such as drawing a circle) but others should be straightforward. For example, if the user has previously moved forward by 10 units, the opposite action is to move backwards 10 units.

Structuring State

4

Learning Outcomes

At the end of this chapter you will be able to:

- Describe how assignment works by *substitution*.

- Apply substitution to determine the result of an expression.

- Describe the terms *state, state space, state transition* and *finite state machine* and their relationship to Python variables.

- Draw *state transition diagrams* for finite state machines.

- Define the term *lexer* and write

simple lexers in Python (e.g. to lex integers and decimal numbers).

- Use all the Python sequence types (list, tuple and dictionary) in programs.

- Describe the similarities and differences between all the various Python types.

- Choose which types to use to solve problems using Python.

So far we have managed to create some useful programs using only statements, functions and variables of type string, integer, float, and function. However, as programs get bigger and more complicated this will not be sufficient. We will have to introduce more ways of structuring our statements and functions, but more immediately we need new ways of structuring our data.

Data (whether input via a user interface, obtained from disk, or embedded in the program itself), and the evolution of that data to produce useful output, is what programs are all about. We need useful ways of structuring data so that we can work with it easily. Let's look at one way of structuring data.

4.1 Structuring Data

4.1.1 Lists

Did you notice when we were looking at the range function on page 88 that we got some interesting output?

```
>>> print range ( 10 )
[0, 1, 2, 3, 4, 5, 6, 7, 8, 9]
>>> print range ( 1 , 5 )
[1, 2, 3, 4]
>>>
```

The Python system has output all the values in the range as a single thing. What is this thing? Let's ask the Python system what the type is, maybe that will give us a hint:

```
>>> print type ( range ( 10 ) )
<type 'list'>
>>>
```

The result of calling the range function is a value that has type list. As it is a value, we must be able to assign the value to a variable. Let's try it:

```
>>> x = range ( 2 , 20 , 3 )
>>> print x
[2, 5, 8, 11, 14, 17]
>>> print type ( x )
<type 'list'>
>>>
```

Well that seems unsurprising, we can use a list just as we used strings, integers and floats – the type has values, we can assign variables and we can do things with them. The big difference, of course, is that list values seems to contain some number of other values. That seems reasonable – think of what we mean by a list in our daily lives: perhaps the most obvious lists people make are shopping lists. Many (but not all) of us write down a list of the things we want and then go out to the shops and buy those things. We might even mark our list as we buy things – in effect we remove items from the list as things get bought.

Lists in Python are not dissimilar. A list is a value to which we can add items and from which we can remove items. Moreover, the order of the items in the list is important. A list is therefore a *mutable sequence*. It is mutable in that we can change the value. It is a sequence because it contains other values in a definite order.

Does this get us anywhere? Well, yes, actually – it is a huge step forward. Till now we have had variables, but not containers. We had to use a variable in our program for every value we needed to store. Containers allow us to implement algorithms where the number of items being processed is not known when we write the program. The significance of this will become apparent.

4.1.2 Prime Numbers Revisited

As an initial example of the use of lists, let's create a version of the program for printing out prime numbers that is far more efficient than the earlier one (Section 3.8.8, page 94). The observation about prime numbers that helps us here is that we only have to try dividing a number by the prime numbers less than the number to know whether the number is prime or not. To do this, we have to store the prime numbers we have already found, and we didn't have the tool to be able to do that before. Now we know about lists, we can do something like:

```
def primes ( n ) :
    '''Print out all the prime numbers less than n.'''
    primeNumbers = [ ]
    for i in range ( 2 , n ) :
        for j in primeNumbers :
            if i % j == 0 :
                break ;
        else :
            primeNumbers += [ i ]
    return primeNumbers
```

```
if __name__ == '__main__' :
    upperLimit = 25
    print 'Primes <' , upperLimit , 'are :' , primes ( upperLimit )
```

which, when executed, gives us:

```
|> python primes.py
Primes < 25 are : [2, 3, 5, 7, 11, 13, 17, 19, 23]
```

The primes function has a variable primeNumbers that is initialized to an empty list – [ ] is the list literal that means a list with no entries in it. Then there is:

```
for i in range ( 2 , n ) :
```

which is an iteration over the list of numbers range (2 , n), where, for each of the values of i, we then iterate over in the list:

```
for j in primeNumbers :
```

Here we now see the true nature of the for loop and why we have the syntax:

```
for <variable> in <sequence> :
    <body>
```

A list is a sequence, so the for loop causes iteration over all the values in the sequence. A for loop is a very general form of loop that can implement counted iteration because the range function creates a list of integer values.

Back in our primes program we have a loop within a loop: the outer loop (variable i) is our sequence of test values and the inner loop (variable j) is of found primes. The body of the inner loop is the check to see if j (which is a prime number from the list of prime numbers) is a factor of i. If it is a factor then we break out and go to the next iteration: if i has no factors from the list of primes, then it is a new prime and we append it to the list of primes. The [i] in:

```
primeNumbers += [ i ]
```

says make a new list containing only the value of i, and the += says append the contents of the list on the right-hand side to the list on the left-hand side, i.e. append the contents of the list [i] to the list primeNumbers. Once all the numbers are tested the function returns a list containing all the prime numbers found.

In the example we have shown a main statement sequence that prints out all the primes less than 25. When executed, we get:

```
|> python primes.py
Primes < 25 are : [2, 3, 5, 7, 11, 13, 17, 19, 23]
```

The print statement knows how to print a list, so it all just works.

This idea of remembering some values and amending them during execution is a critical aspect of what software and computing is about. So much so that there is a word for it: *state*. Before looking at lists in more detail, let's briefly investigate this idea of state.

4.2   State

4.2.1   The States of Things

The *state* of something is the configuration it is in. For example, a light switch can be 'On' or a mobile phone can be 'Ringing'. The *state space* of a device is the set of all states in which the device can exist. So, a light switch has the state space:

{ On , Off }

A mobile phone has a state space along the lines of:

{ Locked , Ready , Ringing , Calling , Connected , On_hold }

Some things can have an infinite state space – or one so large that it cannot sensibly be represented. For example, astrophysicists might contemplate modeling the Universe in a computer simulation by modeling the state of every atom in the Universe. However, this is such a huge amount of data (there are reputed to be 10^{80} protons in the Universe) that it's unlikely to ever be possible. So, for the foreseeable future, let's stick to problems that have a state space that is a bit smaller!

An important property of state is that it changes over time. So, a light can change its state from 'On' to 'Off' and back to 'On'. A mobile phone can go from 'Locked' to 'Ringing' to 'Connected' to 'Ready' to... Changing from one state to another is termed a *state transition*, or just *transition*, and is caused by an *event*. The event "changing the light switch to 'On'" is the event that would move the light from the 'Off' state to the 'On' state. If a mobile phone is in the 'Connected' state then pressing the 'end call' button changes the phone to the 'Ready' state.

4.2.2 Assignment and Substitution

What relevance does this have to programming? A computer has state. Each of our programs has state. The state of a program is the current value of all its variables. An event is the execution of a statement which changes the state of the program. After executing the sequence:

```
a = 5
b = 6
c = 7
```

the program has created the variables a, b, and c, and is in the state:

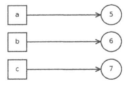

The Python system has created objects to represent the numbers 5, 6 and 7 and has created associations between the variables and the numbers.

If the program then executes the statement:

```
c = 5
```

the program transitions to the state:

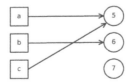

a and b are still associated with the values 5 and 6 respectively, but c has become associated with 5. Thus the role of assignment is to change the associations between variables and values and thereby change the state.

So what is Python actually doing when it is evaluating an expression such as:

```
(a * b)/(a + c)
```

Internally, Python looks back through the information it has collected to see what values have been most recently associated with the variables a, b and c. These values are then *substituted* for the variable names in the expression and the expression evaluated.

Let's see this working in a program:

```
a = 5
b = 6
c = 7
print ( a * b ) / ( a + c )
c = 5
print ( a * b ) / ( a + c )
```

Executing this by typing each line into the interpreter gives:

```
>>> a = 5
>>> b = 6
>>> c = 7
>>> print ( a * b ) / ( a + c )
2
>>> c = 5
>>> print ( a * b ) / ( a + c )
3
>>>
```

Using the notation $[x \setminus 1]$ to mean that 1 is substituted for x in the preceding expression, we can show how the expressions are evaluated. Starting with the first expression:

$$
\begin{aligned}
(a*b)/(a+c)\,[\,a\setminus 5,\,b\setminus 6,\,c\setminus 7\,] \;&=\; (5*b)/(5+c)\,[\,b\setminus 6,\,c\setminus 7\,] \\
&=\; (5*6)/(5+c)\,[\,c\setminus 7\,] \\
&=\; (5*6)/(5+7) \\
&=\; 2
\end{aligned}
$$

The second expression is evaluated in the same way but with a change of associated value for c:

$$
\begin{aligned}
(a*b)/(a+c)\,[\,a\setminus 5,\,b\setminus 6,\,c\setminus 5\,] \;&=\; (5*b)/(5+c)\,[\,b\setminus 6,\,c\setminus 5\,] \\
&=\; (5*6)/(5+c)\,[\,c\setminus 5\,] \\
&=\; (5*6)/(5+5) \\
&=\; 3
\end{aligned}
$$

Clearly we don't need to do this sort of manual evaluation often. However, it is important that we have a model of how the Python system performs evaluation, so that when we do need to investigate how an expression is being evaluated, we can.

4.2.3 Changing State

The state space that a system (a device or a program) has and the transitions between its states are usually represented in a *state transition diagram*. The following is the state transition diagram for a light bulb connected to an on/off switch.

The states of the system are represented by circles and the name of each state is written inside its circle. Transitions between states are represented by *directed arcs* – directed arcs are lines with arrows and hence a direction, which means there is a 'from state' and a 'to state' associated with each directed arc. The sideways 'V' shape in the 'Off' state shows that 'Off' is the state in which the system should start – unsurprisingly this is called the *start state*.

We can write a function to determine which state we transition to from any given state. In the light bulb case, for example:

```
def nextState ( state ) :
    if state == 'Off' :
        state = 'On'
    elif state == 'On' :
        state = 'Off'
    else:
        raise ValueError , 'Attempted to transition from a non-existent state ' + state
    return state
```

Here we have used strings ('On' and 'Off') to represent the states. This is arguably not the right way of doing things, but we will leave discussion of this till Chapter 6.

In this nextState function, we have covered the cases in which state has values 'On', 'Off', and any other string at all. This is an element of what is often called *defensive programming*: we write our program so that it is not possible for it to get into a state it should not be in. In particular, if a light bulb can only be in one of the states 'On' or 'Off', then to be in any other state would be inconsistent – a so-called *inconsistent state*. In this implementation we have chosen to raise an exception when the system appears to be in an inconsistent state. Dealing with this situation is then 'Somefunction else's problem' (SEP).

It is perhaps worth over-emphasizing this point about state: one of the jobs of programmers is to ensure that any program on which they work never ends up in an undesirable state, and especially not an inconsistent state. After all, who actually wants their workstation to crash, or their mobile phone to fail spontaneously, or the ATM into which you just put your debit card to crash and keep hold of your card? When programming always try to take the user's perspective on the system – on some occasions you may be the user of your own systems.

With the definition of nextState in place, we can try it out:

```
>>> print nextState ( 'On' )
Off
>>> print nextState ( 'Off' )
On
>>> print nextState ( 'Half-way' )
Traceback (most recent call last):
  File "<stdin>", line 1, in ?
  File "<stdin>", line 7, in nextState
ValueError: Attempted to transition from a non-existent state Half-way
>>>
```

This function seems to do the right thing with no errors.

4.2.4 Finite State Machines

The light switch system is an example of a *finite state machine* (sometimes called a *finite state automaton*). A finite state machine is a system that transitions between states in its state space, like our light switch moving from 'On' to 'Off' then 'On' again, and so on.

Another example is a set of traffic lights. The following is the state transition diagram for the most usual sort of traffic light system around the world:

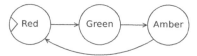

We can write a program that is a traffic light controller:

```
import time

def nextState ( state ) :
    if state == 'Red' :
        state = 'Green'
    elif state == 'Green' :
        state = 'Amber'
    else :
        state = 'Red'
    return state

if __name__ == '__main__' :
    state = 'Red'
    while True :
        print state
        time.sleep ( 5 )
        state = nextState ( state )
```

Strings are definitely not the best way of representing these states, but we will address this in Chapter 6.

Where is defensive programming here? We have written things so that the light goes to red for all inconsistent states. This is a different solution to raising an exception and (arguably) a poorer solution. Although some people would say that it is good for a function such as nextState to ensure a reasonable state as part of a defensive strategy, others would say that this is hiding errors, errors that should be known about as soon as possible. We side with the latter view, and so feel that any inconsistent state should be a exceptional issue, not a hidden one. Raising exceptions is a much better design choice in our view.

Traffic lights never appear alone, they always exist in synchronized groups. More on this in Chapter 6.

In both the light switch and traffic light systems the next state is only determined by the previous state. So, if our light switch is in its 'Off' state, the next state has to be 'On'; if the traffic light system is in its 'Red' state, the next transition has to be to 'Green'. In some finite state machines, however, the next state is determined by the current state *and* an input.

4.2.5 An Example: A Vending Machine

As an example of a finite state machine, let's consider the following simple vending machine that takes tokens as input and dispenses coffee and cola:

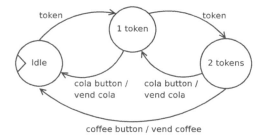

Cola costs the purchaser one token and coffee costs two tokens. Some of the time the system is in the 'Idle' state, but once a token has been placed in the machine it enters the '1 token' state. Notice that the arcs in the state transition diagram are labeled. The arc going from the 'Idle' to the '1 token' states is labeled with 'token', meaning that if the machine is in the 'Idle' state then the event 'token' (which represents the input of a token by the user) will cause it to move to the '1 token' state. If the 'cola button' event occurs (the user presses the 'cola button') while the machine is in the '1 token' state it will output a cola. The syntax 'cola button / vend cola' means that on that particular state transition, 'cola button' is the event (an input) and 'vend cola' is an action, in this case outputting a cola from the machine.

Following the state transitions around, you can work out how a consumer can use the vending machine. For example, if the machine is in 'Idle' state, there are two ways of buying two colas. Firstly you can put two tokens in consecutively (putting the machine in '2 tokens' state) then press the 'cola button' twice. Alternatively, you can put one token in (moving the machine into '1 token' state) then press the 'cola button', and then repeat the same actions.

We could try implementing this in Python now, but we think we would end up doing things in a very awkward way. So we are going to delay implementation until Section 4.5.8 (page 128), when we have introduced more about lists, and, in particular, tuples.

4.3 Representing State

What is the point of all these ideas about state as far as programming and solving problems is concerned? We have to create a representation of the state required to solve the problem in our program. If we have a problem to solve, we have to think about what data is required in the solution and how we should store the data in our program, to provide a good representation of the problem in the computer. Let's use an example to show this.

The 'Towers of Hanoi' is a problem involving three 'towers' and discs of various sizes that fit on the 'towers'. The starting position has all the discs in ascending order of size on one tower:

The Towers of Hanoi puzzle was invented by Édouard Lucas in 1883.

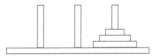

The problem is to move the discs one at a time from one tower to another, never putting a bigger disc on a smaller disc, so that all the discs end up in ascending order on another tower, and to do this using the fewest number of moves. Given the above as a start position the end position would be:

The total state space for the 'Towers of Hanoi' problem depends on the number of discs – if n is the number of discs then the state space has 3^n states. So with three discs ($n = 3$) there are $3^3 = 27$ possible states. By drawing out the complete state transition diagram, we could then search for the path between the start state and the desired end state to see which transitions we had to make. However, this is one of those problems where you probably don't want to do that. Think of using this method with four discs. $3^4 = 81$. That is a lot of states. What about five discs. 243 states. No, this is not a viable method for this problem.

So how can we progress? Let's think about how can we represent the state in our program. One possible representation of the three towers is a trio of lists. What about the discs? Since the discs are all of different sizes, we can represent each disc as an integer. How? As each disc in the problem has a different size, we can order the discs by size, then count them off starting with 1 as the smallest, 2 as the next smallest, etc. In this way we assign an integer to each disc and, moreover, the order of the integers represents the correct order of the discs. So for the problem at hand we have three discs represented by the integers, 1, 2 and 3, and can represent the starting state as:

```
tower1 = [ 3 , 2 , 1 ]
tower2 = [ ]
tower3 = [ ]
```

and the end state as:

```
tower1 = [ ]
tower2 = [ ]
tower3 = [ 3 , 2 , 1 ]
```

> The first item of the lists represents the bottom of the tower. Discs (represented by integers) must appear in order on every list – the list must always be sorted in descending order. Only the items at the ends of the list can be moved.

A move (or state transition) is to take the last item from one list and append it to the end of another list. This represents taking the top disc off one tower and putting it onto another tower – as with the physical version of the game, you can only access the discs at the top of a stack on a tower. The rule that a bigger disc cannot be put on a smaller disc is implemented by not allowing a bigger integer to appear after a smaller integer in the list, i.e. the order of items in any of the lists must always be descending.

So far so good, but what are the moves required to solve the problem? The insight we need is that in order to move the whole set of discs from one tower to another, we can:

1. Move all but the bottom disc to the non-destination tower.
2. Move the bottom disc to the destination tower.
3. Move the discs on the non-destination tower to the destination tower.

Spot the recursive algorithm! Items 1 and 3 of this list are candidates for recursive calls but with a smaller stack of discs to move. Since the size of the stack of discs is smaller, we will eventually make a call with zero items to move. This is clearly the base case, and we have shown that the recursion always moves towards the base case, so we will get termination.

So we have a representation of the problem and we have an algorithm, so the only thing to do now is to write the code:

```python
def move ( source , target ) :
    '''Move a disc from one tower to another checking that the move is legal.'''
    if len ( source ) < 1 :
        raise ValueError , 'Cannot remove a disc from an empty tower.'
    temporary = source[-1]
    del source[-1]
    if len ( target ) > 0 and target[-1] < temporary :
        raise ValueError , 'Cannot place a bigger disc on top of a smaller disc.'
    target.append ( temporary )
    if displayMoves : print 'Move ' , temporary , ': ' ,
```

> The move function includes some features of Python that we haven't seen before. We explain immediately after the listing.

```
def hanoi ( n , source , spare , target ) :
    '''
    Move n-1 discs from the source tower to the spare tower.
    Move one disc from the source tower to the target tower.
    Move n-1 discs from the spare tower to the target tower.
    '''
    if n > 0 :
        hanoi ( n - 1 , source , target , spare )
        move ( source , target )
        if displayMoves : print tower1, ' ' , tower2 , ' ' , tower3
        hanoi ( n - 1 , spare , source , target )

if __name__ == '__main__' :
    tower1 = [ 3 , 2 , 1 ]
    tower2 = [ ]
    tower3 = [ ]
    print 'Problem : ' , tower1 , ' ' , tower2 , ' ' , tower3
    displayMoves = True
    hanoi ( len ( tower1 ) , tower1 , tower2 , tower3 )
    print 'Solution: ' , tower1 , ' ' , tower2 , ' ' , tower3
```

The move function is arguably over-defensive. Analyzing hanoi and the use of move in detail shows that the cases defended against in move cannot actually happen.

There are lots of points to address, all stemming from the move function:

- We use the len function in expressions such as len (source) to find the number of items currently in a list – in this example the number of items currently in the list source.

- We have used the expression source[-1] to reference integer values that represent discs. This is an *indexing* expression. We use brackets after a list variable name to indicate that we want to name a particular item in the list. Using a negative number means we are indexing from the end of the list rather than the beginning. So source[-1] means the value of the last item in the list source.

- We have used the **del** command to remove an item from a list. We could instead have used the assignment source[-1:] = [], but decided to use **del** (we will explain this in Section 4.4.4, page 118).

- We have used the append function in the expression target.append (temporary) to append a new value onto the end of a particular list. We could, equally well, have used the expression target += [temporary]. It really is a matter of choice of style as to which to use.

It looks as if we should have a more detailed look at lists, as they clearly have lots of very useful features that we need to know about in order to do any programming using them.

4.4 Lists and Operations on Them

4.4.1 Indexing

A list is a sequence of items, which means that we can select an item from the list by specifying its position in the sequence. This is called *indexing*. So if we have a list of ten items, we can select the third or seventh item:

Methods

There are some functions that are a little different to the functions we have seen so far. append is just such a function. Instead of the function being called with parameters, for example move (source , target), the function is called on the value associated with a variable, possibly with parameters. So for example target.append (temporary) means call the function append on the value associated with the variable target, with the parameter temporary. Not all functions can be called like this, only special functions. To highlight this "specialness", they are called *methods*. So move is a function, but append is a method.

Only certain types have methods. For example the type list has the method append. This means that the append method can be called on variables of type list. In this case the variable target is of type list and so the call target.append (temporary) works.

We won't be looking at how we can create our own methods until Chapter 6, but this does not stop us using all the predefined methods for the type like list and string.

Note that turtle.left is not a method, it is a function. The difference is that turtle is the name of a package, the Turtle package. This is a different use of the . notation than target.append, where target is a variable.

```
>>> x = [ 'a' , 'b' , 'c' , 'd' , 'e' , 'f' , 'g' , 'h' , 'i' , 'j' , 'k' ]
>>> print x[3]
d
>>> print x[7]
h
>>>
```

Not, perhaps, what might have been expected: the third item in the list is 'c', and the seventh is 'g'. In Python and most other programming languages, when indexing, you start counting with 0 and not 1. So the first item in the list has index 0, the second item has index 1, and so on. When we said we were going to look at the third and seventh items, by using 3 and 7 as indexes, we were actually looking at the items with index 3 and 7, which are the fourth and eighth items.

Starting to count from 0 when thinking about indexing will soon become second nature. At first, though, you may sometimes not do so and this may well lead to an error. Such an error is actually quite common, even with seasoned programmers, so it has a name: *off-by-one error*. Whenever you think indexing in a list is 'off by one' think 'possible indexing error'.

As we noted earlier, you can use negative indexes to index from the end of a list:

```
>>> x = [ 'a' , 'b' , 'c' , 'd' , 'e' , 'f' , 'g' , 'h' , 'i' , 'j' , 'k' ]
>>> print x[-3]
i
>>>
```

Perhaps confusingly, when indexing backwards we start at -1. The issue here is that 0 and -0 are the same, so we cannot use -0 as the first backward index. Hence indexing from the end must start with -1.

Because lists are mutable we are able to change the values in the list using assignment:

```
>>> x = [ 'a' , 'b' , 'c' , 'd' , 'e' , 'f' , 'g' , 'h' , 'i' , 'j' , 'k' ]
>>> x[5] = 'ZZZ'
>>> print x
['a', 'b', 'c', 'd', 'e', 'ZZZ', 'g', 'h', 'i', 'j', 'k']
>>>
```

This seems fairly intuitive: we could have guessed that this is what was going to happen. If we are able to guess correctly what is going to happen when an expression is evaluated or a statement executed, it means two things:

1. The programming language has semantics that are in tune with the way we think.

2. Our understanding of how the programing language executes matches the way the system actually executes.

When both of these are true, programming is going to be fairly straightforward!

4.4.2 Slicing

Indexing in a list is like saying "I'll have that one". Often, though, when we deal with lists, we say "All of them from here to there". That is, we want to take a part of a list as another list. This idea of taking a sub-list, also known as a *slice*, is so important that there is special syntax in Python:

```
>>> x = [ 'a' , 'b' , 'c' , 'd' , 'e' , 'f' , 'g' , 'h' , 'i' , 'j' , 'k' ]
>>> print x[3:7]
['d', 'e', 'f', 'g']
>>>
```

So if there is a colon in the brackets, it is saying 'slice', not 'index'. In this example, the slice starts at index 3 and ends one before index 7: slicing is a "from here, up to, but not including, there" operation that results in a new list.

We can use positive indexes (counting from the front) or negative indexes (counting from the end):

```
>>> x = [ 'a' , 'b' , 'c' , 'd' , 'e' , 'f' , 'g' , 'h' , 'i' , 'j' , 'k' ]
>>> print x[-6:-2]
['f', 'g', 'h', 'i']
>>> print x[2:-2]
['c', 'd', 'e', 'f', 'g', 'h', 'i']
>>> print x[-6:8]
['f', 'g', 'h']
>>> print x[5:-8]
[]
>>>
```

In the last example the indexes did not define a slice, as the first index came after the second. Indexes of a slice must always be such that the first comes before the second – otherwise the result is an empty list.

What happens if we miss out one of the indexes of a slice? In such a situation a default is assumed. If we miss the first index, it is assumed that we mean "start the slice at index 0". If we miss the second index, this means that the slice continues to the end of the list (i.e. ends at index -1):

```
>>> x = [ 'a' , 'b' , 'c' , 'd' , 'e' , 'f' , 'g' , 'h' , 'i' , 'j' , 'k' ]
>>> print x[:6]
['a', 'b', 'c', 'd', 'e', 'f']
>>> print x [8:]
['i', 'j', 'k']
>>> print x[:-4]
['a', 'b', 'c', 'd', 'e', 'f', 'g']
```

```
>>> print x[-4:]
['h', 'i', 'j', 'k']
>>>
```

What happens if we miss both indexes? What do you think? A hypothesis: if the default first index is 0 and the default last index is -1, then we ought to get a copy of the whole list. Let's experiment:

```
>>> x = [ 'a' , 'b' , 'c' , 'd' , 'e' , 'f' , 'g' , 'h' , 'i' , 'j' , 'k' ]
>>> print x[:]
['a', 'b', 'c', 'd', 'e', 'f', 'g', 'h', 'i', 'j', 'k']
>>>
```

Expectation met, hypothesis confirmed.

Cloning

To *clone* something is to make a new thing that is an exact copy of the old thing. Using slicing with the default start and end indexes, as in x[:], is a cloning operation because it results in a new list that is an exact replica of the original list x.

Can we use assignment with slices? Oh yes:

```
>>> x = [ 'a' , 'b' , 'c' , 'd' , 'e' , 'f' , 'g' , 'h' , 'i' , 'j' , 'k' ]
>>> x[2:6] = [ 'AAA' , 'BBB' , 'CCC' ]
>>> print x
['a', 'b', 'AAA', 'BBB', 'CCC', 'g', 'h', 'i', 'j', 'k']
>>>
```

This operation means "replace the slice with the contents of another list". Note that the size of the updated list may be different to before the assignment. Items also may move position in the list. For example, 'g' is now at index 5 whereas it was at index 6.

4.4.3 What's in a List

So far, we have worked only with lists of strings, but there is no restriction on what we can put in a list:

```
>>> x = [ 'Sarah' , 20 , 'James' , 20 , 'Russel' , 10 ]
>>> print x[2]
James
>>> print x[3]
20
>>>
```

A list really can contain an item of any type. A list can even contain other lists:

```
>>> x = [ [ 'Sarah' , 20 ] , [ 'James' , 20 ] , [ 'Russel' , 10 ] ]
>>> print x[2]
['Russel', 10]
>>>
```

It turns out that for sanity of program design, lists rarely contain values of different types. Regularity and structure to the way we represent the state in our program makes algorithms easier to design and implement, and therefore makes programs easier to write.

In the first of the above two examples, we had regularity (the data is string, int, string, int, string, int) but it is not obvious what the structure is. In the second of the above two examples, we have regularity (list, list, list) and we have structure – each list item in the outer list is string followed by int. So say we are writing a game and we need to keep track of the name and speed of a player in a given position, the latter structuring of the data (the outer lists is of positions with each entry structured identically, name followed by speed) will lead to simpler algorithms and hence a simpler program.

4.4.4 Amending Lists

A question: is the following what was intended?

```
>>> x = [ 'a' , 'b' , 'c' , 'd' , 'e' , 'f' , 'g' , 'h' , 'i' , 'j' , 'k' ]
>>> x[5] = [ 'AAA' , 'BBB' , 'CCC' ]
>>> print x
['a', 'b', 'c', 'd', 'e', ['AAA', 'BBB', 'CCC'], 'g', 'h', 'i', 'j', 'k']
>>>
```

This is not really a question we can answer without knowing what the problem is and what the algorithm of solution is. However, the moral of the story is that you need to be careful about syntax when you use indexing, and when you use slicing:

```
>>> x = [ 'a' , 'b' , 'c' , 'd' , 'e' , 'f' , 'g' , 'h' , 'i' , 'j' , 'k' ]
>>> x[5:] = [ 'AAA' , 'BBB' , 'CCC' ]
>>> print x
['a', 'b', 'c', 'd', 'e', 'AAA', 'BBB', 'CCC']
>>>
```

The colon in the brackets makes a huge difference to what the code does.

In the 'Towers of Hanoi' program (page 113) we used a **del** statement and said it was equivalent to source[-1:] = [], but didn't explain. Now we can. **del** removes the item that is the operand. So in the example:

```
>>> x = [ 'a' , 'b' , 'c' , 'd' , 'e' , 'f' , 'g' , 'h' , 'i' , 'j' , 'k' ]
>>> del x[5]
>>> print x
['a', 'b', 'c', 'd', 'e', 'g', 'h', 'i', 'j', 'k']
>>>
```

the **del** removes the 'f' which was x[5]. There is still an x[5] but now the value there is 'g'. Slicing in an assignment can be used to achieve exactly the same result:

```
>>> x = [ 'a' , 'b' , 'c' , 'd' , 'e' , 'f' , 'g' , 'h' , 'i' , 'j' , 'k' ]
>>> x[5:6] = [ ]
>>> print x
['a', 'b', 'c', 'd', 'e', 'g', 'h', 'i', 'j', 'k']
>>>
```

Why have two ways of doing the same thing? Actually they are not the same, they only appear to do the same thing in this circumstance because the outcome in this context is the same. The **del** command can be used in ways very different to the above – though we haven't seen any of those ways just yet.

The same cannot be said for target.append (temporary) and target += [temporary] – these really are just two ways of doing the same thing. First using append:

```
>>> x = [ 'a' , 'b' , 'c' , 'd' , 'e' , 'f' , 'g' , 'h' , 'i' , 'j' , 'k' ]
>>> x.append ( 'ZZZ' )
>>> print x
['a', 'b', 'c', 'd', 'e', 'f', 'g', 'h', 'i', 'j', 'k', 'ZZZ']
>>>
```

Now using +=:

```
>>> x = [ 'a' , 'b' , 'c' , 'd' , 'e' , 'f' , 'g' , 'h' , 'i' , 'j' , 'k' ]
>>> x += [ 'ZZZ' ]
>>> print x
['a', 'b', 'c', 'd', 'e', 'f', 'g', 'h', 'i', 'j', 'k', 'ZZZ']
>>>
```

Although every effort is made to make Python as minimal as possible, trying to ensure only one way of expressing any given action, there are time when this is not possible. This is one of those situations. The effect on Python and Python programming of removing this duplication would be worse than having to deal with there being these two ways of doing things. The consequence is that the decision is one of style. Programmers have to be consistent as to which way of expressing things they use in each program. Having a consistent style of programming is like having a consistent layout of code: it makes the code easier to read and understand. Having code that is easy to read and understand is crucially important in programming.

> ### *Details, Patience and Walk-throughs*
> Care and attention to detail are two of the most useful attributes of a good programmer. Patience is also very useful, especially when things go wrong. Being able to read your code with a clear head is very important. Sometimes having a group of people read and analyze a bit of code can be immensely useful. So much so the whole idea has been formalized under the term *walk-through*.
> The idea of a walk-through, be it by an individual or a group, is to read and analyze code looking for errors in the code but also for poor uses of the programming language or poor algorithms.

4.5 The Mutable and The Immutable: Tuples

4.5.1 Setting the Scene

In the previous section we showed a list of lists:

    [['Sarah' , 20] , ['James' , 20] , ['Russel' , 10]]

As we mentioned then, this is a possible structure for representing information about people in specific positions in some game or puzzle. People may well describe this as a list of *records* – the term record is being used here to indicate that we have data that are treated as a single thing but without specifying a storage mechanism. Here each record is being stored as a list, and all the records stored together in a list. A list is a mutable type and so makes an excellent container of records: we can add and remove items from the list as well as accessing items as needed:

```
>>> data = [ [ 'Sarah' , 20 ] , [ 'James' , 20 ] , [ 'Russel' , 10 ] ]
>>> print data[1]
['James', 20]
>>> print data[1][0]
James
>>>
```

One potential irritant is that by using a list we are saying that the records themselves are mutable containers. So we can expect to be able to do things like:

```
>>> data[1][0] = 26
>>> print data
[['Sarah', 20], [26, 20], ['Russel', 10]]
>>>
```

If the algorithm working the data relies on the first item in each record being a
string representing a name, we now have a problem – it is highly unlikely that
any human is actually called 26. Of course, what is and is not reasonable depends
on the problem at hand: nothing can be said about what is right and wrong that
applies generally. However, it is fairly certain that most algorithms working with
records will want those records to preserve a definite structure at all times. Using
a list in this situation is probably not a good idea. Is there a way of programming
this in a better (more defensive) way? Yes.

4.5.2   What is a Tuple?

As well as lists, Python has tuples. A tuple is like a list in that it is a sequence of
values. A tuple is very different from a list in that a tuple is *immutable*. Once
created, the content of a tuple cannot be changed.

Tuple literals are written as a sequence of values contained in parentheses. So,
for example:

```
[ ( 'Sarah' , 20 ) , ( 'James' , 20 ) , ( 'Russel' , 10 ) ]
```

is a list of tuples. We can show this:

```
>>> x = [ ( 'Sarah' , 20 ) , ( 'James' , 20 ) , ( 'Russel' , 10 ) ]
>>> print type ( x )
<type 'list'>
>>> print type ( x[0] )
<type 'tuple'>
>>>
```

What can we do with tuples? Anything you can do with a list that does not
attempt to change the values in the tuple or the number of items in the tuple. So
we can index and slice:

```
>>> x = ( 'James' , 20 , True , 0.66 )
>>> print x[2]
True
>>> print x[1:3]
(20, True)
>>> print x[-3]
20
>>>
```

Note that the result of a slice of a tuple is a tuple, not a list.

What does being immutable mean for a tuple? If we attempt any change to the tuple, we get an exception:

```
>>> x = ( 'James' , 20 , True , 0.66 )
>>> x[0] = 'Sarah'
Traceback (most recent call last):
  File "<stdin>", line 1, in ?
TypeError: object does not support item assignment
>>>
```

The TypeError exception is raised because the type we were trying to apply the operation to does not support the operation. We can apply assignment to list items but not to tuple items. We can append to a list but not to a tuple.

So why are tuples interesting? Because they provide a very good (and safe) way of representing certain types of data in our program. Say we are doing plane geometry. If we represent a point in the plane with a list containing two values (x coordinate and y coordinate) we could extend the list to have eleven items in it. Not a good way of proceeding unless we spontaneously want to change from two dimensions to eleven dimensions. Instead we use tuples. Once a tuple is created it cannot be changed. We cannot extend a tuple with new items, and we cannot change the value of any items in the tuple – tuples are immutable. A tuple with two items will always be a tuple with two items.

4.5.3 An Example: Distance Finding with Tuples

In plane geometry, the distance, d, between two points, (x_1, y_1) and (x_2, y_2) is calculated using the formula:

$$d = \sqrt{(x_1 - x_2)^2 + (y_1 - y_2)^2}$$

We could write a function that takes four parameters to do this calculation:

```
def distance ( x1 , y1 , x2 , y2 ) :
```

with the x and y coordinates of the points being separate parameters. However, it makes much more sense to write a function that takes two points as parameters – we should write our functions to reflect the concepts in the problem and here the concepts are points, of which there are two. We can achieve this by representing each point with a tuple that is a pair of values. So, here is a function with example uses:

```
import math

def distance ( p1 , p2 ) :
    return math.sqrt ( ( p1[0] - p2[0] ) ** 2 + ( p1[1] - p2[1] ) ** 2 )

if __name__ == '__main__' :
    p1 = ( 1 , 1 )
    p2 = ( 1, 10 )
    print p1 , 'to' , p2 , '=' , distance ( p1 , p2 )
    p1 = ( 0 , 0 )
    p2 = ( 1 , 1 )
    print p1 , 'to' , p2 , '=' , distance ( p1 , p2 )
```

The function for calculating square roots (sqrt), is in the module math, so we import the math module and call the math.sqrt function.

When executed this results in:

```
| > python distance.py
(1, 1) to (1, 10) = 9.0
(0, 0) to (1, 1) = 1.41421356237
```

Python can output tuples without us doing anything special and the results of the calculations look reasonable too – admittedly 1.41421356237 is not exactly $\sqrt{2}$, but it is a reasonable approximation.

4.5.4   The Mutability of Immutables: Variables and Values

We have shown that tuples are immutable, and yet:

```
>>> a = ( 1 , 2 , 3 )
>>> a = a + ( 4 , 5 )
>>> print a
(1, 2, 3, 4, 5)
>>> a = ( 1 , 2 , 3 )
>>> a += ( 4 , 5 )
>>> print a
(1, 2, 3, 4, 5)
>>>
```

The value of a tuple appears to have changed. It hasn't, of course, what we are highlighting here is the distinction between an immutable value and a variable. A tuple is a value that cannot be changed, a variable is a name that can be associated with a value – assignment causes a variable to be associated with a value.

Looking first at the statements:

```
a = ( 1 , 2 , 3 )
a = a + ( 4 , 5 )
```

The statement:

```
a = ( 1 , 2 , 3 )
```

means create a tuple value (1 , 2 , 3) and associate the variable a with this value, giving the state:

The statement:

```
a = a + ( 4 , 5 )
```

means create a new tuple (4 , 5), then create a third tuple that is the sum of the value currently associated with a and (4 , 5), i.e. (1 , 2 , 3 , 4 , 5), and lastly associate the variable a with this newly created value. This leads to the state:

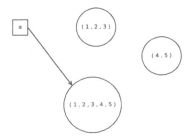

So we are creating values and changing associations, the tuple values themselves never change once created. They are immutable after all.

Why do the statements:

```
a = ( 1 , 2 , 3 )
a += ( 4 , 5 )
```

result in the same state? The statement:

```
a = ( 1 , 2 , 3 )
```

means create a tuple value (1 , 2 , 3) and associate the variable a with this value, giving the state:

exactly as before, it is the same statement after all. The statement:

```
a += ( 4 , 5 )
```

creates a new tuple (4 , 5) and then 'adds' this value to the value associated with the variable a. However, as tuples are immutable, the Python system interprets the += operation to mean that a third tuple should be created which is the sum of the tuple currently associated with a and (4 , 5), i.e. (1 , 2 , 3 , 4 , 5), and that the variable a should then be associated with this value. This leads to the state:

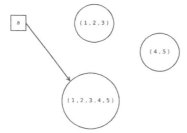

The tuple values have not been changed, we are just creating new immutable tuples and associating variables with them.

Lists on the other hand are mutable. Although the + operator behaves very much the same as the + operator for tuples, the += operator for lists behaves very differently to the one for tuples. The statements:

```
a = [ 1 , 2 , 3 ]
a = a + [ 4 , 5 ]
```

manipulate list values and variables in effectively the same way as happens with tuples. The + expression creates a new list value with which the variable a is associated. The final state has three lists, exactly as the example with tuples had a final state with three tuples. The statements:

```
a = [ 1 , 2 , 3 ]
a += [ 4 , 5 ]
```

however, behave very differently because lists are mutable. The statement:

```
a = [ 1 , 2 , 3 ]
```

causes a list value to be created and for the variable a to be associated with it:

The statement a += [4 , 5] causes the list value associated with a to extend itself to become the value [1 , 2 , 3 , 4 , 5]:

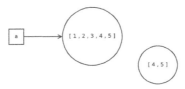

The final state here is very different, we only have two lists – contrast this with the state when working with tuples where we had three tuples in the final state.

Being careful to distinguish the way in which lists and tuples work is not just pedantry. It is a cornerstone of Python that lists are mutable and tuples are immutable. The differences between them are exactly why both exist in Python. The consequence for our programming is that we use lists when a sequence needs to be updated as an integral part of the algorithm, and we use tuples when we do not want values to be updateable. If we do in fact try to treat tuples as updateable by using operations like += then Python ensures that the final result of the operation is correct, even if the way of getting there appears inefficient. Why bother with this? Why not just disallow update-type operation on immutable types? The answer is to do with *polymorphism* which in this context means being able to write functions that can manipulate either lists or tuples without having to know which is being used. Lists and tuples are both sequences and we want to be able to write functions that work with sequences without caring if they are lists or tuples. We are going to leave detailed discussion of polymorphism till Section 7.6. For now the moral of the story is: use the right language feature for the right purpose at the right time – mutable lists for mutable data, immutable tuples for immutable data.

4.5.5 An Interesting (?) Issue

There is one problem relating to tuple literals that you might occasionally come across when working with tuples:

```
>>> a = [ 1 , 2 , 3 ]
>>> a += [ 4 ]
>>> print a
[1, 2, 3, 4]
>>> b = ( 1 , 2 , 3 )
>>> b += ( 4 )
Traceback (most recent call last):
  File "<stdin>", line 1, in <module>
TypeError: can only concatenate tuple (not "int") to tuple
>>> print b
(1, 2, 3)
>>>
```

Although we can have a list of one element, it seems we cannot use parentheses to create a tuple of only one element: [4] is a list, but (4) is an integer:

```
>>> type ( [ 4 ] )
<type 'list'>
```

```
>>> type ( ( 4 ) )
<type 'int'>
>>>
```

Using parentheses with a single value is not treated as a tuple, it is an expression of the type of the item contained. Brackets, [ ], are always list delimiters, which means that we are always specifying a list no matter how many items are listed: [ ], [4], [1 , 2 , 3] are all lists. Parentheses are used both for specifying tuples and for creating higher precedence sub-expressions in expressions, which means there is the potential for doubt about what, for example, (4) means. Where the parentheses surround a sequence of values separated with commas, e.g. (1 , 2 , 3), there is no doubt, it is clearly a tuple and not a sub-expression. Where there is only a single value, it is not clear at all whether it is a tuple or a sub-expression – (4) can either be a tuple or a higher precedence expression. The designers of Python have taken the view that it is a sub-expression. So to have a tuple of length 1, we must include a trailing comma, as in (4 ,):

```
>>> type ( ( 4 , ) )
<type 'tuple'>
>>>
```

With the comma inside the parentheses it cannot be a sub-expression, so it must be a tuple of 1 element. For a tuple of zero elements, there is no problem, we just use ( ):

```
>>> type ( ( ) )
<type 'tuple'>
>>>
```

4.5.6 Tuple Assignment

Python integrates tuples and assignment in a neat and useful way. For example, the following are all valid statement in Python:

```
( a , b ) = ( 1 , 2 )
a , b = ( 3 , 4 )
( a , b ) = 5 , 6
a , b = 7 , 8
```

In this context the comma separated lists do not need parentheses to be treated as tuples.

Each of these assignments statements causes both a and b to be assigned as a single action – at least as far as the program is concerned. Let's convince ourselves that this is indeed the case:

```
>>> ( a , b ) = ( 1 , 2 )
>>> print a , b
1 2
>>> a , b = ( 3 , 4 )
>>> print a , b
3 4
>>> ( a , b ) = 5 , 6
>>> print a , b
5 6
>>> a , b = 7 , 8
>>> print a , b
7 8
>>>
```

Although this feature is called *tuple assignment* (because that is how it is implemented), many people refer to it as *simultaneous assignment* (because that is the effect from a programmer perspective).

Tuple assignment is not restricted to just two variables. Tuples can have any number of items, so tuple assignment can assign any number of variables simultaneously. For example:

    a , b , c , d = 5 , 6 , 7 , 8

The left-hand side must be a tuple of variable names or list items, since only they can be assigned to. The right-hand side is a tuple of expressions – in these examples we have only literals, but any expression can be used. The crucially important restriction is that the number of items on the right-hand side must match the number of items on the left-hand side. If this is not the case a ValueError will be raised. We can show this by experiment:

    >>> a , b = 1 , 2 , 3
    Traceback (most recent call last):
      File "<stdin>", line 1, in ?
    ValueError: too many values to unpack
    >>> a , b , c = 1 , 2
    Traceback (most recent call last):
      File "<stdin>", line 1, in ?
    ValueError: need more than 2 values to unpack
    >>>

Something to remember: when Python executes a tuple assignment, it evaluates *all* the expressions on the right-hand side of the = *before* making any of the assignments. Often, tuple assignment is just a shorthand way of writing a lot of assignments. There is though one idiomatic use where the evaluation then assignment is critical: we can swap values associated with two variables without using an intermediate variable (which is what programming languages without this simultaneous assignment feature have to do):

    >>> a , b = 5 , 6
    >>> a , b = b , a
    >>> print a , b
    6 5
    >>>

The first line is a tuple assignment of literals to variables that causes a to be associated with 5 and b to be associated with 6:

The second line is not magical, it is just the evaluation of some expressions to create the tuple of values on the right-hand side, followed by the assignment of the calculated values to the variables on the left-hand side. The result is that a is associated with the value that b was associated with, and, at the same time, b is associated with the value that a was associated with:

This works exactly because Python evaluates all of the right-hand side expressions before making the assignments. When Python executes this code, on the right-hand side of the assignment the 'old' values for a and b are used. So, Python makes this substitution:

$$a, b = b, a [a \backslash 5, b \backslash 6]$$
$$= 6, 5$$

which is equivalent to:

$$a = 6$$
$$b = 5$$

Hand-evaluating using substitution has given us a clear understanding of what the Python statement means.

Swapping Values

As we have seen, Python allows us to swap the values associated with variable using tuple assignment:

```
a , b = b , a
```

In languages that do not support simultaneous assignment, a third, temporary variable must be introduced, and all the individual assignments performed explicitly:

```
temp = a
a = b
b = temp
```

4.5.7 An Example: Traffic Lights

In the previous example of a traffic light sequencer (page 111) we used a function (nextState) to transition from one state to the next. But what if we want to be able to specify the time between transitions? One approach is to alter the nextState function, inserting wait information and wait code into the function. However, this is almost certainly a bad approach, since it means embedding data that might need to be changed in the functions comprising the program. What we need is a data-oriented approach: we create a representation of the data associated with our solution to the problem, then write code to use the data structure. The code and data are separated, and, if we need to change the waiting time, we can do so by altering the data – there is no need to change the code.

As an example, let's say that our traffic light should be in state 'Red' for 10 s, 'Green' for 10 s, and 'Amber' for 5 s. We can represent this data as a tuple of tuples, leading to the program:

```
import time

states = ( ( 'Red' , 10 ) , ( 'Green' , 10 ) , ( 'Amber' , 5 ) )

if __name__ == '__main__' :
    stateIndex = 0
    while True :
        print states[stateIndex][0]
        time.sleep ( states[stateIndex][1] )
        stateIndex = ( stateIndex + 1 ) % len ( states )
```

The sleep function from the module time causes our program to wait for a given number of seconds.

The expressions states[stateIndex][0] and states[stateIndex][1] perhaps deserve a little explanation. states is a tuple of tuples. This means that states[stateIndex] is a tuple – it is the tuple at index stateIndex in the tuple of tuples. So states[0] is the tuple ('Red', 10). Since the result of the expression states[0] is a tuple, we can index it. So states[0][0] not only makes sense, it delivers the string value 'Red'. Similarly states[0][1] is the integer value 10.

The algorithm we have used in the program is to use an index into the tuple of tuples to select each of the tuples in turn and wait the appropriate number of seconds. Notice how we use the remainder operation (%) so that the index cycles 0 , 1 , 2 , 0 , 1 , 2 , 0 , ... We cannot afford for stateIndex to take on a value that does not represent a valid state of the light. We must catch the case when stateIndex has the value 3 and we add 1 to it to give 4, and set stateIndex to 0. Rather than use if statements, we use the far simpler algorithm of implementing *modulo arithmetic* using the % operator.

Did you also notice that we used len (states) and *not* 3 in the expression that calculates the next value of stateIndex? This use of a calculated value rather than a literal is extremely important: we do not use a literal that may have to change when we can calculate the value we need. This means that the code doesn't have to change when we change something about the data. In this example, what happens if we add a new state, say 'RedAmber', as is required for UK traffic lights:

states = (('Red' , 10) , ('RedAmber' , 2) , ('Green' , 10) , ('Amber' , 5))

If we had used 3 in the code originally, we would now have to edit it. As we used len (states) it just works no matter how many items we have in the tuple of tuples. The point here is that we have not introduced extra data where it is not required.

4.5.8 An Example: A Vending Machine

In Section 4.2.5 (page 111) we presented the state transition diagram for a coffee and cola vending machine. We said then that we wanted to delay implementing it. Now is the time to make good on our promise to actually implement this example.

The core question is: what representation do we use for the finite state machine? We are going to represent the states and transitions with integers. So 'Idle' state will be 0, '1 token' will be 1 and '2 tokens' will be 2. Also, 'Token' transition will be 0, 'Cola button' will be 1 and 'Coffee button' will be 2. There is no problem with states and transitions being represented by the same integers, as a state is never used in code where a transition should be, and vice versa.

```
stateNames = ( 'Idle' , '1 Token' , '2 Tokens' )
transitionNames = ( 'Token' , 'Cola Button' , 'Coffee Button' )

def unknownState ( state ) :
    raise ValueError , 'State ' + str ( state ) + ' is not a known state.'

def unknownTransition ( transition ) :
    raise ValueError , 'Transition ' + str ( transition ) + ' is not a known transition.'

def invalidTransitionFromState ( transition , state ) :
    raise ValueError , 'Invalid transition (' + transitionNames[transition] + \
            ') for state (' + stateNames[state] + ').'

def vendCola ( ) :
    print 'Vending a cola.'
```

We use the function str to create a string from an integer so that we can create strings to output by concatenating a number of them together.

```
def vendCoffee ( ) :
    print 'Vending a coffee.'

def nextState ( state , transition ) :
    if not ( 0 <= state < len ( stateNames ) ) :
        unknownState ( state )
    if not ( 0 <= transition < len ( transitionNames ) ) :
        unknownTransition ( transition )
    if state == 0 :
        if transition == 0 :
            return 1
        else :
            invalidTransitionFromState ( transition , state )
    elif state == 1 :
        if transition == 0 :
            return 2
        elif transition == 1 :
            vendCola ( )
            return 0
        else :
            invalidTransitionFromState ( transition , state )
    elif state == 2 :
        if transition == 1 :
            vendCola ( )
            return 1
        elif transition == 2 :
            vendCoffee ( )
            return 0
        else :
            invalidTransitionFromState ( transition , state )
    else :
        unknownState ( )


if __name__ == '__main__' :
    state = 0
    while True :
        i = input ( 'State ' + stateNames[state] + '. Waiting...' )
        try :
            state = nextState ( state , i )
        except ValueError , exception :
            print exception
```

Notice that we have an infinite loop here. The vending machine should always work, so it is in fact appropriate that we have an infinite loop. Of course, this begs the question of what happens when the machine runs out of cola, coffee, water, etc.

What happens when we run the program? Let's work through a few scenarios. Referring to the diagram on page 111, we can see that if we have the event sequence 0, 1 ('Token', 'Cola button') we should move from 'Idle' state to '1 Token' state and back to 'Idle' state with the vend of a cola:

```
| > python vendingMachine.py
State Idle. Waiting...0
State 1 Token. Waiting...1
Vending a cola.
State Idle. Waiting...
```

So our program does the right thing in this case. Trying a couple of other 'legal' cases:

```
|> python vendingMachine.py
State Idle. Waiting...0
State 1 Token. Waiting...0
State 2 Tokens. Waiting...1
Vending a cola.
State 1 Token. Waiting...1
Vending a cola.
State Idle. Waiting...
```

```
|> python vendingMachine.py
State Idle. Waiting...0
State 1 Token. Waiting...0
State 2 Tokens. Waiting...2
Vending a coffee.
State Idle. Waiting...
```

Should we also try out some error situations? Of course we should:

```
|> python vendingMachine.py
State Idle. Waiting...0
State 1 Token. Waiting...0
State 2 Tokens. Waiting...0
Invalid transition (Token) for state (2 Tokens).
State 2 Tokens. Waiting...
```

```
|> python vendingMachine.py
State Idle. Waiting...1
Invalid transition (Cola Button) for state (Idle).
State Idle. Waiting...2
Invalid transition (Coffee Button) for state (Idle).
State Idle. Waiting...
```

This gives us confidence that the program is actually doing what we want it to do – which is to realize the state machine we described in Section 4.2.5 (page 111).

4.6 Stringing Along

Have you thought that strings are just sequences of characters? Consider the string 'Hello': this is not the same as the string 'oHell', implying that the order of the characters in the string is important, which in turn implies that a string is just a sequence of characters.

Lists and tuples are sequences and support indexing and slicing operations. So if a string is also a sequence, it really implies that we ought to be able to do indexing and slicing of strings. Indeed, we can. Although, lists, tuples and strings are all very different, the fact that they are sequences of values means that they are all similar. To highlight this similarity, these types are collectively called *sequence types*.

Like tuples, and unlike lists, strings are immutable. We can never change a given string. All string operations create new string values.

> Strings are immutable.

4.6.1 Indexing

Indexing allows us to get at the individual elements of a sequence type. We have seen this in action with lists and tuples, and it is also applicable to strings. So if we wanted to know the first letter of the string variable a, we use a[0]:

```
>>> a = 'Some text'
>>> print a[0]
S
>>> print a[1]
o
>>> print a[6]
e
>>>
```

At the risk of stating the obvious: note that the first element has index 0, so if the length is n, then the last element has index $n - 1$.

Off-by-one Errors

Forgetting that indexes start at 0 not 1, and end at *n* - 1 not *n*, is an instance of an *off-by-one error* and everyone gets caught by them from time to time – even the very best programmers. If it happens to you, don't worry about it, simply fix the problem and move on.

The fact that Python supports string indexing means we can iterate over the characters in a string:

```
>>> a = 'Some text.'
>>> for i in range ( len ( a ) ) :
...     print a[i] ,
...
S o m e   t e x t .
>>>
```

The comma (,) at the end of a print statement tells the Python system not to output an end of line.

Even though we have used len (a) to ensure that the loop works for any length of string, using indexing is a low-level way of working. It is more high level to write this as:

```
>>> a = 'Some text.'
>>> for i in a :
...     print i ,
...
S o m e   t e x t .
>>>
```

We can use the for loop directly on the string value because strings, like lists and tuples, are sequences. Remember that the syntax of a for loop is:

```
for <variable> in <sequence> :
    <block>
```

So, if the algorithm only depends on the current character, we use the high-level approach, but if the algorithm requires two or more items from the list then indexing is the way to code things. For example, if we are trying to find repeated letters in a string, we might write:

```
a = 'Assistant poppy sniffer'
for i in range ( len ( a ) ) :
    if i > 0 :
        if a[i] == a[i-1] :
            print '* 2' ,
        else :
            print ', ' + a[i] ,
    else :
        print a[i] ,
```

This algorithm assumes there are no words in the language with triple letters.

which, when executed, outputs:

```
A , s * 2 , i , s , t , a , n , t ,   , p , o , p * 2 , y ,   , s , n , i , f * 2 , e , r
```

and would be very problematic to code without using indexing.

4.6.2 An Example: The Caesar Cipher

Julius Caesar was concerned that any orders he sent to his commanders in the field could be intercepted by the enemy. He therefore invented a system of writing messages so that, if they were intercepted, they would appear to be gibberish. This idea is called *encryption* (or *ciphering*) and the particular algorithm invented by Julius Caesar is called the Caesar Cipher. Suetonius (who wrote a biography of Julius Caesar at the time he was alive) wrote:

> "If he had anything confidential to say, he wrote it in cipher, that is, by so changing the order of the letters of the alphabet, that not a word could be made out. If anyone wishes to decipher these, and get at their meaning, he must substitute the fourth letter of the alphabet, namely D, for A, and so with the other." *Suetonius, Life of Julius Caesar, 56BC*

To encipher a message using this algorithm we need to take each letter and replace it with a letter further up or down the alphabet. The *key* to the message is the number of places around the alphabet we take each replacement letter. Obviously the sender and the recipient must agree (or have a method of agreeing) the same key so that the message can be deciphered. The decoding key for the Caesar Cipher as described by Suetonius is 3, which means that the enciphering key is -3.

To implement this in Python, we have to know which letter is a specific number of letters further up or down the alphabet from a given letter. Say the key for this message is 3. As an experiment, let's add 3 to a letter:

```
>>> print 'a' + 3
Traceback (most recent call last):
  File "<stdin>", line 1, in ?
TypeError: cannot concatenate 'str' and 'int' objects
>>>
```

Clearly, that is not going to be a fruitful direction. What we need is a sequence that we can index into so that we can find the appropriate character.

In the following we have a function for ciphering a whole string that uses a function for ciphering an individual character. To cipher a particular character we use a character string and indexing approach:

```
def cipherCharacter ( character , key ) :
    chars = 'ABCDEFGHIJKLMNOPQRSTUVWXYZabcdefghijklmnopqrstuvwxyz'
    for i in range ( len ( chars ) ) :
        if chars[i] == character :
            return chars[ ( i + key ) % len ( chars ) ]
    return character

def cipherMessage ( message , key ) :
    coded = ''
    for c in message :
        coded += cipherCharacter ( c , key )
    return coded

if __name__ == '__main__' :
    assert cipherCharacter ( 'A' , 3 ) == 'D'
    assert cipherCharacter ( 'Z' , 3 ) == 'c'
    assert cipherCharacter ( 'a' , 3 ) == 'd'
    assert cipherCharacter ( 'z' , 3 ) == 'C'
    assert cipherCharacter ( 'D' , -3 ) == 'A'
    assert cipherCharacter ( 'c' , -3 ) == 'Z'
    assert cipherCharacter ( 'd' , -3 ) == 'a'
```

Note how we use the % operator to get wrap around from z to A.

```
assert cipherCharacter ( 'C' , -3 ) == 'z'
assert cipherMessage ( 'ABCDEFG abcdefg' , 3 ) == 'DEFGHIJ defghij'
assert cipherMessage ( 'TUVWXYZ tuvwxyz' , 3 ) == 'WXYZabc wxyzABC'
```

To test fully the cipherCharacter function we need a very large number of assert statements ($>52^3$, in fact). To test fully the cipherMessage function, we need an infinite number of assert statements, since there are infinite number of strings. Clearly this is impossible. So what can we do? We take a representative sample of all possible situations, a sample that we think covers the most important cases. Hence the restricted number of assertions. We do not claim that the function works, we say that as far as the tests show, there are no errors. This is very different from claiming that our program works.

As always, we review the program after we have finished it. Both functions seem straightforward and do the task asked of them – assuming we only use letters in the messages we are going to encrypt. If this assumption is acceptable then we have no problem. However, we know that computers handle all data internally in the form of numerical values. Is there then a way of implementing cipherCharacters so that it doesn't require the string and indexing approach? Yes there is. Python has the ord function that takes a character value and returns the number used to represent it, and the chr function that takes a number and returns the character that that number represents:

```
>>> print ord ( 'a' )
97
>>> print ord ( 'A' )
65
>>> print chr ( 97 )
a
>>> print chr ( 65 )
A
>>>
```

With these functions, we can dispense with the string and indexing approach, and instead us:

```
def cipherCharacter ( character , key ) :
    return chr ( ord ( character ) + key )
```

which is much smaller, and deals with all the characters including punctuation.

It may not be immediately obvious, but some of the assert statements we had in the previous version of the program that worked then will not work with this version. The problem is that, now we are using the ord and chr functions, we do not get the wrap around from 'z' to 'A' that we had in the previous version. Moreover, we don't know what the numbers are that represent each character. We could find out by continuing the exploration above, but the mapping is machine dependent, i.e. the actual mapping used depends on the computer on which the program is run. We must therefore make our tests a little more abstract. We do this by always performing a mapping in both directions. This means that we do not care what the mapping is, only that it is faithful and consistent. So the full second version of the program looks like this:

```
def cipherCharacter ( character , key ) :
    return chr ( ord ( character ) + key )
```

```
def cipherMessage ( message , key ) :
    coded = ''
    for c in message :
        coded += cipherCharacter ( c , key )
    return coded


if __name__ == '__main__' :
    assert cipherCharacter ( cipherCharacter ( 'A' , -3 ) , 3 ) == 'A'
    assert cipherCharacter ( cipherCharacter ( 'Z' , -3 ) , 3 ) == 'Z'
    assert cipherCharacter ( cipherCharacter ( 'a' , -3 ) , 3 ) == 'a'
    assert cipherCharacter ( cipherCharacter ( 'z' , -3 ) , 3 ) == 'z'
    theString = 'ABCDEFG abcdefg'
    assert cipherMessage ( cipherMessage ( theString , -3 ) , 3 ) == theString
    theString = 'TUVWXYZ tuvwxyz'
    assert cipherMessage ( cipherMessage ( theString , -3 ) , 3 ) == theString
```

We can use the same function for enciphering and deciphering because the Caesar Cipher is *symmetric* – deciphering is applying the same algorithm but with a key that is the negative of the original enciphering key.

Character Encoding

The mapping between characters and their integer representation in the computer is called the *character encoding*. Examples of character encodings are: ASCII, EBCDIC, ISO-8859, ISO-10646 (Universal Character Set, UCS), Unicode. Unicode and UCS are now effectively two names for the same character encoding and is the character encoding everyone is now standardizing on.

Whereas character encodings such as ASCII, EBCDIC and ISO-8859 used a single byte to store the value for a character, Unicode requires more than one byte. The most common ways of representing Unicode are UTF-8 and UTF-16. Linux, Solaris, and Mac OS X use UTF-8 since it is a superset of ASCII, while Windows has ignored this and uses UTF-16LE.

We can of course dispense with the cipherCharacter function and merge the code into cipherMessage, resulting in:

```
def cipherMessage ( message , key ) :
    coded = ''
    for c in message :
        coded += chr ( ord ( c ) + key )
    return coded


if __name__ == '__main__' :
    theString = 'ABCDEFG abcdefg'
    assert cipherMessage ( cipherMessage ( theString , -3 ) , 3 ) == theString
    theString = 'TUVWXYZ tuvwxyz'
    assert cipherMessage ( cipherMessage ( theString , -3 ) , 3 ) == theString
```

Note how the tests know nothing of the character encoding: by encoding and decoding in each test we check that the original message is returned without any need to know anything of the character encoding being used.

At the time of his military activities, Julius Caesar used human scribes to encode and decode messages using a known sequence of characters. We can use our program – which will be a lot quicker:

```
>>> print cipherMessage ( 'We are going to invade Britain.' , 4 )
[i$evi$ksmrk$xs$mrzehi$Fvmxemr2
>>>
```

Our encoded message looks very different from that which Julius Caesar would have seen, as we are working with a very different set of characters – the Romans didn't have all the punctuation and other symbols we are working with.

The encoded message was written on paper and a runner sent with it to the named general. We might send email. When (or if, as the poor runners were invariably major targets) the message reached the general, scribes decoded the message. We achieve the same thing by executing our function on the received message:

```
>>> print cipherMessage ( '[i$evi$ksmrk$xs$mrzehi$Fvmxemr2' , -4 )
We are going to invade Britain.
>>>
```

Of course, this works only because we are using the negative of the key that was used in the encoding and the same character encoding as was used for the encoding process. If either of these are not the case then we get garbage. For example, if we have the wrong key:

```
>>> print cipherMessage ( '[i$evi$ksmrk$xs$mrzehi$Fvmxemr2' , -3 )
Xf!bsf!hpjoh!up!jowbef!Csjubjo/
>>>
```

These days, sending a message using a Caesar Cipher is far from secure. Because people know of the cipher and can use linguistic analysis techniques (i.e. counting the occurrences of symbols in the message and using the known character frequencies in various languages), it does not take long to decipher a message encoded using this cipher. Of course there are many secure ways of encrypting communications, but as this is a book on Python programming, we are not going to investigate them here – even though they are fun.

Invading Britain

Invading Britain was, for a long time, a very popular pastime – Celts, Romans, Angles, Saxons, Jutes, Vikings and Normans all had a go, and were fairly successful at it. Note though that although Julius Caesar did succeed in thoroughly beating the British military (at his second attempt anyway) he didn't, in fact, conquer Britain. That was left to Emperor Claudius nearly 100 years later (43AD) – Britons then became third-class citizens in their own country.

4.6.3   Negative Indices

Just as with lists and tuples, negative indexes can be used with strings – a negative index means index from the end. The fact that this is the same as for lists and tuples shouldn't be a surprise: lists, tuples and strings are all sequence types, and it is important that all indexing features work the same way for all sequence types. Consistency is essential. It helps comprehensibility.

So for a string a, of length n, the first element can be addressed as a[0] or a[-n] and the last element can be accessed as either a[n-1] or a[-1].

4.6.4   An Example: Palindromes

Negative indexes can be very useful in algorithms. As an example, let's write a function for determining whether an input string is a palindrome. A palindrome is a word or phrase that reads the same forwards and backwards. Perhaps the most famous palindrome is:

Able was I ere I saw Elba

assuming that we do not distinguish uppercase and lowercase letters. To implement this test we need a loop that considers two characters at a time (so indexing seems to be the right way forward) in which we work from the beginning and end of the string simultaneously. So negative indexing therefore seems to be the right way of expressing the algorithm:

Note that we only iterate over half the length of the sequence.

```
def isPalindrome ( text ) :
    for i in range ( len ( text ) / 2 ) :
        if text[i] != text[ -( i + 1 ) ] :
            return False
    return True

if __name__ == '__main__' :
    text = raw_input ( 'Enter the text to test: ' )
    if isPalindrome ( text ) :
        print text , 'is a palindrome.'
    else :
        print text , 'is not a palindrome.'
```

The program could be written without negative indexes, but it seems more natural to use them. It seems to express the algorithm simply and clearly.

There is one obvious problem: the string above that we said was a palindrome isn't a palindrome according to this program. The problem is that if we compare characters using the == operator, we distinguish uppercase and lowercase. This means that the program says that:

able was i ere i saw elba

is a palindrome, but that:

Able was I ere I saw Elba

is not. This is not a program error per se. The question that we need to answer is whether case needs to be taken into account. Another issue is whether spaces are significant. Is:

blah h alb

a palindrome?

These are *requirements*: the questions are about what it is that our program is required to do. Such questions can only be answered by looking at the problem and what the end user of the program actually wants the program to do. In this particular case the original problem statement said that:

Able was I ere I saw Elba

is a palindrome. So with this definition, we must say that the current program is wrong. We need to do more work to meet the customer requirement. As case is deemed not to be important in this case, we can simply make strings all lowercase before we start checking – case is then irrelevant in the test. Strings have a method we can use (lower) that creates a new string value (remember strings are immutable) that is a copy of the original string but with all uppercase characters replaced with lowercase equivalents. So, adding this to our isPalindrome function, everything is as it needs to be:

lower is a method on strings so must be called on a string, as in text.lower ( ). It returns a new string.

```
def isPalindrome ( text ) :
    text = text.lower ()
    for i in range ( len ( text ) / 2 ) :
        if text[i] != text[ -( i + 1 ) ] :
            return False
    return True
```

Note that we haven't changed any string values, we have just created a new string value and changed the association of the variable text.

Of course, if the user requirements change, e.g. there is a new definition of palindrome, then we have to revisit the program. But for now we have something that does the job it has been asked to do.

4.6.5 Slicing Strings

In the same way that slicing a list creates a new list and slicing a tuple create a new tuple, slicing a string creates a new string. Here is an example:

```
>>> a = 'ABCDEFGHIJKLMNOP'
>>> print a
ABCDEFGHIJKLMNOP
>>> print a[0:4]
ABCD
>>> print a[2:7]
CDEFG
>>> print a[-6:-3]
KLM
>>>
```

As with all sequence types, we need two numbers to define a slice. a[m:n] gives us *m-n* items in total, beginning with the *m*th element of a and ending at the (*n*-1)th.

Default index values work just as expected:

```
>>> a = 'ABCDEFGHIJKLMNOP'
>>> print a[4:]
EFGHIJKLMNOP
>>> print a[:6]
ABCDEF
>>> print a[:-2]
ABCDEFGHIJKLMN
>>> print a[-2:]
OP
>>> print a[:]
ABCDEFGHIJKLMNOP
>>>
```

Did you notice that using the default start and end indexes for a slice (a[:]) creates a new string that is a clone of the original? Cloning is exactly what this operation does for lists and tuples, and so consistency demands that this be the case for strings, and it is.

4.7 An Example: A Lexer

Lexers are an important class of finite state machine. The job of a lexer is to take a string and output a sequence of *tokens* that represent the words, numbers or symbols in the string. Why is that useful? In a compiler or interpreter (such as the Python system), when you type in a line of code, it is the job of the compiler or interpreter to make sense of what you've given it, or to issue an error message. The first thing the compiler or interpreter does is to split up your line of code into tokens. So if you entered this line into the Python interpreter:

```
>>> sum, diff = ( x + y ) , ( x - y )
```

Python's lexer might create something like the following set of tokens:

```
NAME "sum"
COMMA
NAME "diff"
EQUALS
LPAREN
NAME "x"
PLUS
NAME "y"
RPAREN
COMMA
LPAREN
NAME "x"
MINUS
NAME "y"
RPAREN
```

The next thing that the Python system does is to try and work out what that sequence of tokens means. This process is called *parsing* – we will talk about parsing in Section 4.8.2.

Looking through the list of tokens above you'll probably notice a couple of things. Firstly, whitespace (spaces, tabs, carriage returns, etc.) is not considered. In Python, some whitespace is important, but most isn't – whitespace that delimits blocks needs to be treated carefully, but in expressions whitespace can be ignored once it has been used to separate tokens. Secondly, the lexer has worked out that sum and diff are both names – by looking at the whitespace and symbols, it has concluded that it should separate the words sum and diff from other tokens. Variable names can be as long as we like in Python, so the lexer has to be smart enough to work out that a name is a name without trying to guess how long it might be. Equally, we might have an integer that is very long, 1234567890..., and the lexer should still recognize that it is a number *and* convert it to an int (or some other appropriate type) for the parser to handle.

The following state transition diagram shows how a lexer for integers might work:

This is clearly not a complete state transition diagram, we just show the parts that process integer characters.

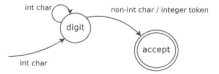

Once the lexer has read one digit it is in its 'digit' state, and it stays in 'digit' state until the next character is not a digit (i.e. one of 0, 1, 2, 3, 4, 5, 6, 7, 8 or 9). On reading a non-digit character the lexer transitions to 'accept' state and outputs the integer value of the character sequence deemed to have been an integer.

So, how should we implement this lexer? Let's introduce an element of prescience and assume that we are going to use this integer lexer as part of a larger program. This means that we should code it as a function. We should also separate input and processing, so let's assume that the lexer function takes a string as parameter.

Because we have read the Python library documentation, we know that there is method isdigit which can be called on a string and which returns **True** if that string contains only digits and **False** otherwise. The method is used by applying it to the string as in: "abc".isdigit ( ), "123".isdigit ( ) or c.isdigit ( ) (where c is of type str). Using functions and methods from the standard Python library saves us having to write them, which is great motivation for actually reading the manuals so as to know what functions and methods are available.

Reading the Python library documentation allows us to know what functions and methods are available and saves work.

Another function that is almost certainly going to be useful is int. This function takes a string that is a sequence of digits and returns the integer value. "Aha", you are saying, "int is the function that solves the problem, so there is no need to write any code". Unfortunately, this is not quite true. If the string provided to int contains non-digit characters a ValueError exception is raised. So the problem is to scan the input so as to create a string that contains only digits that we can then apply int to.

Now we are probably in a position to write the code:

The Python documentation can be found at http://www.python.org/.

```python
def getIntegerValue ( buffer ) :
    for i in range ( len ( buffer ) ) :
        if not buffer[i].isdigit ( ) :
            break
    return int ( buffer [:i] )

if __name__ == '__main__' :
    output = getIntegerValue ( raw_input ( 'Enter a number : ' ) )
    print output , 'of type' , type ( output )
```

The for loop represents being in 'digit' state and the break causes the state change from 'digit' state to 'accept' state. So although it doesn't look obviously as if the code implements the finite state machine, it actually does.

4.8 Dictionaries

4.8.1 Indexing with Non-Integers

All the sequence types allow us to index into values using integer indexes. So, with a list, for example:

```python
>>> x = [ 'blah' , 'foo' , 'bar' ]
>>> print x[1]
'foo'
>>>
```

This is fine for data storage problems where the data is a sequence, but not all data can be sensibly stored as a sequence. Looking back at the examples we used to introduce tuples (page 120):

```python
[ ( 'Sarah' , 20 ) , ( 'James' , 20 ) , ( 'Russel' , 10 ) ]
```

this is a good representation if it is important that the records be in order. If however we were just trying to create an association between strings that are names and some integers, then this would not be a good way of storing the information.

If we want to access the integer associated with a given name, we have to search down the list checking the strings until we find the one we want or come to the end of the list. The problem here is that the data is not structured in a way that makes a 'search by name' algorithm easy. For this, we really need a different form of data storage that a sequence. What we want to be able to do is something like:

valueAssociatedWith ['James']

We need to have a data structure that we can index using something other than an integer. Such a structure is called an *associative array* or *dictionary*.

Python has direct support for this sort of data structure and uses the term *dictionary*. A dictionary is a mutable type that can use any type as an index. An empty dictionary is created using a pair of braces, {}. What appears to be indexing is used with dictionaries for both setting and getting entries in the dictionary. However, these are dictionaries and the indexes do not have to be integers as is the case with sequences. The following shows some of these features in action:

```
>>> a = {}
>>> a [ 'name' ] = 'Jane'
>>> a [ 'age' ] = 26
>>> a [ 0 ] = 'Random data'
>>> print a
{0: 'Random data', 'age': 26, 'name': 'Jane'}
>>> print a [ 'name' ]
Jane
>>>
```

A dictionary is a set of *key*:*value* pairs that can be indexed using the key. Dictionaries are incredibly flexible and have many uses.

4.8.2 Parsing Roman Numerals

An example that introduces the use of dictionaries is parsing Roman numerals. It also introduces parsers, which we said we were going to do in Section 4.7 (page 137).

The problem is to convert a Roman numeral represented as a string into the Arabic numeral of the same value.

Roman numerals are sequences of letters in which the integer value is determined by the letters used and their sequence. Here is a table listing some sample values in Roman and Arabic numerals:

I	1	XI	11	XXI	21	XL	40
II	2	XII	12	XXII	22	L	50
III	3	XIII	13	XXIII	23	LX	60
IV	4	XIV	14	XXIV	24	LXX	70
V	5	XV	15	XXV	25	LXXX	80
VI	6	XVI	16	XXVI	26	XC	90
VII	7	XVII	17	XXVII	27	C	100
VIII	8	XVIII	18	XXVIII	28	D	500
IX	9	XIX	19	XXIX	29	M	1000
X	10	XX	20	XXX	30	MMVI	2006

The letters I, V, X, L, C, D and M are the building block letters and are associated with specific numbers. Letters representing a higher value must precede a letter representing a lower value and all the values are added together to create the number represented. The exception to this rule is that a single letter representing a smaller value may precede a letter of a higher value, in which case the lower value is subtracted from the higher value. So, for example, XI is 10 + 1 = 11, while IX is 10 - 1 = 9.

Although we have shown Roman numerals to be uppercase letters, they can also be lowercase, but case is never mixed: a number is either all uppercase or all lowercase.

> ### Roman Numerals
> The exact format of Roman numerals has changed a little over the centuries and the syntax we've used in this chapter is really Victorian. One particular variant is to avoid the subtractive rule and in particular to write the number 4 as IIII instead of IV – this is often used on clock faces.

Now we need to think about the algorithm we are going to use to convert a Roman numeral into an Arabic numeral. It is not that hard, since the explanation of how the letters form numbers leads directly to the algorithm. We know that the letters are in descending order and added together. If it were just that, everything would be trivial. However we also have the subtractive rule. This means that we have to look ahead to the next character to know what to do with the current character. This means that we have to read characters from the input and use the current character and a lookahead character to decide what to do. We then need a way to convert from Roman numerals to Arabic numerals. This seems like a job for a dictionary: a dictionary is a tool for looking things up and a lookup table is exactly what we need. Using a lookup table avoids the need for a long series of **if**/**elif**/**elif**/... Instead we make the decision in a data-oriented way.

Putting all this together we came up with the following as a first attempt at a solution:

```
numerals = {
    'I' : 1 , 'i' : 1 ,
    'V' : 5 , 'v' : 5 ,
    'X' : 10 , 'x' : 10 ,
    'L' : 50 , 'l' : 50 ,
    'C' : 100 , 'c' : 100 ,
    'D' : 500 , 'd' : 500 ,
    'M' : 1000 , 'm' : 1000
    }

def convertRomanToInteger ( string ) :
    intValue = 0
    for i in range ( len ( string ) ) :
        if i < len ( string ) - 1 and numerals[string[i]] < numerals[string[i+1]]:
            intValue += numerals[string[i+1]] - numerals[string[i]]
        elif i > 0 and numerals[string[i-1]] < numerals[string[i]]:
            pass # Do nothing we must already have processed this.
        else:
            intValue += numerals[string[i]]
    return intValue

if __name__ == '__main__':
    print convertRomanToInteger ( raw_input ( 'Enter a number in Roman numerals : ' ) )
```

To explain what is happening here, let's look at various segments of the program. numerals is a dictionary that contains all the letters used in Roman numerals and which maps the Roman numeral letter to its corresponding integer value (expressed in Arabic numerals as required by Python). The convertRomanToInteger function starts by setting our intValue (the variable that is used to create the integer value that is the result) to zero and iterating over all the characters in the string:

```
def convertRomanToInteger ( string ) :
    intValue = 0
    for i in range ( len ( string ) ) :
```

We must compare each value to the next one along. If the next value is greater than the current one, we subtract the current value from the next one and add it to our total:

```
        if i < len ( string ) - 1 and numerals[string[i]] < numerals[string[i+1]]:
            intValue += numerals[string[i+1]] - numerals[string[i]]
```

If the current value is greater than the previous one, we will already have dealt with it in the previous iteration, so we can skip it – the **pass** statement is a 'do nothing' statement that is required to ensure that there is a body in the elif:

```
        elif i > 0 and numerals[string[i-1]] < numerals[string[i]]:
            pass # Do nothing we must already have processed this.
```

Otherwise, we just add the value of the current letter to the intValue:

```
        else:
            intValue += numerals[string[i]]
```

Having processed the string, all we have to do is return the integer value:

```
    return intValue
```

In the main block we deal with prompting the user, obtaining the input string (using raw_input so there is no processing), call the conversion function, then print the result using Arabic numerals:

```
if __name__ == '__main__' :
    print convertRomanToInteger ( raw_input ( 'Enter a number in Roman numerals : ' ) )
```

So far, so good. This program works as required if the input string is a legal Roman numeral. However it has 'issues':

1. The input 'P' causes an exception (called KeyError) to be raised. This is because when the dictionary is asked to provide the value of P, it finds it does not have such a key.

2. The input IIX results in 8. This is not correct: the rules do not allow a letter for a larger number to follow more than one letter of a lower value. This input should result in an exception.

3. The input IIIIIIIIIIII results in 12, which is the correct value, but is it a legal Roman numeral?

4. The program allows mixed case numbers, but is it correct that this is allowed?

5. The program accepts MIM, MCMIC, MCMXCIX all as representing 1999. Are all of these allowed?

Issue 1 isn't really an error, it is just that the resultant error message is implementation oriented and not user or task oriented. We really ought to introduce some exception handling so that error messages relate to what the user is trying to do rather than reflecting the way the program works.

Issue 2 is a problem because we are only checking one character ahead of the one we are processing. What we are doing here is *parsing*. Parsing is looking at a sequence of tokens and deducing or inferring meaning. In this case we are looking at a sequence of letters that are legal in Roman numerals to discover the number that is being represented. Parsing usually requires *lookahead*. In this case we have a lookahead of 1, i.e. we are looking at the next character as well as the current character when making decisions. The problem we have is that in order to see if there is a failure of the rules of construction of a Roman numeral, we actually need a lookahead of two characters.

You may be asking yourself: "So where does the lexer fit in all this". We introduced the idea of a lexer in Section 4.7 (page 137). The job of a lexer is to turn sequences of characters into sequences of tokens so that a parser can work on the tokens. In the case of parsing Roman numerals, the tokens are the characters, so there is no need for a lexer at all. This, though, is unusual. A parser normally makes use of a lexer to avoid having to deal with characters at all: parsers work with tokens.

You may also be asking yourself: "Is a parser a finite state machine?" Yes, it is. Perhaps then we need to step back and apply finite state machine ideas more explicitly? Actually we are going to stop work on this problem for now. This example is good one for demonstrating proper program testing, so we are going to use it as an example in the program testing chapter (Section 9.4.2 page 289).

4.8.3 An Example: Currency Conversion

At the end of Section 2.13 (page 54) we stated that we needed a new approach to progress the currency conversion program further. There, we were implementing decision making with selection and the code was getting rather messy. We said then we needed a data-oriented approach. What we need is to be able to make use of a dictionary of dictionaries. We can rewrite the program we developed then to be rather more elegant and a lot more easy to evolve:

```
rates = { }
rates['USD'] = { }
rates['GBP'] = { }
rates['AUD'] = { }

rates['USD']['GBP'] = 0.541272
rates['GBP']['USD'] = 1 / rates['USD']['GBP']

rates['USD']['AUD'] = 1.34958
rates['AUD']['USD'] = 1 / rates['USD']['AUD']

rates['GBP']['AUD'] = 2.5060
rates['AUD']['GBP'] = 1 / rates['GBP']['AUD']

fromCurrency = raw_input ( 'Currency being tendered to exchange : ')
toCurrency = raw_input ( 'Currency requested : ')
amount = input ( 'Amount to exchange : ')

try :
    convertedAmount = amount * rates[fromCurrency][toCurrency]
except KeyError , exception :
    print 'Currency ' + str ( exception ) + ' not known at this time.'
else :
    print amount , fromCurrency , 'is', convertedAmount , toCurrency
```

The combination of dictionaries does all the work of storing and, more importantly, searching for rates. Moreover, the program is extensible, since we can easily add new currencies. Exchange rates are data, so having a data structure to store and retrieve the data is clearly sensible.

4.9 A Final Note

Programs that manage state are generally called *imperative* and languages that support them (like Python, Java and C) are called *imperative programming languages*. Making sure that your programs are always in a valid and consistent state, no matter what happens is a tough job. In the following chapters we will introduce some tools and techniques that will support the management of state, thereby making the creation of correct programs easier.

Chapter Summary

In this chapter we have found that:

- List, tuple and dictionary are data types that we can use for structuring data.
- Programs work with state.
- Many systems can be modeled with finite state machines.
- Representing the solution to a problem as a program requires us to represent the data in a way that makes algorithms easy.
- That lexing and parsing are tools for solving some classes of problems.

Self-Review Questions

Self-review 4.1 What are the values of the variables a, b, c and d after the following statements have been executed?

```
a = 1
b = 2
c = a + b
d = a + c
```

Self-review 4.2 How many elements are in the dictionary someData after the following code has been executed?

```
someData = { }
someData['cheese'] = 'dairy'
someData['Cheese'] = 'dairy'
```

Self-review 4.3 Given the following assignment:

```
items = ( ( 3 , 2 ) , ( 5 , 7 ) , ( 1 , 9 ) , 0 , ( 1 ) )
```

without writing a Python program or using the Python interpreter, answer the following:

1. What value is returned by len (items)?
2. What is the value of items[1]?
3. **print** items[2][0] prints 1 but **print** items[3][0] causes a TypeError. Why is this given that items has more than 3 elements?
4. For items[x][y], what values of x and y cause the expression to evaluating to 9?
5. It might at first appear that the type of items[0] and the type of items[4] are the same.
   (a) What are the types of these two expressions?
   (b) Why is the type of items[4] not tuple?
   (c) If it was intended that items[4] be a tuple, how should the assignment be altered, without adding any new values?

Self-review 4.4 What is the output of the following code?

```
a = 1
def f ( ) :
    a = 10
print a
```

Self-review 4.5 Explain why the code in the previous question did *not* display 10.

Self-review 4.6 Referring to the coffee/cola vending machine state transition diagram (page 111), what happens if the consumer puts three tokens into the machine without pressing any buttons?

Self-review 4.7 Which of the following are types mutable and which are immutable: int, list, float, tuple, str.

Self-review 4.8 What happens when the following statement is executed as the first statement of a program?

```
x , y , z = 1 , 2 , x ** 3
```

Self-review 4.9 For each of the following lines, using substitution, hand-evaluate the following sequence:

```
x , y , z = 1 , 2 , 3
z , y , x = x , z , y
x , y , z = ( z + 1 ) , ( x - 2 ) , ( y * 3 )
y , z , x = ( y / x ) , ( x * y ) , ( z ** x )
```

Self-review 4.10 Draw the state space of the following devices:

1. An MP3 or Ogg Vorbis player.
2. A microwave oven.

Self-review 4.11 Draw a state transition diagram for a two-bit binary counter. A binary counter is a digital circuit that has a clock input and an output that gives the number of clock cycles that have been counted. A two-bit binary counter only has two output connections, which can have the value of either 1 or 0. This means that a two-bit counter can count from 0 to $2^2 - 1$ and back to 0 again.

Self-review 4.12 Draw a state transition diagram for a PIN (Personal Identification Number) recognizer. If the user enters '1' followed by '8' followed by '5' followed by '0' followed by 'enter', the machine should enter a state called 'accept'. If the user enters any other combination of numbers, followed by 'enter' the machine should enter a state called 'reject'. Is this program a lexer?

Self-review 4.13 The implementation of cipherCharacter on page 133 has a bug in it even though this bug may never appear in normal use. What is the bug and how can it be fixed?

Self-review 4.14 What are the types of variables a and b in the following code:

```
a = ( 1 )
b = ( 1 , )
```

Self-review 4.15 What is the types and value of y after executing the following code:

```
x = [ 1 , 2 , 3 , 4 , 5 ]
y = x [ : ]
```

Programming Exercises

Exercise 4.1 Examine the following code:

```
a = 10
b = 20
print "Before swapping a=%d, b=%d" % ( a , b )
#Swap values
a = b
b = a
print "After swapping a=%d, b=%d" % ( a , b )
```

1. Try running this small program. What are the values of a and b after the swap?

2. Why is the result not a having the value 20 and b having the value 10 as appears to be the intention from the use of the word swap in the code?

3. Modify the code so that the final result is a having the value 20 and b having the value 1 using simultaneous assignment to swap the values.

4. Many languages, such as C, C++, Java, do not have simultaneous assignment. Modify the program so that it successfully swaps the two values without using simultaneous assignment.

Exercise 4.2 This question is based on a function for stepping through a representation of a pack of cards. The exact nature of the cards isn't important. We use a list to represent pack and in our example we use numbers between 1 and 5 as cards. They could equally be numbers and suits as tuples, strings of character names, etc. Here's the function:

```
# A hand of cards
cards = [ 1 , 5 , 3 , 4 , 2 , 3 , 2 ]

def nextCard ( cards ) :
    next = cards[0]
    newHand = cards[1:] + [ cards[0] ]
    return next , newHand
```

- What is the type of values returned by this function?
- Describe in words what the function does.
- It would be a simple matter for this function to alter the input list so that the first element becomes the last. This would simplify the return value, which is currently two items. Why might this be considered a poorer solution that the function as it is now?
- Write a loop that calls this function repeatedly, printing out the card from the top of the deck each time.
- Using the given function and your answer to the previous question as a starting point, write a program that checks a deck of cards for consecutive identical pairs (a 2 followed by a 2, for example). If a pair is found, a message should be displayed.
- What happens if the input list is empty? Correct the function so that it returns (None , [ ]) when an empty list is used as input.

Exercise 4.3 Write a program to create a frequency table using a dictionary from a set of input values. The program should repeatedly asks the user for an input. The input could be anything at all. As each input is gathered, see if it exists as a key in the dictionary. If it does not exist, associate the input as a key with the number 1. If it does exist, add one to the value already associated with it and add it back to the dictionary. If the value associated with this key is now greater than or equal to 3, print a message that looks something like "Dear user, you have entered the word 'discombobulated' 3 times!"

Frequency tables such as this are often used for storing histogram data. We will look at actually drawing histograms later (Chapter 8). Frequency tables are also used in some sorting algorithms.

Hint: You will need an infinite loop and to use the raw_input function.

Hint: someDict.has_key ('a key') returns a Boolean value indicating whether the dictionary someDict has already got a value associated with the key 'a key'.

Exercise 4.4 Write the Python program that manages the state of the two-bit binary counter from Self-review 4.11

Exercise 4.5 The lexer in Section 4.7 can only recognize non-negative integers. Improve the program by adding code to deal with negative numbers.

Exercise 4.6 Create a program for storing a week's worth of rainfall data. Use a list to store each day's value, entered sequentially by the user. When an entire week has been input, display the days with the minimum and maximum rainfall.

Exercise 4.7 Extend your answer to the previous exercise so that it also displays the mean and standard deviation of the values. The mean is the sum of all the values divided by the number of values. The standard deviation is the square root of the sum of the squares of the difference between each value and the mean, divided by the number of items.

Exercise 4.8 Calculating statistics such as maximum, minimum, mean and standard deviation is a common task. Now that you have a program to do it, package the code up into a function that can be used again in future.

Exercise 4.9 A "wobbly" number is one in which the digits alternate between being higher and lower than the preceding one. Here are some wobbly numbers: 19284756242, 90909, 0909. Using what you have learned about writing lexers, write a function that accepts a list of digits to be checked for wobbliness. If the sequence of digits is wobbly, the function should return **True**, otherwise **False**.

Exercise 4.10 The following code was written before the programmer had drunk their morning coffee, i.e. they were not properly awake at the time. It is supposed to add 3% to all the values in the variable salary_scale. However, there is one very important bug in this code. Find and fix the bug to make sure everyone gets their 3% pay rise!

```
salaryScale = ( 20000 , 21500 , 23000 , 24500 , 26000 , 27500 , 29000 )
for i in range ( len ( salaryScale ) ) :
    salaryScale[i] += salaryScale[i] * 0.03
print salaryScale
```

Exercise 4.11 Starting with the list:

[43 , 1 , 2 , 99 , 54 , 78 , 22 , 6]

write a function to sort the list – i.e. your function should return the list:

[1 , 2 , 6 , 22 , 43 , 54 , 78 , 99]

You can use any method you like to sort the list. Good answers to this problem will work on any list, not just the one we've given here.

Challenges

Challenge 4.1 Imagine a fictional land where monetary units aren't based on decimal orders. In this land, we have 3 basic units of currency:

- The Blink. The smallest unit of currency.
- The Hoojim. Worth 12 Blinks.
- The Bung. Worth 20 Hooja (plural of Hoojim) or 240 Blinks.

1. Write a function called **deBung** that accepts an integer representing a number of Bungs and displays the number of Hooja and Blink it is worth. For example, calling the function like this:

deBung (4)

Will produce the following output:

4 Bungs is worth 80 Hoojim or 960 Blinks.

2. Write a function called enBlinkHoojaBung that takes a number of Blinks and outputs its equivalent in Blink, Hooja and Bung, using the smallest number of coins. Coins in our imaginary land are made of a very heavy metal, so this is important. If the function is called with the value 506, the output should be:

506 Blinks is worth 2 Bung, 1 Hoojim and 6 Blinks.

You will need the remainder operator (%).

3. Rewrite enBlinkHoojaBung so that it returns a tuple of Blinks, Hooja and Bung values instead of writing to the screen. The last example would return (2 , 1 , 6).

Challenge 4.2 Referring back to Exercise 4.2, write a program that uses two hands of cards (two lists) to play a simple game of "snap". No cards change hands, but when two identical cards are played, a message should be printed.

Challenge 4.3 Write a lexer to recognize floating point numbers.

Hint: If your input is the following string: '12345.9876' what do you have to do to each character in the string to generate your float? How are the numbers before the decimal point different to the numbers after the decimal point? Make sure you have an algorithm that works correctly on paper before you start coding and draw a state transition diagram for the scanning part of your lexer.

Functionally Modular

Learning Outcomes

At the end of this chapter you will be able to:

- Use the **global** keyword in Python functions.
- Determine the *scope* of a variable.
- Write programs involving *list comprehensions*.
- Describe the term *functional programming* and identify whether a given piece of code is functional or imperative.
- Write programs in a functional style.
- Describe and use iterators, generators and generator expressions.

- Create and use modules for structuring reusable code.
- Use (with *pydoc*) the special variables __author__, __copyright__, __credits__, __date__, __licence__, __revision__, and __version__ when creating modules.
- Write *higher order functions* that take other functions as arguments or return them as results.
- Use the **lambda**, map and filter functions in functional programs.

In the previous chapter we were looking at issues state and introduced lists and dictionaries. In this chapter we are going to look at some problems using these data structures, and, along the way, we will look at ways of structuring systems to make parts more reusable – this is the idea behind *modules*. Bringing lists and functions together introduces a specific way of thinking about programming. This style is generally called *functional programming*. It introduces a new concept in our understanding of functions: *higher-order functions*.

5.1   An Example: Conway's Game of Life

5.1.1   Introducing the 'Game'

In 1970 John Horton Conway put forward a game that he called The Game of Life. This isn't a game in the usual sense: it is not a game in which players compete against each other with the goal of winning. The Game of Life is a zero-player game, once you set up the initial conditions, the game proceeds without intervention. The Game of Life is played on a two-dimensional rectangular grid in which each cell of the grid is either 'alive' or 'dead'. At each turn, a cell has to decide whether, if it is currently alive, it will remain alive or will die, or, if it is currently dead, whether it will remain dead or will come to life. Each cell interacts with each of its neighbors, of which there are eight:

Of course the cells on the edge of the grid have fewer neighbors. The rules for deciding the next state of a cell are actually quite simple:

1. A live cell with fewer than two neighbors dies (lonely cells die).

2. A live cell with more than three neighbors dies (overcrowded cells die).

3. A live cell with two or three neighbors lives on in the next generation.

4. A dead cell with exactly three live neighbors springs into life.

but it turns out that the game can get very complicated, which is why people love it.

The Game of Life is an instance of a *cellular automaton*. A cellular automaton comprises a potentially infinite, regular grid of cells, in which each cell is in one of a finite number of states – finite state machines again! The grid can be in any finite number of dimensions – the Game of Life is generally a two-dimensional cellular automaton. Time is not continuous for a cellular automaton, it is discrete: there is a distinct sequence of states of the whole system – these are often called generations. The state of the system at time t depends only on the state at time t-1. A given cell of a cellular automaton has a neighborhood or related cells – in the Game of Life a cells' neighborhood is the set of cells 1 step away: the neighborhood comprises the nearest neighbors.

Cellular automata are simple but very interesting and useful models of ecologies – which is what the Game of Life is. Another game that uses a cellular automaton is SimCity (and all its follow-ups). Games like SimCity, which have lots of non-player characters, have to have a model of how those characters behave. The game is played by each character behaving according to a program that is just an implementation of that model. Tamagotchis are another example of games characters whose model tells them when they should sleep, when they need feeding, when they want to play, how healthy they are, and so on. The characters in SimCity are a much more complex example, but all of these are similar in nature to the code we will write to implement the Game of Life.

In fact, cellular automata are important in many forms of simulation as well as in theoretical computing, theoretical biology and mathematics.

5.1.2 Creating a Program

Controls and Representations

How do we go about creating a program to play the Game of Life? Here is the main sequence for a program that creates a 10×8 grid, populates it randomly with live cells (the probability of any cell being alive is 0.4), and then runs three generations:

```
if __name__ == '__main__' :
    createGrid ( 10 , 8 )
    populateGridRandomly ( 0.4 )
    printGrid ( )
    for i in range ( 3 ) :
        calculateNextGeneration ( )
        printSeparator ( )
        printGrid ( )
```

We have decomposed the problem into a sequence of function calls – a classical *functional decomposition* approach to design: some people call it *top-down design*. Taking each of the functions in turn: createGrid has to create a rectangular grid of the specified size:

```
def createGrid ( x , y ) :
    global grid
    grid = [ [ False for j in range ( x ) ] for i in range ( y ) ]
```

This function introduces a number of new ideas. The first statement is a **global** statement. This doesn't do anything directly, it just says that the variable grid used in the function is to be treated as a global variable. This means that the variable will be available everywhere in the program.

The second statement embodies two things:

1. We have chosen to use a list of lists to represent the grid of the game. This is the truly important decision so far: we have to represent the state of the game in some way and a two-dimensional array of Booleans seems a very sensible way. Python does not have two-dimensional array as a built-in data type, so we have to create it using a list of lists. If we have a 2×2 grid, for example, then we need the data structure:

   [[**False** , **False**] , [**False** , **False**]]

2. We have used a feature of Python that we have not used before in this book, *list comprehensions*, to create the list of list data structure.

List comprehensions are a way of creating a list using iteration, but with the for loop is inside the list construct. Instead of having a for loop (or while loop) and constructing the list by appending, we use a list construct and specify what the elements should be using an embedded for loop. In this case the two, nested for loops are simple: they are just asking for repetition. There is more to list comprehensions than we have shown here, but we don't need the extra complexity for this problem.

As ever, the best way of seeing what happens is to try some experiments:

```
>>> def createGrid ( x , y ) :
...     global grid
...     grid = [ [ False for j in range ( x ) ] for i in range ( y ) ]
...
>>> createGrid ( 2 , 3 )
>>> print grid
[[False, False], [False, False], [False, False]]
>>> createGrid ( 4 , 2 )
>>> print grid
[[False, False, False, False], [False, False, False, False]]
>>>
```

> Each cell can be alive or dead, i.e. in one of two states. Booleans have two state so it seems reasonable to use a Boolean to represent the state of a cell. We will choose **True** for alive and **False** for dead.

So createGrid (2 , 3) creates a list with three items each of which is a list with two entries – the array is two across and three down. createGrid (4 , 2) on the other hand creates a list of two items each of which has four items – the array is four across and two down.

With the ability to create grids in place, we need a way of displaying a grid to the user. This is straightforwardly a job for a nested loop:

```
def printGrid ( ) :
    for i in range ( len ( grid ) ) :
        for j in range ( len ( grid[i] ) ) :
            if grid[i][j] : print '#' ,
            else : print '_' ,
        print
```

Not very complicated: we iterate over the rows, and for each row, we iterate over the columns, and for each column, if the value is **True**, we print a hash (#) character, otherwise we print an underline (_) character. So we are printing a # for each live cell, and because we print each column of each row in order, the output represents the grid very nicely.

```
>>> def printGrid ( ) :
...     for i in range ( len ( grid ) ) :
...         for j in  range ( len ( grid[i] ) ) :
...             if grid[i][j] : print '#' ,
...             else : print '_' ,
...         print
...
>>> grid = [ [ False , True , True , False ] , [ True , False , False , True ] ]
>>> printGrid ( )
_ # # _
# _ _ #
>>>
```

This way of printing things only looks right using a font in which the _ and # glyphs have the same width, for example Courier or any other monospace typeface.

The implementation of printSeparator is really quite trivial:

```
def printSeparator ( ) :
    print '\n---------------------------------------\n'
```

Initial and Evolving Populations

Next we need to set the initial state of the grid. Rather than build a user interface immediately, we decided to just have a random selection of live cells at the start. For this we need to write the function:

```
import random
def populateGridRandomly ( x ) :
    random.seed ( )
    for i in range ( len ( grid ) ) :
        for j in range ( len ( grid[i] ) ) :
            if random.random ( ) < x :
                grid[i][j] = True
```

We are using the module random from the standard library to create pseudo-random numbers, so we have to import it. The functions we are using are:

random.seed uses the computer's clock to initialize the random number algorithm. Random number generators do not actually generate numbers randomly, they are predictable – a given generator will give the same sequence of numbers whenever it is started with the same starting value (or seed). By using the current time as the starting value, we get a different sequence.

random.random returns a float in the range [0.0 , 1.0) in which the distribution of numbers is flat, i.e. every number is equally likely.

The effect of executing populateGridRandomly is to pseudo-randomly decide to set each cell to live (**True** represents the cell being live) with a probability of 0.4. So roughly 40% of the cells will be live.

Finally, we have to create the calculateNextGeneration function that moves the grid from this generation to the next generation. As the next generation depends on the current generation, and we have to iterate over all the cells to set the correct liveness value, we are going to have to build a new state and then make it the current state. Setting the liveness in each cell of the next generation, embodying the rules of the game as set out earlier, is clearly a job for a function. However, rather than create a global function, we are going to use Python's ability to have *nested function*. Yes, that's right – we can define new functions within functions. Why would we want to do this? Mostly so that the function is only usable inside the function in which it is defined.

A Functional Digression

Perhaps it is worth taking time out to think about this idea of nested functions a little before progressing the development of the Game of Life code.

In our programs to date we have created a sequence of functions and a main program such that each of the functions could be called from anywhere in the program or the other functions. So for example:

```
def functionA ( ) :                          | > python globalFunctions.py
    print 'A'                                A
                                             A
def functionB ( ) :                          B
    print 'B'                                B
                                             | >
def doAThenB ( ) :
    functionA ( )
    functionB ( )

if __name__ == '__main__' :
    functionA ( )
    doAThenB ( )
    functionB ( )
```

If instead of defining functionA and functionB at the global level, we define them inside doAThenB, then functionA and functionB are not available to be called except within doAThenB. So in the program:

```
def doAThenB ( ) :                           | > python nestedFunctions.py
    def functionA ( ) :                      A
        print 'A'                            B
    def functionB ( ) :                      | >
        print 'B'
    functionA ( )
    functionB ( )

if __name__ == '__main__' :
    doAThenB ( )
```

it is not possible to call functionA or functionB from the main program. The scope of functionA and functionB is the function doAThenB: the functions are not visible anywhere else. If you try to call functionA from the main program, you get an exception and a message something like:

```
Traceback (most recent call last):
  File "nestedFunctions.py", line 10, in <module>
    functionA ( )
NameError: name 'functionA' is not defined
```

We can use this way of defining functions as a way of controlling the ability to use functions. Minimizing the scope of functions is a way of minimizing the possibility of misuse. It is essentially just a safety aid.

Generational Generation

We have now done enough planning to be able to get started on evolving the calculateNextGeneration function. We have decided that we are going to have to create a new list of lists to create the new state based on the old state. So we probably mean something like:

```
def calculateNextGeneration ( ) :
    global grid
    grid = [ [ False for j in range ( len ( grid[i] ) ) ] for i in range ( len ( grid ) ) ]
```

The list comprehension here is basically the same as the one we used in the createGrid function, except that the lengths of the lists are determined by the lengths of the lists in the grid we are going to replace – we can't change the size of the grid part way through the game!

So we have a new grid that is the same size as the old grid, but everything dies immediately – not exactly a Game of Life, just extremely terminal. We clearly need to evolve this function to allow the liveness of the cells to be calculated for the new state. So we add the necessary nested loops:

```
def calculateNextGeneration ( ) :
    global grid
    newGrid = [ [ False for j in range ( len ( grid[i] ) ) ] for i in range ( len ( grid ) ) ]
    def calculateLiveness ( x , y ) :
        return False
    for i in range ( len ( grid ) ) :
        for j in range ( len ( grid[i] ) ) :
            newGrid[i][j] = calculateLiveness ( i , j )
    grid = newGrid
```

Here we have used a nested function. It is right to use a function, but we want to limit its scope, so we nest it.

Clearly this version of calculateNextGeneration leaves everything as terminally dead as previously (since calculateLiveness always returns false), but it gives us a structure that we can evolve further.

We now need to evolve the calculateLiveness function to implement the rules of the game. Since the liveness of a cell in the next generation depends on the liveness of all the neighbors in the current generation, we have to iterate over all the nearest neighbors of the current cell and count the number of live cells that are neighbors. Knowing the neighbor count, we can determine the liveness of the current cell in the next generation with a simple if statement. The rule translates to:

```
if grid[x][y] : return 2 <= count <= 3
else : return count == 3
```

i.e. a live cell stays alive if it has two or three neighbors, otherwise it dies, whereas a dead cell springs to life if it has exactly three live neighbors, otherwise it stays dead.

So we now have the code:

```
def calculateNextGeneration () :
    global grid
    newGrid = [ [ False for j in range ( len ( grid[i] ) ) ] for i in range ( len ( grid ) ) ]
    def calculateLiveness ( x , y ) :
        count = 0
        for i in range ( x - 1 , x + 1 ) :
            for j in range ( y - 1 , y + 1 ) :
                if grid[i][j] : count += 1
        if grid[x][y] : return 2 <= count <= 3
        else : return count == 3
    for i in range ( len ( grid ) ) :
        for j in range ( len ( grid[i] ) ) :
            newGrid[i][j] = calculateLiveness ( i , j )
    grid = newGrid
```

We have used the expression $2 <= count <= 3$ which is true only when count is two or three, so it is equivalent to $(count == 2)$ **or** $(count == 3)$.

However, this is not right for a number of reasons:

- x + 1 and y + 1 are the wrong values for the end points of the iteration – these are the last indexes we want tested, so we must specify one more than this in the range function: iteration continues up to but not including the upper value. So, for example, if we want to use the values 0, 1 and 2, we must specify one more than the largest value in the range function:

    ```
    >>> for i in range ( 0 , 3 ) : print i ,
    ...
    0 1 2
    >>>
    ```

    Getting this wrong was just a slip on our part, creating an off-by-one error. This is easily fixed once it is appreciated what the problem is.

- If x or y are zero or greater than the size of the array, serious problems happen.

    - If x is 0 then the outer loop of the nested loop in calculateLiveness is:

        ```
        for i in range ( -1 , 1 )
        ```

        which leads to a negative index in the access of grid. Likewise if y is 0, the inner loop of the nested loop in calculateLiveness is:

        ```
        for j in range ( -1 , 1 )
        ```

        Negative indexes are describe in Section 4.6.3 (page 135).

        which also leads to a negative index in the access of grid. Negative indexes when accessing grid is the wrong thing to do in this situation, since it means indexing from the end rather than the beginning. This algorithm requires us always to index from the beginning.

    - If the index is greater than the length of the list then, when grid is accessed using that index, an exception is raised – an IndexError, in fact, something like:

        ```
        Traceback (most recent call last):
          File "<stdin>", line 1, in <module>
        IndexError: list index out of range
        ```

Python does not allow non-existent list items to be accessed, so raising an exception is exactly what should happen. We need to either handle the exception if it happens, or better still in this situation, avoid the exception being raised.

We have to add extra code associated with the double loop iteration in calculateLiveness to protect against these indexing problems.

- We count the liveness of the cell itself when calculating how many live cells there are in the neighborhood of the cell, which is wrong – it is only the liveness of surrounding cells that determines the liveness of a cell. We must remove the current cell from the count.

These problems are (relatively) easily addressed by adding extra tests and conditions in the nested loops, giving us:

```
def calculateNextGeneration ( ) :
    global grid
    newGrid = [ [ False for j in range ( len ( grid[i] ) ) ] for i in range ( len ( grid ) ) ]
    def calculateLiveness ( x , y ) :
        count = 0
        for i in range ( x - 1 , x + 2 ) :
            if 0 <= i < len ( grid ) :
                for j in range ( y - 1 , y + 2 ) :
                    if 0 <= j < len ( grid[i] ) :
                        if ( ( i != x ) or ( j != y ) ) and grid[i][j] : count += 1
        if grid[x][y] : return 2 <= count <= 3
        else : return count == 3
    for i in range ( len ( grid ) ) :
        for j in range ( len ( grid[i] ) ) :
            newGrid[i][j] = calculateLiveness ( i , j )
    grid = newGrid
```

The nested loop in calculateLiveness is iterating over all the nearest neighbors of the current cell, counting the number of live cells that are neighbors. This complexity is required because there are edges to the grid and we must not index outside of the grid. We cannot afford to have negative indexes, as that would be indexing from the end rather than the beginning, and we cannot afford to have indexes larger than the size of the lists or we get exceptions. So we carefully check within each loop that the indexes are reasonable. At the heart of the nested loop we increment count if the neighbor is live, except that we do not count the cell itself, we are only counting live neighbors.

This is (probably) the most complicated Python code presented so far in this book. It is worth taking time to look over it, try it out, and ensure that the code makes sense to you.

So the point here is that code is evolved, it doesn't just spring into being whole. You sometimes have to temporarily add print statements to find out what is going on in the execution of the code, and mistakes happen, so check everything.

Executing the Result

The upshot of all this programming is that we now have a program that plays the Game of Life:

```
| > python life_1.py
_ # _ _ # # _ _ _ _
# _ _ _ _ # _ _ # _
_ _ _ _ # # _ # # #
# _ _ # # _ # # _ #
_ # # _ # # _ # # _
_ _ _ _ _ # # _ _ #
_ _ _ _ # _ _ _ _ _
_ _ _ # # _ _ _ _ #
----------------------------------------
_ _ _ _ # # _ _ _ _
_ _ _ _ _ _ _ # # #
_ _ _ # _ _ _ _ _ #
_ # # _ _ _ _ _ _ #
_ # # _ _ _ _ _ _ #
_ _ _ # _ _ # # # _
_ _ _ # # _ _ _ _ _
_ _ _ # # _ _ _ _ _
----------------------------------------
_ _ _ _ _ _ _ _ # _
_ _ _ _ # _ _ _ # #
_ _ # _ _ _ _ _ _ #
_ # _ # _ _ _ _ # #
_ # _ # _ _ _ # _ #
_ _ _ # # _ _ # # _
_ _ # _ _ # _ # _ _
_ _ _ # # _ _ _ _ _
----------------------------------------
_ _ _ _ _ _ _ _ # #
_ _ _ _ _ _ _ _ # #
_ _ # # _ _ _ _ _ _
_ # _ # _ _ _ _ _ #
_ _ _ # _ _ _ # _ #
_ _ _ # # _ _ # _ _
_ _ # _ _ # # # # _
_ _ _ # # _ _ _ _ _
```

but this doesn't really work as an interactive experience. We need to give it a much better user interface. We need a graphical user interface, aka GUI. However, we are going to have to leave this until after the next chapter, as we need to introduce classes before we can do GUI things. We pick this up again in Chapter 12 (page 367).

5.1.3 Improving by Abstracting: More Nested Functions

You probably spotted in the Game of Life code that we ended up with a nested loop in almost all the functions, because each of them was working with all the cells in the grid. Having explicit iteration replicated like this is an indicator that we could perhaps use some form of abstraction to make things simpler.

In this case we can create a function that handles all the iteration over the cells of the grid, applying a function to each cell in the grid:

```
def applyToEachCellOfGrid ( function ) :
    for i in range ( len ( grid ) ) :
        for j in range ( len ( grid[i] ) ) :
            function ( i , j )
```

The parameter to this function is a function, and in particular it is a function that takes two parameters (the indexes of the current cell of interest).

We can now rewrite populateGridRandomly and printGrid to make use of this function:

```
def populateGridRandomly ( x ) :
    random.seed ( )
    def setRandomly ( i , j ) :
        if random.random ( ) < x : grid[i][j] = True
    applyToEachCellOfGrid ( setRandomly )

def printGrid ( ) :
    def printIt ( i , j ) :
        if grid[i][j] : print '#' ,
        else : print '_' ,
        if j == len ( grid[i] ) - 1 : print
    applyToEachCellOfGrid ( printIt )
```

Using the nested function capability allows us to create a local action function that is then passed as a parameter to the applyToEachCellOfGrid function, which iterates over the cells of the grid applying the action function to each cell.

5.2   Functions and Scope

If a function does not explicitly return a value then a special value None is returned.

Introducing the **global** statement and nested functions in the previous section raises a number of issue regarding names. In particular, what is the *scope* of the name of a variable or function. The scope rules for names are the same whether the name is of a variable or of a function, so we use variables as examples here as it is easier.

The *scope* of a variable is that part of your code in which you can refer to the variable. You have probably already noticed that if you create a variable inside a function, you can't refer to it outside that function:

```
>>> def foobar ( n ) :
...     x = 10
...     return n + 10
...
>>> foobar ( 15 )
25
>>> print x
Traceback (most recent call last):
  File "<stdin>", line 1, in ?
NameError: name 'x' is not defined
>>>
```

The variable x inside the function foobar is local to the function and so is only in scope in the function. When we try to print the value of x outside the function foobar, the Python system complains that we haven't defined a variable called x.

As we saw earlier in the Game of Life program, we can use a **global** statement to say that a variable we are using inside a function is actually a global variable, not a local variable:

```
>>> def foobar ( n ) :
...     global x
...     x = 10
...     return n + x
```

```
...
>>> foobar ( 15 )
25
>>> print x
10
>>> x = 25
>>> print x
25
>>>
```

Nesting functions is a way of using scope to hide names of functions that are for internal use only so that they cannot be called unexpectedly. The whole point of having nested functions is that the nested function is scoped to exist only within the enclosing function.

Clearly, then, it is important to understand how Python manages scope, so that whenever we refer to a variable or function name we know which variable or function Python will be using. Python programmers refer to the 'LEGB rule' to explain this. Python has four sorts of scope:

- *L*ocal – names inside a block.

- *E*nclosing – names in the block enclosing the current block.

- *G*lobal – names outside a function in the interpreter or in a file.

- *B*uilt-in – names that are defined by the Python system (e.g. range, len, etc.).

When the Python system needs to look up the value of a variable or find a function name to call, it first looks in the local scope, then it looks in the enclosing scopes, then it looks for a global, then it looks for a built-in. Obviously if there has been a **global** statement then the local and enclosing scopes are ignored and the search is restricted to the global scope.

This rule only applies to names without a period (aka full stop) in. For names with a '.', the lookup searches for names in a module. So the LEGB rule doesn't apply to math.sqrt: instead the name sqrt is looked for in module math.

Assigning to a variable is not the same thing as looking up a variable. Whenever you assign to a variable, a new local variable is created unless there is a **global** statement for the name. This can appear surprising if you use the same name:

```
>>> x = 10
>>> def foobar ( ) :
...     x = 100
...     print x
...
>>> print x
10
>>> foobar ( )
100
>>> print x
10
>>>
```

Because of the assignment in foobar and there is no **global** statement, the x inside foobar is local to foobar and is a different x to the global one.

5.3   Functional Programming with Python

So far we have seen that functions are useful for two reasons:

1. Functions allow us to decompose large tasks into smaller ones. As a general rule, every function you write should perform one task well.

    We already used this approach in the Game of Life program. We started with the main sequence:

    ```
    if __name__ == '__main__' :
        createGrid ( 10 , 8 )
        populateGridRandomly ( 0.4 )
        printGrid ( )
        for i in range ( 3 ) :
            calculateNextGeneration ( )
            printSeparator ( )
            printGrid ( )
    ```

    which decomposed the problem into a sequence of functional calls, each focusing on a specific aspect of solving the problem. This means that when you are writing a particular function, you can forget about all the other tasks the program has to perform and concentrate on the one you are writing.

2. Functions help to avoid duplicate code. If we know that we need to perform some sequence of operations more than once, we place the sequence in a function that gets called as needed. This cuts down the amount of code we need to write. It also diminishes the chances of making a mistake when writing code.

    The function applyToEachCellOfGrid is an example of a function used to avoid duplicating code.

The parameter to applyToEachCellOfGrid is a function and so applyToEachCellOfGrid is an example of a *higher-order function*. A higher-order function is a function that has one or more functions as parameter(s) and/or returns a function. Working with higher-order functions is one of the cornerstones of *functional programming*. The idea is that functions manipulate and combine other functions and then apply them to data in order to achieve the final desired result.

Another feature that is an integral part of the functional programming style is that there is no assignment: functions in functional programming have no *side effects* and are *referentially transparent*.

The terms *side effects* and *referential transparency* were introduced in Section 2.10.3 (page 42).

5.3.1   Being Referentially Transparent

Functional programming has proved very useful in computer science research exactly because it is referentially transparent. The fact that the same function, given the same parameters, will always return the same result means that it is easy to reason about functional programs. Furthermore, it means that mathematical techniques can be used to prove that programs are correct.

Computers, however, are not in general referentially transparent, they are state machines after all. Functions in programming languages that manipulate state, including Python, are generally not referentially transparent: a function might not return the same result if you call it twice with the same parameters. For example:

```
>>> x = 10
>>> def addX ( y ) :
...     return x + y
...
>>> print addX ( 100 )
110
>>> x = 35
>>> print addX ( 100 )
135
>>>
```

In this example, the state of x had an effect on the result of executing the function addX. This makes it difficult to reason about a program that uses addX, because you cannot really say anything constructive about the value being returned.

5.3.2 Having Effects on the Side

In programs that manipulate state, functions can also have *side effects* on the state around them even if they are referentially transparent: a function can change variables declared outside its scope. In Python, if a function does this, it needs to explicitly state that a variable name it refers to is not local to the function. This is what the **global** statement is for:

```
>>> x = 10
>>> def flob ( y ) :
...     global x
...     x += y
...     return 10 * y
...
>>> def addX ( y ) :
...     return x * y
...
>>> print addX ( 100 )
1000
>>> print addX ( 100 )
1000
>>> print flob ( 10 )
100
>>> print flob ( 10 )
100
>>> print addX ( 100 )
3000
>>> print addX ( 100 )
3000
>>> print flob ( 10 )
100
>>> print flob ( 10 )
100
>>> print addX ( 100 )
5000
>>> print addX ( 100 )
5000
>>>
```

So the behavior of addX depends on whether flob has been called or not. addX is not referentially transparent and flob has side effects even though it is ostensibly referentially transparent.

Reasoning about code that uses referentially transparent functions is very much easier than reasoning about programs that use functions with side effects. It is no wonder then that people find it easier to work with programs that use functions with referential transparency and no side effects.

5.3.3 The Programming Imperative

In the above example, to work out the return value of any call of flob or addX, we have to know the value of x at all times. This means that we have to track down every occurrence of calls to flob and addX. In fact, in order to work out the return value from flob or addX, we have to track the whole flow of execution of the program.

Even from this small example, you can see why programs that have and manipulate state (called *imperative programs*) can be difficult to understand. Imperative programming is the programming style in which you tell the computer what to do at each stage. This seems low-level and very computer-oriented. Programming languages should be high-level and human-oriented, as indeed Python is. The corollary here is that functional expression is a high-level way of doing things, easier for humans. This is why many people use a functional programming style as much as possible when using imperative programming languages!

Functional programming is interesting and (because of referential transparency) it is easier to think about and use than imperative programming in many situations. Although Python is an imperative programming language, it has the facilities to be used in a functional programming style. As a practicing programmer it is important that you have experience of both imperative and functional programming styles so that you can use the most appropriate style of programming at all times.

As an example of the sort of 'conflicts' between functional and imperative approaches, let's return to the square spiral program that was used in Chapter 2. Using the final version from that chapter (page 47) as a base, we can come up with a new version that improves on what we had then, given what we know now:

```
import turtle

def drawSideAndTurn ( amount ) :
    turtle.forward ( amount )
    turn ( 90 )

def drawSquareSpiral ( n , increment , maximum ) :
    while n < maximum :
        drawSideAndTurn ( n )
        drawSideAndTurn ( n )
        n += increment

if __name__ == '__main__' :
    turn = turtle.left
    if input ( 'Type False or 0 for an anti-clockwise spiral, True or 1 for a clockwise spiral : ' ) :
        turn = turtle.right
    drawSquareSpiral ( 10 , 10 , 140 )
    input ( 'Press any key to terminate.' )
```

In the functional programming style of programming, control structures such as the while loop:

```
while n < maximum :
    . . .
    n += increment
```

are not used because the side effect of updating the state that the += operation realizes is not permitted in a pure functional program. Likewise, for loops such as:

```
for n in range ( 0 , maximum , increment ) :
    . . .
```

are not allowed either because of the side effect of assigning to the loop variable.

So how can we do iteration in the functional style? We use recursion. Here is the drawSquareSpiral function coded using recursion as iteration:

```
def drawSquareSpiral ( n , increment , maximum ) :
    if n < maximum :
        drawSideAndTurn ( n )
        drawSideAndTurn ( n )
        drawSquareSpiral ( n + increment , increment , maximum )
```

"How does this work as iteration?", you are asking. Let's show this by working through an example call. Let's try:

```
drawSquareSpiral ( 1 , 1 , 3 )
```

We label this Call 1. First the Boolean expression is tested:

$$n < maximum \, [\, n \backslash 1, \, maximum \backslash 3 \,] \quad = \quad 1 < 3$$
$$= \quad True$$

so we execute the block. This calls drawSideAndTurn twice, which causes two sides of a square to be drawn. Then we make the recursive call:

```
drawSquareSpiral ( 2 , 1 , 3 )
```

We label this Call 2. The Boolean expression is tested in this new call:

$$n < maximum \, [\, n \backslash 2, \, maximum \backslash 3 \,] \quad = \quad 2 < 3$$
$$= \quad True$$

so we execute the block. This calls drawSideAndTurn twice, which causes two sides of a square to be drawn. Then we make the recursive call:

```
drawSquareSpiral ( 3 , 1 , 3 )
```

We label this Call 3. The Boolean expression is tested in this call:

$$n < maximum \, [\, n \backslash 3, \, maximum \backslash 3 \,] \quad = \quad 3 < 3$$
$$= \quad False$$

The increased value in the first parameter means that the termination condition for the recursion will eventually be met.

so we do not execute the block, but just return from Call 3. Since the recursive call is the last statement in the block, this means that we also return from Call 2, and thence return from Call 1.

In terms of the calls to drawSideAndTurn, this recursive version of drawSquareSpiral behaves exactly the same as the earlier one that used a while loop – so recursion can be used to create iteration. Indeed, this recursive, 'functional' version of drawSquareSpiral shows the way that iteration is generally programmed when using functional programming languages.

However, this is not a good way of representing iteration in Python. Functional programming languages have mechanisms for handling this use of recursion so

The term for the technique is *tail recursion*.

that execution is efficient. Python does not have this feature, so using recursion to express iteration in Python is very inefficient.

The moral of all this? Python is not a functional programming language, it is an imperative language that fosters a style of programming that employs a lot of the techniques from functional programming. Using a functional approach where possible, and an imperative approach where necessary, is the right way forward. This applies to programming in any programming language: you have to express algorithms in the most appropriate way for the language being used.

> ### Functional Programming Languages
>
> There have been many functional programming languages: Scheme (a variant of Lisp), ML, Hope, Miranda, Caml, Objective Caml, and Haskell are probably the most famous. None of these languages have gained really widespread use, but their impact on the way in which languages like C++, Java, Groovy, Ruby, and Python have developed, and are being used, is very great. One might hypothesize that functional programming is not sufficient for, but it is a really important part of, general-purpose programming. Having said this, languages such as SQL (ubiquitous for database processing) and spreadsheets are examples of functional languages in widespread use.

5.3.4 The Functional Tradition

The use of higher-order functions, having no side effects, and being referentially transparent, means that functional programming is a style of programming in which you try to say what the end result needs to be for a given start point rather than saying how to achieve the end result (as you would in imperative programming). This way of expressing things is called *declarative* and, indeed, some people call functional programming *declarative programming*. The idea of trying to code in as declarative style as possible is gaining great ground, even in the traditionally imperative world of C++ and Java.

The declarative style of expressions leads to a way of thinking about algorithms as evolutions of data rather than being the application of process, which is strange given that 'algorithm' means the steps needed to achieve an end!

Traditionally, functional programming languages have emphasized four functions: **lambda**, map, filter and reduce. **lambda** is a way of creating small anonymous functions that evaluate an expression. map, filter and reduce are higher-order functions that operate on lists. Lists are absolutely critical to functional programming, but the functional languages view of list is a little different to that of Python and the imperative languages. Functional languages do not (generally) support lists as indexable sequences. Instead a list is a structure with a first item and the rest of the list – which is itself a list. This fits well with the use of recursion as a way of expressing algorithms.

5.3.5 Anonymous Functions

So far all our functions, whether they were global or nested, were given a name. There are times though when you want a function but really don't want the hassle of giving it a name. Python provides a keyword, **lambda**, which can be used to create anonymous functions. For example:

```
lambda x , y , z : x + y + z
```

x, y and z are the parameters of the anonymous function – they come before the : and the expression after the : is the body of the function. There is no need for a return statement, it is an integral part of a lambda function that the body is an expression to be evaluated and for that value to be returned from the function. So given that that has to happen, the return is assumed.

The difference between **lambda** and **def** is important here. **lambda** introduces an expression, not a statement, and expressions always return a value. In this case the returned value is a function. **def** on the other hand, introduces a statement. It doesn't return anything, it just assigns the function it defines to the name of that function.

Of course, we can associate the function created by a lambda expression with a variable. So for example:

```
>>> add = lambda x , y , z : x + y + z
>>> add ( 1 , 2 , 3 )
6
>>>
```

Used in this way it is very little different from creating a named function in the first place. So why have them? The answer comes when working with higher-order functions. Higher-order functions take functions as parameters and sometimes you want really don't want to go to the trouble of defining a function.

5.3.6 Processing Lists with map and filter

map and filter are (currently) built-in functions in the Python system that you can use to manage lists. map applies a function to every value in a list. For a function, f, if the list argument to map is $[l_0 , l_1 , l_2 , \ldots , l_n]$, then the returned value is $[f(l_0) , f(l_1) , f(l_2) , \ldots , f(l_n)]$. As you might have guessed, it's often the case that a lambda function is used as a parameter to map. Here is an example:

```
>>> integers = range ( 1 , 21 )
>>> print map ( lambda x : x * 2 , integers )
[2, 4, 6, 8, 10, 12, 14, 16, 18, 20, 22, 24, 26, 28, 30, 32, 34, 36, 38, 40]
>>> print map ( lambda x : ( x + 1 ) / 3 , integers )
[0, 1, 1, 1, 2, 2, 2, 3, 3, 3, 4, 4, 4, 5, 5, 5, 6, 6, 6, 7]
>>> vowels = [ 'a' , 'e' , 'i' , 'o' , 'u' ]
>>> print map ( lambda x : x * 2 , vowels )
['aa', 'ee', 'ii', 'oo', 'uu']
>>> print map ( lambda x : x + 'foobar' , vowels )
['afoobar', 'efoobar', 'ifoobar', 'ofoobar', 'ufoobar']
>>>
```

filter is also a function that applies a function to a list. However, the function that filter applies must return a Boolean: the function must be a *predicate*. filter returns the list of values from the list parameter for which predicate returns **True**. For example:

A predicate is a function that returns a Boolean value.

```
>>> integers = range ( 1 , 21 )
>>> filter ( lambda x : x % 3 == 0 , integers )
[3, 6, 9, 12, 15, 18]
>>> passwords = [ 'foo' , 'bar' , ' verylongpassword' ]
>>> filter ( lambda s : len ( s ) > 6 , passwords )
['verylongpassword']
>>>
```

5.3.7 An Example: Prime Numbers

Let's consider (yet) another way to write the program to print out prime numbers (cf. Section 4.1.2, page 106) , this time using a functional programming approach.

As previously, we use a top-down decomposition approach: our goal is to create a function (primes) that takes an integer parameter and returns a list of all the primes less than that integer. How can we do this functionally? Arguably the simplest algorithm is to have a predicate called something like is_prime, which returns **True** if its parameter is prime, and use that to filter a list of integers. We can generate the integers with the built-in function range. Here's the code for that:

```
def primes ( n ) :
    '''Returns a list of all the primes less than n.'''
    return filter ( is_prime , range ( 2 , n ) )
```

So, now we just need to write the is_prime function. We've given this function a name rather than using an anonymous function because it seems that it might be complicated enough to put in a named function. We can always change things later if this turns out not to be the case.

How should is_prime work? We need to check to see if the number has any factors. If a number has factors then it is not prime – a prime number is one with no factors other than 1 and the number itself. We can use filter to generate the list of factors for a given integer. So, for the number 100, we can generate all the numbers from 2 to 99 and determine which of those numbers are factors of 100, like this:

```
>>> filter ( lambda x : 100 % x == 0 , range ( 2 , 100 ) )
[2, 4, 5, 10, 20, 25, 50]
>>> filter ( lambda x : 97 % x == 0, range ( 2 , 97 ) )
[]
>>>
```

As you can see, if, as in the case with 97 above, there are no factors, then the list returned by filter is empty. So an empty list means that the number is prime. But how can we use this in a Boolean expression? We could use an expression such as **not** len (mylist) == 0. However, Python has a built-in function **bool** that returns a Boolean based on an interpretation of the truth value of its parameter. For list parameters, bool returns **False** for an empty list and **True** for all other lists:

```
>>> print bool ( [ ] )
False
>>> print bool ( [ 1 ] )
True
>>> print bool ( [ 1 , 2 , 3 , 4 ] )
True
>>>
```

So bool (mylist) is equivalent to the expression **not** len (mylist) == 0. Which to use in a program is a question of which better expresses the intention to the reader of the code. There is no right or wrong answer here, only what you prefer. For this example we choose to use the bool function, so our is_prime function looks like:

```
def is_prime ( n ) :
    '''Returns True in n is prime and False otherwise.'''
    return not bool ( filter ( lambda x : ( n % x ) == 0 , range ( 2 , n ) ) )
```

And our functional primes calculator is finished. We can try it out:

```
>>> primes ( 25 )
[2, 3, 5, 7, 11, 13, 17, 19, 23]
>>>
```

BDFL (Benevolent Dictator for Life)

A BDFL is a person who holds dictator-like powers over a project, yet is trusted by users/developers not to abuse this power. Examples include Linus Torvalds for the Linux kernel, and Guido van Rossum for the Python programming language.

Filter, Map and Reduce are Deprecated

Guido van Rossum, Python's BDFL, has announced that the functions filter, map and reduce are deprecated, i.e. he has given notice that these functions will be removed from Python as built-in functions at some time in the future.

filter and map can be replaced by the use of list comprehensions, so there is little loss of functionality. It is really a question of style of programming rather than what can be expressed in Python. BDFL is saying here that list comprehensions are the Python Way of list processing.

As BDFL has said map and filter are not destined to be part of the future of Python, how can we use a functional programming approach? The answer is that list comprehensions can be used to achieve the same functionality just using different syntax.

Here is the prime numbers program written using list comprehensions instead of higher-order functions:

```
def primes ( n ) :
    '''Returns a list of all the primes less than n.'''
    return [ i for i in range ( 2 , n ) if is_prime ( i ) ]

def is_prime ( n ) :
    '''Returns True in n is prime and False otherwise.'''
    return not bool ( [ i for i in range ( 2 , n ) if ( n % i ) == 0 ] )

if __name__ == '__main__' :
    print primes ( 25 )
```

The program uses the same algorithm, avoids side effects and has referentially transparent functions, so it is functional programming. Is it better? The version using higher-order functions is definitely a more traditional approach to functional programming, but BDFL has declared this latter way to be more Pythonic, and he is the BDFL! As we are programming in Python, then the latter is the right way. Were we programming in a different language, we might make a different choice.

Hopefully you spotted the new feature introduced in this code. The two expressions used in the list comprehensions each have an if clause as well as a for clause:

```
i for i in range ( 2 , n ) if is_prime ( i )
i for i in range ( 2 , n ) if ( n % i ) == 0
```

The for clause generates a sequence of values that are then filtered by the if clause before being used in the value expression that creates the values for the list. Using the second of the above:

```
>>> n = 20
>>> print [ i for i in range ( 2 , n ) if n % i == 0 ]
[2, 4, 5, 10]
>>> n = 23
>>> print [ i for i in range ( 2 , n ) if n % i == 0 ]
[]
>>>
```

we find that 20 has a list of values that divide it, whereas 23 is not divisible by any number other than 1 and 23.

This ability to filter the sequence of values generated is what enables list comprehensions to provide the functionality that is provided by filter function.

5.4   An Example: Mean and Standard Deviation

People often use the term *average* when actually they mean *mean*. We use the term mean to avoid confusion with *median*, and *mode* which are other statistics that try a give a measure of average.

In any situation in which you have data, you generally have to calculate the mean and standard deviation of the data. Areas as diverse as marketing and physics work with data and so need to make these calculations. Even in image processing and graphics, these calculations are needed – applying statistical algorithms to image data is one of the cornerstones of image processing. Of course, as anyone familiar with statistics will know, this is just the beginning of analyzing data: there are a whole collection of things that need calculating. For now though we just work with mean and standard deviation – we have to start somewhere!

The mean of a data set is the sum of all the values divided by the number of values. Stating this mathematically:

$$\bar{x} = \sum_{i=0}^{n} x_i$$

The standard deviation of a data set has a rather complicated looking mathematical equation:

$$\sigma = \sqrt{\frac{1}{n} \sum_{i=0}^{n} (x_i - \bar{x})^2}$$

but it turns out to be relatively easy to calculate.

5.4.1   An Imperative Perspective

Prior to the previous section, we would probably have taken an 'imperative programming' view to implementing this calculation: we would most likely have inferred that the summation for both the mean and standard deviation calculations would require an iteration with a pre-initialized variable:

```
import math

def mean ( x ) :
    sum = 0.0
    for i in range ( len ( x ) ) :
        sum += x[i]
    return sum / len ( x )
```

```
def stdDev ( x ) :
    m = mean ( x )
    sumsq = 0.0
    for i in range ( len ( x )) :
        sumsq += ( x[i] - m ) ** 2
    return math.sqrt ( sumsq / len ( x ))
```

Comparing the Python code with the mathematical expression, we see that the mathematical expression is fairly directly represented by the Python code.

Of course, if you have studied means and standard deviations before, you are probably saying to yourself: the above solution requires us to calculate the mean first, so that we can then calculate the standard deviation, but by rearranging the mathematical expression for standard deviation, we can calculate both mean and standard deviation with a single iteration. The equation for standard deviation can be rearranged to:

$$\sigma = \sqrt{\frac{1}{n}\left(\sum_{i=0}^{n} x_i^2\right) - \bar{x}^2}$$

We do not now need to know the mean before we do the summation. In programming terms, we can now calculate the sum and the sum of squares in the same loop. But doesn't that mean we need to be able to return a mean and a standard deviation as the result from a function? Yes, but this is not a problem, we can return a tuple in which the first item is the mean and the second item is the standard deviation:

```
import math

def meanStdDev ( x ) :
    sum = 0.0
    sumsq = 0.0
    for i in range ( len ( x )) :
        sum += x[i]
        sumsq += x[i] * x[i]
    mean = sum / len ( x )
    stdDev = math.sqrt ( sumsq / len ( x ) - mean * mean )
    return ( mean , stdDev )
```

So not only can we pass tuples and lists into a function as a parameter, we can also return tuples and lists as a result.

This now raises the question of which of these approaches is better. Well, actually, that is a fairly meaningless question stated like that. It is only when we add context that we can ask a meaningful question. So if we only need to calculate a mean, the meanStdDev function is not a good solution as it does more work than is needed. Conversely, if we always need to calculate both mean and standard deviation, having two separate functions seems awkward.

5.4.2 A Functional Perspective

Having covered the material on functional programming in the previous section, we should ask ourselves: is there a function we can apply to sum the values rather than creating an explicit loop? Looking at the Python documentation that comes with the system, we discover that there is. Calculating the sum of values in a sequence is such a common operation that an abstraction (in this case a function sum) has been created and put in the standard library:

Reading through the Python library documentation is definitely **A Very Good Idea**.

```
import math

def mean ( x ) :
    return float ( sum ( x ) ) / len ( x )

def stdDev ( x ) :
    return _stdDev ( x , mean ( x ) )

def meanStdDev ( x ) :
    m = mean ( x )
    return ( m , _stdDev ( x , m ) )

def _stdDev ( x , m ) :
    return math.sqrt ( float ( sum ( ( i - m ) ** 2 for i in x ) ) / len ( x ) )
```

Note that we use
the float function to
ensure that we do
float and not integer
divide.

There are a number of things of note here:

- The mean function looks somewhat simpler than before and directly reflects the mathematical definition. It is always good to express a calculation simply and in a way that is directly related to the original requirement.

- We have introduced a *helper function* called _stdDev to express a section of code that is common to both stdDev and meanStdDev. A helper function is one that is internal to the implementation and not intended for use in an application generally. This is a classic use of functions for abstraction to avoid replication of code. We have used a name that begins with an underscore (_) as this is the Python convention for naming a helper function. The reason for making this a helper function rather than an application callable one is that there is a relationship between the data that is the first parameter and the value that is the second parameter that must be assured. If the function was callable from an application, inconsistent values could be provided, and that is definitely not something we want to allow.

- The functions stdDev and meanStdDev have been made much simpler, and code replication avoided, by using a helper function.

- _stdDev not only uses the sum function, it clearly uses a Python feature we haven't seen before. We saw similar expressions used in list comprehensions, but this isn't a list comprehension, it is in fact a *generator expression*. A generator expression is a way of creating a sequence of values using iteration. The expression:

    $(i - m) ** 2$ **for** i **in** x

    says generate the sequence of values calculated by taken each value from the sequence x and evaluating the expression $(i - m) ** 2$, where i is the value of the current item from x. The sum function knows how to work with generator expressions, since they generate sequences and it knows how to deal with sequences.

Some people will say this version of meanStdDev is poor, since it looses the single loop solution and just wraps the nested loop solution. There is some merit to that argument, but, conversely, this version of the function is very clean and simple, and it works for the tests we have run on it. We have the code:

```
def _test ( data , e_mean , e_stdDev ) :
    assert mean ( data ) == e_mean
    assert stdDev ( data ) == e_stdDev
    assert meanStdDev ( data ) == ( e_mean , e_stdDev )

if __name__ == '__main__' :
    _test ( [ 1 , 2 , 3 , 4 ] , 2.5 , 1.11803398874989484820 )
    _test ( [ 1 , 2 , 3 , 4 , 5 ] , 3 , 1.41421356237309504880 )
    _test ( ( 1 , 2 , 3 , 4 ) , 2.5 , 1.11803398874989484820 )
    _test ( ( 1 , 2 , 3 , 4 , 5 ) , 3 , 1.41421356237309504880 )
```

which is not exactly exhaustive testing. We really should have a much fuller test, but we don't have the right technology just yet. We will get to this in Chapter 9.

A quick final note: we test the functions using both list and tuple data. Our functions should work with any and all sequences of values, so we test with a variety to make sure our claims are not empty ones.

5.5 Modularizing Things

5.5.1 Creating Modules

Having created functions for calculating mean and standard deviation, we need a way to avoid repeating these methods in all the programs that use them: we need to be able to share these function across many programs. We know there is a way of doing this because we have used it already. Import statements like:

```
import random
import math
```

clearly indicate that there is a way to collect useful functions into *modules* for reuse. The only question is: how do we package things up?

Well it is fairly simple really, we use files. Here is the mean and standard deviation functions as a module:

Python uses the term *module* for a collection of variables and functions in a single file.

```
'''Functions for calculating mean and standard deviation of a data set.'''
__author__ = 'Russel Winder'
__date__ = '2006-11-12'
__version__ = '1.0'
__copyright__ = 'Copyright (c) 2006 Russel Winder'
__license__ = 'GNU General Public License (GPL)'

import math

def mean ( x ) :
    '''Calculate the mean of the values in the sequence parameter.'''
    return float ( sum ( x ) ) / len ( x )

def stdDev ( x ) :
    '''Calculate the standard deviation of a data set.'''
    return _stdDev ( x , mean ( x ) )

def meanStdDev ( x ) :
    '''Calculate the mean and standard deviation of a data set.'''
    m = mean ( x )
    return ( m , _stdDev ( x , m ) )
```

```
def _stdDev ( x , m ) :
    return math.sqrt ( float ( sum ( ( i - m ) ** 2 for i in x ) ) / len ( x ) )

# A rough and ready test for the module to ensure it is not totally broken.

def _test ( data , e_mean , e_stdDev ) :
    assert mean ( data ) == e_mean
    assert stdDev ( data ) == e_stdDev
    assert meanStdDev ( data ) == ( e_mean , e_stdDev )

if __name__ == '__main__' :
    _test ( [ 1 , 2 , 3 , 4 ] , 2.5 , 1.11803398874989484820 )
    _test ( [ 1 , 2 , 3 , 4 , 5 ] , 3 , 1.41421356237309504880 )
    _test ( ( 1 , 2 , 3 , 4 ) , 2.5 , 1.11803398874989484820 )
    _test ( ( 1 , 2 , 3 , 4 , 5 ) , 3 , 1.41421356237309504880 )
```

A module is just a file that includes the functions (with their documentation strings), and a few variable definitions, along with some documentation strings. In fact, any piece of code in a file can be used as a module: adding the documentation just makes it easier for people to work with the module.

5.5.2 Documenting Modules

There is a program called pydoc which is part of the standard Python system, that generates documentation from a module. So, for example, if we have used the name mean.py for the file of the mean and standard deviation functions module, we can run the command:

```
| > pydoc ./mean.py
```

in the directory that contains the file mean.py, and we get:

```
Help on module mean:

NAME
    mean - Functions for calculating mean and standard deviation of a data set.

FILE
    mean.py

FUNCTIONS
    mean(x)
        Calculate the mean of the values in the sequence parameter.

    meanStdDev(x)
        Calculate the mean and standard deviation of a data set.

    stdDev(x)
        Calculate the standard deviation of a data set.

DATA
    __author__ = 'Russel Winder'
    __copyright__ = 'Copyright (c) 2006 Russel Winder'
    __date__ = '2006-11-12'
    __version__ = '1.0'
```

VERSION
  1.0

DATE
  2006-11-12

AUTHOR
  Russel Winder

Notice how pydoc has used the variables __author__, __date__, and __version__, and made use of them specially. These are *special variables*: they are not used directly in the code, but are used as data for programs like pydoc. Hopefully the names of most special variables – all of which have two underscores (__) at the beginning and end of the name – make it clear what the information provided is.

Of course we have been using a special variable previously: __name__ is a special variable. It is not a variable we set in our code, it is a variable that is set by the Python system that we can use in our code. The Python system stores the name of the module being processed in __name__. If the module is being run from the command line (rather than being imported into another module) then __name__ will be assigned the value '__main__'. So by putting all our script in the block of a:

if __name__ == '__main__' :

statement, we ensure the script code is only executed when it should be.

The **pydoc** command has some useful parameters. If you give a -w option then instead of writing information to the terminal, it generates an HTML file that you can view with any Web browser. So for example we generated and then viewed the documentation for the **mean** module:

You can go even further and use **pydoc** to set up a local Web server that serves all the known documentation as though it were a website.

```
| > pydoc -p 8080
pydoc server ready at http://localhost:8080/
```

and then using a Web browser at the URL http://localhost:8080, we get:

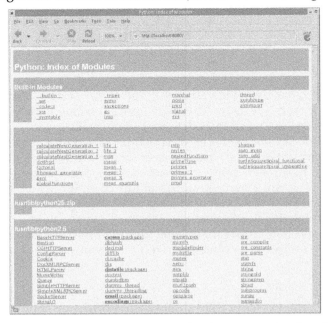

This is a great way of being able to look at all the documentation for all the modules provided as standard with the Python system, as well as all the modules in the directory from which the Web server was started.

5.5.3   Using Modules

Now that we know about modules, our earlier use of the Turtle module becomes clear. The Turtle module is stored somewhere on the computer in a file called turtle.py. The statement **import** turtle is needed to give our programs access to all the functions provided in the Turtle module. Every function in a module is referred to as <module_name>.<name>, so, for example, turtle.forward (100).

The import statement imports all the functions and variables from a module. You can also choose to import only some of the features of a module using a from statement:

```
from <module_name> import <name_list>
```

For example:

from turtle **import** forward, right, left

This means that you can omit the module name when calling the methods. So instead of turtle.forward (100), as we had to say using the import statement, we can use forward (100) – though we can use the module name if we want.

What about using our mean module? Here is a trivial program as an example:

import mean

```
data = [ 10 , 11 , 12 , 13 , 14 ]
print mean.mean ( data )
```

SciPy and NumPy

SciPy (http://www.scipy.org) is a package that provides tools for mathematics, science, and engineering computations. SciPy makes use of NumPy (http://www.numpy.org) which is a package providing a special array type and various linear algebra and Fourier transform functions. If you are doing any mathematics, science, or engineering programs, you should probably think about using SciPy and NumPy.

5.6   Generating Things

In the _stdDev method in the mean module, we used a generator expression. Clearly there is a connection between generator expressions and list comprehensions. In fact, we can think of a list comprehension as being a list created by a generator expression.

The point is that a sequence can either be stored as a data structure, a list or tuple, or it can be created by evaluation of code, a generator expression.

A generator expression is in fact a specific use of a more general feature called a *generator*. A generator is represented in our code by a generator function. A generator function is a little different from a 'normal' function in that it uses a special statement called a yield statement. A generator function is not executed from beginning to end and a value returned as a 'normal' function is. A generator function does a some work and returns a value (using a yield statement, not a return statement), then the next time it is called, starts executing from the statement immediately after the yield statement, i.e. from where it left off. This is very different from a normal function, which would always start again at the beginning.

Let's see an example to introduce the ideas.

5.6.1   An Example: Fibonacci Numbers

In the last chapter (Section 3.7.4, page 81) we created a recursive implementation of a function to generate the sequence of numbers called the Fibonacci Sequence. We didn't create an iterative version then, so it seems time to revisit that example and provide a different implementation.

Being a sequence, it seems that we should be able to create the Fibonacci numbers using a generator expression. Except that it turns out to be quite difficult. A generator expression is a restricted form of generator designed to create a sequence of values from another sequence of values. For generating the Fibonacci numbers, it is easier to use the more general tool – the generator.

Here then is a version of the generator function for generating the Fibonacci numbers coded as a generator:

```
def fibonacciGenerator ( ) :
    previous = 1
    current = 1
    yield current
    while True :
        yield current
        current , previous = current + previous , current
```

This implementation highlights a bug in that the Fibonacci Sequence it generates is different to that of the implementation from Section 3.7.4, (page 81). We will come back to this is Section 9.4.1 (page 287).

The infinite loop (potentially very dangerous) and the tuple assignment are things we have seen before, but what are those yield statements?

The yield statement is for a generator what a return statement is for a function. It says "return this value now to the calling expression and restart here on the next call". yield is very different from **return**. A generator makes a note of which yield statement was last executed and when the generator is called again, it starts executing from the statement following the last-executed yield statement.

Actually, generators are a little bit more intricate than that. When you call the generator function, you don't actually call the generator function per se. Instead, the Python system sees that the function uses a yield statement and instead of calling the function, creates a generator. It is the job of the generator to manage all the calls to the generator function.

So how do we use a generator? Let's show by example:

```
fibonacciNumbers = fibonacciGenerator ( )
for i in range ( 20 ) :
    print fibonacciNumbers.next ( )
```

A generator is a type with methods. The next method must be called on a specific generator. We will follow this up in the next chapter.

The variable fibonacciNumbers is associated with the generator. When we need the next value of the sequence, we call fibonacciNumbers.next ( ) – next is a method understood by generators. This call causes the generator to get the next value from the generator function – the generator function starts executing at the statement after the last yield statement and continues to the next yield statement and returns the value specified.

```
>>> def fibonacciGenerator ( ) :
...     previous = 1
...     current = 1
...     yield current
...     while True :
...         yield current
...         current , previous = current + previous , current
...
>>> fibonacciNumbers = fibonacciGenerator ( )
>>> type ( fibonacciGenerator )
<type 'function'>
>>> type ( fibonacciNumbers )
<type 'generator'>
>>> for i in range ( 5 ) :
...     print fibonacciNumbers.next ( )
...
1
1
2
3
5
>>> for i in range ( 5 ) :
...     print fibonacciNumbers.next ( )
...
8
13
21
34
55
>>> for i in range ( 5 ) :
...     print fibonacciNumbers.next ( )
...
89
144
233
377
610
```

5.6.2 An Example: Prime Numbers

Prime numbers are a great example of the use of generators: any sequence can be created using a generator – even the prime numbers.

All the previous examples of prime number generation have been about creating a function to return a list of the first *n* primes. This is fine if we want a specific number of primes, but what if we don't know how many we will need, we just want to work through them? We can use a generator:

```
def primesGenerator ( ) :                          | > python primes_generator.py
    '''Generate all the prime numbers.'''          2
    yield 2                                        3
    prime = 3                                      5
    primeNumbers = [ prime ]                       7
    yield prime                                    11
    while True :                                   13
        prime += 2                                 17
        for i in primeNumbers :                    19
            if prime % i == 0 :                    23
                break ;                            29
        else :
            primeNumbers += [ prime ]
            yield prime

if __name__ == '__main__' :
    primes = primesGenerator ( )
    for i in range ( 5 ) :
        print primes.next ( )
    for i in range ( 5 ) :
        print primes.next ( )
```

Of course, there is a problem with this implementation: we can only get the next prime, we cannot access any previously calculated primes, even though they are stored in the function. We will address this problem in the next chapter.

5.6.3 Lazy Evaluation

The term *lazy evaluation* is used (particularly in functional programming languages) to describe a technique of delaying evaluation until the result of the evaluation is actually needed. One particular use of this is for describing infinite data structures and, in particular, infinite lists. Clearly we cannot store an infinite list, and in most cases we would never want to. Lazy evaluation means creating only that bit of the infinite list that you actually need for the computation at hand.

Generators are clearly ways of creating potentially infinite lists. However, as we have seen, a generator only creates the sequence, it doesn't do the storing. To create lazily evaluated lists in Python, we need some more infrastructure. The infrastructure we need is that of classes, and that is the topic of the next chapter.

> Chapter Summary
>
> In this chapter we have found that:
>
> - We create two-dimensional list structures using one-dimensional lists – our example was the grid for Conway's Game of Life.
> - The **global** statement is a way of subverting the standard scope rules to create global variables.
> - Nested functions are a mechanism for controlling the scope of functions.
> - Higher-order functions can be used to abstract control flow features.
> - LEGB (local, enclosing, global, built-in)) is the lookup resolution rule. It is the expression of the Python scope rules.
> - Functional programming is an alternative approach to imperative programming.
> - map and filter are the 'standard' higher-order functions of functional programming, though list comprehensions can be used instead – and are more Pythonic according to BDFL.
> - Module are a way to make code reusable.
> - Using generators allows us to generate (potentially infinite) sequences of values.
> - The yield statement is the tool for making generator functions.

Self-Review Questions

Self-review 5.1 Which names are *local*, which are *global* and which are *built-in* in the following code fragment?

```
space_invaders = [ ... ]
player_pos = ( 200 , 25 )
level = 1
max_level = 10

def play ( ) :
    . . .
    while ( level < max_level +1 ) :
        if len ( space_invaders ) == 0 :
            level += 1
            continue
    . . .
```

Self-review 5.2 What is special about a *recursive* function?

Self-review 5.3 What is a *side effect*?

Self-review 5.4 What does the term *referential transparency* mean?

Self-review 5.5 What list of lists does the following list comprehension evaluate to?

```
[ [ '#' for col in range ( 3 ) ] for row in range ( 3 ) ]
```

Self-review 5.6 What is the result of executing the following code?

```
def dp ( l1 , l2 ) :
    def p ( ll1 , ll2 , n ) :
        return ll1[n] * ll2[n]
    r = 0
    for i in range ( len ( l1 )) :
        r += p ( l1 , l2 , i )
    return r

print dp ( [ 1 , 2 , 3 ] , [ 4 , 5 , 6 ] )
```

Self-review 5.7 In Python modules, what is the following code idiom used for?

```
if __name__ == '__main__':
    . . .
```

Self-review 5.8 What is wrong with the following code?

```
from turtle import *
turtle.forward ( 100 )
```

Self-review 5.9 What are the following special variables used for?

1. __author__
2. __date__
3. __copyright__
4. __version__
5. __revision__
6. __license__
7. __credits__

Self-review 5.10 What is the result of executing the following Python code?

```
l = [ i for i in range ( 1 , 100 ) ]
map ( lambda x : x ** 3 , l )
```

Is there a better way of expressing the algorithm in Python?

Self-review 5.11 What is the result of the following Python code?

```
import string
v = [ 'a' , 'e' , 'i' , 'o' , 'u' , 'A' , 'E' , 'I' , 'O' , 'U' ]
filter ( lambda x : x in string.uppercase , v )
```

Self-review 5.12 What is a generator in Python?

Self-review 5.13 What does the Python keyword yield mean?

Self-review 5.14 What does the following Python function do?

```
def geni ( n ) :
    for i in range ( n ) :
        yield i
```

Self-review 5.15 Using the documentation on the Python website, find out what the exception StopIteration is used for.

Programming Exercises

Exercise 5.1 The following Python code represents a Tic-Tac-Toe board as a list of lists:

$$[\, [\, '\#' \, , \, 'o' \, , \, 'x' \,] \, , \, [\, '\#' \, , \, '\#' \, , \, 'o' \,] \, , \, [\, 'x' \, , \, '\#' \, , \, 'o' \,] \,]$$

The # symbols represent blank squares on the board. Write a function print_board that takes a list of lists as an argument and prints out a Tic-Tac-Toe board in the following format:

```
 | o | x
-----------
 |   | o
-----------
x |   | o
```

Exercise 5.2 Convert the following iterative functions into recursive functions:

1.
```
def sum_even ( n ) :
    total = 0
    for i in range ( 2 , n + 1 , 2 ) :
        total += i
    return total
```

Any iterative function can be recoded as a recursive function, and any recursive function can be recoded as an iterative function.

2.
```
def min ( l ) :
    m = 0
    for i in l :
        if i<m : m = i
    return m
```

3.
```
def prod ( l ) :
    product , i = 1 , 0
    while i < len ( l ) :
        product *= l[i]
        i += 1
    return product
```

Hint: You may find it useful to add an extra parameter to the recursive version of min.

Exercise 5.3 Convert the following recursive functions into iterative ones:

1.
```
def sum_odd ( n , total ) :
    if n == 1 : return total
    elif n % 2 == 0 : return sum_odd ( n - 1 , total )
    else : return sum_odd ( n - 2 , total + n )
```

2.
```
def max ( l , n ) :
    if l == [ ] : return n
    elif l[0] > n : return max ( l[1:] , l[0] )
    else : return max ( l[1:] , n )
```

3.
```
def mylen ( l , n ) :
    if l == [] : return n
    else : return mylen ( l[1:] , n +1 )
```

Exercise 5.4 The following code is a module that provides functions for drawing some simple shapes using the Python Turtle module. Copy the code into a file called shape.py and add in:

- Documentation for the module and its functions.
- Special variables such as __date__.
- Some simple testing.

Make sure you use pydoc to generate a webpage containing your documentation.

```
__author__ = 'Sarah Mount'

from turtle import *

def square ( n ) :
    for i in range ( 4 ) :
        forward ( n )
        left ( 90 )

def rectangle ( s1 , s2 ) :
    for i in range ( 2 ) :
        forward ( s1 )
        left ( 90 )
        forward ( s2 )
        left ( 90 )

def pentagon ( s ) :
    for i in range ( 5 ) :
        forward ( s )
        left ( 360 / 5 )
```

Exercise 5.5 Use map and **lambda** to turn a list of integers from 1 to 100 into a list of even numbers from 2 to 200.

Exercise 5.6 Use filter to generate a list of odd numbers from 0 to 100.

Exercise 5.7 Use a list comprehension to generate a list of odd numbers from 0 to 100.

Exercise 5.8 Write a generator function (using the yield keyword) that generates factorial numbers.

Exercise 5.9 Ackermann's Function is defined as:

$$A(m,n) = \begin{cases} n+1 & \text{if } m = 0 \\ A(m-1,1) & \text{if } m > 0 \text{ and } n = 0 \\ A(m-1,A(m,n-1)) & \text{if } m > 0 \text{ and } n > 0 \end{cases}$$

Write a recursive Python function to implement Ackermann's Function. How many recursive calls will be required to evaluate $A(2,3)$?

Exercise 5.10 In Section 4.6.4 (page 135) we introduced palindromes as words or phrases that read the same forwards and backwards, and showed implementations using iteration and negative indexing. For this question we say that 'deed', 'peep' and 'a man, a plan, a canal, panama!' are all palindromes – so we do not make spaces significant. Write a recursive function implementation of isPalindrome to test whether or not a string is a palindrome.

Exercise 5.11 The first five rows of Pascal's Triangle are:

$$
\begin{array}{ccccccccc}
 & & & & 1 & & & & \\
 & & & 1 & & 1 & & & \\
 & & 1 & & 2 & & 1 & & \\
 & 1 & & 3 & & 3 & & 1 & \\
1 & & 4 & & 6 & & 4 & & 1 \\
 & & & & \cdot & \cdot & \cdot & & \\
\end{array}
$$

Each number is generated by adding the two above it. Write a recursive function to generate the first n lines of Pascal's Triangle.

Challenges

Challenge 5.1 Create a module for playing Tic-Tac-Toe.

Hint: You may want to consider the following functions:

1. *print_board () – from the programming exercise above, except that you will want to use a global board variable, rather than a function argument.*

2. *has_won () – check to see whether either player has won. This function should return the string 'o' or 'x' if either the o or x player has won and '#' if neither player has won. A player wins in Tic-Tac-Toe if they have three of their counters in a row, a column or a diagonal.*

3. *place_counter (sq , counter) – place the counter on a particular square of the board. The first argument should be a number between 0 and 8 and the second argument should be either 'o' or 'x'. You should consider the squares on the board to be numbered as in the diagram below.*

   ```
   0 | 1 | 2
   ----------
   3 | 4 | 5
   ----------
   6 | 7 | 8
   ```

   Using a numbering such as this one makes the answer to this challenge simpler!

4. *next_play () – This function should ask the user for the next move they want to play. You should make sure that the user knows whether x or o is currently playing. You can assume that the user will enter an integer value. You should still check that the integer the player has provided is between 0 and 8 inclusive.*

5. *play () – This is the top-level function that tells Python how to play Tic-Tac-Toe. The algorithm for game play is:*

- *If one of the players has won the game, print a message on the screen to congratulate them.*
- *If no-one has won the game, then:*
  - *Use the next_play function to get the current player's next move.*
  - *Play the next move by calling the place_counter function.*
  - *Print the new board.*
  - *Change the current player – either from 'x' to 'o' or from 'o' to 'x'.*

You will also need two global variables, one to store the current state of the board and one to say which player is playing next.

Below is an outline of the module to get you started – make sure you add some documentation and make good use of Python's special variables, like __author__ and __version__.

```python
board = [ [ '#' for col in range ( 3 ) ] for row in range ( 3 ) ]
o_playing = True
def play ( ) :
    # Your code here!
def next_play ( ) :
    # Your code here!
def has_won ( ) :
    # Your code here!
def place_counter ( ) :
    # Your code here!
def print_board ( ) :
    # Your code here!

if __name__ == '__main__':
    play ( )
```

Challenge 5.2 One reason for selecting a recursive version of an algorithm over an iterative one, or vice versa, is running time. There are various ways of assessing whether one algorithm is faster than another. Big O notation is a very important one – we will come to this in Chapter 10. A technique for assessing the speed of programs implementing algorithms is to executing benchmarks. Benchmarks require us to be able to time the execution of a program. Python helps us here, as it provides a module called timeit that can be used to time the execution of Python expressions. Here is an example of the timeit module in use:

```python
>>> import timeit
>>>
>>> def is_prime ( n ) :
...     return not bool ( filter ( lambda x: n%x == 0, range ( 2 , n ) ) )
...
>>> def primes ( n ) :
...     return filter ( is_prime , range ( 2 , n ) )
...
>>> t = timeit.Timer ( 'primes ( 100 )' , 'from __main__ import primes' )
```

```
>>> print t.timeit ( 500 )
1.47258400917
>>>
```

Here, we have written some code to time one of our prime number generators, and found out how long it has taken Python to execute the code 500 times. We did this by creating an object called timeit.Timer that took a call to our primes function as its first argument. The second argument, 'from __main__ import primes' tells the timeit module where it can find the primes function – in this case in the __main__ namespace.

The argument to the timeit method, 500, means 'execute the code 500 times'. Python code generally executes very quickly, so timing a very short piece of code that only runs once can be inaccurate. So, instead, we can ask timeit to time the code over several hundred or thousand runs, which will give us more accurate information. In the example above, the code took 1.47258400917 s to run.

For this challenge, test the time of execution of all the prime number generators we have presented in this book, timing them using the timeit module, to determine which is the fastest.

Challenge 5.3 Chess is played on an 8×8 board. A *queen* may attack any piece on the same row, column or diagonal as herself.

The Eight Queens Problem involves placing eight queens on a chess board in such a way that no queen is attacking any other – so, there must be at most one queen on any row, column or diagonal.

There are 92 solutions to the Eight Queens Problem and the challenge is to write a program that finds all of them.

Hint: Think about how to represent the board. A list of lists of Booleans might be a sensible choice, but are there other options? Whatever you use, you will probably want to make sure that you can print chess boards in a human-readable format, such as this:

```
Q X X X X X X X
X X Q X X X X X
X X X X X Q X X
X Q X X X X X X
X X X X X X X Q
X X X Q X X X X
X X X X X X Q X
X X X X Q X X X
```

The Eight Queens Problem is the subject of the classic paper, *Program Development by Stepwise Refinement* by Nicklaus Wirth. You can find his paper at the ACM 'classics' website: http://www.acm.org/classics/dec95/

Classy Objects

6

Learning Outcomes

At the end of this chapter you will be able to:

- Create classes and use objects to create applications.

- Define the term *abstract data type* and write classes to implement new abstract data types.

- Overload built-in functions using operator overloading methods.

- Implement new exception types.

A couple of dangling problems from earlier chapters provide the introduction to this chapter. In Chapter 4 we introduced state and finite state machines. In particular, in Section 4.5.7 (page 127) we created a program to sequence a traffic light. We noted then that lights never appear individually but always in synchronized groups. The program as we left it was not really a good starting point for building a simulation – we didn't quite have the right abstractions. Functions and modules are very helpful but we are an abstraction short: we need to be able to combine the state of a light and functions operating on that state into a single value to represent the light. By using an *object* to represent a traffic light, we can use the traffic light just like any other value in our programs. In particular, we can pass it around as a function parameter and we can clone it. Moreover, we can easily have many traffic lights, all with similar and/or related behaviors.

At the end of the last chapter we stated that we wanted to be able to create a lazily evaluated list of prime numbers so that the list could be used like any other list. The problem with the list-based implementations we have created so far is that they provide a fixed list of primes, so we had to know exactly how many, or up to which value of, prime number we want. The problem with the generator-based implementation is that it only delivers a sequence of values and, although it stores a list of primes, it doesn't provide access to that list. What we want to be able to do is access the list that is inside the generator function. We could use a **global** statement to make the list a global item, but that will not enable the list we use to expand itself when needed. A list is a list, it is a data structure we can do things to, but it cannot initiate actions. Also, of course, having a global list leaves it open to being incorrectly amended and that may lead to an inconsistent state – something that must be considered anathema. So whilst modules are an excellent tool for reuse, as seen so far, they only deal with functions and global data. We need a new abstraction that allows a list and a generator to work in symbiosis to create a lazily evaluated list of prime numbers.

Both these 'problems' are leading to the need for an abstraction that allows us to bind data values (state) and functions into a single abstraction: we need *objects*, and the associated concept of *class*.

6.1 Objects Are Good

To date we have used variables and functions, and can create modules. We can almost certainly create a traffic light simulation using global variables to hold the states of the lights, and functions that take a light as a parameter to manipulate the states as needed. Indeed this would be the way of doing things in many programming languages (C, Ada, for example). However, this is not the Pythonic Way. Like languages such as C++, and Java, Python supports *object-oriented programming*, and using this approach to programming is generally considered to be the right way of proceeding when creating large programs.

Of course, this begs the questions, "What is object-oriented programming?", and indeed, "What is an object?". In fact, we have been dealing with objects indirectly already, though we haven't discussed them explicitly until now. For example, when we introduced generators at the end of the last chapter (Section 5.6, page 177), we used expressions like:

In computing, *object* is a word with a definite meaning.

```
primes.next ()
```

but carefully (!) avoided explaining things. primes is a variable, not a module, so how can we call the next method? The answer is that the variable is associated with an object and objects have *methods*: a generator is an object with a method next that can be called. Methods are the entry points that are used to ask an object to do something: methods are functions within an object.

Functions that are parts of objects are called *methods*.

When we were creating the Game of Life program in the previous chapter, we used the module random and, in particular, two of the functions defined in that module: random.seed and random.random. Although we used the functions as functions, internally they use objects. Indeed, we can use random number generator objects directly:

```
>>> import random
>>> r = random.Random ()
>>> r.random ()
0.35504954450565551
>>> r.random ()
0.76348784528130653
>>> r.random ()
0.46062079064093542
>>>
```

In this statement sequence, we create a variable r that is associated with an object created by calling the function random.Random. We then call the random method on the object three times, each call giving us a new float in the range [0.0, 1.0).

The mathematical notation [0.0, 1.0) describes the range from and including 0.0 up to but not including 1.0.

So why is this interesting? Why would we want to do this? In the case of generating random numbers, there are different sorts of random number generator. Also it means we can have multiple independent sources of random numbers if we can create multiple objects.

The idea of objects is basically straightforward: an object collects together some state and some functions so that the whole can be treated as a single entity. In the previous chapter we used generators: a generator is an object that maintains the state of the generation of the sequence of values and provides methods (in particular next) that allow use of the generator. Random number creation objects have state, allowing them to compute new random numbers and have a method random that creates and returns the next number. In both cases, the inner workings of the object are hidden. We don't really need to know how the object works (unless we are programming it), only that it does, and how to use it.

> An object *is a way of abstracting state and functions into a single identifiable entity.*

Object-oriented programming is a style of programming in which a collection of objects is created and the objects are allowed to communicate with each other, where communication is achieved using method calls. This is quite a different way of working than the purely function-oriented approach we have worked with so far. The object-oriented approach has brought with it a lot of new jargon. The most obvious is that a function that is part of an object is called a *method*, highlighting the fact that it is not just a function, it is a function associated with a specific object.

So, in the example above r has the type random.Random. A random.Random is a random number generator that holds data, some of which is Python code to manipulate other data. r.random ( ) is a call to a method that manipulates state held within the object associated with r and returns a value.

Strings, lists, tuples and dictionaries are all objects. In fact we have already seen methods used on some of these:

- Page 114 the append method of list.

- Page 136 the lower method of string.

- Page 139 the isdigit method of string.

6.2 Objects Have Class

Class is another word that has been given a special meaning in computing. A class is a description of the state and methods comprising an object. An object is an *instance* of a class.

In the example above the module random has a class Random. An instance of the class is created by calling random.Random ( ) – the name of the class is used as a function that we call to create an instance of that class. We associate this newly created instance with the variable r by assignment. So r is associated with an object of type random.Random that is an *instance* of the class random.Random: when we created the object (r = random.Random ( )) we *instantiated* random.Random. It is important to learn the jargon: when you read books or documentation you need to understand the terms and the way they are used. Perhaps more importantly, when you talk to other programmers, you need to be able to communicate with them, and as a programmer you are expected to know the jargon. The more we use the jargon (correctly, of course!), the more comprehensible it becomes – just like learning any language.

People often talk about *instantiating* a class to create an object.

> *Object-oriented Programming*
>
> Object-oriented programming (OOP) was invented in the 1960s with the Simula programming language. It did not become really popular until the 1990s with the rise of Smalltalk, C++, and Java. Most modern languages have some sort of facility for using the key features of OOP – classes, objects and inheritance, and Python is no exception. No matter what sort of programming you go on to do, it is almost certain that you will need objects, classes and object-oriented programming.

6.3 An Example: Craps Dice

6.3.1 Introduction

Let's look at creating a program to play craps. This will involve creating an abstraction to represent a die since craps is a game played using two six-sided dice.

> *Craps, the Game*
>
> Craps is played with two six-sided dice. The dice are thrown by a player and, if the total is 7 or 11, the player wins. If the total is 2, 3, or 12, the player loses. If the total is 4, 5, 6, 8, 9, or 10 then the player makes a series of throws until either the same number is thrown again or a 7 is rolled. If the player rolls the same number again the player wins; if they roll a 7, the player loses.

Craps only actually gets interesting when you realize that it is a game on which bets are made. It is a gambling game. This means the player generally loses, and the house (the people who run the game) generally wins. However, some people seems to derive fun from losing money... which makes it a business opportunity!

To start, we look just at the generation of the dice rolls and the winning or losing: we are going to ignore all the issues of betting for now.

6.3.2 First Roll: Just Do It

The mathematical notation [1, 6] describes the range from and including 1 up to and including 6.

Clearly, we need to be able to roll six-sided dice in the program. This is really a question of generating random integers in the range [1, 6]. The random module has a function that does just what we need, randint:

```
>>> import random
>>> print random.randint ( 1 , 6 )
1
>>> print random.randint ( 1 , 6 )
4
>>> print random.randint ( 1 , 6 )
6
>>> print random.randint ( 1 , 6 )
3
>>>
```

We can use this to generate the following program that plays one turn:

```
import random

def roll ( ) :
    '''Roll a 6-sided die and return the result.'''
    return random.randint ( 1 , 6 )
```

```
if __name__ == '__main__' :
    random.seed ()
    value = roll () + roll ()
    print value
    if value == 7 or value == 11 : print "Win"
    elif value == 2 or value == 3 or value == 12 : print "Lose"
    else :
        while True :
            throw = roll () + roll ()
            print throw
            if throw == 7 : print "Lose" ; break
            if throw == value : print "Win" ; break
```

This program does the job of rolling the dice so, in a sense, the problem is solved. However...

6.3.3 Second Roll: Objectify

Although the program in the previous subsection does the job, it isn't an example of doing things in an object-oriented way. So, ignoring the question "Why bother, we already have a working system?" let's investigate the Object-Oriented Way.

First we create a class that represents a die:

```
class Die :
    '''A class representing a die.'''

    def __init__ ( self ) :
        '''Initialize the die with 1 showing.'''
        self.generator = random.Random ()
        self.current = 1

    def roll ( self ) :
        '''Roll the die and return the new value showing.'''
        self.current = self.generator.randint ( 1 , 6 )
        return self.current
```

This clearly needs some explanation. We have created a new class, Die, that has two methods (__init__ and roll) and two variables that make up the state of the die (self.generator and self.current). We have given the class a documentation string and each of the functions a documentation string. Documenting things is always good; running pydoc on this file results the output shown in Figure 6.1.

> Modules can contain class definitions as well as functions and variables.

Each *instance method* (a method defined as part of a class) in a class has at least one parameter. In this case the two methods (__init__ and roll) have only one parameter. The first parameter of any instance method is a reference to the object being worked with. Conventionally, this first parameter is named self to highlight its role, but as it is just a variable, any legal variable name is acceptable. Having said this, it is always good to follow convention, as it makes reading the code easier.

> Method names that start and finish with two underscores indicate that the methods are special to the Python system.

__init__ is a special method called the *constructor*. It is the method called when a new instance is created. The statement a = Die () causes the Python system to create a new object and then call Die.__init__ to do the initialization of the newly created object.

This constructor has two statements, both of which are assignments to *instance variables* (i.e. variables that comprise the state of an object). So an object instantiated from class Die has a state comprising two variables, one (self.generator) a reference to a random.Random object and one (self.current) a reference to an integer value. The statements of the constructor create and initialize the state of the object. Initializing the state is very important, as it provides certainty and safety – a strong element of defensive programming!

roll is an instance method, so it has the mandatory first parameter (self) that refers to the object being manipulated. As with any method, its role is to offer some sort of service to code using instances of the class. roll's purpose is to change the current value of the die, and return the new value. This service models the action of rolling a die and observing the value on the top face.

So, an object combines state and computation: an object has a current state and that state can be evolved by the action of the methods called. We can visualize the state of an object diagrammatically. An object is a container, in which the variables are references to other objects:

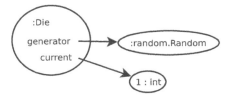

In object-oriented programming an instance of an object can be used to represent something in the world. In this case an instance of Die represents a six-sided die with a particular side uppermost, showing the current value. This idea of an object representing something in the world is actually at the heart of the object-oriented way of thinking about programs. The object-oriented way is to create a collection of objects that send messages to each other (by calling methods) and by doing so alter the state of the system. Contrast this with the functional programming way of thinking which emphasizes the evolution of data by the application of functions, and the use of higher-order functions.

Figure 6.1

The output from running pydoc on the file craps_2.py which is the file name of the file in which the module is stored.

```
Help on module craps_2:

NAME
    craps_2

FILE
    craps_2.py

CLASSES
    Die

    class Die
     |  A class representing a die.
     |
     |  Methods defined here:
     |
     |  __init__(self)
     |      Initialize the die with 1 showing.
     |
     |  roll(self)
     |      Roll the die and return the new value showing.
```

During the 1990s the imperative, object-oriented approach beat the declarative, functional approach in the war of ideas about how to build large systems. Rightly or wrongly, there is now a generally held belief that the object-oriented way is the right way of building large systems – software development doctrine is that the object-orientation is the correct approach. It is noticeable though that there is an increasing move towards more and more declarative expression in the use of all programming languages. In effect there is an acceptance that the functional approach has great relevance even within object-oriented programming. So the current dogma is: use classes and objects to provide structure to programs and use functional programming techniques whenever possible within the methods of classes.

Back to the example. We have a class to represent a die: how can we use it to create our craps program? In fact the solution is not very different from what we had before:

```python
if __name__ == '__main__' :
    a = Die ()
    b = Die ()
    value = a.roll () + b.roll ()
    print value
    if value == 7 or value == 11 : print "Win"
    elif value == 2 or value == 3 or value == 12 : print "Lose"
    else :
        while True :
            throw = a.roll () + b.roll ()
            print throw
            if throw == 7 : print "Lose" ; break
            if throw == value : print "Win" ; break
```

Basically we have just changed from using function calls to creating a couple of objects and calling methods on them. So we seem to have created complexity (using a class instead of a function) for no real gain. At this stage of the development of this program, the benefits of using the object-oriented approach have not become apparent; as we extend the program, they will.

Looking at the class definition and the main code block, there appears to be an inconsistency. In the class we define the method roll as:

```python
def roll ( self ) :
```

and yet in the calling code we call it as:

```python
a.roll ()
```

Clearly methods are very special. Instance methods must have a first parameter, and yet when they are called they can have no parameter. But they do have to be called for a particular object, so there is that as a possible parameter. The Python system converts a call of the form:

$$<variable>.<method>(\{<parameter>\}*)$$

into execution of the method:

$$<method>(self,\{<parameter>\}*)$$

of the class of the object that the variable is associated with. Since we call a.roll with no parameters, the method Die.roll is called with self associated with the same object with which a is associated. self is a reference to the object that the method roll is called on – in this case, the same object that is referred to by a.

The { }* in these syntax specifications denote that the material within the braces can appear zero or more times.

6.3.4   Third Roll: Re-Present

Let's change the way in which output is displayed. Instead of printing the sum of the values of the dice, let's have a print out of the value of each die, but not as a number, as the dots representation of a six-sided die. A relatively small change to the program gives us the desired behavior:

```
import random

class Die :
    '''A class representing a die.'''

    representations = [
        '***\n***\n***\n' , # Have to populate position 0 but it's never used.
        ' \n * \n \n' ,
        ' * \n \n * \n' ,
        ' * \n * \n * \n' ,
        '* *\n \n* *\n' ,
        '* *\n * \n* *\n',
        '* *\n* *\n* *\n'
        ]

    def __init__ ( self ) :
        '''Initialize the die with 1 showing.'''
        self.generator = random.Random ( )
        self.current = 1

    def __str__ ( self ) :
        '''Create a string representation of the die face showing.'''
        return Die.representations[self.current]

    def roll ( self ) :
        '''Roll the die and return the new value showing.'''
        self.current = self.generator.randint ( 1 , 6 )
        return self.current

if __name__ == '__main__' :
    a = Die ( )
    b = Die ( )
    value = a.roll ( ) + b.roll ( )
    print a , '\n' , b , '\n' , value
    if value == 7 or value == 11 : print "Win"
    elif value == 2 or value == 3 or value == 12 : print "Lose"
    else :
        while True :
            throw = a.roll ( ) + b.roll ( )
            print '------'
            print a , '\n' , b , '\n' , throw
            if throw == 7 : print "Lose" ; break
            if throw == value : print "Win" ; break
```

There are a couple of new features here: we have a variable representation at the same level as the method definitions, and we have a method called __str__.

Because the variable representation is defined in the class rather than being created in the constructor, it is a *class variable* rather than an instance variable. Instance variables comprise the state that is unique to each object and we always have to refer to them using self, so for example self.generator, self.current. Class variables are shared by all the instances of the class. No matter how many objects there are of a given class, there is only one value associated with a class variable and it is shared by all instances of the class. In this case, no matter how many instances of Die there are, there is only one Die.representations variable that is shared by them all. The upshot of this is that all instances of Die have the same presentation. So a and b have their own instances of self.generator and self.current, but they share a single Die.representation.

The __str__ method is a special method (the two underscores at beginning and end of the name indicate this). This method is called automatically by the Python system when a request to print the value of an object is made. So the sequence:

```
a = Die ()
print a
```

causes the Python system to call Die.__str__ for the object a to create a string representation of the object that can be printed out.

> If you use self.representation instead of Die.representation in your code, it will execute the same. However, the convention is always to use the class name for accessing class variables.

When this new version of the code is executed, we get something like:

```
|> python craps_3.py
* *
 *
* *

* *

* *

9
------
 *
 *
 *

* *
* *
* *

9
Win
|>
```

> When you execute this code you will get a different output, since the result is supposed to be random.

What's so important about this? The critical point is that the code for handling the string representation of the die is in the Die class. The code that makes use of a Die object doesn't have to worry about how to create the representation for printing. If we had not been using classes we would have had to write a function to create the string representation of the dice values, and this would directly impact our main code. By separating the issues into main algorithm issues and representation issues, we have neatly partitioned the problem. This is *separation of concerns*, which is one of the cornerstones of programming.

6.3.5 Stringing Along

It is perhaps worth looking at another example of the use of __str__. Say, we were going to write a program that had to deal with information about people. We might perhaps, start with the class:

```
class Person :
    def __init__ ( self , name ) :
        self.name = name
    def __str__ ( self ) :
        return 'My name is: ' + self.name
```

The constructor requires a parameter that sets the name of the person represented by the new instance. The name is stored as part of the state of the object. Whenever Python needs to create a string representation of the object, for a print statement for example, then the __str__ method is called automatically behind the scenes by the Python system. So the sequence:

```
person = Person ( 'Russel' )
print person
person = Person ( 'Sarah' )
print person
person = Person ( 'James' )
print person
```

when executed, results in:

```
|> python person.py
My name is: Russel
My name is: Sarah
My name is: James
|>
```

6.4 An Example: Prime Numbers

We must now be in a position to implement a lazily evaluated list of prime numbers. We said we needed a way of coordinating state and methods in order to implement this, and this is what classes give us.

6.4.1 What is the Problem?

Before wading into code though, let's review what it is we actually want. The list of prime numbers is an infinite list. Clearly we cannot create all of it since no computer is big enough to deal with the infinite. This is why we want lazy evaluation; we only want to generate that part of the whole list that we actually need, and need here is determined by demand – we create the list as we need it.

So we are creating a class, instances of which need to behave like lists – although we should say sequence type here. This implies that we need to be able to ask for the nth value, i.e. we need to ensure that we can index into the sequence. However we do not want to allow assignment of items in the sequence. So we are creating a self-generating, lazily evaluated, read-only sequence.

What other ways of accessing the sequence do we want to offer? Well, perhaps the following:

The largest prime smaller than a given number.
The smallest prime larger than a given number.

6.4.2 Priming the Pump

Now we have some requirements we should start to think about implementation. Clearly we are going to need a list instance variable to store the primes we have calculated to date. Also, we know that we can use a generator to act as a mechanism for calculating the values to populate the list as we need them. So we can imagine what the constructor and generator method might be:

```
def __init__ ( self ) :
    self.data = [ ]
    self.primes = self.__generator ( )

def __generator ( self ) :
    prime = 2
    self.data += [ prime ]
    yield prime
    prime += 1
    self.data += [ prime ]
    yield prime
    while True :
        prime += 2
        for i in self.data :
            if prime % i == 0 : break ;
        else :
            self.data += [ prime ]
            yield prime
```

The constructor (__init__) creates an instance variable (self.data) to hold the list of evaluated primes, and an instance variable (self.primes) associated with the generator object created by calling the generator function – a method in this case. We have called the generator method __generator, i.e. with leading double underscore, to indicate that this is not a method that code using the class will use directly – it is a method that is private to the class. Methods named in this way will not be documented, i.e. they will not appear in the output of the pydoc command – people won't try and use what they do not know about!

The body of __generator is just a minor variation on the code from Section 5.6.2 (page 179) so there are no new things there.

We can implement the methods for finding the prime smaller or bigger than a given value quite easily now:

```
def getLargestPrimeLessThan ( self , value ) :
    i = 0 ;
    while True :
        if i == len ( self.data ) : self.primes.next ( )
        if self.data[i] >= value : return self.data[i - 1]
        i += 1

def getSmallestPrimeGreaterThan ( self , value ) :
    i = 0 ;
    while True :
        if i == len ( self.data ) : self.primes.next ( )
        if self.data[i] >= value : return self.data[i]
        i += 1
```

We will address the fact that these look almost identical in the next subsection.

The algorithm used here is to search up the list of known primes until we find the value we are looking for. Of course, we have to ensure the section of the list we want actually exists. If it doesn't, we must create it. Here is the evaluation happening as needed – if we need to test the value and it isn't there, then we need it, so we create it by calling on the generator to deliver the next prime number.

So all that remains is to provide a means of allowing indexing into the sequence, i.e. we need to support:

```
a = PrimeList ( )
print a[20]
```

to give us the twenty-first prime number. Implementing indexing requires us to use another method that is special to the Python system. Just as __init__ (constructor) is special to Python, the __getitem__ method is special: it is the method that the Python system uses to deal with indexing. So the expression a[20] results in the Python system finding and calling __getitem__ (self , index) with self referring to the same object as a and index associated with the value 20. It is the responsibility of the __getitem__ method to deliver the correct value from the sequence. Here is our first version of this method for our primes list:

```
def __getitem__ ( self , index ) :
    if not ( 0 <= index < len ( self.data ) ) :
        for i in range ( index - len ( self.data ) + 1 ) :
            self.primes.next ( )
    return self.data[index]
```

6.4.3 The Prime Directive

We noted in the previous subsection that the functions getLargestPrimeLessThan and getSmallestPrimeGreaterThan are almost identical, and that we need to do something about this. The prime directive in programming is to avoid any and all unnecessary duplication of code and to use all abstraction tools available (functions, classes and modules in Python) to remove duplication when it occurs. Clearly we have to investigate whether the duplication in these two functions is necessary, and, if it is not, find some mechanism that deals with the commonality whilst allowing the necessary different behavior.

The observation that moves things forward is that both methods have in common that they ensure the existence of the list of primes up to and one beyond the value that is the parameter. The difference between them is that one method returns the last prime in the search and the other the one before it.

We can use this observation to rewrite the methods as:

We create a private method by using two leading underscores and no training underscores.

```
def __getSmallestPrimeGreaterThan ( self , value ) :
    '''Ensure that the list has all the primes up to and including the first prime larger
    than the value and return the index.'''
    i = 0 ;
    while True :
        if i == len ( self.data ) : self.primes.next ( )
        if self.data[i] >= value : return i
        i += 1

def getLargestPrimeLessThan ( self , value ) :
    return self.data[self.__getSmallestPrimeGreaterThan ( value ) - 1]

def getSmallestPrimeGreaterThan ( self , value ) :
    return self.data[self.__getSmallestPrimeGreaterThan ( value )]
```

We have created a private method to do the search and ensure the existence of the primes in the list, but instead of returning a prime value, it returns the index of the point at which the search ended. This is the index we need for getSmallestPrimeLess Than and one greater than the index we need for getLargestPrimeSmallerThan. So we just need to use the value returned by __getSmallestPrimeGreaterThan to index into self.data appropriately. We have now decreased the code duplication to something much more acceptable.

6.4.4   The Full Module With Some Tests

Now we have a first draft of a module that provides a class that implements the read-only, lazily evaluated sequence of prime numbers:

```
'''
A class implementing a lazily-evaluated sequence of prime numbers.
'''

__author__ = 'Russel Winder'
__date__ = '2006-11-16'
__version__ = '1.1'
__copyright__ = 'Copyright (c) 2006 Russel Winder'


class PrimeList :

    def __init__ ( self ) :
        self.data = [ ]
        self.primes = self.__generator ( )

    def __generator ( self ) :
        '''Generator method that creates a generator for the infinite list of prime numbers.'''
        prime = 2
        self.data += [ prime ]
        yield prime
        prime += 1
        self.data += [ prime ]
        yield prime
        while True :
            prime += 2
            for i in self.data :
                if prime % i == 0 : break ;
            else :
                self.data += [ prime ]
                yield prime

    def __getitem__ ( self , index ) :
        '''Method implementing indexing so that the instance of this type can be indexed
        like any sequence.'''
        if not ( 0 <= index < len ( self.data ) ) :
            for i in range ( index - len ( self.data ) + 1 ) :
                self.primes.next ( )
        return self.data[index]

    def __getSmallestPrimeGreaterThan ( self , value ) :
        '''Ensure that the list has all the primes up to and including the first prime larger
        than the value and return the index.'''
        i = 0 ;
        while True :
            if i == len ( self.data ) : self.primes.next ( )
            if self.data[i] >= value : return i
            i += 1
```

```
        def getLargestPrimeLessThan ( self , value ) :
            return self.data[self.__getSmallestPrimeGreaterThan ( value ) - 1]

        def getSmallestPrimeGreaterThan ( self , value ) :
            return self.data[self.__getSmallestPrimeGreaterThan ( value )]

if __name__ == '__main__' :
    primes = PrimeList ()
    list = [ ]
    for i in range ( 10 ) : list += [ primes[i] ]
    assert list == [ 2 , 3 , 5 , 7 , 11 , 13 , 17 , 19 , 23 , 29 ]
    assert primes.getLargestPrimeLessThan ( 9 ) == 7
    assert primes.getLargestPrimeLessThan ( 29 ) == 23
    assert primes.getLargestPrimeLessThan ( 50 ) == 47
    assert primes[30] == 127
    assert primes.getSmallestPrimeGreaterThan ( 20 ) == 23
    assert primes.getSmallestPrimeGreaterThan ( 44 ) == 47

# Problem:
#
# primes.getLargestPrimeLessThan ( 2 ) fails if the primes list is not empty
# due to negative indexing issues.
```

We have put some tests in the module so we can ensure that it isn't totally broken. This isn't a complete test, but we will come to that in Chapter 9.

You probably spotted the comment at the end of the file: we have identified a problem with this implementation and have written a comment about it as a reminder to do something about it. This problem really must be addressed and a new version of the module created. However, for the purposes of this chapter, we have a 'final result' for this problem.

6.5 An Example: Traffic Lights

6.5.1 A Reusable Abstraction

In Section 4.5.7 (page 127) we implemented a traffic light using a tuple of tuples to store the state space information. The problem with that implementation (and all the previous ones) is that it is not a good basis for building a traffic light system. This is because the previous programs are complete programs rather than abstractions that enable us to build complex systems. So the obvious next step is to create the necessary abstractions, and that means classes.

Here is an initial version of a class to represent a traffic light:

```
import time

class TrafficLight :
    '''A standard three-light traffic light.'''

    states = ( 'Red' , 'Green' , 'Amber' )

    def __init__ ( self , timings ) :
        if len ( timings ) != len ( self.states ) :
            raise ValueError , "Incorrect number of timing values."
        self.timings = timings
        self.current = 0
```

```
    def sequence ( self ) :
        while True :
            print self.states[self.current]
            time.sleep ( self.timings[self.current] )
            self.current = ( self.current + 1 ) % len ( self.states )

if __name__ == '__main__' :
    light = TrafficLight ( ( 10 , 10 , 5 ) )
    light.sequence ( )
```

The abstraction here is a three-color traffic light that follows the sequence 'Red', 'Green', 'Amber' with the time that the light spends in each state set by a parameter to the constructor. We have used a tuple, but we could also use a list: the class only needs the object associated with timings in the constructor to be a sequence – i.e. it needs to find its length and be able to index it. Whether to use a tuple or a list is really a matter of whether a mutable or immutable data structure is a better tool for implementing the program under development. In general, immutable is safer, so as part of our 'defensive programming' approach we take the safer approach until we need to do something different.

6.5.2 At the Crossroads

We now have a reusable abstraction: what can we do with it? One obvious application is to control the lights at a crossroads. Let's assume we have a north–south road crossing an east–west road and that we need lights to control the crossing. We could do something very simple and just sequence things so that first one road, then the other road, is on green.

But how can we have one light sequence then a different light sequence with the traffic light class we have? The problem is that the loop controlling behavior is currently in the sequence method: we need to change the code so that we can have external synchronization. We have to put the coordination in our main block and make the sequencing method just do a single timed sequence from 'Red' to 'Red':

```
import time

class TrafficLight :
    '''A standard three-light traffic light.'''

    states = ( 'Red' , 'Green' , 'Amber' )

    def __init__ ( self , identifier , timings ) :
        if len ( timings ) != len ( self.states ) :
            raise ValueError , "Incorrect number of timing values."
        self.identifier = identifier
        self.timings = timings
        self.current = 0
        print self.identifier + ' initial state: ' + self.states[self.current]

    def sequence ( self ) :
        for i in range ( len ( self.timings ) ) :
            print self.identifier + ': ' + self.states[self.current]
            time.sleep ( self.timings[self.current] )
            self.current = ( self.current + 1 ) % len ( self.states )
        print self.identifier + ': ' + self.states[self.current]
```

```
if __name__ == '__main__' :
    eastWestLight = TrafficLight ( 'East--West' , ( 5 , 5 , 2 ) )
    northSouthLight = TrafficLight ( 'North--South' , ( 5 , 5 , 2 ) )
    while True :
        eastWestLight.sequence ()
        northSouthLight.sequence ()
```

The TrafficLight constructor sets the initial state as before (assumed to be 'Red' to avoid accidents), but we have added a way of identifying the particular light. The sequence method has been changed so that it only performs a 'Red' to 'Red' sequence. There now has to be an external agent that controls sequencing, and that is our main program.

Of course, this example is a bit boring just doing text output. To give it life, we need some graphics. Unfortunately, we need a few more concepts before we can wade in, so we leave this for now and return to it in the next chapter (Section 7.9.3).

6.6 Abstract Data Types (ADTs)

6.6.1 Brief Introduction to ADTs

An *abstract data type* (ADT) is a type with values where the internal structure of the values are unknown and unknowable. The point is that because the internal structure is unknown and unknowable, it can be changed without there being any effect on the programs that use the type.

> If you think the idea of an ADT is very like that of a class, then you are thinking along exactly the right lines!

Say we were trying to create the concept of a queue as might be needed in modeling and simulation work. A queue is a 'thing' to which items can be added at one end and taken from the other.

> *Queues and Queuing*
>
> Queuing is a well-known human activity: we queue to buy concert tickets, we queue to get on airplanes, we queue up a list of tracks to play on music players. We even queue when buying from Web-based shopping sites: we select our purchases and the Web application queues them for credit card validation, for parcel packing and sending, and finally to get delivered.
>
> Queues have structure: you join at the end of the queue, and leave from the start of the queue; you cannot join the queue anywhere except the end (well not without a big fight erupting); and you cannot leave from the middle of the queue (well you can but not with the same effect as leaving from the start of the queue).
>
> Queues and queuing are very important in all our lives. In fact, queuing is so important in the human world, there is even a mathematics for it: Queuing Theory. It is not just a thing for 'maths geeks', Queuing Theory is used in the Internet to route packets as efficiently as possible.

The concept of a queue is an abstract one: there are instances of queues, but there is no 'the queue'; a queue is a type. The important thing about a queue is that it is a container in which the order of retrieval of items is the same as the order of their insertion. Many people like to think of a queue as a first-in–first-out list (FIFO, or sometimes last-in–last-out, LILO). Of course, a queue is a FIFO container, but it is not a list. We may use a list to implement a queue but a queue is not a list.

Let's develop our ideas about the queue type. We can give names to the operations: 'add' inserts a value at the end of the queue, and 'remove' extracts a value from the beginning of a queue. We can say various things about these operations.

We cannot remove from an empty queue. We can always add to a queue. If we add an item to an empty queue and immediately retrieve an element from the queue, then we get the item we just added. We can even express these ideas in a quasi-mathematical way:

```
Type Queue
Operations
    create : → Queue
    add : item × Queue → Queue
    remove : Queue → item × Queue
Axioms
    remove ( add ( i , create ) ) == i
```

In the days before object-orientation, ADTs were constructed using data structures and functions. We don't have to do this in Python, of course, but just to show what we are talking about, we could write:

```python
def create ( ) : return [ ]

def add ( queue , item ) :
    queue += [ item ]

def remove ( queue ) :
    item = queue[0]
    del queue[0]
    return item
```

which we could test with code such as:

```python
q = create ( )
add ( q , 1 )
assert remove ( q ) == 1
add ( q , 3 )
add ( q , 'c' )
assert remove ( q ) == 3
assert remove ( q ) == 'c'
```

People still use this way of realizing ADTs in languages that do not support object-orientation, for example C. Python is, of course, a high-level object-oriented language so...

6.6.2   Classes and ADTs

Being able to realize abstract data types easily was one of the driving forces behind the idea of a class in object-oriented programming. A class allows us to specify the methods of an ADT, and it allows for the internal structure of the values of the type to be hidden from code using the type. So for example, we can write the queue type as a class:

```python
class Queue :

    def __init__ ( self ) :
        self.data = [ ]

    def add ( self , item ) :
        self.data += [ item ]

    def remove ( self ) :
        item = self.data[0]
        del self.data[0]
        return item
```

which we can use as in this code:

```
q = Queue ( )
q.add ( 1 )
assert q.remove ( ) == 1
q.add ( 3 )
q.add ( 'c' )
assert q.remove ( ) == 3
assert q.remove ( ) == 'c'
```

If you are saying to yourself "So what, what's the real difference between these two queue implementations?" then that is fine. In a sense that is a major part of the point. There are many different ways of implementing ADTs. It is the ADTs that are the important design tools: how they are realized in a given language is just (!) a programming issue.

6.6.3   Overloading Operators

As you may have noticed, Python allows operators to be applied to many different types. For example, '+' can be applied between integer, floats, characters, lists, and tuples. So there is a version of '+' that works with integers and a version that works with floats, etc.:

```
>>> print 1 + 2
3
>>> print 1.0 + 2.0
3.0
>>> print 'a' + 'c'
ac
>>> print [ 1 , 2 ] + [ 3 , 4 ]
[1, 2, 3, 4]
>>> print ( 1 , 2 ) + ( 3 , 4 )
(1, 2, 3, 4)
>>>
```

This works as follows: when the Python system is reading and parsing the program, it converts expressions like a + b into method calls on objects. + calls the method __add__. Here is a table of just some of the binary operator mappings:

+	__add__	-	__sub__	*	__mul__	/	__div__
&	__and__	|	__or__	^	__xor__		
<	__lt__	<=	__le__	>	__gt__	>=	__ge__
==	__eq__	!=	__ne__				

The documentation that comes with the Python system gives a full list of the operator/method mapping – see Section 3.4 "Special Method Names" in the Reference Manual. Rather than replicate it all here, we ask you to look at the manual.

6.6.4   An Example: Queue

Continuing with the example of an ADT for a queue: as a container type it has to have a size so, we should support the len function. A queue is a sequence, so what about indexing and iteration. We decide that we want the queue type to be a black box so that the entries in the queue cannot be seen – the only operations are inserting at the end and extracting from the front. This means we do not need to support indexing, either for getting or setting values. Which means we do not need to investigate what is needed to support those operations for this example. What might be interesting though is to support += as a synonym for the add operation. Putting all this together:

```
class Queue :
    def __init__ ( self ) :
        self.data = []
    def __str__ ( self ) :
        return str ( self.data )
    def __len__ ( self ) :
        return len (self.data )
    def __iadd__ ( self , item ) :
        self.add ( item )
        return self
    def add ( self , item ) :
        self.data += [ item ]
    def remove ( self ) :
        item = self.data[0]
        del self.data[0]
        return item
```

```
if __name__ == '__main__' :
    q = Queue ()
    q.add ( 1 )
    assert q.remove () == 1
    q.add ( 3 )
    q.add ( 'c' )
    assert len ( q ) == 2
    assert q.remove () == 3
    assert q.remove () == 'c'
    assert len ( q ) == 0
    q += 3
    q += 'c'
    assert len ( q ) == 2
    assert q.remove () == 3
    assert q.remove () == 'c'
    assert len ( q ) == 0
```

The __iadd__ method implements the += operator.

6.6.5 An Example: Stack

Another classic data structure that appears in almost all books on programming is the stack. A stack is like a queue in that it is a container with controlled access to the items in the container. A stack is very different to a queue in that it is a first-in–last-out (FILO, or last-in–first-out, LIFO) container. Basically, a stack is a container in which you put items in at the top and take them off the top. Think of plate stackers used in canteens: you can put plates on the top of the stacker and the stack of plates moves down. Only the top plate is accessible: all the others are contained in sequence but hidden within the stacker. When a plate is removed from the stacker the one underneath is 'exposed' and becomes available until there are no more plates left in the stack.

Given that we already have a queue type, a stack type really is quite straightforward to implement:

```
class Stack :
    def __init__ ( self ) :
        self.data = []
    def __str__ ( self ) :
        return str ( self.data )
    def __len__ ( self ) :
        return len (self.data )
    def __iadd__ ( self , item ) :
        self.add ( item )
        return self
    def add ( self , item ) :
        self.data += [ item ]
    def remove ( self ) :
        index = len ( self.data ) - 1
        item = self.data[index]
        del self.data[index]
        return item
    def push ( self , item ) :
        self.add ( item )
    def pop ( self ) :
        return self.remove ()
```

```
if __name__ == '__main__' :
    s = Stack ()
    s.push ( 1 )
    assert len ( s ) == 1
    assert s.pop () == 1
    s.add ( 3 )
    s.push ( 'c' )
    assert len ( s ) == 2
    assert s.pop () == 'c'
    assert s.remove () == 3
    assert len ( s ) == 0
    s += 3
    s += 'c'
    assert len ( s ) == 2
    assert s.remove () == 'c'
    assert s.pop () == 3
    assert len ( s ) == 0
```

6.6.6 An Example: Matrix

Lots of applications in graphics and data manipulation require data transformations that are handled very well by matrices. So, for example, in plane geometry we can represent rotation by the matrix:

$$\begin{pmatrix} \cos\theta & -\sin\theta \\ \sin\theta & \cos\theta \end{pmatrix}$$

Multiple rotations can be represented by applying multiple rotation matrices. Moreover, other transformations like shear and translation can also be represented by matrices and combinations of matrices. Applying multiple transformations requires multiplying matrices together to create a compound transformation matrix. It seems that it might be wise to have an ADT to represent matrices to make implementing matrix using algorithms as easy as possible.

For plane geometry, we know that the matrices we need are all 2×2 matrices. For three-dimensional geometry, we need 3×3 matrices. But rather than limit ourselves to one application of matrices, we can and should create a general matrix type that can then be applied in specific circumstances. So what we are going to do is assume that a matrix is a rectangular structure of numbers. We might think of the following as a good starting point:

```
class Matrix :
```

We use list comprehensions here to create a rectangular two-dimensional store of floats.

```
    def __init__ ( self , rows , columns ) :
        self.rows = rows
        self.columns = columns
        self.data = [ [ 0.0 for column in range ( columns ) ] for row in range ( rows ) ]

    def __str__ ( self ) :
        result = ''
        for row in range ( self.rows ) :
            result += '| '
            for column in range ( self.columns ) :
                result += str ( self.data[row][column] ) + ' '
            result += '|\n'
        return result[ : len ( result ) - 1 ]

if __name__ == '__main__' :
    m = Matrix ( 2 , 2 )
    print m
```

A major problem with specifying a new matrix by specifying its size, as we have above, is that there is only one matrix value that we can create for each size – the matrix with all entries being 0.0. In order to get any other matrix value, we have to create the zero matrix and amend the entries appropriately. Is there a better way? Yes, we have a different constructor, one that takes as a parameter a representation of the matrix that can be used to construct the internal representation. So we need a constructor that takes a parameter that is a rectangular structure containing the data for the matrix – sequence of sequences perhaps? This brings an important issue: we must not use the data structure passed as a parameter as the representation of the matrix. Why is this? There are two reasons:

1. The internal data structure may be different to the parameter data structure so explicit construction is always best.

2. Even if the internal and parameter data structure have the same structure, the matrix implementation must not share the data structure with the program using the type.

The first is really separation of concerns in disguise. It may be that the sequence of sequence idea is not the best data structure to use to represent the matrix, but it is definitely the right data structure for code using matrices to create easily. The matrix constructor should never impose the internal data structure on the code using the matrix.

The second point is perhaps even more important. It is a question of who "owns" the data structure and therefore has permission to change it. Types such as matrix, when passed a data structure, should not assume that they have the right to change the data structure they are passed – ownership of the data structure remains with the calling program. Types like matrix should always construct a new data structure internally, copying values as necessary from the parameter to create the internal representation of the matrix.

Taking all this into account, here is the beginnings of a module:

> There is an interesting, intentional bug in this code that we shall investigate in Section 9.4.4.

```
'''Class to represent a matrix including overloads of operators.'''
__author__ = 'Russel Winder'
__date__ = '2006-12-02'
__version__ = '1.0'
__copyright__ = 'Copyright (c) 2006 Russel Winder'
__licence__ = 'GNU General Public Licence (GPL)'


class Matrix :

    def __init__ ( self , data ) :
        # Ensure parameter is rectangular whilst creating the internal representation.
        self.data = []
        columns = len ( data[0] )
        for row in data :
            if len ( row ) != columns : raise ValueError , 'Data is not a rectangular structure.'
            self.data += [ row[:] ]

    def __str__ ( self ) :
        result = ''
        for row in self.data :
            result += '| '
            for i in row :
                result += str ( i ) + ' '
            result += '|\n'
        return result[ : len ( result ) - 1 ]

    def __ensureSameShape ( self , m ) :
        if len ( self.data ) != len ( m.data ) or len ( self.data[0] ) != len ( m.data[0] ) :
            raise ValueError , 'Matrices not of the same shape.'

    def __add__ ( self , m ) :
        self.__ensureSameShape ( m )
        n = Matrix ( self.data )
        for row in range ( len ( self.data ) ) :
            for column in range ( len ( self.data[0] ) ) :
                n.data[row][column] += m.data[row][column]
        return n
```

```python
def __sub__ ( self , m ) :
    self.__ensureSameShape ( m )
    n = Matrix ( self.data )
    for row in range ( len ( self.data ) ) :
        for column in range ( len ( self.data[0] ) ) :
            n.data[row][column] -= m.data[row][column]
    return n
```

We can have both classes and functions in a module!

```python
def __eq__ ( self , m ) :
    try : self.__ensureSameShape ( m )
    except ValueError : return False
    for row in range ( len ( self.data ) ) :
        for column in range ( len ( self.data[0] ) ) :
            if self.data[row][column] != m.data[row][column] : return False
    return True
```

zeros and unit are examples of matrix creation functions – they are functions that create specific instances of the class.

```python
def zeros ( rows , columns ) :
    return Matrix ( [ [ 0.0 for column in range ( columns ) ] for row in range ( rows ) ] )

def unit ( rows , columns ) :
    m = Matrix ( [ [ 0.0 for column in range ( columns ) ] for row in range ( rows ) ] )
    for i in range ( min ( rows , columns ) ) :
        m.data[i][i] = 1.0
    return m

if __name__ == '__main__' :
    z = zeros ( 2 , 2 )
    u = unit ( 2 , 2 )
    assert u == u + z
    assert u == z + u
    assert u == u - z
    a = Matrix ( ( ( -1.0 , 0.0 ) , ( 0.0 , -1.0 ) ) )
    assert a == z - u
```

As previously, we have a test script in our module. The test here is not really a proper test, it is there just to ensure that our implementation is not totally broken. We will address how to test things properly in Chapter 9.

You have probably spotted that we haven't implemented multiplication in this class, despite saying earlier it was the prime reason why we needed an abstract data type for matrices. We are going to be a bit mean and leave this as an exercise (see Exercise 6.4, page 214).

Assuming that we have implemented multiplication of matrices, how can we use it? Let's write a program to draw a triangle and a transformed triangle using the Turtle package. First we need a function to draw a triangle:

```python
import turtle

def drawTriangle ( points ) :
    turtle.up ()
    turtle.goto ( points[0][0] , points[0][1] )
    turtle.down ()
    turtle.goto ( points[1][0] , points[1][1] )
    turtle.goto ( points[2][0] , points[2][1] )
    turtle.goto ( points[0][0] , points[0][1] )
```

Clearly we have made some assumptions about how the data is presented to this function. In particular, we are assuming that points is a sequence of three objects, each of which is a sequence of two items. The model here is that the function is being given the (x, y) coordinates of three points in the plane describing a triangle.

How can we create and transform triangles? First we need an example triangle:

```
coordinates = ( ( -10.0, -10.0 ) , ( 0.0 , 40.0 ) , ( 60.0 , 60.0 ) )
```

coordinates is a sequence of three pairs which fits very nicely with the assumptions made by the drawTriangle function. We can confidently expect then that a call such as:

```
drawTriangle ( coordinates )
```

will draw a triangle – assuming the data presented actually describes a triangle of course!

Now we need a transformation matrix. Let's undertake a rotation by 90° anti-clockwise. By default, the Turtle package works in radians and 90° anti-clockwise is $\pi/2$, so the angle θ in the rotation matrix needs to be $\pi/2$, which means the matrix we want is:

```
from math import pi , cos , sin
from matrix import Matrix

theta = pi / 2
rotationMatrix = Matrix ( (
    ( cos ( theta ) , -sin ( theta ) ) ,
    ( sin ( theta ) , cos ( theta ) )
    ) )
```

We have used the **from** form of the **import** statement to import specific variable and function names so that we can use them in our code without specifying the module name – it makes the code look more like the mathematical expression.

To transform a coordinate using this transformation matrix, we need to have the coordinates as a matrix. The 2×2 transformation matrix pre-multiplies the coordinate matrix, so we need a 2×1 matrix of the coordinate data. The result of the multiplication is then a 2×1 matrix of the transformed coordinate. We have the coordinates as a sequence of sequences, so we ought be able to use list comprehensions to create a sequence of matrices. First though how do we construct a matrix representing a coordinate from a sequence representing a coordinate?

The matrix Matrix (((0.0 ,) , (40.0 ,)) is the 2×1 matrix that represents the same coordinate as (0.0 , 40.0). So if the variable c is associated with a sequence representing a coordinate, the 2×1 matrix Matrix (((c[0] ,) , (c[1] ,)) represents the same coordinate.

We use this to create a list of all three matrices using list comprehension:

```
coordinateMatrices = [ Matrix ( ( ( c[0] , ) , ( c[1] , ) ) ) for c in coordinates ]
```

> Following the approach of being declarative, we use list comprehensions rather than explicit iteration to work with the sequences that specify the triangles.

Now we can do the transformation of the triangle again using list comprehension to work on all three points in a single expression:

```
newCoordinateMatrices = \
    [ rotationMatrix * coordinateMatrices[i] for i in range ( len ( coordinateMatrices ) ) ]
```

> Here we are using the * operator which invokes the __mul__ method of the matrix class.

The drawTriangle function requires a sequence of sequences representation of the coordinates and we have a sequence of matrices representation. So we need to extract the necessary information. At this stage of the development of the matrix class we haven't prepared a neat and sophisticated way of doing this so we will have to delve in to the internals of the matrix representation:

```
newCoordinates = \
    [ ( newCoordinateMatrices[i].data[0][0] , newCoordinateMatrices[i].data[1][0] ) \
        for i in range ( len ( newCoordinateMatrices ) ) ]
```

We *must* put thinking about how to avoid having to do this on the 'todo list' for this matrix class development project.

Now with all this in place, we can draw both the original and rotated triangles:

```
drawTriangle ( coordinates )
drawTriangle ( newCoordinates )
```

The result of running this code is the drawing:

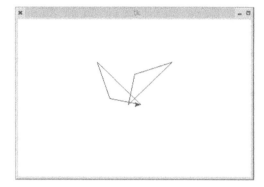

> **NumPy**
>
> If you are interested in using matrices in real programs, you may want to investigate the NumPy library (http://numpy.scipy.org/) rather than try and develop the above matrix implementation into a 'production quality' system – NumPy is already production quality.

6.7 An Example: Poker Dice

For the next phase of our investigation of classes, we are going to return to dice games. We are going to create a program for playing poker dice. The dice are still six-sided dice but now the sides have A, K, Q, J, 10, 9 on them. This is just a representation issue, and using classes to separate concerns, offers an easy way to handle this.

We know that in poker dice, we have five six-sided dice and they have to be rolled. So, following the idea of capturing the 'things' in the problem as instances of classes, we need a class for the die and a class for the 'hand' comprising five dice. Ignoring the playing of the game for the moment, we have the following program to act a basis from which to work:

```
import random

class Die :
    '''A class representing a die.'''
```

Poker Dice, the Game

The game is played with a set of five poker dice. Poker dice are six-sided dice, but instead of the traditional spots, each side has a playing card value symbol. The values in order of rank are:

> ace, king, queen, jack, ten, nine

There is no notion of suits in poker dice.

At each round of the game, players put an equal stake into the pot. Then, in sequence, each player has three rolls of the dice. All dice must be rolled in the first round, but then a selection is rolled for the second or third rolls. Once a die has not been rolled, it may not be rolled again for that player's current turn. The object is to make the best poker hand. After the final throw of a player's turn, the value of the hand is noted and the dice pass to the next player. The highest hand wins the pot.

Poker dice hand values are the same as that of the card game Poker. The hands are ranked from highest to lowest as:

> Five of a kind
> Four of a kind
> A full house (three of a kind and one pair)
> A straight (9-10-J-Q-K or 10-J-Q-K-A)
> Three of a kind
> Two pairs
> One pair

Higher numbers outrank lower numbers. So, five aces beats five kings, a high straight (aces high) beats a low straight (kings high), A full house consisting of three queens and two nines beats a full house consisting of three nines and two queens, and so on.

A popular variation in the event of ties is to use 'kickers'. This is the value of the poker dice that do not contribute to a made hand. For example, let's say two players both roll four of a kind. Player 1 has four queens and a king. Player 2 has four queens and a nine. The spare die is the kicker, so in this example Player 1 has a king kicker and Player 2 has a 9 kicker. Therefore Player 1 wins the pot.

In the event of a dead tie where two or more players make hands of equal strength, traditionally another round would be played between these players to determine the winner. If you prefer, the winning players may split the pot, i.e. divide the pot equally between the winning players. This rule should be agreed prior to playing.

```python
representations = [ 'A' , 'K' , 'Q' , 'J' , '10' , '9' ]

def __init__ ( self ) :
    '''Initialize the die with A showing.'''
    self.generator = random.Random ( )
    self.current = 0

def __str__ ( self ) :
    '''Create a string representation of the die face showing.'''
    return Die.representations[self.current]

def roll ( self ) :
    '''Roll the die and return the new value showing.'''
    self.current = self.generator.randint ( 0 , 5 )
    return self.current

class Hand :
    '''A class to represent a hand at dice poker.'''
```

```
def __init__ ( self ) :
    '''initialize a hand of 5 dice.'''
    self.hand = [ Die ( ) , Die ( ) , Die ( ) , Die ( ) , Die ( ) ]

def __str__ ( self ) :
    '''Create a string representation of the hand.'''
    result = '['
    for i in range ( len ( self.hand ) ) :
        result += ' ' + str ( self.hand[i] )
    return result + ' ]'

def roll ( self , rollset = [ 0 , 1 , 2 , 3 , 4 ] ) :
    '''Roll the dice of the given index in the hand.'''
    for i in rollset : self.hand[i].roll ( )

if __name__ == '__main__' :
    hand = Hand ( )
    hand.roll ( )
    print hand
```

It seems natural to use a list of dice to represent the hand: we want the hand to be mutable, so a list rather than a tuple seems more appropriate.

> **Reducing Things**
>
> Anyone who has studied and liked the functional approach to programming would look at this implementation of __str__ and say, why not do this as:
>
> ```
> def __str__ ( self ) :
>     '''Create a string representation of the hand.'''
>     return '[' + reduce ( lambda L , v : L + ' ' + str ( v ) , self.hand , '' ) + ' ]'
> ```
>
> The reason is that BDFL has deprecated reduce (i.e. reduce will be removed from future versions of Python), so we do things the hard way to ensure we do not build obvious obsolescence into our software from the outset.

Chapter Summary

In this chapter we have found that:

- Values in Python programs are objects.
- Objects are instances of classes.
- A constructor is called to initialize a newly created object.
- Classes are ways of describing abstract data types (ADTs).
- Python supports operator overloading.
- Separation of concerns is an important design principle.
- Classes can be used to implement new exception types.

Self-Review Questions

Self-review 6.1 Explain the roles of r, random, and ( ) in:

```
r.random ( )
```

Self-review 6.2 What is an object?

Self-review 6.3 Why are classes important?

Self-review 6.4 What is a method?

Self-review 6.5 Why is a method different than a function?

Self-review 6.6 Why is the method name __init__ special, and for what reason(s)?

Self-review 6.7 What is an *abstract data type*?

Self-review 6.8 Why is there an apparent difference between the number of parameters in the definition of a method and the number of arguments passed to it when called?

Self-review 6.9 What does self mean? Is it a Python keyword?

Self-review 6.10 Is the method bar in the following code legal in Python?

```
class Foo :
    def __init__ ( self ) :
        self.foo = 1
    def bar ( flibble ) :
        print flibble.foo
```

Self-review 6.11 What is *operator overloading*?

Self-review 6.12 Which operators do the following methods overload?

1. __add__
2. __eq__
3. __lt__
4. __or__
5. __ne__
6. __div__
7. __ge__

Self-review 6.13 What is the difference between a queue and a stack?

Self-review 6.14 Why is it usually thought to be a bad thing to use **global** statements?

Self-review 6.15 What does the __ mean in the name __foobar in the following class?

```
class Foo :
    def __init__ ( self ) :
        self.__foobar ()
    def __foobar ( self ) :
        print 'foobar'
```

Self-review 6.16 What new facilities for encapsulation do classes offer?

Programming Exercises

Exercise 6.1 Create a class to represent a single die that can have any positive integer number of sides. This kind of die might be used when playing role-playing games (RPGs).

Exercise 6.2 Write a class to represent an RPG character's money pouch. Money should be stored as an integer, with methods for adding money and removing money. The removing method should take a value as parameter. If there is enough money, the value is removed from the money in the pouch and **True** is returned. If there is not enough money, **False** is returned.

Exercise 6.3 Write a simple RPG character class. The character should have a name, a money pouch and an inventory. The name should be stored as a string, the money pouch should be an instance of the pouch from the previous exercise and the inventory should be a dictionary in which keys are item names and values are the number of items held by the player.

Ensure that there are methods for adding items to, and removing items from, the inventory.

There should be a __str__ method that returns something that can be printed. For example:

print playerA

Might display:

```
-------------------------
Duncan Disorderly
-------------------------
Money: 235 gold pieces
-------------------------
Knapsack contains:

  Arrow: 12
  Rubber Sword: 1
  Felt tipped pen: 2
  Imitation fur coat: 23
-------------------------
```

Exercise 6.4 Implement the multiplication operation for the Matrix class.

Exercise 6.5 Implement __getitem__ for the Matrix class so that we can rewrite the drawTriangle function to work with a triplet of 2×1 matrices:

```
def drawTriangle ( coordinateMatrix ) :
    turtle.up ()
    turtle.goto ( coordinateMatrix[0][0][0] , coordinateMatrix[0][1][0] )
    turtle.down ()
    turtle.goto ( coordinateMatrix[1][0][0] , coordinateMatrix[1][1][0] )
    turtle.goto ( coordinateMatrix[2][0][0] , coordinateMatrix[2][1][0] )
    turtle.goto ( coordinateMatrix[0][0][0] , coordinateMatrix[0][1][0] )
```

Exercise 6.6 Write a class Account that stores the current balance, interest rate and account number of a bank account. Your class should provide methods to withdraw, deposit and add interest to the account. The user should only be allowed to withdraw money up to some overdraft limit. If an account goes overdrawn, there is fee charged.

Exercise 6.7 Write a small class to represent the light switch state machine from Section 4.2. Provide a single method to change the state of the switch and method called isOn which returns **True** if the switch is on and **False** if it is off. Make sure you override the __str__ method so that light switches can be printed to the console.

Exercise 6.8 Write a program which *uses* the Stack class. Your program should begin by printing a menu to the user:

> 1. Add new data to stack
> 2. Print stack
> 3. Remove datum from stack
> 4. Exit

You should allow the user to enter 1, 2, 3 or 4 to select their desired action and you should write code to implement the four possible options.

Exercise 6.9 Amend your program from Exercise 6.8 to use a Queue as the data structure used to store data in.

Exercise 6.10 A *priority queue* is an abstract data type similar to the queue introduced in Section 6.6.1 and Section 6.6.4. A priority queue associates a priority with each stored item and always stores the items so that the elements with the highest priority are at the 'top' of the queue and are the first to be removed – i.e. the items in a priority queue are sorted by priority. Create a PriorityQueue class based on the Queue class:

1. The add method should take two parameters, an item to store and a priority, which should be an integer.

2. The add method should ensure that when new data is added to the priority queue, it is added as a tuple which contains both the data and its priority. Make sure that data is always stored in priority order.

3. The remove method should return queue items, not tuples – i.e. the priority associated with the returned item can be ignored.

Challenges

Challenge 6.1 Currently, the *n*-faced die (see Exercise 6.1) is unable to display its spots and must instead rely on displaying a number.

Your task is to write a function that returns a string representation of the die face for a given number. For example, this:

```
print makeFace ( 9 )
```

might display:

```
***
***
***
```

The algorithm is up to you, but do remember about integer division and the remainder operator (%)

Now that you can make faces with an arbitrary number of spots, add this functionality to your *n*-sided die class.

Challenge 6.2 Extend your RPG character class to hold values for health points (HP), attack points (AP) and defence points (DP).

Add an attack method that takes a character instance as a parameter. This is your opponent.

If the character's AP is greater than the opponent's DP, the difference is subtracted from the opponent's HP. So, if I attack with a power of 7 and my opponent has a defence power of 6, they lose 1 health point. If they have a defence power of 9, they sustain no damage.

Write a program that demonstrates your character class by creating two characters that take it in turns to bop each other until one of them runs out of HP.

Inheriting Class

In the previous chapter we used two different classes, both called Die, one for the craps program and one for the poker dice programs. Although the classes were different, there was a lot of commonality. In particular, the craps Die and the poker dice Die both represent a six-sided die, but they have different marks on the sides. So the dice are the same and have the same behavior, yet they are different. What we really want to do is to capture the "sameness", and, at the same time, admit the difference. All object-oriented programming languages have support for this: it is called *inheritance*.

7.1   Inheritance: Modeling and Reuse

One of the strengths of the object-oriented approach to programming is that it provides a clean way of reusing code. Programs often consist of millions of lines of code, written by many teams of programmers, sometimes even from more than one company. It is therefore essential to have mechanisms for modularizing and reusing code. Reuse of software cuts development time and costs. This means that not only do programmers like it, so do accountants. In fact, even in a relatively small program, being able to reuse code can make your programs easier to read and maintain, and make them quicker to write. *Inheritance* is one of the major tools for code reuse, and it is probably the single biggest reason for the popularity of object-oriented programming. Having said this, inheritance has to be used correctly – all too often people use it for the wrong sort of reuse. Inheritance supports one form of code reuse, but it is more than that: inheritance has a special place in terms of the structure of the system being developed.

With inheritance, one class 'inherits' all the data and methods of its parent. So, if you have several classes that are all rather similar, instead of having to retype all the code to define some of their methods, you can use inheritance to say "this class has all the data and methods of it's parent and these new ones as well". This sounds exactly what we need for the six-sided die.

In most programming languages, the terms subclass and superclass are used: the 'parent' class is called the *superclass* and the 'child' class is called the *subclass*. We can tell Python that we want a class to have a particular superclass by using an extension to the class declaration syntax:

```
class <name> ( <superclass> ) :
    . . .
```

As a very simple example, in the following, the class Child inherits all the capabilities of its superclass Parent:

```
>>> class Parent :
...     def foo ( self ) :
...             print 'foo'
...
>>> class Child ( Parent ) :
...     def bar ( self ) :
...             print 'bar'
...
>>> c = Child ()
>>> c.bar ()
bar
>>> c.foo ()
foo
>>> p = Parent ()
>>> p.foo ()
foo
>>> p.bar ()
Traceback (most recent call last):
  File "<stdin>", line 1, in ?
AttributeError: Parent instance has no attribute 'bar'
>>>
```

An *attribute* is a name that is part of the state of an object. Methods are searched for using the attributes, so if a method name cannot be found, an AttributeError is raised.

All the methods defined in the superclass (Parent) can be used by an object of that class and by any subclass: an object of the subclass (Child) has all the methods of the superclass as well as those defined in the class. So for the object referred to by c there are methods bar (from the class) and foo (from the superclass) available. The object referred to by p on the other hand only has a method foo.

We can represent this relationship between classes diagrammatically:

where the arrow points from the subclass to the superclass.

If you are asking "What is the superclass of the class Parent?" then you are asking a very good question. The answer is that, in this example, Parent doesn't have a superclass. However, this does point to some complications. Python currently (Python 2.5) has two sorts of class: 'old-style' classes and 'new-style' classes. What we have presented so far have all been 'old-style' classes: any class with no explicit superclass, and any subclass of such a class, is an 'old-style' class.

What is a 'new-style' class? Any class that inherits from a Python built-in type, for example, int or float is a 'new-style' class. Also there is a special type called object that is the supertype of all 'new-style' classes. So if we had written:

> **class** Parent (object) :

in the above example, Parent and Child would have been 'new-style' classes. So what is the difference?

```
>>> class Parent ( object ) :
...     def foo ( self ) :
...         print 'foo'
...
>>> class Child ( Parent ) :
...     def bar ( self ) :
...         print 'bar'
...
>>> c = Child ()
>>> c.bar ()
bar
>>> c.foo ()
foo
>>> p = Parent ()
>>> p.foo ()
foo
>>> p.bar ()
Traceback (most recent call last):
  File "<stdin>", line 1, in ?
AttributeError: 'Parent' object has no attribute 'bar'
>>>
```

Not a lot, it seems: the only difference here is the message of the AttributeError! Actually this is a bit unfair as there are actually many differences between 'old-style' and 'new-style' classes, it is just that none of the differences really affect our use of classes at this stage of our learning. For now we don't need to worry about the differences.

There is, however, an important point that we can introduce with this 'new-style' classes version. All 'new-style' classes have to have a superclass – except the class object, which is unique amongst 'new-style' classes in having no superclass. So in this example, Parent is a subclass of object and Child is a subclass of Parent and hence is a subclass of object. We can represent this relationship diagrammatically:

where, as previously, the arrow points from the subclass to the superclass. The point that Child is a subclass of object because it is a subclass of Parent, which is a subclass of object, is a linchpin of the idea of an *inheritance hierarchy*. People often reinforce this by talking about *direct subclass/direct superclass* and *indirect subclass/indirect superclass*. Child is a direct subclass of Parent because Child names Parent as its superclass in its class declaration. Child is an indirect subclass of object because object is not a direct superclass of Child but there is an *inheritance chain* that connects Child to object – in this case Child is a direct subclass of Parent, which is a direct subclass of object, so Child is an indirect subclass of object.

Inheritance is important and useful whenever several types need to share the same capabilities and are conceptually related. What we mean here is that there must be an 'is-a' relationship between the subclass and the superclass: when thinking about the two classes it must be the case that the subclass concept is a special case of the superclass concept.

So, for example, an apple is a fruit, and so is a pear, so if we have a system in which fruit is a class then both apple and pear can be subclasses because an apple is a fruit and a pear is a fruit. If we are modeling trees in an orchard, apple tree and pear tree are both trees, so classes representing apple tree and pear tree can be subclasses of the tree class. In the realms of transport, we can have vehicles. Cars are vehicles, trucks are vehicles; there is an 'is-a' relationship, so inheritance is appropriate.

7.2   And The Point Is . . .

Many graphical programs (e.g. games) deal with points in space. These might be two or three dimensional and will probably have methods to do things like finding the distance between the point and the origin, finding the distance between the point and another point, and so on. We may decide, as a design decision, that we have two-dimensional points as a class and then three-dimensional points as a subclass:

```
import math

class Point2d :
    def __init__ ( self , x , y ) :
        self.x = x
        self.y = y
    def __str__ ( self ) :
        return 'Point2d (' + str ( self.x ) + ',' + str ( self.y ) + ')'
    def distance ( self ) :
        return math.sqrt ( self.x ** 2 + self.y **2 )

class Point3d ( Point2d ) :
    def __init__ ( self , x , y , z ) :
        Point2d.__init__ ( self , x , y )
        self.z = z
    def __str__ ( self ) :
        return 'Point3d (' + str ( self.x ) + ',' + str ( self.y ) + ',' + str ( self.z ) + ')'
    def distance ( self ) :
        return math.sqrt ( self.x ** 2 + self.y **2 + self.z ** 2 )

if __name__ == '__main__':
    p1 = Point2d ( 16 , 16 )
    p2 = Point3d ( 25 , 25 , 25 )
    print p1 , 'is:' , p1.distance ( ) , 'from the origin.'
    print p2 , 'is:' , p2.distance ( ) , 'from the origin.'
```

Point3d inherits the __str__ and distance methods from Point2d but *overrides* them providing new definitions.

which when executed produces:

```
|> python point.py
Point2d ( 16 , 16 ) is: 22.627416998 from the origin.
Point3d ( 25 , 25 , 25 ) is: 43.3012701892 from the origin.
|>
```

We are making the decision that a Point3d is a Point2d, and so Point3d is a subclass of Point2d. Another way of thinking about this is in terms of *substitutability*: wherever the code expects to be using an object of a given class, then if we substitute an object of a subclass of that class then the code must work. So for the code above, we can use an instance of Point3d wherever the code expects an instance of Point2d, because Point3d is a subclass of Point2d, and a Point3d object is substitutable for a Point2d object.

> ### A Dimensional Argument
>
> If you have worked with two- and three-dimensional points in mathematics, you may well be saying to yourself "But isn't a three-dimensional point more general than a two-dimensional point: a two-dimensional point is a restriction on a two-dimensional point, so it should be the subclass." The first part of this statement is very true, but the deduction is wrong because the ideas of generality and restriction are different in computing. In object-oriented programming, generality is about having less state and fewer constraints, whereas in geometry generality is about being able to describe more and so involves more state – diametrically opposed definitions of generality! The upshot is that when writing code in any object-oriented language, it is the state that determines which is the superclass and which is the subclass. Subclasses always have more state and/or more restrictions than the superclass. So in this points example, the two-dimensional point is the superclass as it has less state than the three-dimensional point. Substitutability also comes into play: we can use a three-dimensional point wherever we need a two-dimensional point, but we cannot do the reverse.

7.3 A Dungeon Full of Dice

In the Dungeons & Dragons role-playing game, a number of different dice are used: four-sided, six-sided, eight-sided, and twenty-sided. Also, there are times when a 'percentage' needs to be generated, and this usually means using two ten-sided dice to create a number between 1 and 100, equivalent to a 100-sided die.

Wouldn't it be good if we could avoid replicating code by abstracting the notion of die and then applying it in ways to create the different number of sides? This is exactly what inheritance can give us:

```
'''
Module containing various dice-related classes.
'''

__author__ = 'Russel Winder'
__date__ = '2006-11-21'
__version__ = '1.0'
__copyright__ = 'Copyright (c) 2006 Russel Winder'
__licence__ = 'GNU General Public Licence (GPL)'

import random
```

```
class Die :
    '''A class representing a die.'''

    def __init__ ( self , sides ) :
        '''Initialize the die.'''
        self.sides = sides
        self.generator = random.Random ()
        self.current = 1

    def __str__ ( self ) :
        '''Create a representation of the die face showing.
        Assumes faces show 1..n for an n-sided die.'''
        return str ( self.current )

    def value ( self ) :
        '''Return the current value of the die.'''
        return self.current

    def roll ( self ) :
        '''Roll the die and return the new value showing.'''
        self.current = self.generator.randint ( 1 , self.sides )
        return self.value ()

class D4 ( Die ) :
    '''A 4-sided die.'''
    def __init__ ( self ) : Die.__init__ ( self , 4 )

class D6 ( Die ) :
    '''A 6-sided die.'''
    def __init__ ( self ) : Die.__init__ ( self , 6 )

class D8 ( Die ) :
    '''A 8-sided die.'''
    def __init__ ( self ) : Die.__init__ ( self , 8 )

class D10 ( Die ) :
    '''A 10-sided die.'''
    def __init__ ( self ) : Die.__init__ ( self , 10 )

class D20 ( Die ) :
    '''A 20-sided die.'''
    def __init__ ( self ) : Die.__init__ ( self , 20 )

class D100 ( Die ) :
    '''A 100-sided, or percentage, die.'''
    def __init__ ( self ) : Die.__init__ ( self , 100 )
```

We have a generic Die class that is really just a way of generating and storing a random integer in a given range. The number of sides on the die is determined by a parameter to the constructor.

Looking at the D4 class, we see that the declaration includes Die in parentheses after the class name. This indicates that Die is the superclass of D4. All the methods of Die are automatically methods in D4 because D4 is a subclass of Die. So although we have not declared them, D4 has methods __str__, value, and roll because they are part of the superclass. The subclass inherits all the methods of the superclass.

One thing we do need to specify is the number of sides for the die. This means the subclass has to have a constructor so that it can properly call the superclass constructor. So D4 must define a constructor so that it can call the Die constructor with the parameter 4. This is what the line:

```
Die.__init__ ( self , 4 )
```

does. We have to call it like an ordinary function call because that is the way it has to be. We call the superclass constructor Die.__init__ as a function with the self object and the constructor parameter, 4.

The other dice are handled is exactly the same way, and with almost identical code. All that is different is the name of the class and the parameter value in the superclass constructor call.

Note that we have to call the superclass constructor explicitly from our constructor. In some languages (e.g. C++, Java) there are (complicated) rules that govern when a superclass constructor has to be called explicitly and when it is called automatically. Python has simplified this: superclass constructors always have to be called explicitly.

7.4 Craps and Poker Dice

What do the craps and poker dice programs look like? First craps:

```python
import die

class CrapsDie ( die.D6 ) :
    '''A class representing a die used for the craps program.'''

    representations = [
        '***\n***\n***\n' , # Have to populate index 0 as padding.
        ' \n * \n \n' ,
        ' * \n \n * \n' ,
        ' * \n * \n * \n' ,
        '* *\n \n* *\n' ,
        '* *\n * \n* *\n',
        '* *\n* *\n* *\n'
        ]

    def __str__ ( self ) :
        '''Create a representation of the die face showing.'''
        return self.representations[self.current]

if __name__ == '__main__' :
    a = CrapsDie ()
    b = CrapsDie ()
    value = a.roll () + b.roll ()
    print a , '\n' , b , '\n' , value
    if value == 7 or value == 11 : print "Win"
    elif value == 2 or value == 3 or value == 12 : print "Lose"
    else :
        while True :
            throw = a.roll () + b.roll ()
            print '------'
            print a , '\n' , b , '\n' , throw
            if throw == 7 : print "Lose" ; break
            if throw == value : print "Win" ; break
```

Using the dice classes from the previous section the CrapsDie is easy to define: we subclass a standard six-sided die and put some special print processing in it.

The poker dice game looks like:

```
import die

class PokerDie ( die.D6 ) :
    '''A class representing a poker die.'''

    representations = [ '' , 'A' , 'K' , 'Q' , 'J' , '10' , '9' ] # NB have to fill index 0.

    def __str__ ( self ) :
        '''Create a representation of the die face showing.'''
        return self.representations[self.current]

class Hand :
    '''A class to represent a hand at dice poker.'''

    def __init__ ( self ) :
        '''initialize a hand of 5 dice.'''
        self.hand = [ PokerDie () , PokerDie () , PokerDie () , PokerDie () , PokerDie () ]

    def __str__ ( self ) :
        '''Create a string representation of the hand.'''
        result = '['
        for i in range ( len ( self.hand ) ) :
            result += ' ' + str ( self.hand[i] )
        return result + ' ]'

    def roll ( self ) :
        '''Roll all 5 dice in the hand.'''
        for i in range ( len ( self .hand ) ) :
            self.hand[i].roll ()

if __name__ == '__main__' :
    hand = Hand ()
    hand.roll ()
    print hand
```

As with the craps die, the PokerDie class simply adds different output to a standard six-sided die.

The CrapsDie class and the PokerDie are related to each other, but they share a common superclass (Die.D6). We have captured the commonality (they are both six-sided die) and enabled reuse of code, but have kept the difference (the six sides have different symbols). It is not sensible to substitute a PokerDie where a CrapsDie is required or vice versa, so it is right they they do not have a subclass–superclass relationship, they are siblings in an inheritance hierarchy. Diagrammatically, we have:

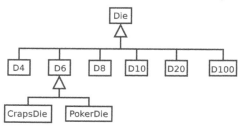

where, as before, the arrow points to the superclass from the subclass. Here we are showing that lines can combine to show that a superclass has many subclasses.

Association and Aggregation

There is clearly a relationship between Hand and PokerDie in the Poker Dice example, but it is definitely not any form of inheritance relationship. The relationship between them is called *association*: an instance of Hand has the ability to call methods on an instance of PokerDie, so there is an association between Hand and PokerDie.

The relationship between Hand and PokerDie is a special case of association called *aggregation*. An instance of Hand has a data structure (in this case a list) that has references to many instances of PokerDie, so a Hand is an aggregation of PokerDies. This is often called a 'has-a' relationship to clearly distinguish it from inheritance, which is an 'is-a' relationship.

7.5 Hello, the Graphical Way

Earlier in this book we used the Turtle package for drawing images on the screen. Whenever we drew a picture, the Turtle package automatically put a *frame* on the screen, giving us a *canvas* on which to draw. The Turtle package makes use of the Tkinter package, which is a package for doing user interface graphics on the computer screen that comes as standard with the Python distribution. Idle (the program development environment that comes with Python) is another example of use of the Tkinter package.

In this section we are going to investigate programming graphical user interfaces (GUIs) using Tkinter as it introduces some new ideas about programming, gives us some insights into how the Turtle package works, and is fun.

7.5.1 The Straightforward

In Section 1.2 (page 3) we saw a program that wrote the string Hello. to the console. As a variation on the theme, let's investigate using Tkinter to create a frame on the desktop into which we write the string. The complete program is:

```
from Tkinter import Label
from Tkinter import Tk

root = Tk ( )
widget = Label ( root , text = 'Hello.' )
widget.pack ( )
root.mainloop ( )
```

and when executed it results in the following appearing on the screen.

Importing Things

We use a from statement:

```
from Tkinter import Tk
```

as this means we do not have to specify the module name in our code when we use functions and classes from the module. If we had used:

> **import** Tkinter

we would have had to use the names Tkinter.Frame and Tkinter.Label in our code. However using the **from** statement, the Python system already knows the module name, so we can just use the names Frame and Label. Which you use in your code is a matter of coding style. The important thing is not which to choose, but is to be clear and consistent, i.e. to have a good coding style. We believe that the source code presented in the book has a good, coherent style. It is not the only good style possible. Feel free to disagree with our style, but always ensure that all your programs exhibit a clear, consistent and coherent style.

Why are we pushing this 'party line' about programming style? It is all to do with code readability. A coding style that is clear and consistent is easier to read. It leads to code that is easier to get right and to evolve.

Widgets

The various components of user interfaces, such as the label in the above example, are generally called *widgets*. Menus, buttons, scrollbars, labels, etc. are all widgets. Widgets are represented by objects.

Programmers often use the term widget to mean both the user interface component and the object that represents it. Normally the context makes it clear what is meant, but there is some scope for confusion.

Framing the Questions

Hopefully, you are asking a few questions about this program, for example:

1. Why do we have to have an object created by the call of the Tk function?

2. Why is the second parameter to the Label function call an assignment?

3. Why is there a call to the method pack?

4. Why is there a call to the method mainloop?

A Tkinter program has to have a main frame. The Tk function call creates and initializes an object that does everything needed to create and display the main frame – this is abstraction at work, we don't need to know anything about the operating system, graphics, etc., it is all done for us.

The call of the Label function creates an object representing a *widget* that can be placed in the frame. The first parameter to the Label function ensures that the label object knows which frame object it is working with. The assignment used as the second parameter is an example of *named parameters* which is a very important feature of the Python function call mechanism.

Naming those Parameters

The functions that create Tkinter widgets can take a (very) large number of parameters. It would be truly awful if we had to list all the parameters for all widget creation calls. Fortunately, Python has a way of passing parameters to functions in such a way that we only have to specify those parameters for which we want to provide non-default values: *named parameters*.

The Label function requires us to provide one *positional parameter* – in this case we use a reference to the frame, root. All other parameters that this function uses have default values, so we do not have to provide any further parameters unless we want to use non-default values. In this case we want to specify the text that is to be the label. Looking in the manual page for Tkinter.Label, we find that the parameter named text is the one to which we need to provide a value. So we use the named parameter mechanism: as the second parameter to the Label call, we provide what looks like an assignment. In effect it is; we are assigning a value to a function parameter by name rather than by position in the parameter list. All the other parameters to the Label call use their *default value*

This example is only really giving a hint as to the true power of the Python function call mechanism. Here we have highlighted that the default value/named parameter mechanism is going to make using packages both easy and hard. It is easy because we can make use of the default values to simplify our code, it is hard because we have to have a good manual available so that we can readily find the information we need about which parameters we use as named parameters. The Python community knows this and so there are invariably good manuals associated with each package. Also of course there is pydoc to access the information that is contained in the package source code. You may want to investigate the result of typing 'pydoc Tkinter.Label'. Remember though that this information is not intended for learners, it is intended for programmers who know Python and need to have quick, definitive access to information.

Packing Things Away

Why call the method pack on the widget? Well, we haven't specified any size or position information for the label or the frame, and yet the system needs to know this information to display things on the screen. What the pack method does is to cause the label and frame to calculate size and position based on the content of the label and frame and any properties that have been set for the widget packing. In this case, the string 'Hello.' is the content, and we have specified no properties, so calling pack asks the label object and the frame object to size and position themselves around that string.

The Main Event

Which leaves us with the question of why we have the call to the method mainloop.

User interface programs are different from the programs we have written so far. Until now, our programs have started at the beginning, done something, and then stopped. User interface programs are examples of a type of program called *event-driven programs*. In event-driven programs, the program sets up objects and data structures and then processes events from the outside world.

All Tkinter programs are event-driven programs, even the ones such as those above that appear to have no interaction. The mainloop method contains all that is needed to deal with all the events and event handling. To set things going, we just have to call mainloop. It causes the frame to display itself, and all the action to happen.

You can see the event handling at work by using the mouse to click on the ✗ button of the frame. The operating system creates an event (called 'close') that is passed to the program associated with the frame. The mainloop method gets the event and processes it for us, causing the program to terminate. There is clearly a

The **✗** button is on the top left of the frames shown in this book. It may appear elsewhere for you. The position depends on operating system and window manager settings.

lot going on behind the scenes, but that is the whole point: abstraction is about being able to use a package without having to know all the details of what is happening inside the package.

7.5.2 Buttoning Up

Tkinter is clearly intended to support interaction using keyboard, mouse and screen, so we should show an example of an interactive program. The following is a variant of a program from the standard Python documentation:

```python
from Tkinter import Button
from Tkinter import Frame
from Tkinter import Tk

class HelloFrame ( Frame ) :

    def __init__ ( self , master ) :
        Frame.__init__ ( self , master )
        self.createButtonBar ()
        self.pack ()

    def hello ( self ) :
        print 'Hello.'

    def createButtonBar ( self ) :
        # Show how to do things the long way, each of the properties is set indiually.
        self.quitButton = Button ( self )
        self.quitButton[ 'text' ] = 'Quit'
        self.quitButton[ 'fg' ] = 'blue'
        self.quitButton[ 'command' ] = self.quit
        self.quitButton.pack ( { 'side' : 'left' } ) # Use a dictionary parameter -- old-fashioned.
        # Show how to do things using named parameters.
        self.helloButton = Button ( self , text = 'Hello' , command = self.hello )
        self.helloButton.pack ( side = 'left' )

if __name__ == '__main__' :
    root = Tk ()
    helloFrame = HelloFrame ( root )
    root.title ( 'Hello' )
    root.mainloop ()
```

When executed, this program displays a control panel with two buttons:

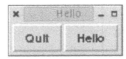

which prints Hello. on the terminal when the 'Hello' button is pressed, and quits when the 'Quit' button is pressed.

A Tkinter-based program has to have a frame in which all the graphics action happens. We have chosen here to make our class a subclass of the Tk Frame class. This is not essential: there are other ways of achieving the same goal, but as this is a chapter about inheritance it seems appropriate to use inheritance where it is reasonable to do so.

Tkinter Widgets

The following widget types are available using Tkinter:

Button	A simple button, used to execute a command or other operation.
Canvas	A widget used for drawing graphs and plots, create graphics editors, or for implement custom widgets.
Checkbutton	A widget presenting a variable that can have two distinct values. Clicking the button toggles between the values.
Entry	A text entry field.
Frame	A container widget. The frame can have a border and a background, and is used to group other widgets when creating an application or dialog layout.
Label	A widget for displaying text or an image.
Listbox	A widget for displaying a list of alternatives. The listbox can be configured to create radiobutton or checklist behavior.
Menu	A menu pane. Used to implement pulldown and popup menus.
Menubutton	A widget implementing pulldown menus.
Message	A widget for displaying text. Similar to the label widget, but can automatically wrap text to a given width or aspect ratio.
Radiobutton	A widget presenting a set of values, one of which is the currently selected one. Clicking the button sets the variable to that value, and clears all other radiobuttons associated with the same variable.
Scale	A widget for setting a numerical value by dragging a 'slider'.
Scrollbar	Standard scrollbars for use with canvas, entry, listbox, and text widgets.
Text	A widget for displaying formatted text. Allows you to display and edit text with various styles and attributes. Also supports embedded images and windows.
Toplevel	A container widget displayed as a separate, top-level window.

In the constructor of our class, we make a call to the method createButtonBar which is defined in our class. Then there is a call to the method pack which does not appear to exist in our class. It does, of course: pack is a method inherited from Frame, so is a method in our class that we can call.

This interface (just two buttons) doesn't really need that much design, so we let Tkinter size and arrange the widgets: we use the pack method with no parameters (accepting all the default values) to say "Arrange these widgets in whatever way you see fit." The result is exactly as we intended so the defaults do the right thing in this case.

The hello method provides the action associated with a press of the 'Hello' button. It is not the name that makes the association between button push and method execution: we make the association explicitly when we create the button by providing a named parameter for the command parameter. The 'Quit' button is associated with the quit method, which is defined in the Frame class and inherited by the Hello class. quit just does what it says: it causes the Python system to terminate execution, clearing up whatever it must to terminate tidily.

The createButtonBar method creates the two buttons ready for packing. We have shown two different styles of setting up widgets, the long way and the short way. One is not better than the other; they are just useful in different circumstances. The 'Quit' button is created and then set up using individual property assignments. Clearly the object created by the call to Button is a dictionary, since we are assigning values to keys – properties are keys in a dictionary. The 'Hello' button is created and set up at the same time using the named parameters feature. In this situation, using named parameters is probably more appropriate, but neither is right or wrong per se.

When packing the 'Quit' and 'Help' buttons, we have, for the first time, used parameters. The purpose of the parameters is to set explicit constraints on the packing. For both the 'Quit' and 'Hello' buttons we say that we want them to be packed on the left side. For the 'Quit' button we specify this using a dictionary literal parameter, whilst for the 'Hello' button we use a named parameter. Although both of these techniques achieve the goal, named parameters are now officially preferred over using an explicit dictionary literal. The reason is to do with the internal working of the package and the Python system. As we can and are using Tkinter as a "black box", we don't worry about the details, we just choose to follow the preferred style, accepting that there is a good reason for the preference.

In this code, we have shown different ways of setting up the widgets. However, in a real program, we would not mix styles in this way. Instead we would choose a style and use it consistently throughout the code. Consistency aids in reading and comprehending code and so is a 'good thing'. Conversely, chaotic style is obfuscating and so is a 'bad thing'.

This leads us to the main block. We create an instance of our class, set the window title, and then call the mainloop method. Our 'Hello' program has set up two buttons and is ready to process events. The mainloop method contains all that is needed to wait for events – in this case button presses – and then call the methods specified in our program at the appropriate time. In this case when the user presses the 'Quit' button the quit method is executed, and when the user presses the 'Hello' button, the hello method is executed.

7.5.3 Getting the Message

Always check to see if the widget you want already exist in the library before setting about programming something.

Writing a message to the console is not a particularly GUI way of interacting with the user. What we really want is for the press of the button to do something using user interface widgets. A quick search of online materials about Python ascertains that there is a module called tkMessageBox which provides functions for creating various 'off the shelf' interaction boxes. A quick read of the tkMessageBox documentation reveals that there is a function showinfo that does exactly what we need.

We change our program's behavior just by changing the hello method:

```
def hello ( self ) :
    tkMessageBox.showinfo ( 'Hello' , 'Hello.' )
```

Everything else remains the same – except that we have to put an import statement:

```
import tkMessageBox
```

at the top of the file to ensure correct access to the module.

With this version of the program, when we press the 'Hello' button we get a 'pop-up dialog':

Pressing the 'OK' button on this dialog makes it go away, exactly as we would expect. In fact, you have to press the 'OK' button for the 'Quit' and 'Hello' buttons on the main frame to become clickable again. The message box is called a *modal dialog*, which means that it is the only part of the application that is active when displayed.

HCI is Needed for User Interfaces

Designing and implementing good user interfaces is a seriously non-trivial task that really needs knowledge of programming, the physics of the interaction devices, ergonomics and (arguably most importantly) the cognitive psychology of users. The field of human–computer interaction (HCI) brings all these issues together and it is from this field that we can get good, usable user interface designs.

A really good user interface seems natural and intuitive, almost transparent to the user's use of the system. Creating a really good user interface is generally achieved by having HCI professionals involved in the design, implementation and evaluation of the user interface.

7.6 Polymorphism

7.6.1 What's the Point?

The example in Section 7.2 (page 220) presented the classes Point2d and Point3d. Point3d overrides the method distance (for calculating the distance between two points), since the method inherited from Point2d does not perform the correct calculation for a Point3d. Even if this was not the case, Point3d would still have a distance method, since it inherits from Point2d. The inheritance relationship provides a guarantee that the subclass has all the methods of the superclass.

Why is this interesting? Even though instances of Point2d and Point3d have different types, there are some methods that can be guaranteed to exist. This means we can do things like the following:

```
from point import Point2d, Point3d

points = [ ]
points.append ( Point2d ( 23 , 24 ) )
points.append ( Point3d ( 22 , 22 , 22 ) )
points += [ Point3d ( 0 , 0 , 100 ) , Point2d ( 1000 , 1000 ) ]
points.append ( Point3d ( -100 , 0 , 100 ) )
points += [ Point3d ( 25 , -50 , 25 ) , Point2d ( -99 , 45 ) ]
for p in points :
    print p.distance ( )
```

which, when executed, results in:

```
| > python pointList.py
33.2415402772
38.1051177665
100.0
1414.21356237
141.421356237
61.2372435696
108.747413762
| >
```

We have called the method distance using the variable p, but a different method is called depending on which object is currently associated with the variable: different objects do different things given the same method call. The actual method called depends on the object the method is being called on.

This programming language feature is known as *polymorphism* – Greek for 'many shapes'. If some objects all guarantee to have a specific set of methods, and if we implement our algorithms working on those objects using only that set of methods, then we do not have to know the exact class that was used to instantiate each of the objects. It is the set of methods that we can use that govern what we can do, the exact class of the object is not actually important.

It is not necessary for the objects to be instantiated from classes in an inheritance hierarchy for this approach to work. What matters is whether the methods needed are part of the object being used. However, having a common superclass and using only the methods of that class is one way of ensuring that all objects have the methods required.

Polymorphism is very important concept in programming, indeed it is one of the cornerstones of object-oriented programming. To emphasize this, let's cover the same point with a couple more examples.

7.6.2 Rolling a Handful of Dice

In our dice examples, we set things up so that polymorphic behavior is possible. All our die classes are direct or indirect subclasses of Die and so all have a roll method. This means that we can always roll a die without ever knowing what type it actually is.

```
>>> import die
>>>
>>> dice = [ die.D6 ( ) , die.D4 ( ) , die.D20 ( ) ]
>>> for i in dice :
...     print i.roll ( )
...
5
4
12
>>>
```

7.7 Shaping Up

A classic example of polymorphism is that of a 'shape library'. The idea is to define an inheritance hierarchy of shape descriptions all with a common superclass so that there is a guarantee that methods are defined. We can then use this hierarchy to show polymorphism by calling the methods without actually knowing the type of the object being worked with.

Here is a start at a hierarchy of classes that might be useful for a vector graphics system. Each shape can determine its own area and perimeter:

```
class Shape :
    def getArea ( self ) : return 0.0
    def getPerimeter ( self ) : return 0.0
```

```
class Rectangle ( Shape ) :
    def __init__ ( self , side1 , side2 ) :
        self.side1 = side1
        self.side2 = side2
    def getArea ( self ) : return self.side1 * self.side2
    def getPerimeter ( self ) : return ( 2 * self.side1 ) + ( 2 * self.side2 )

class Square ( Rectangle ) :
    def __init__ ( self , side ) :
        Rectangle.__init__ ( self , side , side )

class Circle ( Shape ) :
    def __init__ ( self , radius ) :
        self.radius = radius
    def getArea ( self ) :
        import math
        return math.pi * self.radius * self.radius
    def getPerimeter(self):
        import math
        return 2 * math.pi * self.radius

if __name__ == '__main__' :
    r = Rectangle ( 2 , 4 )
    assert r.getArea ( ) == 8
    assert r.getPerimeter ( ) == 12
    r = Square ( 4 )
    assert r.getArea ( ) == 16
    assert r.getPerimeter ( ) == 16
    r = Circle ( 4 )
    assert r.getArea ( ) == 50.26548245743669181504
    assert r.getPerimeter ( ) == 25.13274122871834590752
```

We can iterate through lists of shapes and call the methods common to all shape types without knowing the exact type of the shape object:

```
from shapes import Rectangle
from shapes import Square
from shapes import Circle

shapes = [ Rectangle ( 1 , 2 ) , Square ( 77 ) , Circle ( 70 ) , Rectangle ( 86 , 99 ) , Square ( 6 ) ]
for s in shapes :
    print s.getArea ( ) , ',' , s.getPerimeter ( )
```

which results in:

```
2 , 6
5929 , 308
15393.8040026 , 439.822971503
8514 , 370
36 , 24
```

Using the polymorphism of objects that have a common superclass (Shape in this case), we can use methods that all Shape objects have without finding out which subclass of Shape was used to instantiated the object.

7.8   Multiple Inheritance

The shapes example of the previous section obviously leads to the question: "How do we draw the shapes?" Why don't we 'connect' our shapes classes to the Turtle module? Here is a module that defines some drawable shapes, with a small test:

```
import shapes
import turtle

class Drawable :
    def goto ( self , x , y ) :
        turtle.up ()
        turtle.goto ( x , y )
        turtle.down ()
    def draw ( self , x , y ) : pass

class DrawableRectangle ( Drawable , shapes.Rectangle ) :
    def __init__ ( self , side1 , side2 ) :
        shapes.Rectangle.__init__ ( self , side1 , side2 )
    def draw ( self , x , y ) :
        self.goto ( x , y )
        turtle.goto ( x + self.side1 , y )
        turtle.goto ( x + self.side1 , y + self.side2 )
        turtle.goto ( x , y + self.side2 )
        turtle.goto ( x , y )

class DrawableSquare ( DrawableRectangle ) :
    def __init__ ( self , side ) :
        DrawableRectangle.__init__ ( self , side , side )

class DrawableCircle ( Drawable , shapes.Circle ) :
    def __init__ ( self , radius ) :
        shapes.Circle.__init__ ( self , radius )
    def draw ( self , x , y ) :
        self.goto ( x , y )
        turtle.circle ( self.radius )

if __name__ == '__main__' :
    r = DrawableRectangle ( 20 , 40 )
    assert r.getArea () == 800
    assert r.getPerimeter () == 120
    r.draw ( 60 , 50 )
    r = DrawableSquare ( 40 )
    assert r.getArea () == 1600
    assert r.getPerimeter () == 160
    r.draw ( 10 , 10 )
    r = DrawableCircle ( 40 )
    assert r.getArea () == 5026.548245743669181504
    assert r.getPerimeter () == 251.3274122871834590752
    r.draw ( -40 , -50 )
    raw_input ( 'Press any key to terminate: ' )
```

This is not quite inheritance as we described earlier: there are two superclasses.

Figure 7.1 shows the result of executing this program.

Clearly there is a new Python feature here: we have more than one superclass! Most of the code here is fairly standard: we import the Rectangle, Square, and Circle classes from the shapes module. The Drawable class defined here is nothing special: it is the superclass for all drawable shapes. Drawable defines a support method, goto, since all drawing will use this, and it defines a draw method for which it provides no code – the **pass** statement is a statement that does nothing, it is there just to ensure that there is a statement in the method body, as required by Python.

Now what about those superclasses? We define the classes DrawableRectangle and DrawableCircle, both of which have two superclasses – we have a list of two superclasses in the method definition. A DrawableRectangle is both a Drawable and a Rectangle. Likewise, DrawableCircle is both a Drawable and a Circle.

What does this multiple inheritance mean? The subclass inherits all the variables and methods from more than one superclasses. The order of the superclasses in the class definition defines the order in which the names are searched for. In the case of DrawableRectangle, names are first looked up in DrawableRectangle. If not found there, Drawable is searched. If not found there, Rectangle is searched. If not found there, Shape is searched. If a name is still not found an exception is raised.

Clearly, multiple inheritance introduces some extra complexities over single inheritance, but this just means being more careful when using it.

7.9 Non-Linear Data Structures

Lists and tuples are useful ways of structuring data but they are clearly linear – they are sequences and sequences are linear. Although dictionaries are not sequences, they are effectively linear, since they just provide a mapping between a set of keys and their associated values. The world, though, is full of non-linear structures. Family trees, for example, are clearly not linear – highlighted by the use of the term 'tree' to describe a structure with many branches. Inheritance hierarchies are generally not linear structures. We will also find that creating user interfaces means that we have to create non-linear structures of widgets. So trees are important in computing as well as in the real world.

It is perhaps helpful to have representative diagrams:

A linear data structure is one in which each node can only have 0 or 1 children.

A sequence

A binary tree

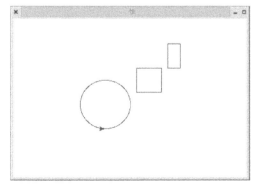

Figure 7.1

The result of drawing some shapes.

The Diamond Problem

Many people believe that multiple inheritance is a bad idea because of the Diamond Problem. The designers of Java definitely believed this, so Java does not allow multiple inheritance. What is the Diamond Problem? In an inheritance hierarchy where multiple inheritance is allowed, you can have situations such as:

Classes B and C are distinct subclasses of the common superclass A. Class D then multiply inherits from both B and C. So for Python, the Diamond Problem is: "When does A get searched during name lookup?" Python has a simple algorithm to deal with this:

- List all the classes to be searched as though there was no multiple inheritance. This gives: D, B, A, C, A.
- Remove all but the last occurrence of any repeated class names. This gives: D, B, C, A.

Python doesn't therefore have any difficulties with multiple inheritance.

On the left we have a sequence. The items in the structure are ordered, so we can count them off, as shown. Lists, tuples, and strings are sequences; the items in them are strictly ordered. On the right, we have a tree structure. Each node in the tree can have 0, 1 or 2 child nodes. Since the maximum number of children a node can have is 2, we have a *binary tree*.

7.9.1 Representing and Evaluating Expressions

For our first example of non-linear data structures, we are going to look at representing and evaluating arithmetic expressions. In Section 4.7 (page 137) we introduced the idea of a lexer and a parser. The task of a lexer is to take a sequence of characters and create tokens from them. The token sequence is then passed to a parser which creates an data structure to represent the meaning of the original character sequence. So, for example, the character sequence:

    2 + 3 * 4

is a character sequence that represents an arithmetic expression which, when evaluated, results in the integer value 14. We can show that this is so by using the Python system:

    |> python -c 'print 2 + 3 * 4'
    14
    |>

Clearly the Python system is lexing and parsing the expression so that it can be evaluated.

Parsing and lexing is generally controlled by a grammar – every language has rules and the grammar of a language is that set of rules. For natural languages such as English, Chinese, Spanish, etc., the grammar is generally quite complicated. Programming languages, on the other hand, tend to have much simpler grammars, ones that can be written down relatively straightforwardly. If we restrict ourselves to lexing and parsing only arithmetic expressions with no variables and no parentheses (brackets) then the grammar is actually simple:

> <*digit*> :: (0 | 1 | 2 | 3 | 4 | 5 | 6 | 7 | 8 | 9)
> <*number*> :: <*digit*>* .? <*digit*>*
> <*expression*> :: <*number*>
> | <*expression*> + <*expression*>
> | <*expression*> - <*expression*>
> | <*expression*> * <*expression*>
> | <*expression*> / <*expression*>

So, our language has numbers, which are like floats (a string of digits followed, optionally, by a decimal point and another string of digits) and expressions. Expressions can be a number or two expressions added, or subtracted, or multiplied, or divided together. So, the following are all valid expressions:

> 1000
> 1 + 3
> 1 * 2 + 3 / 4 - 5

and the following are invalid:

> 1000 +
> 1 * / 3
> 1 && 2

The question now is: "How are we going to represent the expression once lexed and parsed?" Clearly we are going to use objects, but what are the classes of the objects?

We will have a class Exp which will be the superclass of all objects used in the representation of the expression. One subclass of Exp will be Num, which represents numeric values. Other subclasses will be Add, Sub, Mul and Div to represent the operators in expressions. Each operator has a left and right operand which themselves can be expressions – very recursive. Each rule of the grammar is represented using an object of a specific class. The core of the Exp class will be methods to:

- Return a string representation (__str__).

- Evaluate the expression represented by the object (evaluate).

We represent expressions as trees of objects of types appropriate for the parts of the expression. So we represent the expression 1 + 2 with the diagram:

which, in terms of objects, really means:

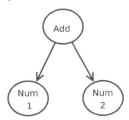

In a diagram like this, the 1, 2 and + are *nodes*. The + node has two *child nodes*, 1 and 2. Nodes with no children are called *leaf nodes*.

which we can construct in a Python program with the expression:

Add (Num (1) , Num (2))

The function calls cause the creation of the objects with the desired connections: the Num calls create objects with no children, and the Add call creates an object with two children – the two Num objects.

Now consider the expression 1 + 2 - 5 * 6, which can be drawn:

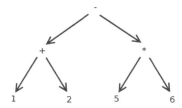

with the obvious interpretation in terms of objects, and represented as objects in Python:

Sub (Add (Num (1) , Num (2)) , Mul (Num (5) , Num (6)))

This is clearly not linear, it is definitely a *tree*, a *binary tree* in fact. Why is this? A binary tree is a tree in which each node has zero, one or two children.

So having created our tree representation of the expression, it is easy to evaluate: we call the evaluate method on the top object (usually called the *root node*) which then recursively evaluates its left and right nodes and then calculates the result.

Therefore to evaluate the tree that represents 1 + 2 - 5 * 6, we evaluate the - node by evaluating the left node then the right node and subtracting the latter from the former:

- The left node is the expression 1 + 2, so we evaluate the left node (1) then the right node (2) and add the two, returning the value 3.

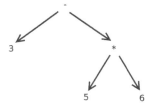

- The right node is the expression 5 * 6, so we evaluate the left node (5) then the right node (6) and multiply the two to return 30.

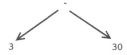

- The overall result is 3 - 30, i.e. -27.

-27

Being able to call methods on objects and rely on polymorphism makes this very straightforward to program:

```
class Exp :
    def __str__ ( self ) : return ''
    def eval ( self ) : return 0

class Num ( Exp ) :
    def __init__ ( self , num ) : self.num = num
    def __str__ ( self ) : return str ( self.num )
    def eval ( self ) : return self.num

class Add ( Exp ) :
    def __init__ ( self , left , right ) :
        self.left = left
        self.right = right
    def __str__ ( self ) : return '(' + str ( self.left ) + ') + (' + str ( self.right ) + ')'
    def eval ( self ) : return self.left.eval () + self.right.eval ()

class Sub ( Exp ) :
    def __init__ ( self , left , right ) :
        self.left = left
        self.right = right
    def __str__ ( self ) : return '(' + str ( self.left ) + ') - (' + str ( self.right ) + ')'
    def eval ( self ) : return self.left.eval () - self.right.eval ()

class Mul ( Exp ) :
    def __init__ ( self , left , right ) :
        self.left = left
        self.right = right
    def __str__ ( self ) : return '(' + str ( self.left ) + ') * (' + str ( self.right ) + ')'
    def eval ( self ) : return self.left.eval () * self.right.eval ()

class Div ( Exp ) :
    def __init__ ( self , left , right ) :
        self.left = left
        self.right = right
    def __str__ ( self ) : return '(' + str ( self.left ) + ') / (' + str ( self.right ) + ')'
    def eval ( self ) : return self.left.eval () / self.right.eval ()

if __name__ == '__main__' :
    def test ( exp ) : print exp , ' Evaluates to:' , exp.eval ()
    expr = []
    expr.append ( Add (Num ( 1 ) , Num ( 2 ) ) )
    expr.append ( Sub ( Add ( Num ( 1 ) , Num ( 2 ) ) , Mul ( Num ( 5 ) , Num ( 6 ) ) ) )
    expr.append ( Div ( Sub ( Add ( Num ( 1 ) , Num ( 2 ) ) , Mul ( Num ( 5 ) , Num ( 6 ) ) ) , Num ( 2 ) ) )
    map ( test , expr )
```

When executed this results in:

```
|> python expressionEvaluation.py
( 1 ) + ( 2 )  Evaluates to: 3
( ( 1 ) + ( 2 ) ) - ( ( 5 ) * ( 6 ) )  Evaluates to: -27
( ( ( 1 ) + ( 2 ) ) - ( ( 5 ) * ( 6 ) ) ) / ( 2 )  Evaluates to: -14
|>
```

exactly as anticipated. If that last one made you think that the answer should be -13.5 then remember that currently division between ints delivers an int in Python.

Trees, recursion and polymorphism combine here to make things straightforward. Of course, this begs the question of how we do the lexing and parsing.

This is a big area of study, and deserves a book to itself. Rather than do the topic injustice by giving a too cursory introduction here, we are going to leave this as a dangling thread in this book. We strongly recommend reading one of the many excellent textbooks on lexing and parsing, it is an important topic in computing.

7.9.2 GUI Trees

Building graphical user interfaces (GUIs) is a matter of creating a non-linear structure of widgets. Each widget in the GUI is represented by an object and each object has to know which widget is its parent.

Say for example we want to create the interface:

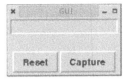

where we have a text entry box at the top, a display area in the middle, and two buttons side-by-side at the bottom. In terms of widgets we have the structure:

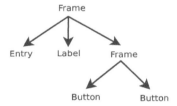

The overall container is a Frame that has an Entry, Label, and Frame widget stacked vertically. The contained Frame widget has two Button widgets laid out horizontally.

This technique of using Frame widgets to provide 'boxes' in which to put and lay out widgets, and then use them as widgets, is the whole purpose of Frame: it is a tool for creating appropriate layouts of widgets. Clearly, the widget structure of a user interface is invariably going to be tree structured rather than linear.

What about the code? It is really a question of writing the statement in the constructor to realize the required object structure. We make calls of the various methods with appropriate parameters, and it all works:

```
import Tkinter
import tkMessageBox

class GuiFrame ( Tkinter.Frame ) :

    def __init__ ( self , master ) :
        Tkinter.Frame.__init__ ( self , master )
        self.entry = Tkinter.Entry ( self )
        self.entry.pack ()
        self.label = Tkinter.Label ( self )
        self.label.pack ()
        buttonBar = Tkinter.Frame ( self )
        buttonBar.pack ()
        resetButton = Tkinter.Button ( buttonBar , text = 'Reset' , command = self.reset )
```

```
        resetButton.pack ( side = 'left' )
        captureButton = Tkinter.Button ( buttonBar , text = 'Capture' , command = self.capture )
        captureButton.pack ( side = 'right' )
        self.pack ()

    def reset ( self ) :
        self.label [ 'text' ] = "

    def capture ( self ) :
        self.label [ 'text' ] = self.entry.get ()

if __name__ == '__main__' :
    root = Tkinter.Tk ()
    frame = GuiFrame ( root )
    root.title ( 'GUI' )
    root.mainloop ()
```

Note that we only make the variables that refer to objects we need to work with in methods other than the constructor into instance variables. The Entry object and the Label object have to be accessible in other methods of the class, so we make the variables that refer to them instance variables. The contained Frame object and its two Button objects don't need to be accessed in our program once they are set up, so the variables referring to them in the constructor are simply local variables.

The point here is that we don't just add instance variables to the class unnecessarily. Our defensive programming approach means that we only make a variable into an instance variable if it is essential that it be so. Anything else should be kept as local as possible. Where many methods need to access an object, the variable referring to it needs to be an instance variable of the class. If this is not the case then do not make it an instance variable. The idea here is to minimize the scope of variables, and thus minimize the chances of things going wrong.

You may now be thinking: "Why not just use local functions in the constructor rather than methods?" True, we could indeed do this:

```
import Tkinter
import tkMessageBox

class GuiFrame ( Tkinter.Frame ) :

    def __init__ ( self , master ) :
        Tkinter.Frame.__init__ ( self , master )
        entry = Tkinter.Entry ( self )
        entry.pack ()
        label = Tkinter.Label ( self )
        label.pack ()
        def reset () :
            label [ 'text' ] = "
        def capture () :
            label [ 'text' ] = entry.get ()
        buttonBar = Tkinter.Frame ( self )
        buttonBar.pack ()
        resetButton = Tkinter.Button ( buttonBar , text = 'Reset' , command = reset )
        resetButton.pack ( side = 'left' )
        captureButton = Tkinter.Button ( buttonBar , text = 'Capture' , command = capture )
        captureButton.pack ( side = 'right' )
        self.pack ()
```

```
if __name__ == '__main__' :
    root = Tkinter.Tk ( )
    frame = GuiFrame ( root )
    root.title ( 'GUI' )
    root.mainloop ( )
```

It is difficult to say definitively whether the method approach or the local function approach is a better way of proceeding. Restricting the scope of a name to the smallest possible region of a program is always a good idea since it minimizes the possibility of unexpected error. On the other hand placing local functions within a method is arguably not as clear as having all functions and methods separated. Often this is a matter of personal choice. When many people are working together, they need to discuss these issues and come to a consensus as to the style the group will use. Sometimes, especially in large companies, someone will create a style manual that defines the 'house style' and everyone is expected to stick to it even if they disagree with it.

There is a document laying out Guido van Rossum's view on the coding style issue, *Style Guide for Python Code*, which can be found at http://www.python.org/dev/peps/pep-0008. Not everyone agrees with all of that document, as you can tell from the style of code in this book.

The point is not that there is one true way, the point is that that consistency of style in a given body of code is most important.

7.9.3 An Example: A Traffic Light

We said at the end of Section 6.5 (page 202) that we should create a graphical representation of a traffic light. As a starting point we want something like:

that then sequences through the states. What we have here is three lights stacked vertically. We could find out how to draw three circles on a single widget (this is possible), but it seems a better idea to create classes to represent each light. We can encapsulate behavior and representation so that our traffic light class can be concerned with sequencing three lights and not with issues of how the lights are represented. It is all down to the separation of concerns and using classes to create abstractions.

Based on the code from Section 6.5 (page 200), we came up with:

```
import time
import Tkinter

class TrafficLight ( Tkinter.Frame ) :
    '''A standard three-light traffic light.'''

    class Light ( Tkinter.Canvas ) :
        '''An individual light to be part of a traffic light.'''
        def __init__ ( self , master , color ) :
            size = 30
```

```
            halfPadding = 2
            Tkinter.Canvas.__init__ (
                self , master ,
                width = size + 2 * halfPadding , height = size + 2 * halfPadding )
            self.id = self.create_oval (
                halfPadding , halfPadding ,
                size + halfPadding , size + halfPadding ,
                fill = 'black' )
            self.color = color
        def on ( self ) : self.itemconfigure ( self.id , fill = self.color )
        def off ( self ) : self.itemconfigure ( self.id , fill = 'black' )

    states = ( ( True , False , False ) , ( False , False , True ) , ( False , True , False ) )

    def __init__ ( self , master , timings ) :
        Tkinter.Frame.__init__ ( self , master )
        if len ( timings ) != len ( self.states ) :
            raise ValueError , "Incorrect number of timing values."
        self.timings = timings
        self.current = 0
        self.lights = (
            TrafficLight.Light ( self , 'red' ) ,
            TrafficLight.Light ( self , 'yellow' ) ,
            TrafficLight.Light ( self , 'green' )
            )
        self.lights[0].on ( )
        for l in self.lights : l.pack ( )
        self.pack ( )

    def sequence ( self ) :
        for i in range ( len ( self.timings ) ) :
            time.sleep ( self.timings[self.current] )
            self.current = ( self.current + 1 ) % len ( self.states )
            for i in range ( len ( self.lights ) ) :
                if self.states[self.current][i] : self.lights[i].on ( )
                else : self.lights[i].off ( )

if __name__ == '__main__' :
    root = Tkinter.Tk ( )
    eastWestLight = TrafficLight ( root , ( 5 , 5 , 2 ) )
    root.mainloop ( )
```

We have a class Light in our class TrafficLight, which inherits from Tkinter.Canvas. A Light is therefore a drawing area where we can draw things – because it is a subclass of Tkinter.Canvas. In particular, we are going to draw a circle of some color. The use of halfPadding in the size calculations is to make sure that the circle is smaller than and centered on the square that is the canvas. A Light object has two methods, on and off that switch the light on and off by causing a change in the state of the drawing. In particular, we change the fill color of the circle.

The states class variable has changed dramatically. Instead of being a trio of strings, it is now a trio of tuples, each of three Booleans. What we have done is to change the states from strings to specifications of which light is on and which light is off for a given state. We have assumed that the red light is light 0, the amber light is light 1 and the green light is light 2.

The constructor for TrafficLight changes quite a lot as well. We create a tuple of Light objects being very careful that 0 is red, 1 is amber and 2 is green to coordinate with the states class variable. This need for coordination is called *coupling* and is generally something to minimize as much as possible. Here though we have coupling that is central to the correctness of our implementation. Fortunately though it is only an issue for the implementation of the class: users of the class never need to know of the coupling.

Of course there is one huge drawback to this code: the traffic light doesn't actually do anything, it just sits there, red, all the time. The problem is that we have no events for the Tkinter system to respond to to make the sequencing happen. We have just created the representation and the ability to do something. To actually animate things we need a new feature: we need *threads*.

Rather than delve into threads immediately, we leave this program for now and come back to it after we have introduced threads (Section 11.3).

7.10 Quack, Quack

You may be thinking "What on earth have ducks got to do with programming?" But we really do want to introduce ducks. We're not going to discuss ducks per se, but we do want to introduce the Duck Test, 'duck typing' and look again at polymorphism. There are many expressions of the Duck Test, but all of them are something like:

> If it looks like a duck, walks like a duck, swims like a duck, and quacks like a duck, then it must be a duck.

This is an example of *inductive reasoning*. Some say this is an example of *inducktive reasoning* and others that it is *deducktive reasoning*, but what it definitely isn't is *deductive reasoning*. Logic and philosophy are a very big area and this is a book on programming, so let's get on with the reason for introducing the Duck Test.

The Duck Test

The origins of the 'Duck Test' quote are shrouded in the mists of time. Wikipedia (http://en.wikipedia.org/wiki/Duck_test), and other sources, state that in Richard Immerman's book*The CIA in Guatemala: The Foreign Policy of Intervention* (University of Texas Press, 1982) there is a quote of a comment made in 1950 by Richard Patterson, the then United States Ambassador to Guatemala:

> Suppose you see a bird walking around in a farm yard. This bird has no label that says 'duck'. But the bird certainly looks like a duck. Also, he goes to the pond and you notice that he swims like a duck. Then he opens his beak and quacks like a duck. Well, by this time you have probably reached the conclusion that the bird is a duck, whether he's wearing a label or not.

Some sources appear to indicate that, the rather more 'sound byte' form:

> If it walks like a duck, and quacks like a duck, it must be a duck.

is due to Ronald Reagan in a conversation with Lyn Nofziger, 1967-08-31.

7.10.1 Duck Typing

When we introduced polymorphism earlier (Section 7.6, page 231), we emphasized the role of the inheritance hierarchy in providing the foundation for polymorphism. In programming languages such as C++, inheritance is required for polymorphic behavior. Programming language like Java introduce *interfaces* that can be *conformed to* by objects.

An interface is a specification of a set of methods. An object conforms to an interface if it has all the methods required by the interface. Interfaces as well as classes are types and so type correctness can be checked at compile time. This ensures that there are as few errors as possible to be detected at run time.

Python, like other *dynamic programming languages* such as Groovy, Ruby, Lua, Smalltalk, etc., does not bother with explicit interfaces and compile time type checking. Parameters to functions and methods have no type until they are executed. All functions and methods are polymorphic: we don't actually know the type of the object associated with a variable.

If we have a function that we designed to be given some form of die:

```
def rollEm ( a , b ) :
    a.roll ( )
    b.roll ( )
```

the variables a and b don't actually know what the type of the object is going to be until the code executes. It is an assumption that the objects these variables refer to will have a method roll. At run time, an attempt is made to execute the roll method on the objects the variables refer to, and if the calls succeed, execution continues. However, there is the possibility that the object may not have a roll method. In this situation, an exception is raised – an AttributeError. The error message, if the exception is not handled, will look something like:

```
Traceback (most recent call last):
  File "<stdin>", line 1, in <module>
  File "<stdin>", line 2, in rollEm
AttributeError: X instance has no attribute 'roll'
```

where X will be the type of the object passed as a parameter that is associated with the variable a.

In the context in which the function was written – playing with dice and expecting the parameters to be die objects – the exception can never occur. However, the function makes no assumptions that the parameter objects are die objects. The function is fully polymorphic. We can pass it any object that has a roll method. As long as the object has roll in its interface it can be used: if it behaves like a die, then it must be a die – even if it isn't.

Here then is why it is called 'duck typing'. A function or method in Python only cares about the methods actually available in the object it is working with at the time it is working with it: there is no notion of checking to see whether the object is of the right class. If the object has the methods that are required to be there, there is no problem. If the object has the methods we need, then it is of the right type.

A trivial example of this is:

```
import die

class Duck :
    def __str__ ( self ) : return 'quack'
    def roll ( self ) : pass

things = [ die.D6 ( ) , Duck ( ) , die.D4 ( ) , Duck ( ) ]
```

> Methods are stored in the state of an object using attributes. If searching for a method fails to find an attribute of the right name, an AttributeError is raised.

```
for t in things :
    print t

for t in things :
    t.roll ()

for t in things :
    print t
```

which, when executed results in:

```
| > python duck.py
1
quack
1
quack
4
quack
3
quack
| >
```

The list contains some objects, not all of which are die. Moreover they are not all objects instantiated from the same inheritance hierarchy. Yet they can be used by the function rollEm polymorphically because all the objects have all the methods needed by rollEm.

So 'duck typing' is really the ultimate in substitutability: we don't bother with types, we just try it and see what happens. The Pythonic Way of programming is to assume that things will be correct and deal with failure if it happens.

Duck Typing

The Python Tutorial give this definition of Duck Typing:

> Pythonic programming style that determines an object's type by inspection of its method or attribute signature rather than by explicit relationship to some type object ("If it looks like a duck and quacks like a duck, it must be a duck.") By emphasizing interfaces rather than specific types, well-designed code improves its flexibility by allowing polymorphic substitution. Duck-typing avoids tests using type or isinstance. Instead, it typically employs hasattr tests or EAFP programming.

EAFP

EAFP is the acronym for "it's easier to ask for forgiveness than permission" – reputedly first applied to computer programming by Grace Hopper. The definition from the Python Tutorial is:

> This common Python coding style assumes the existence of valid keys or attributes and catches exceptions if the assumption proves false. This clean and fast style is characterized by the presence of many try and except statements. The technique contrasts with the LBYL style that is common in many other languages such as C.

LBYL here stands for 'look before you leap' and describes the style of programming in which the state is checked before a function or method call is made to ensure that the call will not fail.

7.10.2 Not Everyone Likes Ducks

Although 'duck typing' is standard in all dynamic programming languages (Python, Groovy, Ruby, Lua, etc.), it is not universally agreed that it is a good thing. People who program in C, C++, Java, Eiffel, etc., tend to be very strong proponents of what has been called the LBYL or "look before you leap" style of programming. In the LBYL style strong type checking prior to execution and rigidly correct types are the order of the day. The emphasis is on all interfaces being checked and found correct before execution of any calls. Groovy allows elements of this style of programming, even though it is a dynamic programming languages. The Python programming language currently has no way of enforcing *programming to interfaces*, which means that all method calls on objects are check at compile time to ensure that parameters are of the correct types.

Many people feel that whilst dynamic languages are fine for prototyping, final production systems must be programmed in languages with strong typing – i.e. programming to interfaces should be enforced. The most extreme example of this is Eiffel. That language supports the full *Design by Contract* approach to programming, which involves not only programming to interfaces but also having full pre- and post-conditions for every method call.

The dynamic programming community says, "If a program has a proper test suite then there is no need for programming to interfaces and design by contract." Certainly it is true that having a proper test suite is important but all the arguments between the camps gets very polarized very quickly.

Clearly though we must now discuss how to do testing properly in Python. However, before we can cover that topic properly, we need to introduce a little more on input/output in Python, and in particular how to work with files. So the next chapter is on file handling then we will look at proper testing.

> Chapter Summary
>
> In this chapter we have found that:
>
> - Inheritance is a relationship between classes.
> - Inheritance is an 'is-a' relationship between types.
> - Aggregation is a 'has-a' relationship between classes.
> - Polymorphism is a consequence of inheritance.
> - Tkinter is a package for supporting user interface graphics.
> - Multiple inheritance is a way of allowing an object to have more that one type.
> - Tree data structures are a form of non-linear data structure.
> - Ducks seems to have a role in dynamic programming.
> - Polymorphism is important in programming.

Self-Review Questions

Self-review 7.1 What do the terms 'subclass' and 'superclass' mean in object-oriented programming?

Self-review 7.2 What does the following declaration mean?

```
class Foo ( Bar ) :
```

Self-review 7.3 What is the built-in name object in Python?

Self-review 7.4 What is the difference between single and multiple inheritance?

Self-review 7.5 What is the Diamond Problem in multiple inheritance?

Self-review 7.6 Define the terms:

1. Association.
2. Aggregation.

Self-review 7.7 In graphical user interfaces, what are:

1. Widgets.
2. Callbacks.
3. Events.
4. Event loops.
5. Event handler.

Self-review 7.8 What does the pack method do in Tkinter widgets?

Self-review 7.9 What is a modal dialog box?

Self-review 7.10 What is polymorphism? How is it related to object-oriented programming? Give a short example of a piece of code that exploits polymorphism.

Self-review 7.11 Using the expression evaluator from Section 7.9.1 (page 236), draw the object diagram that represents the following Python expression:

Mul (3 , Div (Add (1 , 2) , Sub (5 , 8)))

What does that expression evaluate to?

Self-review 7.12 What is duck typing?

Self-review 7.13 What does the name self mean? Is self a Python keyword?

Self-review 7.14 Explain what is happening in the following code:

```
class Foo ( Bar ) :
    def __init__ ( self ) :
        Bar.__init__ ( self )
        return
```

Programming Exercises

Exercise 7.1 Extend the traffic light program to include a short red+amber 'prepare to go' state as is used for traffic lights in the UK, and other places.

Exercise 7.2 Create a subclasses of your Account class (from Exercise 6.6) called CreditAccount in which the user is charged a set amount for every withdrawal that is made. If the user is overdrawn, the withdrawal charge is doubled.

Exercise 7.3 Create a subclasses of your Account class (from Exercise 6.6) called StudentAccount in which new accounts start off with a balance of £500 and an overdraft of up to £3000 is allowed, with no charges for withdrawal.

Exercise 7.4 Create versions of:

1. DrawableRectangle
2. DrawableSquare
3. DrawableCircle

that work using the Tkinter package.

Exercise 7.5 Create a class called Number and two subclasses Binary and Roman for dealing with different sorts of number representation. The constructors to Binary and Roman should take a string argument so that you can use them like this:

```
b = Binary ('11010101')
r = Roman ('MCMLXXVIII')
```

In your Number class you need to have methods that are common to all types of number representation:

1. You'll want a private method called __to_int that returns an ordinary integer representation of the calling object.
2. You'll need to override the built-in method __str__ that returns a string representation of the number which the calling object represents.
3. You'll need to override the __int__ method that is used by calls to the int function which converts its argument to an integer.

In all three classes you'll need an __int__ method that calls the __to_int method in the calling object – even though Binary and Roman are subclasses of Number, they still need an __int__ method of their own. Why is this? If you're not sure you have understood why this works, when you've finished this exercise, comment out the definition of __int__ in Binary and Roman and see what happens.

You'll need to override __to_int in the Binary and Roman classes. For the method in Roman, you may want to use the algorithm in Section 4.8.2 to parse a Roman numeral into an integer. Make the LUT (lookup table) a class variable (rather than an instance variable).

For the Binary class, you'll need to convert between binary and decimal. As a reminder of the algorithm, here's an example:

$$1010101 \rightarrow 1 \times 2^6 + 0 \times 2^5 + 1 \times 2^4 + 0 \times 2^3 + 1 \times 2^2 + + 0 \times 2^1 + 1 \times 2^0$$

When you have written all your classes you'll need to test them. Below is the beginnings of a test program you can use to help you:

```
def test ( ) :
    data = [
        ( Binary ( '0' ) , 0 ) , ( Binary ( '1' ) , 1 ) ,
        ( Binary ( '10' ) , 2 ) , ( Binary ( '11' ) , 3 ) ,
        ( Binary ( '100' ) , 4 ) , ( Binary ( '101' ) , 5 ) ,
        ( Binary ( '10101010101' ) , 1365 ) ,
        ( Roman ( 'I' ) , 1 ) , ( Roman ( 'II' ) , 2 ) ,
        ( Roman ( 'IV' ) , 4 ) , ( Roman ( 'VI' ) , 6 ) ,
        ( Roman ( 'IX' ) , 9 ) , ( Roman ( 'X' ) , 10 ) ,
        ( Roman ( 'XI' ) , 11 ) , ( Roman ( 'MM' ) , 2000 ) ,
        ( Roman ( 'MCMLXXVIII') , 1978 )
        ]
    for entry in data :
        assert int ( entry[0] ) == entry[1]

if __name__ == '__main__' :
    test ( )
```

When your code works you should get no assertion failures when you execute the test program.

Exercise 7.6 On page 236 we introduced the Diamond Problem of object-oriented programming languages and explained how Python deals with it. In this exercise you will explore how Python handles multiple inheritance.

Below are class definitions that exhibit the Diamond Problem. Start off by drawing a diagram to show the inheritance relationships between the five classes.

Create objects that are instances of classes D and E. Call the **foobar** and **barfoo** methods in both objects. What is the difference between the output from the two objects? Why does this happen?

```
class A :
    def foobar ( self ) :
        print 'Class A'
    def barfoo ( self ) :
        print 'barfoo from class A!'
class B ( A ) :
    def foobar ( self ) :
        print 'Class B inherits from A'
    def barfoo ( self ) :
        print 'barfoo from class B!'
class C ( A ) :
    def foobar ( self ) :
        print 'Class C inherits from A'
    def barfoo ( self ) :
        print 'barfoo from class C!'
class D ( B , C ) :
    def __init__ ( self ) :
        return
class E ( C , B ) :
    def __init__ ( self ) :
        return
```

Exercise 7.7 Write a program that takes a list of Point objects (from Section 7.2, page 220) and draws them with the Turtle module. Your code should be polymorphic. A Point2D object represents a point on the screen, but if you need to move the turtle to a point represented by a Point3D object, just ignore the *z* component.

Here is some test data to get you started:

```
square = [
    Point2D ( 0.0 , 0.0 ) , Point2D ( 100.0 , 0.0 ) , Point2D ( 100.0 , 100.0 ) ,
    Point2D ( 0.0 , 100.0 ) , Point2D ( 0.0 , 0.0 )
]
rectangle = [
    Point2D ( 0.0 , 0.0 ) , Point2D ( 200.0 , 0.0 ) , Point2D ( 200.0 , 100.0 ) ,
    Point2D ( 0.0 , 100.0 ) , Point2D ( 0.0 , 0.0 )
]
pentagon = [
    Point2D ( 0.0 , 0.0 ) , Point2D ( 100.0 , 0.0 ) , Point2D ( 131.0 , 95.0 ) ,
    Point2D ( 50.0 , 154.0 ) , Point2D ( -30.0 , 95.0 ) , Point2D ( 0.0 , 0.0 )
]
square3 = [
    Point3D ( 0.0 , 0.0 , 1.0 ) , Point3D ( 100.0 , 0.0 , 1.0 ) , Point3D ( 100.0 , 100.0 , 1.0 ) ,
    Point3D ( 0.0 , 100.0 , 1.0 ) , Point3D ( 0.0 , 0.0 , 1.0 )
]
square23 = [
    Point3D ( 0.0 , 0.0 , 1.0 ) , Point2D ( 100.0 , 0.0 ) , Point2D ( 100.0 , 100.0 ) ,
    Point3D ( 0.0 , 100.0 , 1.0 ) , Point2D ( 0.0 , 0.0 )
]
```

Hint: To draw these shapes elegantly, it would be sensible to lift the 'pen' of the turtle off the screen before moving from the origin to the first point.

Exercise 7.8 Write a version of the Caesar cipher from Section 4.6.2 (page 131) with a simple GUI. Allow users to enter text in a text box, then generate an enciphered version of the text when they press a button. Let users change the key that is used by the cipher either by providing a text box to enter the key, or a drop-down list of available keys.

You should research the HCI literature to see which of these two options the HCI community believe is a better choice of data entry in this context.

Exercise 7.9 Extend the Caesar cipher GUI by adding a button that causes deciphering (rather than enciphering) of the text in the text box.

Exercise 7.10 Write a simple color picker using Tkinter. You should provide the user with three sliders (using the Tkinter.Scale class) which they can use to set red, green and blue values. Whenever a slider is moved, a callback should be issued that changes the background color in a Canvas widget.

Exercise 7.11 Extend your answer to the previous exercise to allow users to also select specific colors from a drop-down list. Here is a random list of colors that you may want to include:

255 255 255	white	255 215 0	gold
0 0 0	black	139 69 19	SaddleBrown
47 79 79	dark slate gray	160 82 45	sienna
0 0 128	NavyBlue	205 133 63	peru
30 144 255	dodger blue	245 245 220	beige
70 130 180	SteelBlue	245 222 179	wheat
175 238 238	PaleTurquoise	244 164 96	SandyBrown
85 107 47	DarkOliveGreen	210 180 140	tan
124 252 0	LawnGreen	210 105 30	chocolate
0 255 0	green	178 34 34	firebrick
154 205 50	YellowGreen	255 140 0	dark orange
240 230 140	khaki	255 69 0	OrangeRed
255 255 224	LightYellow	255 0 0	red
255 255 0	yellow	255 105 180	hot pink

The three numbers are the red, green, and blue (RGB) values used by a screen to generate the color of the associated name name.

Challenges

Challenge 7.1 Write a GUI for the expression evaluator in Section 7.9.1. Let the user enter an expression and press a button to have that expression evaluated. To make this a bit simpler, you might want to start out with a GUI where the user enters a Python expression such as this:

Add(1, 2)

You'll need to turn the string from the user into a real Python object. Fortunately, Python provides a function called eval that does that. Here's an example of eval in action:

```
>>> class Foo :
...     def __init__ ( self ) :
...         return
...     def foo ( self ) :
...         print 'foobar!'
...
>>> eval ( 'Foo ( ).foo ( )' )
foobar!
>>>
```

Note that you can only use eval with expressions, not with statements!

Challenge 7.2 This challenge is to create a GUI that allows you to apply various image processing algorithms to images. To do this you will need an image processing library. Python doesn't come with one as standard, but you can download the Python Imaging Library (PIL) from http://www.pythonware.com/ – it is free. You will also need the PIL handbook http://www.pythonware.com/library/pil/handbook/, which is the best documentation available for the library.

The GUI should allow you to select an image, maybe using a list-box or a modal dialog from the tkFileDialog module. You will also need some buttons that apply transformations to the current image and display the processed image. To get you started, we have provided some code below that uses Tkinter to display an image, and some examples of image processing using PIL.

The *negative* of an image has the amount of red, green and blue in each image inverted. The negative of a red pixel (255, 0, 0) is a cyan pixel (0, 255, 255). The negative of a black pixel (0, 0, 0) is a white pixel (255, 255, 255). So to create the negative of an image, we just have to subtract the current red, green and blue values of each pixel from 255. Here's an example image and the code that implements the transformation:

'''Produces the negative of a positive color image.'''

```
__author__ = 'Sarah Mount'
__date__ = '2006-09'
__version__ = '1.0'
__copyright__ = 'Copyright (c) 2006 Sarah Mount'
__licence__ = 'GNU General Public Licence (GPL)'

import Image , sys , viewport

if __name__ == '__main__' :
    title = 'Color->Negative Using Python Image Library'
    filename = sys.argv[1]
    image = Image.open ( filename , 'r' )
    image.load ( )
    negative = image.point ( lambda pixel : 255 - pixel )
    viewport.display_image ( negative , title )
```

Two things to note here. Firstly, the PIL library stores the red, green and blue pixel values of an image as separate list elements (rather than storing a list of three-tuples). Secondly, each PIL image has a method called point that allows us to apply a transformation on each pixel value in the image. point can be used in two ways: you can either pass it a function or **lambda** expression to apply to each pixel value, or you can pass it a lookup table. Above we have used a **lambda** expression.

The PIL library also defines a number of *filters* that can be used to perform transformations on images. These are located in the ImageFilter module. To use a filter, you create an instance of a filter class and pass it to the filter method of an image object.

This example creates an *embossed* version of the image in which the edges of the objects in the image appear raised above the surface of the image:

```
'''Emboss an image.'''

__author__ = 'Sarah Mount'
__date__ = '2006-09'
__version__ = '1.0'
__copyright__ = 'Copyright (c) 2006 Sarah Mount'
__licence__ = 'GNU General Public Licence (GPL)'

import Image , ImageFilter , sys , viewport

if __name__ == '__main__' :
    filename = sys.argv[1]
    image = Image.open ( filename , 'r' )
    image = image.filter ( ImageFilter.EMBOSS ( ) )
    viewport.display_image ( image ,
                    'Image Embossed Using Python Image Library' )
```

Below is the code for the viewport module that we have used in the examples above:

```
'''View a PIL image on a Tkinter canvas.'''

__author__ = 'Sarah Mount'
__date__ = '2006-09'
__version__ = '1.0'
__copyright__ = 'Copyright (c) 2006 Sarah Mount'
__licence__ = 'GNU General Public Licence (GPL)'

import Tkinter , Image , ImageTk , sys

def display_image ( pil_image, title ) :
    '''Take a PIL image and display it in a GUI.'''
    root = Tkinter.Tk ( )
    root.title ( title )
    im_width, im_height = pil_image.getbbox ( )[2:4]
    canvas = Tkinter.Canvas ( root, width=im_width, height=im_height )
    canvas.pack ( side=Tkinter.LEFT, fill=Tkinter.BOTH, expand=1 )
    photo = ImageTk.PhotoImage ( pil_image )
    item = canvas.create_image ( 0, 0, anchor=Tkinter.NW, image=photo )
    Tkinter.mainloop ( )

if __name__ == '__main__' :
    filename = sys.argv[1]
    image = Image.open ( filename , 'r' )
    display_image ( image , 'Tk Viewport' )
```

Filing Things Away

8

Learning Outcomes

At the end of this chapter you will be able to:

- Write programs that open, read and write files on disk.

- Make use of iterators with files.

- Explain why parsing is needed for input and write simple parsers.

- Explain the terms 'serialization', 'marshaling', 'deserialization' and 'unmarshaling' and why they are important for input/output.

- Use dictionaries as ways of creating indexes onto lists of data.

Surprisingly, we have managed to get to this point in the book without mentioning data storage and files. There is no point in having a computer program that can do wonderful things with data but has no actual data to work with. True, we can get data from the users, but they don't want to type in all the information all the time, they want to have data stored on disk and used by our program. So this chapter is about files and the data they contain, and how to get that data into and out of Python programs.

8.1   Files are There Somewhere

A file is a thing with a name that is managed by the operating system that runs a computer. The operating system provides various operations for working with files. This means that it is impossible to say anything general about how files are stored or even how they are named. On the various Unix-like systems, for example, Linux, Solaris, Mac OS X, FreeBSD, OpenBSD, etc., you see paths like:

> /home/users/russel/Checkouts/PythonForRookies/trunk/SConstruct

Each / is a separator. All the names except the last are names of directories and the last may be a directory or a file. A directory is a 'container' that can contain files and other directories.

On Windows, you see paths like:

> C:\home\users\russel\Checkouts\PythonForRookies\trunk\SConstruct

Here C: represents a disk and the separator is \, but the concepts of directory and file are basically the same.

Every operating system manages disks, stores data, and does almost everything in its own, usually unique, way. Fortunately, when programming with Python, we don't have to worry about these issues. The Python systems hides all the differences between the operating systems: it provides a way of working with files that is the same on all operating systems. The only potential problem is the way of naming files, but Python has ways of dealing with them as well, enabling programs to be truly operating system independent.

When working with files, we talk about *paths* (as we did above) which are the 'addresses' of files in the file store. Paths can be *absolute* or *relative*. An absolute path always starts with the separator character (possibly preceded by a disk name on Windows: this is not needed for Unix-like operating systems since they handle disks as part of a global file store) and specifies the file with respect to the root of the file store. A relative path doesn't start with the separator character and is the position of the file relative to the current directory. The current directory is the one from which a program is started.

There are generally two special directory names, '.' and '..', that are immensely useful when working with relatively paths. '.' means the current directory – apparently redundant but nonetheless very useful! '..' means the parent of the current directory and allows us to go up the hierarchy. The root directory is unique, in that its '..' entry refers to itself – there is no parent so this is reasonable meaning.

8.2 Files are Sequences

8.2.1 Lining it Up

Python has a built-in type file that does all the hard work of dealing with the operating system when opening and managing files. We create an object of this type, passing a path as parameter, and the Python system does everything that is necessary to get the operating system to provide access to the contents of the file. As far as our program is concerned the file object can be used as a sequence that we can iterate over. So for example:

A relative path with no directory components means the file is in the current directory.

```
theFile = file ('nameCheck.py')
for line in theFile :
    print line
```

The path here is nameCheck.py, a relative path that is just the name of a file, no directories. This means the file must be in the same directory as that in which we execute the program. The variable theFile is associated with the file object that is created. We then iterate over each line of the file using a standard for loop because the file object creates the abstraction of a file as a sequence of lines of characters. Running the program we get:

```
|> python nameCheck.py
theFile = file ('nameCheck.py')

for line in theFile :

    print line

|>
```

This is not quite what we expected. The issue here is that the print statement appends an end-of-line at the end of the output, and the string associated with line has the end-of-line in the data from the file. So we get double-spaced output. There are two ways of dealing with this: we can either stop the print statement from outputting an extra end-of-line by putting a comma at the end of the statement:

```
theFile = file ( 'nameCheck.py' )
for line in theFile :
    print line ,
```

which results in:

```
| > python nameCheck.py
theFile = file ( 'nameCheck.py' )
for line in theFile :
    print line
| >
```

or we can strip the end-of-line from the end of the string with normal string operations:

```
theFile = file ( 'nameCheck.py' )
for line in theFile :
    print line[:-1]
```

which results in the same output as shown above.

The real point of these examples is that a file object can be used in a for loop to process files one line at a time. In each loop, the line from the file is presented as a string on which we can use all the Python tools of string processing.

8.2.2 Floating Away

The programs in the previous subsection give us a framework for dealing with lines of text in a file, but what if our file contains numbers and we want to process the numbers as numbers. Say we have a file that contains:

```
1.0 4.5
3.4
3.4 5.6 99.3
```

The only thing we know is that there is a sequence of floating point numbers that are separated by spaces and newlines. The problem is that the numbers are represented in string form, as a sequence of characters in the file, and we want to deal with the values as floats. This is not really a problem using Python: we can quite easily create a list of floats from the file. The solution is to use the split method on strings to create a list of strings from the current line of data from the file, and then use list comprehension to create a list of floats from the list of strings. It is probably easier to just show the code:

```
theFile = file ( 'theData.txt' )
theData = [ ]
for line in theFile :
    theData += [ float ( i ) for i in line.split ( ) ]
print theData
```

The only tricky bit is that we are processing the file line by line, so we have to append newly created lists of floats to **theData** – the variable we are using to accumulate the final result. As the end-of-line is the same as space in this context, i.e. it separates floating point numbers, there is no extra complexity.

When this program is executed, we get the output:

```
|> python readTheData.py
[1.0, 4.5, 3.3999999999999999, 3.3999999999999999, 5.5999999999999996, 99.299999999999997 ]
|>
```

which looks a bit surprising. The problem relates to the fact that float values are held with finite precision. We are seeing one of the consequences of the very small variations that are inevitably associated with using float numbers. The variations are tiny numerically, but have a disproportionate effect when printing things out!

The important point is that we have easily created a list of floats from a file containing a sequence of floats represented as strings.

> ### Numerical Analysis
> There are algorithms in which even the tiniest of variations in the input values can cause huge changes in the results. Such algorithms are termed *ill-conditioned* – as opposed to *well-conditioned* algorithms, which give answers that change little for small changes of input values. The study of values and algorithms is called *numerical analysis* and is a very important field for solving problems involving floating point numbers.

In case you were wondering, yes, what we are doing here is parsing. We are taking a sequence of characters from a file, assuming the content is a whitespace-separated sequence of floating point values and creating a list of float values. The grammar we are working with for this lexing and parsing is:

```
<digit> :: ( 0 | 1 | 2 | 3 | 4 | 5 | 6 | 7 | 8 | 9 )
<number> :: -? <digit>* .? <digit>*
<file-content> :: ( <number> <whitespace> )*
```

The fact that almost all the hard work is being done by built-in Python functions is testimony to the fact that Python has the right abstractions and the right built-in functions.

8.2.3 Floating an Alternative

If we know that a file we want to parse is relatively small, we can read it all into memory at once instead of working line by line. The read method on a newly opened file causes the whole file to be read.

Getting the whole file in as a single string allows us to get rid of the iteration and do things in a far more declarative style:

```
theFile = file ( 'theData.txt' )
theData = [ float ( i ) for i in theFile.read ().split ( ) ]
print theData
```

But this does rely on the file being small. By small we mean files from a few bytes to a few millions of bytes. The exact meaning of small depends on the amount of memory available on the computer – reading the whole file in requires having sufficient memory to hold all the characters of the file in memory. When files get to be many billions of bytes, there is no way you want to attempt to read the whole thing in at once. There are, however, ways of dealing with this. Processing files line by line, as in the previous subsection, is one solution. Using alternative file-like types, such as mmap, is another. At this stage of our learning programming though, it is highly unlikely that we will need to process files of these very large sizes. So we are not going to go into further detail on this here, but instead assume all our files are small.

8.2.4 An Example: Plotting Data

Visualizing data is generally a far better way of getting a 'feel' for the data than just staring at the numbers. Let's say we have some data stored in a file, and let's say they are all individual floating point values. We can look at the numbers:

```
3.4 5.6 98.3
1.01 4.56 3.48
3.5 5.6 99.3 1.03 4.52
3.42 3.45 5.7 98.8
```

but it is hard to make sense of them. Sorting the data helps a little:

```
1.01 1.03
3.4 3.42 3.45 3.48 3.5
4.52 4.56
5.6 5.6 5.7
98.3 98.8 99.3
```

but really we need a visual representation. For data sets such as this a histograms or bar chart can be a really useful visual aid. By creating 'bins' (some people calls these 'buckets') that collect values in a given range, we can create counts of values in each bin and can then create a histogram or bar chart. So if we create bins to hold values in the ranges 0–1, 1–2, 2–3, 3–4, 4–5, 5–6, >5 for the above data, we can show the data as:

0–1	1–2	2–3	3–4	4–5	5–6	> 5
0	2	0	5	2	2	3

Even though the data is still presented as numbers, it is being displayed in a way that has a visual/spatial element to it that helps comprehension. In particular, we can get a 'feel' for the distribution of the values across the range.

Let's say these ideas inspire us to write a program for reading data from a file and creating some bins for the data and then printing them out. We might come up with something such as:

```python
def getData ( fileName ) :
    return [ float ( i ) for i in file ( fileName ).read ().split () ]

def createBins ( data , numberOfBins ) :
    minimum = int ( min ( data ) - 1 )
    maximum = int ( max ( data ) + 1 )
    binWidth = ( maximum - minimum ) / numberOfBins
    bins = [ [] for i in range ( numberOfBins ) ]
    low = minimum
    high = minimum + binWidth
    for i in range ( numberOfBins ) :
        bins[i] = [ str ( low ) + '--' + str ( high ) , 0 ]
        for d in data :
            if low < d < high : bins[i][1] += 1
        low , high = high , int ( high + binWidth )
    return bins
```

This program is in a file called createBins.py, so it is a module called createBins.

```
if __name__ == '__main__' :
    for bar in createBins ( getData ( 'dataForPlotting.txt' ) , 10 ) :
        print bar[0] , bar[1]
```

which, when executed, gives us:

```
|> python createBins.py
0--10 12
10--20 0
20--30 0
30--40 0
40--50 0
50--60 0
60--70 0
70--80 0
80--90 0
90--100 3
|>
```

showing us that the data is actually extremely bimodal. Of course, drawing these bins as a histogram will make things more visual and comprehensible, and highlight more the bimodal nature of the data. So we create a Tkinter module to draw histograms as a prerequisite to actually drawing this data. As a first step on this path we have:

```
import Tkinter

def plot ( data ) :
    numberOfBins = len ( data )
    root = Tkinter.Tk ()
    width , height = 400 , 300
    canvas = Tkinter.Canvas ( root , width = width , height = height )
    canvas.pack ()
    numberOfStripes = 2 * numberOfBins + 1
    barWidth = width / numberOfStripes
    unitHeight = 300 / ( max ( [ datum[1] for datum in data ] ) + 2 )
    for i in range ( numberOfBins ) :
        canvas.create_rectangle (
            ( 2 * i + 1 ) * barWidth , unitHeight ,
            ( 2 * i + 2 ) * barWidth , ( data[i][1] + 1 ) * unitHeight ,
            fill = 'black' )
    root.mainloop ()

if __name__ == '__main__' :
    plot ( [
        [ '1--2' , 1 ] ,
        [ '2--3' , 3 ] ,
        [ '3--4' , 1 ]
        ] )
```

This program is in a file called histograms.py, so it is a module called histograms.

Figure 8.1 shows the result when the program is executed, but it is not quite the result we expected. We have something of a fundamental bug! The histogram is being drawn upside-down. The bars are being drawn with zero at the top and increasing frequency going down; the reverse of the way histograms are normally drawn. The bug in the program is quite easy to find and fix, so were are going to leave this as an exercise in debugging for the reader, see Self-review 8.5 (page 276).

Assuming we have fixed the bug in the above code, we can write a program to draw our data. We don't need to write much to do this, as we already have all the functions we need in the programs from earlier in this section.

```
import createBins
import histograms
if __name__ == '__main__' :
    histograms.plot ( createBins.createBins ( createBins.getData ( 'dataForPlotting.txt' ) , 10 ) )
```

Figure 8.2 shows the result of executing this program. It clearly reinforces beyond doubt that the data is definitely bimodal.

The advantage here is that because we ensure that a program is actually a module, what we presented previously as programs can be reused because they are just modules. We can therefore make use of the data reading and bin creating functions from the **createBins** module and (the corrected version of) the histogram drawing function from the **histograms** module. This is what software reuse is about.

We now have the beginnings of some tools that could be made into some useful histogram creation software. As a test, let's create a very large number of random numbers in the range [0, 100) and see what happens. To do this we have to write some data to a file:

```
import random
import createBins
import histograms
if __name__ == '__main__' :
    fileName = 'temporary.txt'
    theFile = file ( fileName , 'w' )
    for i in range ( 2000 ) :
        theFile.write ( str ( 100 * random.random () ) + '\n' )
    theFile.close ()
    histograms.plot ( createBins.createBins ( createBins.getData ( fileName ) , 10 ) )
```

To open a file for writing, creating it it if doesn't exist, we must specify a second parameter to the file function call. 'w' says we are going to write to the file.

Figure 8.1

The result of the first histogram drawing program.

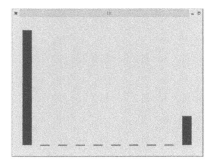

Figure 8.2

The result of executing the histogram plotting program with the bimodal data.

We have used the method write on the file object to write a string to the file. When we have written all the data we are going to write, we close the file. Closing the file ensures that all the data is actually written to the file – operating systems invariably use clever buffering techniques to minimize the amount of reading and writing to disk, closing the file ensures all buffers are flushed and the data really is written to disk.

Because we are using random numbers, every execution of the program is different. One execution gave us the result shown in Figure 8.3. This shows that the random number generator is not particularly biased; it is creating a fairly flat distribution – at least with the bins we are using.

Looking at the program, you may be asking the question: "Why do we have to close the file only to open it again?" We can envisage changing the getData function so that the parameter is a file object rather than a string. Or we could be really sophisticated and change getData so that it works correctly if the parameter is of type string or of type file. The point is that if getData can work with a file object then there is no need to close the file after writing it in the main program. Instead, we can open and write the file object in the main code and then pass the object to getData for reading. There is no necessity for the information to actually be on the disk, hence there is no requirement to close the file to ensure the operating system buffers are flushed to disk. We are not going to follow this line of development here, instead we are going to leave it as exercises – see Exercise 8.1, (page 277), and Exercise 8.2, (page 277). This doesn't mean this direction is not important, it is just that the issues are best investigated by actually doing the programming rather than reading about a solution. If you do want to look at our answers to these exercises then you will find them on the website: http://www.pythonforrookies.org – but do try creating your own answers before looking at ours.

There is another issue that is going to lead to a programming exercise: the histogram currently has no labels and most importantly there is no indication of what frequencies the bars on the histogram represent. Without data about the bins that the bars are displaying, and data about what the lengths of the bars actually represent, the histogram is just art, it contains no information. In order to make the histogram meaningful and useful, we must add appropriate annotations so that it is a visual presentation of data – which it is not just at the moment. Making these changes is a really good programming exercise so we are going to make it just that: see Exercise 8.3 (page 277).

Figure 8.3

An execution of the histogram plotting program with a large amount of random data in the range [0, 100).

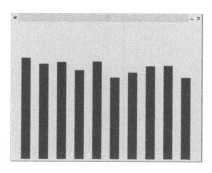

8.3 Files Can Store Data

In this section we are going to do three things:

1. Investigate a few more of the operations we can do with files.

2. See how we can use files to store data from our programs.

3. Prepare the ground for the next section. We are going to develop a small database to store information about books in a library, so we need to be able to store data permanently.

> ### The 3 Rs
>
> The 3 Rs are Reading, Recording and Reckoning. People who say it is Reading, Writing and Arithmetic clearly have problems with spelling, and people who say it is Reading, 'Riting and 'Rithmetic are just having a laugh.

8.3.1 Recording, Reopening and Reading

Say that for we are working with a dictionary, for example:

```
stuff = {}
stuff [ 'flob' ] = 'adob'
stuff [ 'blah' ] = 'blah blah'
```

and we need to store the data between executions of the program. We need to write this data to disk so that we can read it back in again when we next run the program. We could construct our own system for writing the information to disk so that we can read it in again, or we could make use of the facilities that Python already has for doing this. If the programming language already has the tools for doing the job, don't reinvent them, use them.

Python has two techniques for doing the necessary writing and reading of data. The first is to read and write string representations of the data, and that is the approach we are going to investigate here. The second is to use the Pickle module. *Pickling* is important, but it is the sort of thing that is core to a second course on programming.

We have already seen that Python uses the str function as a tool for creating a string representation of a value. In fact, Python has a second tool for creating string representations and that is the repr function. Why have two mechanisms? The str function is for creating a string representation that you might display to a user. The repr function has a different role: it must generate a string representation of the value that can be parsed by the Python system to regenerate the value. It seems like repr is the tool we need for saving state between executions of the program.

We save the state simply by writing a string representation of the data:

```
fileName = 'burble.txt'

theFile = file ( fileName , 'w' )
theFile.write ( repr ( stuff ) )
theFile.close ( )
```

which writes the data to the file as:

```
{'flob': 'adob', 'blah': 'blah blah'}
```

> Python uses the term *pickling* for the activity that in other language is called *serialization* or *marshaling*.

> The repr function is similar the str function: it generates a string representation of the value. The difference is that repr must write a parsable string where str has no such constraint.

But what about reading the data back in? Are we going to have to write our own parser? No – Python already has one. The function eval parses strings that are Python expressions and returns the value ready to be used in a Python program. So as long as the data we read from file is just a Python expression, we use eval to do all the parsing. Fortunately, when we wrote the dictionary to disk, we carefully ensured (by using the repr function) that what we wrote is a Python literal! This means we can write:

```
theFile = file ( fileName )
newStuff = eval ( theFile.read ( ) )
```

and newStuff is a variable associated with the dictionary value that we wrote. This is something we can check by executing:

```
assert stuff == newStuff
```

which does not raise an exception as the values associated with the two variables are indeed the same. The object associated with stuff and the object associated with newStuff are different objects but represent the same value because they are both dictionaries and have the same set of key–value pairs.

8.3.2   Avoiding Reopening

In the program in the previous subsection, we create a dictionary, wrote it to disk, close the file and then immediately reopen it. We ought be able to avoid having to close and reopen the file. We can:

```
stuff = {}
stuff [ 'flob' ] = 'adob'
stuff [ 'blah' ] = 'blah blah'

fileName = 'burble.txt'

theFile = file ( fileName , 'w+' )
theFile.write ( repr ( stuff ) )
theFile.flush ( )

theFile.seek ( 0 )
newStuff = eval ( theFile.read ( ) )

assert stuff == newStuff
```

If we want to read the file after we write it without closing and reopening, we must specify 'w+' as the mode of opening.

Instead of closing the file, we flush the file. Whereas the close method causes the operating system to release all resources associated with opening the file, the flush method ensures that the information is actually on the disk and not just held in a buffer by the operating system. close implies a flush.

Compared to processors and memory disks are immensely slow. For this reason operating systems have highly sophisticated buffering systems for managing disks. This includes not writing information to disk until it is a good time to do so. The flush method demands that the operating system write out all data to disk immediately: executing the method causes the operating system to flush the buffers.

What does the seek method do? A file object has a notion of current position in the file. Thinking of a file as a sequence of characters, each character has a position in the file. The current position in the file is the index of the character the file is currently dealing with. In the program above after the write call, the current position is the last character in the file. After the flush, the current position is therefore the last character of the file. However, when we read the file, we want to read the whole file from the beginning. This means we have to reposition the current position to be the first character in the file. The seek method places the current position at the index specified as the parameter. So by specifying 0 to the seek method we say "go to the beginning of the file" to be able to read the whole file.

Opening a file in the way we have shown so far always sets the current position to the first character in the file, which is why we haven't worried about explicit positioning in the file previously. If we do not reset the current position after the flush in this program, the next read reads from the current position to the end of the file, therefore reading nothing. So if we do not close and reopen the file, we have to explicitly set the current position, hence the use of the seek method call.

8.3.3   Them Modes, Them Modes, . . .

When opening files, we have seen the function file used with one parameter (the name of the file to open) and two parameters (the name of the file to open and a mode specification). We didn't really address what the modes were, we just slipped them in. They are however, important, and shouldn't be ignored. The possible modes of opening a file are:

r   Open the file for reading only. If the file does not exist, raise an exception. *This is the default if no mode parameter is give.*

r+   Open the file for reading and writing with the current position at the beginning of the file. If the file does not exist, raise an exception.

w   Open the file for writing only. If the file exists, delete its contents. If the file does not exist, create it.

w+   Open the file for writing and reading. If the file exists, delete its contents. If the file does not exist, create it.

a   Open the file for writing. If the file exists, do not delete the contents, but set the current position to the end of the file. If the file does not exist, create it.

a+   Open the file for writing and reading. If the file exists, do not delete the contents, but set the current position to the end of the file. If the file does not exist, create it.

This table is just a summary of the modes. For further details you should consult the Python manual.

8.4   A Development: Managing Books

Some people like books and may even have a sizable collection; a library at home. Many of these people even like to catalog their collection. However, very few of these people have enough books to warrant using a commercial library cataloging system. There is then a need for a small scale library cataloging system. We have identified a requirement.

8.4.1   The Problem and Its Solution

The problem we are going to solve is the creation of a software system for keeping records of books. We will implement a Python system that allows us to create, query, and manage entries (usually called *records*) in our database. We will do the implementation as a staged activity:

1. Think about what data we want to store and how we want to work with it.

2. Decide on how to represent our data both in memory and on disk.

3. Create a user interface that allows the data to be created, queried and managed.

It will turn out that we do not get to do 3 in this chapter – but then this is a chapter on files and file handling.

8.4.2   Dictionaries Are Good

A book has various items of data associated with it that we might want to store, for example:

> Author name, book title, book subtitle, publisher,
> cover (hardback/softback), page count, category

It seems quite natural to think of this data being stored either as a tuple or as a dictionary. Using a tuple implies having records with a fixed structure and ordering of data – we have to know that the first item in the tuple is the author name, the second the book title, etc., and we have to provide values for all fields for all books. Perhaps then a dictionary is a better idea, since we can then use keys that are not just integers, and we can more easily add new fields without having to completely rewrite the database. So it seems dictionaries are going to be a good way of representing the records.

A database is a collection of records, so we will need to decide how to store these. The most obvious solution is to put all the dictionaries of the records into a list. This makes searching for specific entries difficult – to find all the books by a given author, we have to search the list testing to see whether each record has the author name we are searching for. This is possible, but inelegant – we have to search all the records every time we want to locate specific data. It would be better if we created indexes into the data, so that once we have done whatever searching is needed to create the indexes, we can avoid the need for further searching by using the index to locate specific records. We might want to create author indexes, publisher indexes, book category (science fiction, romance, etc.) indexes. Dictionaries make great ways of implementing indexes. The insight that moves us forward here is that we can store the data in a list and create dictionaries that provide indexes to the items in the list. The data is held as objects and the list and the dictionaries have references to the objects: the objects can be shared by many lists and dictionaries.

In any database-like system it is essential that each record has a unique property (usually called a *primary key*) that can be used to create the main index. Generally, authors don't write two different books with the same title, so we might think that author name and book title form a unique property? Yes and no. Author name and book title certainly are a unique property, but they are two distinct properties of the book and so form a *compound key*. Compound keys are harder to work with than *simple keys* (keys comprising a single property), so we should avoid using compound keys if possible. Also of course, authors produce editions of a book so actually the compound key would need to consist of author name, book title, edition number.

8.4.3 ISBNs

Fortunately for us there is a unique key associated with every book: it is called the ISBN. ISBN stands for International Standard Book Number.

The original ISBN was a ten-digit number that uniquely identified a book published after 1967. As from 2007-01-01, ISBNs are thirteen-digit numbers. The terms ISBN-10 and ISBN-13 have been introduced to be able to specify which variety of number an ISBN is in situations where there could be doubt. The core rule is that ISBN for books published 1967–2007 means ISBN-10 and for books published after 2007 ISBN mean ISBN-13.

Books published before 1967 do not have an ISBN, so we cannot use it as a unique identifier for such books. We are going to make a simplifying assumptions for now: let's assume all our books have an ISBN. If, later on, we find we have some that do not, we can worry about the problem then.

A few books have two ISBNs. For example *Structure and Interpretation of Computer Programs* by Harold Abelson and Gerald Jay Sussman with Julie Sussman, was published in 1985 by MIT Press with the ISBN 0-262-01077-1 and by McGraw-Hill with the ISBN 0-07-000-422-6. This is not a problem because each of these ISBNs uniquely identifies the same book.

If you look at the copyright page of this book, you will find its ISBN is:

ISBN 978-1-84480-701-7

ISBNs are numbers, but when printed they are always preceded by the letters ISBN (or ISBN-10 or ISBN-13 when both are printed).

The Structure of ISBNs

You probably spotted that the examples of ISBNs above are not listed as just decimal digits, they have structure, using a hyphen to separate the parts – some people use spaces rather than hyphens but this is frowned upon. ISBNs are structured:

prefix A three digit prefix. *For ISBN-13, not present in ISBN-10.*

group Specifies the country, area or language area of the book. Comprises 1 to 5 digits.

publisher Specifies the publisher within the group. Comprises 1 to 7 digits.

book Specifies the book the publisher published in the group.

check digit A single digit calculated from the other digits of the ISBN.

Clearly there is complexity in the group, publisher, and book parts but we don't need to worry about that since we are only analyzing existing numbers we are not assigning new ones. If you are interested, there are a number of books and websites that explain the details.

At first sight an ISBN-10 appears to be just an ISBN-13 without the prefix. This is not true: the group number, publisher number and book number are the same in ISBN-13 and ISBN-10, but the check digit is usually different – the algorithm for calculating the check digit is different between the two types of ISBN.

All ISBN-10s can be converted to ISBN-13 but only very specific ISBN-13s can be converted to ISBN-10. The ISBN-13 prefix for ISBN-10s is 978. So if you see an ISBN-13 with this prefix it can be converted to an ISBN-10. For any other ISBN-13 prefix there is no ISBN-10 equivalent.

ISBN-13s appear to be what we should use for our keys, but to handle books that were published before ISBN-13 came into being we have to know how to convert from ISBN-10 to ISBN-13.

ISBN-10 Check Digit

In a sense we don't really need to bother with trying to understand the algorithm for calculating the ISBN-10 check digit: there will be no new ISBN-10s issued; we can assume that all ISBN-10s that are in use are correct; and we will not need to convert from ISBN-13 to ISBN-10, only the other way. On the other hand, the ISBN-10 check digit can be X which needs some explanation.

The formula for an ISBN-10 check digit is:

$$check\ digit_{ISBN10} = \left(11 - \left(\sum_{i=1}^{9} w_i\, d_i \right) \bmod 11 \right) \bmod 11$$

where d_i is the ith digit of the ISBN-10 working from left to right, and w_i is the weight for the digit: $w_i = 11 - i$.

So for example, this book has ISBN-10 1-84480-701-0. To show that 0 is the correct checksum, we do the calculation. We multiply the digits by their weight and sum the products:

digit	1	8	4	4	8	0	7	0	1	
weight	10	9	8	7	6	5	4	3	2	
	10	72	32	28	48	0	28	0	2	220

We divide 220 by 11, giving us 20 remainder 0, and, as the remainder is 0, the checksum is 0.

To implement this as a function we have to be decisive about how we are going to represent ISBNs in our program – without a representation, we have no idea what code to write. The most obvious representation is as a string, so we can work with ISBNs as they are written in books – though we will probably drop the 'ISBN' at the beginning of each number. This raises a few issues:

- Working with characters means we have to transform to integers to do the calculations. This is fairly straightforward since we have the int function. We just have to be certain that we only pass it strings that are decimal digits. We can use the **in** operator to ensure that a character is one of a specific list.

- We need to deal with the fact that the number has hyphens at unknown places in the number. This means we need to not process these characters. It also means we cannot use indexing into the string to find the characters we need to process, since we don't know, a priori, where the hyphens will be.

Bearing the above in mind, we can write the function as:

The **in** operator returns **True** if the value of the left operand is in the right operand, which must be a sequence or set type.

```
def isbn10CheckDigit ( isbn ) :
    isbn10Sum = 0
    weight = 10
    for c in isbn :
        if not ( c in '0123456789' ) :
            if c == '-' : continue
            else : raise ValueError , 'ISBN not just decimal digits and hyphens.'
        isbn10Sum += weight * int ( c )
        weight -= 1
        if weight == 1 : break ;
    return ( 11 - ( isbn10Sum % 11 ) ) % 11
```

We use the weight value to terminate the loop in case the ISBN parameter already contains the check digit. Another example of defensive programming. Another aspect of defensiveness is that even though we only process decimal digit characters and ignore hyphens, we raise an exception if we see any other character – ISBNs are supposed to use hyphens to separate the components, so any other character is treated as an error and flagged as such.

There is a surprise in store with this implementation: not only does it work with strings, it works with lists and tuples! Our 'make sure things are not totally broken' test for this function is:

```
if __name__ == '__main__' :
    # Python for Rookies, ISBN-10 1-84480-701-0
    assert isbn10CheckDigit ( '1844807010' ) == 0
    assert isbn10CheckDigit ( '1-84480-701-0' ) == 0
    # Developing Java Softweare 3rd edition, ISBN-10 0-470-09025-1
    assert isbn10CheckDigit ( '0470090251' ) == 1
    assert isbn10CheckDigit ( '0-470-09025-1' ) == 1
    # HCI 2005, ISBN-10 1-84628-192-X
    assert isbn10CheckDigit ( '184628192X' ) == 10
    assert isbn10CheckDigit ( '1-84628-192-X' ) == 10
    # HCI 2006, ISBN-10 1-84628-588-7
    assert isbn10CheckDigit ( '1846285887' ) == 7
    assert isbn10CheckDigit ( [ '1' , '8' , '4' , '6' , '2' , '8' , '5' , '8' , '8' , '7' ] ) == 7
    assert isbn10CheckDigit ( ( '1' , '-' , '8' , '4' , '6' , '2' , '8' , '-' , '5' , '8' , '8' , '-' , '7' ) ) == 7
```

This works because strings, lists and tuples are all sequences and the only assumption we have made in our function is that the parameter is a sequence that can be indexed. This is polymorphism working well.

Did you spot test code that we used an X as the check digit? It is not completely obvious from the formula and the code of the function, but the check digit can have the value 10, which is not a single digit as required for the ISBN check digit. This is why the check digit can be a single decimal digit or X: if the check digit has value 10, it is written as an X in the ISBN-10.

ISBN-13 Check Digit

Although we are going to use ISBN-13s as our primary keys, many books have only an ISBN-10 printed in them. This means that we need to be able to convert an ISBN-10 to an ISBN-13. Hence we need to know how to calculate the correct ISBN-13 check digit. The formula is:

$$check\ digit_{ISBN13} = \left(10 - \left(\sum_{i=1}^{12} w_i\, d_i \right) \bmod 10 \right) \bmod 10$$

where d_i is the ith digit of the number reading left to right (as with ISBN-10) and the weight w_i is:

$$w_i = \begin{cases} 1 & i \in \{1,3,5,7,9,11\} \\ 3 & i \in \{2,4,6,8,10,12\} \end{cases}$$

This is very different from the ISBN-10 calculation even though the formula look fairly similar. For example, this book has ISBN-13 978-1-84480-701-7. To show that 7 is the correct checksum, we do the calculation. We multiply the digits by their weight and sum the products:

This means that the first digit has weight 1, the second digit has weight 3, the third digit has weight 1, the fourth digit has weight 3, and so on.

digit	9	7	8	1	8	4	4	8	0	7	0	1	
weight	1	3	1	3	1	3	1	3	1	3	1	3	
	9	21	8	3	8	12	4	24	0	21	0	3	115

We divide 113 by 10, giving us 11 remainder 3. Subtracting 3 from 10 we have 7 as the checksum.

As with the ISBN-10 formula, the ISBN-13 formula is straightforward to implement:

This code is in file isbnCheckDigit.py so it can be used as module isbnCheckDigit.

```
def isbnCheckDigit ( isbn ) :
    isbnSum = 0
    def __isbnWeight ( n ) :
        if ( n % 2 ) == 0 : return 1
        else : return 3
    digitCount = 0
    for c in isbn :
        if not ( c in '0123456789' ) :
            if c == '-' : continue
            else : raise ValueError , 'ISBN not just decimal digits and hyphens.'
        isbnSum += __isbnWeight ( digitCount ) * int ( c )
        digitCount += 1
        if digitCount == 12 : break
    return ( 10 - ( isbnSum % 10 ) ) % 10


if __name__ == '__main__' :
    # Python for Rookies, ISBN 978-1-84480-701-7
    assert isbnCheckDigit ( '9781844807017' ) == 7
    assert isbnCheckDigit ( '978-1-84480-701-7' ) == 7
    # Developing Java Softweare 3rd edition, ISBN 978-0-470-09025-1
    assert isbnCheckDigit ( '9780470090251' ) == 1
    assert isbnCheckDigit ( '978-0-470-09025-1' ) == 1
    # HCI 2005, ISBN 978-1-84628-192-1
    assert isbnCheckDigit ( '9781846281921' ) == 1
    assert isbnCheckDigit ( '978-1-84628-192-1' ) == 1
    # HCI 2006, ISBN 978-1-84628-588-2
    assert isbnCheckDigit ( '9781846285882' ) == 2
    assert isbnCheckDigit ( [ '9', '7', '8', '1', '8', '4', '6', '2', '8', '5', '8', '8', '2' ] ) == 2
    assert isbnCheckDigit ( ( '9', '7', '8', '-', '1', '-', '8', '4', '6', '2', '8', '-', '5', '8', '8', '-', '2' ) ) == 2
```

ISBN-10 → ISBN-13

To convert an ISBN-10 to an ISBN-13 the algorithm is:

1. Prepend 978 to the ISBN-10.

2. Remove ISBN-10 check digit.

3. Calculate and append ISBN-13 check digit.

which is easy to implement given the function we created above:

```
import isbnCheckDigit

def isbn10ToIsbn13 ( isbn10 ) :
    isbnBase = '978-' + isbn10[:-1]
    return isbnBase + str ( isbnCheckDigit.isbnCheckDigit ( isbnBase ) )
```

```
if __name__ == '__main__' :
    assert isbn10ToIsbn13 ( '1-84480-701-0' ) == '978-1-84480-701-7'
    assert isbn10ToIsbn13 ( '0-470-09025-1' ) == '978-0-470-09025-1'
    assert isbn10ToIsbn13 ( '1-84628-192-X' ) == '978-1-84628-192-1'
```

For the moment we create a new module for the conversion code and simply import the checksum calculation function from another module. As we evolve the program, we may well decide to rearrange things and put various functions together in the same module. This is fine, it is the evolutionary nature of system development.

8.4.4 Having Some Data

We now have some ISBN-related code, but we need to use all the ideas we have collected so far to design a system to store data about the books we have. Earlier, we decided that we were going to use a list to store our data, with each record being a dictionary of information about a book. Here is an example of what we mean:

```
[
    {
    'title' : 'Python for Rookies' ,
    'author' : ( 'Sarah Mount' , 'James Shuttleworth' , 'Russel Winder' ) ,
    'publisher' : 'Cengage Learning' ,
    'date' : 2008 ,
    'ISBN' : '978-1-84480-701-7'
    } ,
    {
    'title' : 'Developing Java Software, Third Edition' ,
    'author' : ( 'Russel Winder' , 'Graham Roberts' ) ,
    'publisher' : 'Wiley' ,
    'date' : 2007 ,
    'ISBN' : '978-0-470-09025-1'
    }
]
```

We put this data into a file called bookData.py.

Editing the Python source code representation of the data is not intended to be the final user interface for the application, but to get the core of our system in place this is not a bad way of progressing. We know we can read from disk and write to disk this form of the data. So as a mechanism for prototyping the functionality, it is a sound strategy.

At this stage, we probably should be thinking in terms of classes and objects. Managing the database seems like a very good area to be using classes and objects, so let's assume we are going to develop a class BookDatabase. As a first step we can write the code needed to create instances of the class and for those instances to read the initial data:

```
class BookDatabase :

    def __init__ ( self , fileName = 'bookDatabase.txt' ) :
        self.file = file ( fileName , 'a+' )
        self.file.seek ( 0 )
        theData = self.file.read ( )
        if len ( theData ) == 0 : self.database = [ ]
        else : self.database = eval ( theData )
```

repr is a special
method used for
creating string
representations of
an object. This
method must return
a string
representation that
can be parsed to
recreate the original
value.

```
    def __repr__ ( self ) :
        return self.database.__repr__ ()

if __name__ == '__main__' :
    import sys
    if len ( sys.argv ) > 1 :
        db = BookDatabase ( sys.argv[1] )
    else :
        db = BookDatabase ()
    print db
```

We have decided that the default file name for the data is to be 'bookDatabase.txt'. The user may, of course, specify a different file to use. If the file to be used as a database does not exist, it is created – using an opening mode of a+ gives us this behavior. This opening mode leaves the current position at the end of the file, so in order to read the file we have to reset the current position to the beginning of the file.

Note that we do not assume the file has any data in it. If the file is empty we create an empty list as the database, otherwise we assume that the file contains a valid Python list literal – if there are any errors in the file then the evaluation will fail and an exception be raised.

The __repr__ method is a special method that is similar the __str__ method. The difference is that whilst the __str__ method can produce any string form that is desired for the object, the __repr__ method must produce a string representation of the object that can be parsed by the Python system to recreate the original value. In this case, we need to generate a source code form of the dictionary that stores all the data.

The __repr__ method of an object is called whenever the repr function is applied to an object. So:

```
x = BookDatabase ()
y = repr ( x )
```

causes the BookDatabase.__repr__ method to be called on the object referred to by x.

The design decisions made so far are not cast in stone: they can be changed and the code changed appropriately. The whole point is that we are evolving a prototype, and when doing this we must be prepared to revisit all design decisions – and be prepared to rewrite the whole program if we completely change the design!

8.4.5 Storing The Data

The program above simply reads in a database and prints it to screen. The __repr__ method is used to create the string for the print statement because a __repr__ method is defined, but a __str__ is not. The Python system searches for suitable method to create a string representation for the print statement in a defined order: __str__ is used if it exists, if it doesn't __repr__ is used if it exists, and if that doesn't exist there is a standard default method built in. All that remains is to decide how to write the data to disk? Maybe we should create a method called writeBack that allows us to do this?

Given that we hold the whole database in memory as a list, and we want to write the whole thing to disk whenever there is a call to writeBack, we probably want to open and close the file for each write. This means we can use the w+ opening mode to cause any previous contents of the file, if they exist, to be deleted. This requires a change to the way we work with the file in the class. Instead of storing the file, we actually just want to store the file name. So now we have:

```
class BookDatabase :

    def __init__ ( self , fileName = 'bookDatabase.txt' ) :
        self.fileName = fileName
        theFile = file ( self.fileName , 'a+' )
        theFile.seek ( 0 )
        theData = theFile.read ()
        if len ( theData ) == 0 : self.database = []
        else : self.database = eval ( theData )
        theFile.close ()

    def __repr__ ( self ) :
        return self.database.__repr__ ()

    def writeBack ( self ) :
        theFile = file ( self.fileName , 'w+' )
        theFile.write ( repr ( self.database ) )
        theFile.close ()

if __name__ == '__main__' :
    import shutil
    sourceName = 'bookData.py'
    destinationName = 'bookDatabase.txt'
    shutil.copyfile ( sourceName , destinationName )
    db = BookDatabase ()
    db.writeBack ()
    d1 = eval ( file ( sourceName ).read () )
    d2 = eval ( file ( destinationName ).read () )
    assert d1 == d2
```

The test code uses the data from earlier that we put in the file bookData.py.

which gives us a database we can open and read, and then write to disk whenever we want. Notice that we only open the file when we actually need to get at the contents. This means that we are not keeping operating system resources tied up when we don't need them. Also, if there is a problem with our program, there is no chance of corrupting the file unless the problem occurs when we do the reading and writing. The downside of this is that writing the file to disk will take a little longer, because Python has to work with the operating system to open and close the file on every database write operation. But this is a reasonable price to pay: the trade-off favors data safety over raw speed.

So defensiveness here means not keeping files open unless we need them. This 'rule of programming' is in the same category as the rule 'keep variables local': it is all about minimizing the use of resources and maximizing our chances of detecting any errors. These rules are guidelines to help us think about what we are doing.

8.4.6 Creating Indexes

We now have a way of managing a database both in memory and on disk. Clearly we want to write a user interface that allows us to add records to the database. We will need to gather the data for the record and insert it into the database. Of course, there are details such as: what happens if an attempt is made to insert a new record for an ISBN that is already in the database? The problem is really: how can we make queries on the database? It is also certain that people will want to search for books by title, author, publisher, ISBN, etc.

We stated earlier that it is a bad idea to have to search each record every time we want to make a query, but how can we avoid it? Say the query is "All books by Sarah Mount". What we really want is to have a dictionary with 'Sarah Mount' as a key and a list of all books she wrote as data: what we need is an author index. We will also want a publisher index, possibly a publication date index (by year), and definitely an ISBN index – it is the primary index after all. A title index is probably not a good idea, but an index of words in titles may be a very good idea so that we can search for books with 'Philosophy' in the title, for example.

We clearly need to create a number of indexes. What is an index? It is a mapping between a key and a value. This seems like a dictionary! So in an author index the key is the author name, but what is the value? If we were creating a database using a database management system (DBMS), we would need a unique key for each record. So if we were using a DBMS, we would have a special index, the primary index, using the unique, primary key that held all the data, and other indexes would use the primary key to refer to the entries. However, we are working with objects in memory, so things are actually much easier: we can just share the dictionary objects that are the book records in all the indexes. This removes a complete layer of index lookup. Do remember though that we can only do this because we are working with objects in memory, rather than storing them on disk.

We steam ahead and write a new method for our class :

```
def createIndex ( self , fieldName ) :
    index = { }
    for record in self.database :
        index[ record[ fieldName ] ] = [ record ]
    return index
```

which we can use thus:

```
indexByISBN = db.createIndex ( 'ISBN' )
```

However, there is a problem with this code. We said the value associated with each key should be a list of all records that have the value for the index key, but here it is not – all the indexed values are single item lists: we have used assignment and not any form of list appending. Also, what happens if the record doesn't have the key the index is being made for. And what happens if the data in the record is a list – we don't really want lists as keys in the index. We are going to have to evolve this further for it to be useful.

Dealing with missing keys is a question of handling KeyError exceptions. Whenever there is a read of a dictionary using a key, the Python system checks to see if an item with that key already exists, and if it does not, raises a KeyError. If however, the access is an assignment and an entry with that key doesn't exist, then it is created.

Dealing with record values that are lists or tuples and not just strings or numbers means we have to iterate over them rather than using them directly as keys. Doing this is straightforward, but knowing when to do it requires Python technology we haven't used before: we have to ask what the type of an item is, and for this we need the isinstance function:

```
def createIndex ( self , fieldName ) :
    index = { }
    for record in self.database :
        try :
            datum = record[ fieldName ]
            def addToIndex ( key , datum ) :
                try : index [ key ] += [ datum ]
                except KeyError : index [ key ] = [ datum ]
            if isinstance ( datum , list ) or isinstance ( datum , tuple ) :
                for item in datum : addToIndex ( item , record )
            else :
                addToIndex ( datum , record )
        except KeyError : pass
    return index
```

We have used a local function definition to abstract the process of actually append-ing an item, which avoids code replication. The body of this local method uses an exception handling trick that exemplifies the EAFP approach so common in Python. We attempt to append the newly found record to the list of a key we assume exists. If the key is in the index, fine, no more needs to be done. If it is not in the index, a KeyError exception is raised, and by handling this we can assign the list of the record, causing the entry to be created. We therefore try the normal situation first, and if that fails, we take alternative action to deal with the case.

EAFP – easier to forgive that to ask permission: try the usual case and if it fails, deal with the problem.

This method still makes many assumptions about the data, but it appears to do the job we are asking of it with the data we have tried it with. This is not to say it works in general, it just works for the data we have tried.

At this point we have probably done as much as we can without thinking about user interface issues and what functionality is actually required by the user. This gives us an excuse not to do anything more on this development in this chapter, since this is a chapter about files and file handling.

8.5 Rounding Off

Having given what we hope is an interesting and useful introduction to using files, it is difficult to write much more that is general and useful without either just presenting information that is in the manual, or writing a whole 500-page book. Moreover, file handling techniques tend to be very specific to applications: it is difficult to say things that apply generally, useful information tends to be application and domain specific.

Chapter Summary

In this chapter we have found that:

- Opening files makes a connection between a program and a file.
- Operating systems buffer information and so files must be flushed or closed to ensure data is written.
- We can use iteration to read files as strings – each string being a line from the file.
- We can parse simple file structures to convert from text representation to internal representation of data.
- The 'current position' maintained by file objects controls how we use files.
- We can manage a permanent store of data using the repr and eval functions.
- That we can use multiple indexes on data to provide multiple views of that data.

Self-Review Questions

Self-review 8.1 We can store the contents of dictionaries, lists and tuples in a file and, using eval, retrieve them while keeping their type and structure. Does this mean that the operating system specifically supports these types?

Self-review 8.2 Why should we not use the write mode ('w') when we wish to add data to an existing file?

Self-review 8.3 What mode *should* be used when adding data to an existing file?

Self-review 8.4 If you search your computer's hard disk, you may find that many files have the same name. Readme.txt, for example, appears many times on our hard disks. These files are distinct and normally have different contents. How is it that the operating system can maintain separate files of the same name?

Self-review 8.5 What is 'wrong' with the histogram drawing algorithm on page 260?

> *Hint: The problem is not in the code structure but in the assumption about coordinates.*

Self-review 8.6 What are the special files . and .. for?

Self-review 8.7 What is the 'root' directory in a file system and what is it's .. file?

Self-review 8.8 In the os module Python has a variable called os.sep which has the value '/' on UNIX machines and '\' on Windows computers. What do you think this variable is used for?

Self-review 8.9 What are *buffers* and why does Python use them when opening files?

Self-review 8.10 What does the flush method do?

Self-review 8.11 What does the special method __repr__ do and why is it different to the __str__ method?

Self-review 8.12 What does Python's eval function do?

Self-review 8.13 What exception is raised when Python tries to open a file which does not exist?

Self-review 8.14 The check digit in ISBNs tells us whether an ISBN is valid. Can you think of any other computing related activities where check digits (or check sums) are used?

Self-review 8.15 Why do some ISBN numbers end with an X?

Programming Exercises

Exercise 8.1 Amend the getData method so that the parameter is a file object rather than a file name. Change the histogram drawing program removing the closing of the file and execute it to show that the amended getData method works as it should.

Exercise 8.2 Amend the getData method so that the parameter can be either a string giving the name of the file to be read, or a file object of an already open file.

Hint: Use the isinstance function to separate the three cases.

Exercise 8.3 Evolve the histogram drawing code (your corrected version from Self-review 8.5 rather than the faulty version on page 260) so that the bars have labels that show which bin the data is for, and so that there are indications of what the lengths of the bars represent. One approach would be to draw an axis down the side with tick marks and values. It may also be sensible to write the actual count of items in the bin above the bar, perhaps resulting in something like:

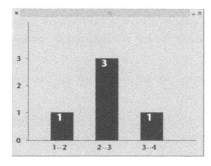

Exercise 8.4 Look at the following program:

```
file = open ( 'words.dat' , 'w' )
word = "
while word != 'END' :
    word = raw_input ( 'Enter a word (enter END to quit): ')
    file.write ( word + '\n' )
file.close ()
```

This is a very simple program for storing a list of words in a file. When executed it expects the user to enter some words, one per line, finishing with the word "END".

1. What is the name of the file containing the words?
2. How many words are stored in the file?
3. Write a program to read the data file and display a numbered list of the contents, such as:

```
1: chicken
2: apple
3: fox
4: aubergine
5: END
```

4. Note that "END" is always the last word displayed. This isn't really the behavior we want, since "END" is meant as a command, not a word. Change the program so that it no longer stores "END" in the file.

5. There's still a problem: we can't put the word "END" into the file even if we wanted to. Maybe we should use the empty string (") to signal the user's desire to quit? Modify the program to use the empty string to terminate user input.

Exercise 8.5 Using your answer to the previous question as a starting point, write a program that counts the number of times each word appears in the data file. Its output might look like this:

> Carrot: 3
> Cheese: 1
> Egg: 6
> Tomato: 2

Exercise 8.6 It would be nice if we had a graphical display of word frequency for the previous exercise. Use the histogram module from earlier in the chapter to display the word frequencies as a histogram.

Exercise 8.7 Write a program to say how many lines of text there are in a text file the name of which is obtained by prompting and reading input from the user.

Exercise 8.8 Write a program to read the contents of a text file and display it in a Tkinter text box.

Exercise 8.9 Write a program to store a list of contact names and telephone numbers, similar to the contact lists you might find on a mobile phone. The data needs to be stored in a file so that it is *persistent* – that is, the data available at the beginning of a new execution of the program is the same as at the end of the previous execution.

Exercise 8.10 Extend the program written for the previous exercise so that as new contacts are added, the program checks for duplicate names and numbers. If the new contact's name is already in the database, the message "This person is already entered." should appear. If the telephone number is already in the database, the program should display "This person's telephone number is already in the database. This could be an error, or a second contact at the same company. Add anyway?" If the user enters "Y", the contact is added.

Challenges

Challenge 8.1 Write a program to display a simple form of digital book. "Books" are text files in which each block (page) of text is followed by a double dash (--).

When a book is displayed, the first block of text is shown and the program should wait for the user to press the enter key before displaying the next.

Challenge 8.2 Extend the previous challenge so that it is possible to skip forward by an arbitrary number of pages. This should be achieved by allowing the user to enter a number before pressing the enter key. If the number is positive, the given number of pages are skipped. If there is no number, the next page is displayed.

Challenge 8.3 Further extend the book reader so that it can accept negative numbers for skipping pages. Entering -1 should go back to the previous page. There are many ways to achieve this.

Testing, Testing

Learning Outcomes

At the end of this chapter you will be able to:

- Describe how unit testing is used in a larger development cycle and why it is important.

- Use PyUnit to create and execute unit tests.

- Develop code using a unit-test-centered approach.

In the early days of software development, programmers used to define requirements for programs, write code to implement those requirements, then test their code. Well, at least that is what students were told they were supposed to do. In reality, programs were often released before they were properly tested – all too often leading to the situation in which users were using software that had clear and obvious bugs.

Some Infamous Bugs

In November 1979 NORAD appeared to detect a Soviet missile launch. It was, in fact, a system test, but this was not indicated in the control room. This incident is reputed to be the inspiration behind the film *War Games*.

In the period 1985–7, the Therac-25 medical accelerator caused at least five deaths. There was a problem in the operating system that caused incorrect and potentially lethal doses of radiation to be applied to patients.

On January 15, 1990, a large part of the AT&T US national telephone network crashed due to problems in the synchronization software. The episode lasted for nine hours while programmers searched for and corrected the cause. An estimated 60,000 people were left without telephone service. AT&T estimated at least $60 million in lost revenue. The incidental damage to businesses is hard to estimate, but was presumably much larger. The public safety and national security implications of such a large telephone system outage are incalculable.

On February 25, 1991, an Iraqi Scud missile evaded Patriot anti-missile defenses and hit the Dhahran American Army barracks because of a software flaw that prevented correct tracking. The missile strike left 28 dead and around 100 wounded.

On March 23, 2003, a Patriot missile system incorrectly identified an RAF jet as an Iraqi missile and brought it down, killing two people. The problem is believed to be in the Patriot targeting software.

In modern software development, developers design and implement their tests first, before they've written the program which needs testing. The idea is that by writing tests first, potential issues relating to the design and implementation of the program will be brought to light. This test-first approach to programming has been formalized into a whole process of programming called *Test-Driven Development* (TDD).

Proponents of modern 'agile' software development approaches, such as eXtreme Programming (XP) maintain that testing is as much about developing code as it is about catching bugs and getting your code ready for use:

> The most common misconception about unit testing frameworks is that they are only testing tools. They are development tools same as your editor and compiler. Don't keep this powerful development tool in reserve until the last month of the project, use it throughout. Your unit testing framework can help you formalize requirements, clarify architecture, write code, debug code, integrate code, release, optimize, and of course test.
>
> — http://www.extremeprogramming.org/rules/unittestframework.html

Not only do tests help to develop code, they help to document the code by making it clear what the program ought to do. Thus, when we come back to a program after some time away from it, having forgotten everything about it, we can read the test code and re-remember what the program is supposed to do, and thence how it does it. Also, if we have to work on a program that somebody else has written, the tests give us a very quick introduction to the program and its functionality.

We have emphasized the absolute necessity for programmers always to test their programs – not only in the paragraphs above, but also in the whole of this book. Until now though, we have not *really* tested our programs properly despite this message – this is not hypocrisy! The reason for not yet doing testing properly has been that we did not have the right tools, and it seems wrong to try and do things in an inappropriate way. We did do some simple tests, but we left things at that. Now that we have introduced classes and inheritance, we are in a position to correct the deficiency and do our testing properly.

What can we test to show how it is all done? There are four obvious candidates – we left these points dangling earlier in the book:

- When writing a program to generate the Fibonacci numbers in Section 3.7.4 (page 82), we stated that we would test the program more thoroughly when we had the right tools. This was reinforced in a marginal note in Section 5.6.1 (page 177), where the claim was made that there was a bug in the implementation.

- When creating the program to convert numbers represented in Roman numerals into numbers represented in Arabic numerals (Section 4.8.2, page 140), we stated that we ought to test the program we wrote but that we didn't, at that time, have the right tools.

- When generating prime numbers in Section 6.4.4, we said that testing the code properly would be delayed until we had the right tools for the job.

- When creating a class to realize matrices in Section 6.6.6, we said we still didn't have quite the right tools – although we had classes, we hadn't covered inheritance.

It seems reasonable therefore to use these as the primary examples of testing correctly, now that we have all the required infrastructure in our tool bag.

xUnit

Testing programs has been around since programs have existed – in reality this means since the early 1940s. However, it was not until the mid-1990s, with the arrival of unit test frameworks and the integration of unit testing with code development, that testing took its rightful place in the overall process of software development.

The first really successful unit test framework was sUnit, which was a unit testing framework for Smalltalk. This rapidly generated a whole collection of unit test frameworks collectively called xUnit. So for example, Check, cppUnit, JUnit, NUnit are examples of unit testing frameworks for C, C++, Java and C# respectively. The frameworks all have the same basic aims and goals, but they have different ways of working so as to work well with the programming language they are aimed at.

For Python there have, in the past, been two or three useful unit testing frameworks. However, these have now been absorbed into a single standard framework called PyUnit. Although the framework is named PyUnit, the Python module is called unittest.

9.1   Introducing PyUnit

Testing is so important to programming, and has such a standard structure and approach, that it seems right and correct that there should be a standard way of doing things. Moreover, that standard way of doing things should be realized in the standard library to save everyone having to replicate the code needed.

> I am really impressed with the effect of unit testing on the quality of my code since I started using PyUnit about two months ago. I know that the extra effort has saved me literally days of looking for subtle bugs. Writing the unit tests first is also a very good inoculation against over-engineering.
>
> — Terrel Shumway, http://pyunit.sourceforge.net/

The Python module unittest is the standard framework for writing unit tests in Python – despite the module name, it is generally referred to as PyUnit. In its simplest form of use, PyUnit provides a class unittest.TestCase that we can subclass to access the functionality of the unit test framework.

The documentation for PyUnit (under the module name unittest) in the Python distribution is good and extensive. There is even more material to be found at the website http://pyunit.sourceforge.net.

9.2   Testing Things

How should we test our code? We write a test program that 'exercises' the classes, methods and functions comprising the program we are testing. So, for example, with the function that calculates the nth Fibonacci number, we know what the results should be. This means that we can write a program that calls the function and checks that the correct result was calculated. We 'assert' things about the code – we make assertions in our test program. So, for example, we know that the eleventh item in the Fibonacci Sequence, F_{10}, has the value 55, so we can write a test program:

```python
import unittest
from fibonacci_handledException import fibonacci

class Fibonacci_Test ( unittest.TestCase ) :
    def test_Ten ( self ) :
        self.assertEqual ( 55 , fibonacci ( 10 ) )

if __name__ == '__main__' :
    unittest.main ()
```

We import the PyUnit framework (unittest) and the fibonacci function. We then define a class, which we have called Fibonacci_Test, that is a subclass of unittest.TestCase and so is a class that uses the PyUnit framework. This particular class has just one method, test_Ten. This is a test method. Classes that are PyUnit test classes can have methods of any name, but only methods that start with the four letters test are test methods. Completing our test program is a call to the function unittest.main. This function is the entry into the PyUnit framework that causes it to execute all the test methods. In this case, when executed, we get:

```
|> python fibonacci_Test.py
.
-----------------------------------------------------------------
Ran 1 test in 0.000s

OK
```

An '.' indicates that
a test method
succeed.

So it seems our test worked and our fibonacci (10) call did indeed generate the value 55.

The method assertEqual is inherited from unittest.TestCase and throws an exception if its parameters are not equal to each other. In the code above, no exception was thrown, as the values were equal; the test did not fail. If instead we had written:

```
self.assertEqual ( 54 , fibonacci ( 10 ) )
```

the program would have output:

An 'F' indicates that
a test method failed
due to an assertion
failing.

```
F
=========================================================
FAIL: test_Ten (__main__.Fibonacci_Test)
-----------------------------------------------------------------
Traceback (most recent call last):
  File "fibonacci_Error_Test.py", line 9, in test_Ten
    self.assertEqual ( 54 , fibonacci ( 10 ) )
AssertionError: 54 != 55


-----------------------------------------------------------------
Ran 1 test in 0.001s

FAILED (failures=1)
```

The assertion we made about the result of the call to the fibonacci function fails, we get an exception, and the PyUnit framework reports this.

9.3 Building Tests

Now that we have the technology, how do we use it? The idea is to build up a set of test methods that try enough cases to give us confidence that our code contains no errors. We must bear in mind though something that Edsger W Dijkstra raised:

> Program testing can be a very effective way to show the presence of bugs, but is hopelessly inadequate for showing their absence.
>
> — Edsger W Dijkstra, *The Humble Programmer*, ACM Turing Lecture 1972.

There is an important way of thinking here: we do *not* say we think our program works or that our tests show that the program works. We say that our tests do not show any bugs in our program. There is a corollary:

The idea of unit testing is to try and find bugs in our program.

A successful test is one that finds a bug. A test that does not find a bug does not give us any extra information about our program, it just increases our confidence that the program will work in the situations in which we need it to work.

This discussion of approach and mind-set is a critically important facet of programming. The way a programmer approaches unit testing is possibly the most important indicator of whether a person is a good programmer or a bad programmer. A good programmer cares about testing and doing it right.

What values should we test for the Fibonacci number function? We should test some values to make sure we get the answers we expect, but we should also test the error handling to make sure that our function fails when it should, and handles failure conditions appropriately. So we build up some more tests:

```
import unittest
from fibonacci_handledException import fibonacci

class Fibonacci_Test ( unittest.TestCase ) :
    def test_One ( self ) :
        self.assertEqual ( 1 , fibonacci ( 1 ) )
    def test_Five ( self ) :
        self.assertEqual ( 5 , fibonacci ( 5 ) )
    def test_Ten ( self ) :
        self.assertEqual ( 55 , fibonacci ( 10 ) )
    def test_MinusOne ( self ) :
        self.assertRaises ( ValueError , fibonacci , -1 )

if __name__ == '__main__' :
    unittest.main ()
```

When executed, this gives us:

```
....
----------------------------------------------------------------
Ran 4 tests in 0.000s

OK
```

So far so good. But isn't this writing of vast numbers of methods all of which are basically the same rather tedious? Yes, it is. We should use the full power of Python to create our test methods:

```
import unittest
from fibonacci_handledException import fibonacci

class Fibonacci_Test ( unittest.TestCase ) :

    def test_Correct ( self ) :
        data = ( 0 , 1 , 1 , 2 , 3 , 5 , 8 , 13 , 21 , 34 , 55 , 89 , 144 )
        for i in range ( len ( data ) ) :
            self.assertEquals ( data[ i ] , fibonacci ( i ) )

    def test_Negative ( self ) :
        for i in range ( -5 , -1 ) :
            self.assertRaises ( ValueError , fibonacci , i )
```

This attitude and approach to testing and programs is the core of professional programming.

assertRaises (e , f , p) asserts that when the method that is the second parameter (f) is called with the third parameter (p), i.e. when f (p) is executed, the result is the exception that is the first parameter (e).

In test_Correct, the index of an item in the tuple (i) is used as the parameter to the fibonacci call with the item itself being the expected value.

```
if __name__ == '__main__' :
    unittest.main ()
```

Only two test methods, but an awful lot of assertions about the expected results of the fibonacci function:

```
..
-------------------------------------------------------------------
Ran 2 tests in 0.001s

OK
```

Even with just two test methods, we have a good selection of test cases and no bug has been highlighted in the fibonacci function. It seems fair to have confidence that the fibonacci function does indeed behave as it should.

It is important that tests are extensive, and very easy to run.

What do we mean by extensive?

There should be tests for all the situations that could be met by the program. We cannot try, at least in general, every possible case, though that would be the ultimate in extensive, so we need to try sample cases from each category. Taking the fibonacci function as an example, we can clearly distinguish three categories of input: negative numbers, non-negative numbers (including zero), and non-numbers. All negative parameters and all non-numbers should result in an exception being raised. For all non-negative parameters n, fibonacci should return the value of the nth number in the Fibonacci Sequence – where the sequence starts with the 0th item which has value 0. So we choose a few negative values to ensure that exceptions are raised and the first few (we chose 13) of the sequence, to make sure they are calculated correctly. We then make the assumption that all negative parameters will throw an exception because some of them do in our tests, and the assumption that all positive parameters will be correctly calculated because the first 13 are. Assuming our assumptions are reasonable, these tests are sufficient to give us confidence that our implementation of the Fibonacci function has no bugs.

The term *coverage* is generally used when talking about how extensive tests are. If a test has more coverage then it is testing more of the code. There are even tools for most languages to help calculate a correct measure of coverage.

Have you spotted a problem? We mentioned non-numbers, but we have no tests for them. Clearly, we need more tests in our test program. But what to test for and how to test it? First let's find out what happens when we try calling fibonacci with, for example, a string:

```
>>> print fibonacci ('one')
Traceback (most recent call last):
  File "<stdin>", line 1, in <module>
  File "<stdin>", line 9, in fibonacci
TypeError: unsupported operand type(s) for -: 'str' and 'int'
>>> print fibonacci ([])
Traceback (most recent call last):
  File "<stdin>", line 1, in <module>
  File "<stdin>", line 9, in fibonacci
TypeError: unsupported operand type(s) for -: 'list' and 'int'
>>>
```

It seems that the expressions n - 1 and n - 2 get executed for strings and lists and lead to a TypeError being raised. Maybe this is what we need to happen? For now the answer is yes, so we extend the test program by adding a few more tests:

```
def test_EmptyString (self) :
    self.assertRaises (TypeError , fibonacci , '')
```

```
def test_NonEmptyString ( self ) :
    self.assertRaises ( TypeError , fibonacci , 'one' )

def test_EmptyList ( self ) :
    self.assertRaises ( TypeError , fibonacci , [ ] )

def test_NonEmptyList ( self ) :
    self.assertRaises ( TypeError , fibonacci , [ 1 , 2 , 3 ] )

def test_EmptyTuple ( self ) :
    self.assertRaises ( TypeError , fibonacci , ( ) )

def test_NonEmptyTuple ( self ) :
    self.assertRaises ( TypeError , fibonacci , ( 1 , 2 , 3 ) )

def test_EmptyDictionary ( self ) :
    self.assertRaises ( TypeError , fibonacci , { } )

def test_NonEmptyDictionary ( self ) :
    self.assertRaises ( TypeError , fibonacci , { 1 : 1 , 2 : 2 , 3 : 3 } )
```

When we run the tests, we get:

```
|> python fibonacci_Test_4.py
..........
----------------------------------------------------------------------
Ran 10 tests in 0.002s

OK
|>
```

For the example non-numbers we have chosen, a TypeError is raised exactly as should happen. We should perhaps add more tests of this sort, but for now let's assume that all non-numbers will cause this exception.

What do we mean by easy to run?

The tests should require little work to execute and should execute quickly. In this case, we just have to execute the command python fibonacci_Test.py, and as we can see from the output above, execution takes significantly less than 1 second. Why is this important? We should execute the tests after any changes we make to either the code being tested or the testing code: make a change, run the tests. This is only possible if the tests are quick and easy to run – but remember, tests do need to be extensive, which is actually more important than speed of execution.

The real importance of unit testing is that the test is automated and can be run repeatedly. Tests must be run regularly and often.

9.4   Some Examples

9.4.1   Generating Fibonacci Numbers

Having tested the recursive implementation of a function to create the Fibonacci Sequence, what about testing the version that is a generator from Section 5.6.1 (page 177)? We came up with the test:

```
import unittest
from fibonacci_generator import fibonacciGenerator

class Fibonacci_Test ( unittest.TestCase ) :

    def test_Correct ( self ) :
        fibonacciNumbers = fibonacciGenerator ()
        data = ( 0 , 1 , 1 , 2 , 3 , 5 , 8 , 13 , 21 , 34 , 55 , 89 , 144 )
        for i in range ( len ( data ) ) :
            self.assertEquals ( data[ i ] , fibonacciNumbers.next () )

if __name__ == '__main__' :
    unittest.main ()
```

However, when we execute this, we get:

```
F
========================================================
FAIL: test_Correct (__main__.Fibonacci_Test)
--------------------------------------------------------
Traceback (most recent call last):
  File "fibonacciGenerator_Test.py", line 13, in test_Correct
    self.assertEquals ( data[ i ] , fibonacciNumbers.next () )
AssertionError: 0 != 1


--------------------------------------------------------
Ran 1 test in 0.001s

FAILED (failures=1)
```

Our test code looks reasonable, yet we have a failure. What can be wrong? Looking at the assertion failure, it says that when we expected to get a 0, we actually got a 1. Our test says that the first number in the Fibonacci Sequence is 0, whilst our generator delivers 1 as the first item. Back to the definition: what is the first number in the Fibonacci Sequence, 0 or 1? From the definition we gave in Section 3.7.4 (page 81) it is clearly 0: $F_0 = 0$. Our generator code has been wrong all the time. This is certainly because we did not test the code.

The moral of this story is always test all your code.

Perhaps an even more important moral of the story is that ad hoc testing, as we had before, can give you erroneous confidence that the code has no bugs. Only rigorous and extensive testing can really give us the confidence that our code is not broken.

Where do we go from here? We have found a bug in our code, so we just fix it. The corrected code is:

The corrections are that previous = 0 replaces previous = 1 and yield previous replaces yield current.

```
def fibonacciGenerator () :
    previous = 0
    current = 1
    yield previous
    while True :
        yield current
        current , previous = current + previous , current
```

The problem was that we had not used the correct code for the start up of the generation. By initializing previous to 0 instead of 1 and yielding previous instead of current for the very first value returned by the generator, we fix the bug.

.

Ran 1 test in 0.000s

OK

9.4.2 Roman Numerals

The next code in need of proper testing is the Roman numerals program from
Section 4.8.2 (page 140). Again, we need to test not only various correct situations,
but also various error situations. As a start we came up with:

```
import unittest
from romanNumerals import convertRomanToInteger

class RomanNumerals_Test ( unittest.TestCase ) :

    def testNormalCorrectUpper ( self ) :
        data = (
            ( 1 , 'I' ) , ( 2 , 'II' ) , ( 3 , 'III' ) , ( 4 , 'IV' ) , ( 5 , 'V' ) , ( 6 , 'VI' ) , ( 7 , 'VII' ) ,
            ( 8 , 'VIII' ) , ( 9 , 'IX' ) , ( 10 , 'X' ) , ( 11 , 'XI' ) , ( 12 , 'XII' ) , ( 13 , 'XIII' ) ,
            ( 14 , 'XIV' ) , ( 15 , 'XV' ) , ( 16 , 'XVI' ) , ( 17 , 'XVII' ) , ( 18 , 'XVIII' ) ,
            ( 19 , 'XIX' ) , ( 20 , 'XX' ) ,
            ( 1988 , 'MCMLXXXVIII' ) , ( 1990 , 'MXM' ) ,
            ( 1999 , 'MIM' ) , ( 1999 , 'MCMIC' ) , ( 1999 , 'MCMXCIX' ) ,
            ( 2000 , 'MM' ) , ( 2007 , 'MMVII' )
            )
        for datum in data :
            self.assertEqual ( datum[0] , convertRomanToInteger ( datum[1] ) )

    def testNormalCorrectLower ( self ) :
        data = (
            ( 1 , 'i' ) , ( 2 , 'ii' ) , ( 3 , 'iii' ) , ( 4 , 'iv' ) , ( 5 , 'v' ) , ( 6 , 'vi' ) , ( 7 , 'vii' ) ,
            ( 8 , 'viii' ) , ( 9 , 'ix' ) , ( 10 , 'x' ) , ( 11 , 'xi' ) , ( 12 , 'xii' ) , ( 13 , 'xiii' ) ,
            ( 14 , 'xiv' ) , ( 15 , 'xv' ) , ( 16 , 'xvi' ) , ( 17 , 'xvii' ) , ( 18 , 'xviii' ) ,
            ( 19 , 'xix' ) , ( 20 , 'xx' ) ,
            ( 1988 , 'mcmlxxxviii' ) , ( 1990 , 'mxm' ) ,
            ( 1999 , 'mim' ) , ( 1999 , 'mcmic' ) , ( 1999 , 'mcmxcix' ) ,
            ( 2000 , 'mm' ) , ( 2007 , 'mmvii' )
            )
        for datum in data :
            self.assertEqual ( datum[0] , convertRomanToInteger ( datum[1] ) )

    def testUnusualButCorrectUpper ( self ) :
        data = (
            ( 4 , 'IIII' ) , ( 5 , 'IIIII' ) , ( 6 , 'IIIIII' ) , ( 7 , 'IIIIIII' ) , ( 9 , 'VIIII' ) ,
            ( 10 , 'VIIIII' ) , ( 11 , 'VIIIIII' ) , ( 14 , 'XIIII' ) , ( 15 , 'XIIIII' ) ,
            ( 16 , 'XIIIIII' ) , ( 17 , 'XIIIIIII' ) , ( 19 , 'XVIIII' ) , ( 20 , 'XVIIIII' ) ,
            ( 21 , 'XVIIIIII' ) , ( 22 , 'XVIIIIIII' ) , ( 24 , 'XXIIII' ) , ( 25 , 'XXIIIII' ) ,
            ( 26 , 'XXIIIIII' ) , ( 27 , 'XXIIIIIII' )
            )
        for datum in data :
            self.assertEqual ( datum[0] , convertRomanToInteger ( datum[1] ) )
```

These tests are each
structured similarly
and use a data
structure that is a
tuple of tuples
(actually a tuple of
pairs). The for loop
iterates over each
pair in the tuple, the
first item is the
Arabic
representation, and
the second is the
string holding the
Roman numeral
representation.

```
        def testUnusualButCorrectLower ( self ) :
            data = (
                ( 4 , 'iiii' ) , ( 5 , 'iiiii' ) , ( 6 , 'iiiiii' ) , ( 7 , 'iiiiiii' ) , ( 9 , 'viiii' ) ,
                ( 10 , 'viiiii' ) , ( 11 , 'viiiiii' ) , ( 14 , 'xiiii' ) , ( 15 , 'xiiiii' ) ,
                ( 16 , 'xiiiiii' ) , ( 17 , 'xiiiiiii' ) , ( 19 , 'xviiii' ) , ( 20 , 'xviiiii' ) ,
                ( 21 , 'xviiiiii' ) , ( 22 , 'xviiiiiii' ) , ( 24 , 'xxiiii' ) , ( 25 , 'xxiiiii' ) ,
                ( 26 , 'xxiiiiii' ) , ( 27 , 'xxiiiiiii' )
                )
            for datum in data :
                self.assertEqual ( datum[0] , convertRomanToInteger ( datum[1] ) )

        def testIncorrectDigitsUpper ( self ) :
            data = ( 'A' , 'B' , 'E' , ':' , 'P' , ',' , )
            for datum in data :
                self.assertRaises ( ValueError , convertRomanToInteger , datum )

        def testIncorrectDigitsLower ( self ) :
            data = ( 'a' , 'b' , 'e' , ':' , 'p' , ',' , )
            for datum in data :
                self.assertRaises ( ValueError , convertRomanToInteger , datum )

        def testNotCorrectUpper ( self ) :
            data = ( 'IIV' , 'IIIV' , 'IVV' , 'IVX' )
            for datum in data :
                self.assertRaises ( ValueError , convertRomanToInteger , datum )

        def testNotCorrectLower ( self ) :
            data = ( 'iiv' , 'iiiv' , 'ivv' , 'ivx' )
            for datum in data :
                self.assertRaises ( ValueError , convertRomanToInteger , datum )


if __name__ == '__main__' :
    unittest.main ()
```

When we run this with the implementation from Section 4.8.2 though, we get:

An 'E' indicates a a test method failed for some reason other than an assertion fail.

```
EE..FF..
============================================================
ERROR: testIncorrectDigitsLower (__main__.RomanNumerals_Test)
------------------------------------------------------------
Traceback (most recent call last):
  File "romanNumerals_Test.py", line 65, in testIncorrectDigitsLower
    self.assertRaises ( ValueError , romanNumerals.convertRomanToInteger , datum )
  File "unittest.py", line 320, in failUnlessRaises
    callableObj(*args, **kwargs)
  File "../structuringState/romanNumerals.py", line 19, in convertRomanToInteger
    intValue += numerals[string[i]]
KeyError: 'a'


============================================================
ERROR: testIncorrectDigitsUpper (__main__.RomanNumerals_Test)
------------------------------------------------------------
Traceback (most recent call last):
  File "romanNumerals_Test.py", line 60, in testIncorrectDigitsUpper
    self.assertRaises ( ValueError , romanNumerals.convertRomanToInteger , datum )
  File "unittest.py", line 320, in failUnlessRaises
```

```
    callableObj(*args, **kwargs)
  File "../structuringState/romanNumerals.py", line 19, in convertRomanToInteger
    intValue += numerals[string[i]]
KeyError: 'A'


======================================================
FAIL: testNotCorrectLower (__main__.RomanNumerals_Test)
------------------------------------------------------
Traceback (most recent call last):
  File "romanNumerals_Test.py", line 75, in testNotCorrectLower
    self.assertRaises ( ValueError , romanNumerals.convertRomanToInteger , datum )
AssertionError: ValueError not raised


======================================================
FAIL: testNotCorrectUpper (__main__.RomanNumerals_Test)
------------------------------------------------------
Traceback (most recent call last):
  File "romanNumerals_Test.py", line 70, in testNotCorrectUpper
    self.assertRaises ( ValueError , romanNumerals.convertRomanToInteger , datum )
AssertionError: ValueError not raised


------------------------------------------------------
Ran 8 tests in 0.005s

FAILED (failures=2, errors=2)
```

The reason for this test failure is that we have written the test class to specify what we want the Roman numerals program to do but the code from Section 4.8.2 (page 140) does not implement the requirements as codified in the tests. Assuming the test program correctly reflects the real requirements of what the program is to do, the implementation code is wrong. We must therefore amend it until the tests pass. In this case, we need to add better error case handling. This turns out to be relatively straightforward, though the code does look quite a lot different, as we have to use different control structures to allow some of the error cases to be handled. In particular:

- We change the way iteration is handled so we can add processing to enforce the rule that only one smaller value character can precede a higher value character. This stops IIX from being legal. In effect we are looking ahead two characters in our parse of the number to support error handling.

- We add handling of KeyError to deal with incorrect characters in a number. We raise a ValueError. So we turn an implementation/representation oriented exception into a more user-oriented exception.

```python
import sys

numerals = {
    'I' : 1 , 'i' : 1 ,
    'V' : 5 , 'v' : 5 ,
    'X' : 10 , 'x' : 10 ,
    'L' : 50 , 'l' : 50 ,
    'C' : 100 , 'c' : 100 ,
    'D' : 500 , 'd' : 500 ,
    'M' : 1000 , 'm' : 1000
    }
```

The program is almost completely rewritten. The best way of seeing the difference is to refer back to the previous version on page 142.

```
def convertRomanToInteger ( string ) :
    intValue = 0
    i = 0
    while i < len ( string ) :
        try :
            if i < len ( string ) -2 and numerals[string[i]] < numerals[string[i+2]]:
                raise ValueError , 'Incorrect sequence of letters.'
            if i < len ( string ) - 1 and numerals[string[i]] < numerals[string[i+1]]:
                intValue += numerals[string[i+1]] - numerals[string[i]]
                i += 2
            elif i > 0 and numerals[string[i-1]] < numerals[string[i]]:
                raise ValueError, 'This cannot be happen.'
            else:
                intValue += numerals[string[i]]
                i += 1
        except KeyError :
            ( e_type , e_value , e_trace ) = sys.exc_info ()
            raise ValueError , 'The letter ' + str ( e_value ) + \
                ' is not allowed in a Roman number.'
    return intValue

if __name__ == '__main__' :
    print convertRomanToInteger ( raw_input ( 'Enter a number in Roman numerals : ' ) )
```

The function sys.exc_info returns a tuple with three items, the actual type of the exception, the value that caused the exception and a trace of the execution.

When we execute the test program with this as the implementation then we get:

```
........
----------------------------------------------------------------
Ran 8 tests in 0.002s

OK
```

We don't claim the code is bug free, but we can claim that there are no test failures and that the implementation should work correctly in the expected use cases.

Some issues are still left to worry about:

- Should we be stopping numbers such as IIIIIIIIIII, for example, from being legal?

- Should we be forbidding mixed case numbers? (Probably yes, because observation indicates that mixed case is never used, numbers are either all uppercase or all lowercase.)

- Are MCMIC, MCMXCIX and MIM all valid representations of 1999? Why does MCMXCIX appear to be the preferred representation?

- Is MCMCXCVIII a valid representation of 2098?

- Is MXMVII a valid representation of 1998?

To answer these questions, we need to find out more about the rules of Roman numerals. When we find the answers, we first extend the tests with the results of our researches. This means that tests will fail when the test is run. Consequently, we have to amend our code until the tests do not fail.

We are not going to work through these questions here, instead we are going to leave them as a challenge for the reader – see Challenge 9.1 (page 308). See the website (http://www.pythonforrookies.org) for our thoughts on these questions.

9.4.3 Prime Numbers

Although we implemented a class for a lazy list of prime numbers in Section 6.4 (page 196), we claimed then that we hadn't tested the class properly. Clearly we should test it.

The tests we have in the module are not actually bad, they are just very basic. Except that there is one issue, all the tests worked with the same prime generator. We really ought to use a different generator for each test to ensure that the starting state for any test is known and controlled.

The PyUnit framework gives us a way of doing this. The framework guarantees that if there is a method called setUp in the test class, it will be called before each test method of that test class is called. This means that we can put code for setting up state into this function to guarantees that the state is the same for all test methods.

In this example we use this feature to set up a brand new prime number generator for each test method:

```python
import unittest
from primeList_2 import PrimeList

class PrimeList_Test ( unittest.TestCase ) :

    def setUp ( self ) :
        self.primes = PrimeList ()

    def test_Beginning ( self ) :
        list = [ ]
        for i in range ( 10 ) :
            list += [ self.primes[i] ]
        self.assertEqual ( [ 2 , 3 , 5 , 7 , 11 , 13 , 17 , 19 , 23 , 29 ] , list )

    def test_Indexing ( self ) :
        self.assertEquals ( 127 , self.primes[ 30 ] )

    def test_getLargestPrimeLessThan ( self ) :
        data = ( ( 9 , 7 ) , ( 29 , 23 ) , ( 50 , 47 ) )
        for datum in data :
            self.assertEquals ( datum[ 1 ] , self.primes.getLargestPrimeLessThan ( datum[ 0 ] ) )

    def test_getSmallestPrimeGreaterThan ( self ) :
        data = ( ( 20 , 23 ) , ( 44 , 47 ) )
        for datum in data :
            self.assertEquals ( datum[ 1 ] , self.primes.getSmallestPrimeGreaterThan ( datum[ 0 ] ) )

if __name__ == '__main__' :
    unittest.main ()
```

This program doesn't test the code for caching the values of prime numbers, it only tests the use of the PrimeList type.

When this code is executed, we get:

```
|> python primeList_Test.py
....
----------------------------------------------------------------------
Ran 4 tests in 0.002s

OK
```

The only real question here is whether the tests are extensive enough for us to have good confidence that the class is working as it should.

9.4.4 Matrices

In Section 6.6.6 (page 206) we implemented a matrix class, but we didn't do a proper test, we just did a superficial test. In this section we are going to investigate creating a proper test class. Actually we are just going to investigate testing addition. We are going to slide over subtraction and multiplication – not because we are trying to cheat in any way, but simply because the programs get longer than is sensible for presentation in a book and the important points can be made by just looking at the testing of one operation.

We are going to assume that we are working with the Matrix class that results from answering Exercise 6.4 and Exercise 6.5.

Let's get started with a test class for testing matrix addition – knowing that we should do something analogous for subtraction and multiplication to be able to make any reasonable claim that we are properly testing the Matrix class. Creating the tests for subtraction and multiplication will make an excellent exercise once we have covered addition – see Exercise 9.2 (page 307).

```python
import unittest
from matrix import Matrix , zeros , unit

class Matrix_Test ( unittest.TestCase ) :

    def test_Zeros ( self ) :
        xRange = 2
        yRange = 4
        matrix = zeros ( xRange , yRange )
        for x in range ( xRange ) :
            for y in range ( yRange ) :
                self.assertEquals ( 0 , matrix[x][y] )

    def test_Unit ( self ) :
        xRange = 2
        yRange = 4
        matrix = unit ( xRange , yRange )
        for x in range ( xRange ) :
            for y in range ( yRange ) :
                if x == y :
                    self.assertEquals ( 1 , matrix[x][y] )
                else :
                    self.assertEquals ( 0 , matrix[x][y] )

    def test_AddIntegerCorrect ( self ) :
        # data is a tuple of triplets, the first two are the matrices to be added, the third is
        # the expected answer.
        data = (
            ( Matrix ((( 1 , 1 ) , ( 1 , 1 ))) , Matrix ((( 2 , 2 ) , ( 2 , 2 ))) ,
              Matrix ((( 3 , 3 ) , ( 3 , 3 )))) ,
            ( Matrix ((( 1 ,) , ( 1 ,) , ( 1 ,) , ( 1 ,))) , Matrix ((( 2 ,) , ( 2 ,) , ( 2 ,) , ( 2 ,))) ,
              Matrix ((( 3 ,) , ( 3 ,) , ( 3 ,) , ( 3 ,)))) ,
            ( Matrix ((( 1 , 1 , 1 , 1 ) ,)) , Matrix ((( 2 , 2 , 2 , 2 ) ,)) ,
              Matrix ((( 3 , 3 , 3 , 3 ) ,)))
            )
        for datum in data :
            # Addition should be commutative so try both ways round.
            self.assertEqual ( datum[2] , datum[0] + datum[1] )
            self.assertEqual ( datum[2] , datum[1] + datum[0] )
```

```
    def test_AddDoubleCorrect ( self ) :
        # data is a tuple of triplets, the first two are the matrices to be added, the third is
        # the expected answer.
        data = (
            ( Matrix ((( 1.0 , 1.0 ) , ( 1.0 , 1.0 ))) , Matrix ((( 2.0 , 2.0 ) , ( 2.0 , 2.0 ))) ,
                Matrix ((( 3.0 , 3.0 ) , ( 3.0 , 3.0 )))) ,
            ( Matrix ((( 1.0 ,) , ( 1.0 ,) , ( 1.0 ,) , ( 1.0 ,))) , Matrix ((( 2.0 ,) , ( 2.0 ,) , ( 2.0 ,) , ( 2.0 ,))) ,
                Matrix ((( 3.0 ,) , ( 3.0 ,) , ( 3.0 ,) , ( 3.0 ,)))) ,
            ( Matrix ((( 1.0 , 1.0 , 1.0 , 1.0 ) ,)) , Matrix ((( 2.0 , 2.0 , 2.0 , 2.0 ) ,)) ,
                Matrix ((( 3.0 , 3.0 , 3.0 , 3.0 ) ,)))
            )
        for datum in data :
            # Addition should be commutative so try both ways round.
            self.assertEqual ( datum[2] , datum[0] + datum[1] )
            self.assertEqual ( datum[2] , datum[1] + datum[0] )

    def test_AddIntegerError ( self ) :
        # data is tuple of pairs which should not be addable due to different shapes.
        data = (
            ( Matrix ((( 1 , 1 ) , ( 1 , 1 ))) , Matrix ((( 2 ,) , ( 2 ,) , ( 2 ,) , ( 2 ,)))) ,
            ( Matrix ((( 1 ,) , ( 1 ,) , ( 1 ,) , ( 1 ,))) , Matrix ((( 2 , 2 , 2 , 2 ) ,))) ,
            ( Matrix ((( 1 , 1 , 1 , 1 ) ,)) , Matrix ((( 2 , 2 ) , ( 2 , 2 ))))
            )
        for datum in data :
            self.assertRaises ( ValueError , Matrix.__add__ , datum[0] , datum[1] )

    def test_AddDoubleError ( self ) :
        # data is tuple of pairs which should not be addable due to different shapes.
        data = (
            ( Matrix ((( 1.0 , 1.0 ) , ( 1.0 , 1.0 ))) , Matrix ((( 2.0 ,) , ( 2.0 ,) , ( 2.0 ,) , ( 2.0 ,)))) ,
            ( Matrix ((( 1.0 ,) , ( 1.0 ,) , ( 1.0 ,) , ( 1.0 ,))) , Matrix ((( 2.0 , 2.0 , 2.0 , 2.0 ) ,))) ,
            ( Matrix ((( 1.0 , 1.0 , 1.0 , 1.0 ) ,)) , Matrix ((( 2.0 , 2.0 ) , ( 2.0 , 2.0 ))))
            )
        for datum in data :
            self.assertRaises ( ValueError , Matrix.__add__ , datum[0] , datum[1] )

if __name__ == '__main__' :
    unittest.main ()
```

When we tried this with our answer to Exercise 6.4 and Exercise 6.5, we got:

```
E.E...
============================================================
ERROR: test_AddDoubleCorrect (__main__.Matrix_Test)
------------------------------------------------------------
Traceback (most recent call last):
  File "matrix_Test.py", line 64, in test_AddDoubleCorrect
    self.assertEqual ( datum[2] , datum[0] + datum[1] )
  File "../../Answers/SourceCode/classyObjects/matrix.py", line 40, in __add__
    n.data[row][column] += m.data[row][column]
TypeError: object does not support item assignment

============================================================
ERROR: test_AddIntegerCorrect (__main__.Matrix_Test)
------------------------------------------------------------
Traceback (most recent call last):
```

```
File "matrix_Test.py", line 48, in test_AddIntegerCorrect
  self.assertEqual ( datum[2] , datum[0] + datum[1] )
File "../../Answers/SourceCode/classyObjects/matrix.py", line 40, in __add__
  n.data[row][column] += m.data[row][column]
TypeError: object does not support item assignment
```

```
----------------------------------------------------------------------
Ran 6 tests in 0.003s
```

```
FAILED (errors=2)
```

This was unexpected, but immediately the work of finding the problem (debugging) and correcting it started. The first step is to check that the test program is actually correct. Looking through it is detail, yes, the test program is correct. This means that there really must be something wrong with the Matrix class.

The error message is saying that the += operator cannot be applied to the data that is n.data[row][column]. How can this be? The datum is either an integer or a float held in a sequence. Of course, there are two sorts of sequence: mutable (lists) and immutable (tuples). The += operator can only be used for item assignment with mutable sequences. Clearly then we are attempting to use the operator on an immutable sequence. But the matrix is represented as a list of lists, so the data structure should be a mutable sequence. Clearly in this case, it is not. How can this be? We are using tuples to initialize the matrix, so maybe there is something there?

One experiment we should try is to use lists rather than tuples for the initialization. On changing all the tuples used to initialize matrices into lists, we find we get the test result:

```
......
----------------------------------------------------------------------
Ran 6 tests in 0.004s
```

```
OK
```

All the tests pass. But we must not just leave it there, we now know there is a bug in the Matrix class and it is to do with initialization using tuples rather than lists.

Step 1 is to extend the test class so that it includes the list initialization and the tuple initialization – always add tests to a test class, never remove them.

Step 2 is to look at the constructor:

```
def __init__ ( self , data ) :
    # Ensure parameter is rectangular whilst creating the internal represnetation.
    self.data = []
    columns = len ( data[0] )
    for row in data :
        if len ( row ) != columns :
            raise ValueError , 'Data is not a rectangular structure.'
        self.data += [ row[:] ]
```

to try to decide what it is about this code that is different for lists and tuples. It may not be entirely obvious, but the line:

```
self.data += [ row[:] ]
```

creates a new list whose contents will be appended to self.data, but it creates clones of the rows. This means that tuples are created if tuples are the input and lists are created if lists are the input. So we create a list of tuples instead of a list of lists if the initializing data consists of tuples. Clearly this is not what we want, we definitely need a list of lists: the algorithms used to implement addition, subtraction and multiplication rely on the data structure being mutable. So this line of our code is wrong.

Instead of cloning row, we must iterate over it and individually copy the objects from it into a newly created list. We can do this easily with a list comprehension:

```
self.data += [ [ x for x in row ] ]
```

This ensures that we create a list of lists as required by the rest of the code no matter what sort of sequence is used to initialize the matrix.

With this change in place, when we run the tests, we get:

```
..........
----------------------------------------------------------------------
Ran 10 tests in 0.005s

OK
```

Much better! Of course, we cannot say that the Matrix class is correct, but we can say that it appears to do matrix addition correctly, and we have fixed a bug we didn't know we had until we started creating the proper test.

> Of course, we can just use
> self.data = data[:] to clone the data all in one go, but we still have to make the check that the data is rectangular.

9.5 Test-Driven Development

The most formalized of the test-first approaches to software development is called Test-Driven Development (TDD). In this way of working, code in the program under development is only ever written in response to a unit test failure. The only real way of explaining this is to show an example.

Let's develop a function to calculate factorials. We have done this already, but the point is that because the function is simple, straightforward, and we have done it before, it means we can concentrate on the process of development and really show what TDD means.

9.5.1 Getting Started

Although we know the mathematical definition of factorial and can write a recursive implementation directly from the mathematical definition, the TDD process requires us to write tests and only when there is a test failure do we write any code for the software being developed. Since we know that factorial$(0) = 1$, we can write the test:

```
import unittest
from tdd_factorial_1 import factorial

class Factorial_Test ( unittest.TestCase ) :

    def test_zero ( self ) :
        self.assertEquals ( 1 , factorial ( 0 ) )

if __name__ == '__main__' :
    unittest.main ()
```

Running this test we get:

```
Traceback (most recent call last):
  File "tdd_factorial_1_Test.py", line 2, in ?
    from tdd_factorial_1 import factorial
ImportError: No module named tdd_factorial_1
```

because we haven't written any code for the function. In TDD this is said to be a 'Red' – a Red is a test failure. The term stems from the support tools used with sUnit and Smalltalk development and JUnit and Java development where green is shown if all tests pass and red is shown if any tests fail.

So we have a Red, which means we must deal with the problem so that we get a Green. In TDD, we create the minimal change possible to get a Green, so we write:

```
def factorial ( x ) :
    return 1
```

It is true that this is not a good implementation of factorial, but it causes the tests to pass:

```
.
----------------------------------------------------------------------
Ran 1 test in 0.000s

OK
```

Green. . . so this is the right code to write. What we have is a program that correctly calculates factorial for the cases we have tested.

9.5.2 Extending the Coverage

The next step is to extend the requirements by extending the test – we know that factorial(1) = 1:

```
import unittest
from tdd_factorial_3 import factorial

class Factorial_Test ( unittest.TestCase ) :

    def test_zero ( self ) :
        self.assertEquals ( 1 , factorial ( 0 ) )

    def test_one ( self ) :
        self.assertEquals ( 1 , factorial ( 1 ) )

if __name__ == '__main__' :
    unittest.main ()
```

Running the tests:

```
..
----------------------------------------------------------------------
Ran 2 tests in 0.000s

OK
```

Green – our implementation is still valid for the tests we have. So we progress adding more tests:

```
import unittest
from tdd_factorial_3 import factorial

class Factorial_Test ( unittest.TestCase ) :

    def test_zero ( self ) :
        self.assertEquals ( 1 , factorial ( 0 ) )
```

```python
    def test_one ( self ) :
        self.assertEquals ( 1 , factorial ( 1 ) )

    def test_two ( self ) :
        self.assertEquals ( 2 , factorial ( 2 ) )

if __name__ == '__main__' :
    unittest.main ()
```

Running this code give us:

```
.F.
============================================================
FAIL: test_two (__main__.Factorial_Test)
----------------------------------------------------------------
Traceback (most recent call last):
  File "tdd_factorial_3_Test.py", line 13, in test_two
    self.assertEquals ( 2 , factorial ( 2 ) )
AssertionError: 2 != 1


----------------------------------------------------------------
Ran 3 tests in 0.002s

FAILED (failures=1)
```

Red – we need to amend the function to get a Green:

```python
def factorial ( x ) :
    if x <= 1 : return 1
    else : return 2
```

Note that we do the minimum amount of work to get a Green. Let's continue in this way for a while. We add the test method:

```python
    def test_three ( self ) :
        self.assertEquals ( 6 , factorial ( 3 ) )
```

which give us a Red, so we amend the code to:

```python
def factorial ( x ) :
    if x <= 1 : return 1
    elif x == 2 : return 2
    else : return 6
```

to get a Green. Then we add the test method:

```python
    def test_four ( self ) :
        self.assertEquals ( 24 , factorial ( 4 ) )
```

which give us a Red, so we amend the code to:

```python
def factorial ( x ) :
    if x <= 1 : return 1
    elif x == 2 : return 2
    elif x == 3 : return 6
    else : return 24
```

to get a Green.

At this point we have a mass of methods, which has been great for development, but it looks ugly and what is worse, the function implementation is looking ugly. In TDD, having noticed this, we stop development to reflect on what we have and, if appropriate, *refactor* our code. Basically we rewrite the code so it looks nicer.

Refactoring is the transforming of an implementation that gives Green to a better implementation that gives Green.

9.5.3 Leaping in the Light

This is the point at which we take the leap and introduce a more sophisticated version of the algorithm: we have a test system that allows us to catch obvious problems. We make a change to the function:

```
def factorial ( x ) :
    if x <= 1 : return 1
    else : return x * factorial ( x - 1 )
```

and immediately run the tests. Green. We should though add some more tests. Let's do this by adding a single test method with a more sophisticated approach to checking, on the assumption that we do not need the fine grain testing of having multiple methods:

```
def test_correct ( self ) :
    data = ( ( 0 , 1 ) , ( 1 , 1 ) , ( 2 , 2 ) , ( 3 , 6 ) , ( 4 , 24 ) , ( 7 , 5040 ) , ( 11 , 39916800 ) ,
            ( 21 , 51090942171709440000 ) )
    for datum in data :
        self.assertEquals ( datum[1] , factorial ( datum[0] ) )
```

Green. Now we have a reasonable implementation that passes its tests, which are themselves looking a lot more comprehensive. Note though that we do not remove any test methods, we leave the ones we already have in place – even though in some sense the testing replicates tests we have just introduced. We are protecting against *regression*: if we only ever add tests, every time we run the test program we are checking that our code passes all previous tests so we have not reintroduced any errors we had fixed in the past.

A *regression* is when a part of the program that used to work stops working due to a change in the system.

We have had a go at some correct values, what about incorrect ones? We should have dealt with some negative values – factorial is not defined for negative values. So let's add a test for negative values:

```
def test_negative ( self ) :
    for datum in range ( -10 , -1 ) :
        self.assertRaises ( ValueError , factorial , datum )
```

Red:

```
..F....
========================================================
FAIL: test_negative (__main__.Factorial_Test)
--------------------------------------------------------
Traceback (most recent call last):
  File "tdd_factorial_7_Test.py", line 28, in test_negative
    self.assertRaises ( ValueError , factorial , datum )
AssertionError: ValueError not raised


--------------------------------------------------------
Ran 7 tests in 0.002s

FAILED (failures=1)
```

So we amend the code:

```
def factorial ( x ) :
    if x < 0 : raise ValueError , 'Factorial is only defined for positive integers.'
    if x <= 1 : return 1
    else : return x * factorial ( x - 1 )
```

Green. We now have confidence that the function should work as expected. In fact, we have sufficient confidence that we release the function for others to use.

9.5.4 Things Not Thought Of

All goes well for a while, then someone reports the factorial function is broken:

```
>>> print factorial ( x )
59.0625
>>>
```

The only way to get a float as a result of calling our factorial function is if the parameter is a float. Should we be allowing types other than integer as parameters? Clearly we should not allow non-numeric parameters. Fortunately, by luck, we get an error for lists and tuples anyway:

```
>>> print factorial ( [ 1.0 , 2.0 ] )
Traceback (most recent call last):
  File "<stdin>", line 1, in ?
  File "<stdin>", line 4, in factorial
TypeError: unsupported operand type(s) for -: 'list' and 'int'
>>> print factorial ( ( 1.0 , 2.0 ) )
Traceback (most recent call last):
  File "<stdin>", line 1, in ?
  File "<stdin>", line 4, in factorial
TypeError: unsupported operand type(s) for -: 'tuple' and 'int'
>>> print factorial ( factorial )
Traceback (most recent call last):
  File "<stdin>", line 1, in ?
  File "<stdin>", line 4, in factorial
TypeError: unsupported operand type(s) for -: 'function' and 'int'
>>>
```

but this is hardly the right sort of error message: the message says things about the implementation of the factorial function when the caller wants information about what they did wrong in calling the factorial function. So, in good TDD style, we amend the test code first. We add the methods:

```
def test_list ( self ) :
    self.assertRaises ( ValueError , factorial , [ 1.0 , 2.0 ] )

def test_tuple ( self ) :
    self.assertRaises ( ValueError , factorial , ( 1.0 , 2.0 ) )
```

which gives us a Red:

```
..E...E..
===========================================================
ERROR: test_list (__main__.Factorial_Test)
-------------------------------------------------------------------
Traceback (most recent call last):
  File "tdd_factorial_8_Test.py", line 31, in test_list
    self.assertRaises ( ValueError , factorial , [ 1.0 , 2.0 ] )
  File "unittest.py", line 320, in failUnlessRaises
    callableObj(*args, **kwargs)
  File "tdd_factorial_7.py", line 4, in factorial
    else : return x * factorial ( x - 1 )
TypeError: unsupported operand type(s) for -: 'list' and 'int'


===========================================================
ERROR: test_tuple (__main__.Factorial_Test)
```

```
----------------------------------------------------------------
Traceback (most recent call last):
  File "tdd_factorial_8_Test.py", line 34, in test_tuple
    self.assertRaises ( ValueError , factorial , ( 1.0 , 2.0 ) )
  File "unittest.py", line 320, in failUnlessRaises
    callableObj(*args, **kwargs)
  File "tdd_factorial_7.py", line 4, in factorial
    else : return x * factorial ( x - 1 )
TypeError: unsupported operand type(s) for -: 'tuple' and 'int'


----------------------------------------------------------------
Ran 9 tests in 0.019s

FAILED (errors=2)
```

So we change the implementation:

```
def factorial ( x ) :
    if type ( x ) != type ( 0 ) : raise ValueError , 'Factorial is only defined for integers.'
    if x < 0 : raise ValueError , 'Factorial is only defined for positive integers.'
    if x <= 1 : return 1
    else : return x * factorial ( x - 1 )
```

and we get a Green. What is more, we get some sensible errors *and* we fixed the floating point problem at the same time:

```
>>> factorial ( 4 )
24
>>> factorial ( [ ] )
Traceback (most recent call last):
  File "<stdin>", line 1, in ?
  File "<stdin>", line 2, in factorial
ValueError: Factorial is only defined for integers.
>>> factorial ( -1 )
Traceback (most recent call last):
  File "<stdin>", line 1, in ?
  File "<stdin>", line 3, in factorial
ValueError: Factorial is only defined for positive integers.
>>> factorial ( 1.5 )
Traceback (most recent call last):
  File "<stdin>", line 1, in ?
  File "<stdin>", line 2, in factorial
ValueError: Factorial is only defined for integers.
>>>
```

This illustrates a situation for which we have no test case: float parameters. Immediately we add the test method:

```
def test_float ( self ) :
    data = ( 2.4 , 5.6 , 20.5 )
    for datum in data :
        self.assertRaises ( ValueError , factorial , datum )
```

and we still have Green. Now we begin to have some real confidence in the function, we re-release it and await bug reports.

After a while, someone reports back: "Yes the factorial function is working fine, but factorial is actually defined for floating point numbers, it is called the Gamma Function."

The Gamma Function is not an everyday function, so you may never have come across it. It is an extension of factorial that works with real numbers and complex numbers. We don't need to worry about it because probably the best answer to the query is: "Yes the Gamma Function is important and for non-negative integers the Gamma Function is factorial, but factorial is definitely only defined for non-negative integers, the Gamma Function is a different function. If you need the Gamma Function then we should start a new development of a new function."

9.5.5 Refactoring for Fun and Profit

Some time later, someone reports that the factorial function fails for large parameters. In particular, they report that factorial (1000) fails with a very long error message that ends:

```
RuntimeError: maximum recursion depth exceeded in cmp
```

We have found one of the few situations in which recursion in Python has a real problem: there are very few of these. We must change our implementation: we must refactor our code. This is fine, we have a ready-made test suite, so we can amend with confidence.

The change we make is straightforward, we replace the recursive implementation with an iterative implementation:

```
def factorial ( x ) :
    if type ( x ) != type ( 0 ) : raise ValueError , 'Factorial is only defined for integers.'
    if x < 0 : raise ValueError , 'Factorial is only defined for positive integers.'
    if x <= 1 : return 1
    else :
        rv = 1
        for i in range ( 2 , x ) :
            rv *= i
        return rv
```

and, of course, run the tests:

```
F.F...F.F.
==========================================================
FAIL: test_correct (__main__.Factorial_Test)
----------------------------------------------------------
Traceback (most recent call last):
  File "tdd_factorial_10_Test.py", line 24, in test_correct
    self.assertEquals ( datum[1] , factorial ( datum[0] ) )
AssertionError: 2 != 1


==========================================================
FAIL: test_four (__main__.Factorial_Test)
----------------------------------------------------------
Traceback (most recent call last):
  File "tdd_factorial_10_Test.py", line 19, in test_four
    self.assertEquals ( 24 , factorial ( 4 ) )
AssertionError: 24 != 6


==========================================================
FAIL: test_three (__main__.Factorial_Test)
----------------------------------------------------------
Traceback (most recent call last):
```

```
    File "tdd_factorial_10_Test.py", line 16, in test_three
      self.assertEquals ( 6 , factorial ( 3 ) )
  AssertionError: 6 != 2


  ========================================================
  FAIL: test_two (__main__.Factorial_Test)
  ----------------------------------------------------------------
  Traceback (most recent call last):
    File "tdd_factorial_10_Test.py", line 13, in test_two
      self.assertEquals ( 2 , factorial ( 2 ) )
  AssertionError: 2 != 1


  ----------------------------------------------------------------
  Ran 10 tests in 0.001s

  FAILED (failures=4)
```

What is wrong? If we have only the test_correct test method, we have problems progressing without further investigation – this is a drawback to the strategy of having a single test method with multiple data values tested. However, we have data from the test_two, test_three, and test_four test methods. Let's tabulate the data:

parameter	expected	actual
2	2	1
3	6	2
4	24	6

Hmmm... there is a definite pattern emerging. The actual for any parameter is the expected of the previous parameter. This means that the final multiplication is not happening in the calculation of the result.

Looking back at the code, the likely offender must be the for loop control:

```
    for i in range ( 2 , x ) :
```

What an embarrassing slip. We have forgotten that range creates a list of values up to but not including the final value. Instead of the above, we should have written:

```
    for i in range ( 2 , x + 1 ) :
```

so that the value x is included in those being multiplied together. Making this change and running the tests we get:

```
    ..........
    ----------------------------------------------------------------
    Ran 10 tests in 0.011s

    OK
```

Green. However, we are not quite finished. We must add a new test case. We add a new tuple in the test_correct function for factorial (2000). This number has over 5700 digits, so it is not really sensible to print it in this book, but that does not stop us adding it as a test in the unit test. Having done that we get a Green.

9.5.6 Summarizing TDD

It is true that the above example risks trivializing TDD because the example is very simple. Hopefully though you can see past this to the important message:

- The tests should always pass – Green is the only state in which to leave code. Never leave a code in a Red state, fix it now, not later.

- Any new feature of the program must be preceded by creating a test that causes a Red – leading to development to reacquire Green status.

- Any reports of problems should lead to immediate extension of the tests to capture the problem – this may lead to development work to reacquire Green if the state goes to Red.

- Never amend the code without first running the tests to ensure a Green state, then extend the tests to capture the new feature, then run the tests regularly and often as the code is being developed.

- Never remove tests from a test class.

Some people think that TDD is too rigid and constraining, and that developing software should be a more holistic activity – develop some code here, some tests there. What is not in doubt is that unit tests are an essential part of software development, and that the tests should be extensive and have good coverage.

Chapter Summary

In this chapter we have found that:

- Unit testing is A Good Thing.
- Unit test frameworks are A Good Thing.
- PyUnit is the standard unit test framework for Python programming.
- The very basic tests we have been providing previously can easily be replaced by PyUnit tests.
- Taking pride in unit testing is a mark of programmer professionalism.
- Test-Driven Development (TDD) is a process of software development that integrally involves unit testing.

Self-Review Questions

Self-review 9.1 What is unit testing?

Self-review 9.2 Why is unit testing important?

Self-review 9.3 What is PyUnit?

Self-review 9.4 What is unittest?

Self-review 9.5 What does this line of code mean?

```
class Fibonacci_Test ( unittest.TestCase ) :
```

Self-review 9.6 What is an assertion?

Self-review 9.7 What does the following line mean:

```
self.assertEqual ( 55 , fibonacci ( 10 ) )
```

Self-review 9.8 When is a method a unit test method?

Self-review 9.9 What do 'Red' and 'Green' mean in the context of unit testing?

Self-review 9.10 Why are the terms 'Red' and 'Green' used in the context of unit testing?

Self-review 9.11 What is 'coverage'?

Self-review 9.12 What is 'refactoring'?

Self-review 9.13 Why is unit testing important for refactoring?

Self-review 9.14 Using the Web, look up the term *eXtreme programming*, which has been mentioned in this chapter. What are the main features of this method and how does unit testing fit into it?

Self-review 9.15 Debugging code thoroughly usually gives rise to a few exceptions. To debug code efficiently, it's important that you understand what Python's different exception types mean. What are the following exceptions used for in Python:

- AssertionError
- ImportError
- IndexError
- KeyError
- NameError
- TypeError
- ValueError

Programming Exercises

Exercise 9.1 Although much of this chapter has been about testing, another fundamental skill is being able to identify and correct errors once your testing has uncovered them. The following pieces of code all contain simple errors. Identify the errors in each program and suggest possible tests to detect them and solutions to fix them:

1.  ```
    for i in range(1, -10, 1):
        print i
    ```

2.  ```
    l = [1, 2, 3, 4, 5]
    l[6] = 6
    ```

3.  ```
    print [1, 2, 3].append([4, 5])
    ```

Hint: In most cases there will be more than one possible solution. Give some consideration to which fixes would be best to use in different situations.
    ```

Exercise 9.2 Complete the Matrix class test by adding test methods to deal with the subtraction and multiplication operations.

Exercise 9.3 Write a test program for the queue implementation from Section 6.6.4 (page 204).

Exercise 9.4 Write a test program for the stack implementation from Section 6.6.5 (page 205).

Exercise 9.5 Write a test program for the Account class from Exercise 6.6 (page 215), the CreditAccount class from Exercise 7.2 (page 249), and the StudentAccount class from Exercise 7.3 (page 249).

Exercise 9.6 Below is the start of a test suite; the exercise is to write a module that passes it. Your code will provide functions to calculate various sorts of average on lists of data:

- mode – the most frequent datum appearing in the list.
- median – the middle value in the list of (sorted) data.
- mean – the total of the data divided by the number of values.

```
import average, unittest

class TestMe ( unittest.TestCase ) :

    def setUp ( self ) :
        self.zeros = [ 0.0 for i in range ( 1 ,10 ) ]
        self.ints = [ i for i in range ( -10 , 10 ) ]
        self.foobar = [ i for i in range ( -10 , 10 ) ] + [ 2 , 2 , 2 , 2 , 2 , 2 , 2 , 2 ]

    def test_mode ( self ) :
        self.assertEquals ( 0.0 , average.mode ( self.zeros ) )
        self.assertEquals ( 0 , average.mode ( self.ints ) )
        self.assertEquals ( 2 , average.mode ( self.foobar ) )

    def test_mean ( self ) :
        self.assertEquals ( 0.0 , average.mean ( self.zeros ) )
        self.assertEquals ( -1 , average.mean ( self.ints ) )
        self.assertEquals ( 0 , average.mean ( self.foobar ) )

    def test_median ( self ) :
        self.assertEquals ( 0.0 , average.median ( self.zeros ) )
        self.assertEquals ( 0 , average.median ( self.ints ) )
        self.assertEquals ( 2 , average.median ( self.foobar ) )

    if __name__ == '__main__':
        unittest.main ()
```

Exercise 9.7 The test suite for the previous task is a good start, but not very complete. Add some more test cases. In particular, you should test for:

- Handling data that isn't in a sequence.
- Handling data that is in a sequence but isn't numeric.

Exercise 9.8 Use PyUnit to test the following functions in the random module:

- randint
- random
- choice

Exercise 9.9 If you have completed the exercise above, you will have noticed that the random module contains both functions and classes. The classes represent various sorts of random number generator, and many of the available functions are duplicated as methods in each of the classes. Write a test suite to test the randint, random and choice methods in the random.Random class.

Exercise 9.10 Some programs cannot be easily tested using unit test modules such as PyUnit. GUIs, in particular, need both unit testing (to exercise application logic) and testing that exercises the graphical components of the program.

For this exercise you need to thoroughly test the Turtle module. Although you are already familiar with this code, you should make sure that you plan your testing carefully and exercise as many of the available functions as possible. In particular, you should note that many functions in turtle are not graphical, and so *can* be tested with PyUnit.

Exercise 9.11 Some data is more interesting to test than others. UK postcodes (unlike US zip codes) are particularly interesting because they have lots of special cases. Most postcodes consist of two letters, one number, a space, a number and two letters. For example, James' office postcode is CV1 5FB. However, many postcodes are slightly different, such as PO10 0AB, SW1A 0AA and SAN TA1.

Read about British postcodes on Wikipedia http://en.wikipedia.org/wiki/UK_postcodes and write a table of test data that would thoroughly exercise a postcode parser.

Challenges

Challenge 9.1 We left these questions as questions for the reader in Section 9.4.2 (page 289):

1. Should we be stopping numbers such as IIIIIIIIIII, for example, from being legal?

2. Should we be forbidding mixed case numbers?

3. Are MCMIC, MCMXCIX and MIM all valid representations of 1999? Why does MCMXCIX appear to be the preferred representation?

4. Is MCMCXCVIII a valid representation of 2098?

5. Is MXMVII a valid representation of 1998?

Challenge 9.2 In this challenge you will be developing a program using Test-Driven Development (TDD), which we introduced in Section 9.5 (page 297). Make sure you follow the principles of TDD strictly. The purpose of this challenge is not just to give you more programming practice, but to give you experience of developing a whole program using TDD.

In Chapters 6 and 7 we developed the Die class and its various subclasses. For this challenge you will write a game of Snap, which should be played on the console (i.e. you don't need to write a GUI unless you want to). You will probably want to include the following components, but the detailed design of the code is up to you:

- A pack of cards. You will probably want to use a subclass of Die for this. You don't have to model a standard pack of 52 cards, it's up to you.

- Some part of your program should control the game. This component should be responsible for knowing whose turn it is to play and when the game has been won (or drawn if you run out of cards).

- An interface. Some component of your program should be responsible for communicating with the user. Following good HCI principles, you should make sure that the user is always aware of the state of the game (including their score).

Note that because users are playing with a pack of cards, when one card is (randomly) played, it cannot be used again. So you need some way to ensure that cards are not played twice – perhaps by keeping track of which cards have already been played. This code could be placed in various components of the program. Think about where would be most sensible to put it (but remember, you can always refactor your code later on).

Challenge 9.3 In Section 9.4.4 (page 294) of this chapter, we wrote a test class for the matrix module from Section 6.6.6 (page 206). In this challenge we will give you code for another module that uses matrices to perform some simple graphics operations. The code comes with some simple tests, your job is to test the code thoroughly using PyUnit.

In graphics applications such as the GIMP or Photoshop and in animations, shapes and objects are often moved, scaled and rotated automatically. This is often done using a technique called homogeneous coordinates, in which 3D matrices are used to manipulate 2D images.

To convert a 2D point into a homogeneous 3D point we make the following transformation:

$$(x, y) \mapsto (x, y, 1)$$

and to convert back to an ordinary 2D point the following transformation needs to be performed:

$$(x,y,h) \mapsto \left(\frac{x}{h}, \frac{y}{h}\right)$$

To perform a transformation (rotation, translation or scaling) on a point, the point needs to be multiplied by a transformation matrix. In the code below we have created a class called HomogMatrix which is a subclass of the Matrix class you have seen before. This class has methods to convert vectors to and from their homogeneous counterparts. The module also has functions to perform transformations on vectors and code to draw shapes (made from lists of vectors) with the Python turtle.

Make sure you spend some time looking through this code in order to understand it, before you begin to write some test cases for the HomogMatrix class and the later functions.

```
'''Provides functions to rotate, scale and translate points
    using homogeneous matrices.'''

__author__ = 'Sarah Mount <s.mount@wlv.ac.uk>'
__date__ = '2007-05-30'
__version__ = '1.0'
__copyright__ = 'Copyright (c) 2007 Sarah Mount'
__licence__ = 'GNU General Public Licence (GPL)'

from matrix import Matrix
import copy, math, turtle

class HomogMatrix ( Matrix ) :
    def __init__ ( self , data ) :
        Matrix.__init__ ( self , data )
    def __ensure2D ( self ) :
        if len ( self.data ) != 1 or len ( self.data[0] ) != 2 :
            raise ValueError , 'Matrix not a 2D vector.'
    def __ensure3D ( self ) :
        if len ( self.data ) != 1 or len ( self.data[0] ) != 3 :
            raise ValueError , 'Matrix not a 3D vector.'
    def de_homo ( self ) :
        '''Convert a homogeneous 3D point into a 2D point.'''
        self.__ensure3D ()
        m1 = self.data[0][0] / self.data[0][2]
        m2 = self.data[0][1] / self.data[0][2]
        return HomogMatrix ( [ [ m1 , m2 ] ] )
    def en_homo ( self ) :
        '''Convert a 2D point into a homogeneous 3D point.'''
        self.__ensure2D ()
        d = copy.copy ( self.data )
        d[0] = list ( d[0] )
        d[0] += [1.0]
        return HomogMatrix ( d )
    def __mul__ ( self , m ) :
        mm = HomogMatrix ( Matrix.__mul__ ( self , m ) )
        return HomogMatrix ( mm )
```

```python
    def __add__ ( self , m ) :
        mm = HomogMatrix ( Matrix.__add__ ( self , m ) )
        return HomogMatrix ( mm )
    def __sub__ ( self , m ) :
        mm = HomogMatrix ( Matrix.__sub__ ( self , m ) )
        return HomogMatrix ( mm )

def translate ( v , ( tx , ty ) ) :
    '''Translate 2D vector v by (t1, t2)'''
    if not isinstance ( v , HomogMatrix ) :
        raise ValueError , 'Matrix not homogeneous'
    t_data = [
        [ 1.0 , 0.0 , 0.0 ] ,
        [ 0.0 , 1.0 , 0.0 ] ,
        [ tx , ty , 1.0 ] ]
    t = Matrix ( t_data )
    v_h = v.en_homo ()
    translated = v_h * t
    return translated.de_homo ()

def scale ( v , ( sx , sy ) ) :
    '''Scale vector v by (sx, sy).'''
    if not isinstance ( v , HomogMatrix ) :
        raise ValueError , 'Matrix not homogeneous'
    s_data = [
        [ sx , 0.0 , 0.0 ] ,
        [ 0.0 , sy , 0.0 ] ,
        [ 0.0 , 0.0 , 1.0 ] ]
    s = HomogMatrix ( s_data )
    v_h = v.en_homo ()
    scaled = v_h * s
    return scaled.de_homo ()

def rotate ( v , theta ) :
    '''Scale vector v by (sx, sy).'''
    if not isinstance ( v , HomogMatrix ) :
        raise ValueError , 'Matrix not homogeneous'
    r_data = [
        [ math.cos ( theta ) , math.sin ( theta ) , 0.0 ] ,
        [ -math.sin ( theta ) , math.cos ( theta ) , 0.0 ] ,
        [ 0.0 , 0.0 , 1.0 ] ]
    r = Matrix ( r_data )
    v_h = v.en_homo ()
    rotated = v_h * r
    return rotated.de_homo ()

def draw ( points ) :
    '''Draw a shape made from a list of points.'''
    turtle.clear ()
    turtle.up ()
    turtle.goto ( points[0][0] )
    turtle.down ()
    for point in points[1:] :
        turtle.goto ( point[0] )
```

```
if __name__ == '__main__':
    # Test data -- some simple shapes made from lists of points.
    # A point is a 2D vector [[x, y]]
    shapes = {
        'square' : [
            HomogMatrix ( [ [ ( 0.0 , 0.0 ) ] ] ) ,
            HomogMatrix ( [ [ ( 100.0 , 0.0 ) ] ] ) ,
            HomogMatrix ( [ [ ( 100.0 , 100.0 ) ] ] ) ,
            HomogMatrix ( [ [ ( 0.0 , 100.0 ) ] ] ) ,
            HomogMatrix ( [ [ ( 0.0 , 0.0 ) ] ] ) ] ,
        'rectangle' : [
            HomogMatrix ( [ [ ( 0.0 , 0.0 ) ] ] ) ,
            HomogMatrix ( [ [ ( 200.0 , 0.0 ) ] ] ) ,
            HomogMatrix ( [ [ ( 200.0 , 100.0 ) ] ] ) ,
            HomogMatrix ( [ [ ( 0.0 , 100.0 ) ] ] ) ,
            HomogMatrix ( [ [ ( 0.0 , 0.0 ) ] ] ) ] ,
        'pentagon' : [
            HomogMatrix ( [ [ ( 0.0 , 0.0 ) ] ] ) ,
            HomogMatrix ( [ [ ( 100.0 , 0.0 ) ] ] ) ,
            HomogMatrix ( [ [ ( 131.0 , 95.0 ) ] ] ) ,
            HomogMatrix ( [ [ ( 50.0 , 154.0 ) ] ] ) ,
            HomogMatrix ( [ [ ( -30.0 , 95.0 ) ] ] ) ,
            HomogMatrix ( [ [ ( 0.0 , 0.0 ) ] ] ) ]
    }
    for shape in shapes.keys ( ) :
        print shape , ':'
        for vector in shapes[shape] :
            print vector
        draw ( shapes[shape] )
        print

def draw_transform ( trans , data , s , t ) :
    '''Apply matrix transformation to a shape and draw the transformed
    shape with the turtle. trans should be a function. data is used by the
    trans function. s should be a key (for the shapes dict). t should be a
    string.'''
    ss = map ( lambda v : trans ( v , data ) , shapes[s] )
    print t , s , ':'
    for v in ss : print '\t' , v
    print
    draw ( ss )

# Draw transformed shapes
draw_transform ( translate , ( -100.0 , -100.0 ) , 'square' , 'translated' )
draw_transform ( translate, ( -200.0 , -200.0 ) , 'pentagon' , 'translated' )
draw_transform ( scale, ( 1.5 , 0.2 ) , 'rectangle' , 'scaled' )
draw_transform ( scale, ( 0.25 , 0.25 ) , 'pentagon' , 'scaled' )
draw_transform ( rotate , 45.0 , 'square' , 'rotated' )
draw_transform ( rotate , 20.0 , 'pentagon' , 'rotated' )

raw_input ( 'Press any key to exit.' )
```

Algorithms and Data Structures

Learning Outcomes

At the end of this chapter you will be able to:

- Describe and implement simple algorithms for searching and sorting, such as *binary search* and *bubble sort*.

- Implement binary trees and write programs to traverse them.

- Understand the meaning of measurements in *Big O* notation.

- Choose between alternative algorithms based on their *Big O* measurements.

- Choose between compound data structures based on the *Big O* measure of their store and retrieval operations.

Programming is about creating programs that execute algorithms on data. Having the right representation of the data needed to solve the problem at hand, and having a good realization of the algorithm to work the data, are what programming is all about. Moreover, ensuring that the algorithm and its implementation are efficient is important to the quality of the program. Having an uncomplicated program that does the required job, and is easy to write and evolve, is critically important. Having a program that not only runs correctly, but runs quickly, is also important.

So far the main data structures we have used are sequences (lists, tuples and strings) and dictionaries. Sequences are data structures in which items are indexed by their position in the sequence, whereas dictionaries are data structures in which items are accessed by a key. We have used sequences as general storage mechanisms for working with collections of data, whilst we have used dictionaries where we needed to index data so that we could access it easily.

We have also introduced queues and stacks as data structures that have very specific add and remove properties. Queues and stacks are *closed data structures* because it is not possible to investigate what values the data structures contain; the data structure controls access to values and only particular values can be observed. Conversely sequences are *open data structures* as we can iterate over the data structure observing all the values. Why is this an issue? With an open data structure there is a model of how data is stored. For example a list is a sequence so we have the model that values are stored in some sort of consecutive way. For closed data structures, there is no such model; the data structure is opaque, we have no model for the way the data is stored. This opaqueness of the implementation is core to the idea of an *abstract data type*. The type offers a way of storing values and a set of methods (the *public interface*) for managing instances of the type, but there is no access to the internal representation. Why is this a good thing? It means that the implementation of the abstract data type can be changed without affecting code that uses instances of the type. For example, we could create an implementation of a stack and others could write applications using it. Later we find that we can implement the stack in a far more efficient way, so we change the stack type. As long as we do not change the public interface of the stack type, then no application code needs to be changed, yet the new version of stack gets used and the application becomes more efficient.

Abstract data types are then one of the tools for supporting separation of concerns. By designing the public interfaces of our types well, we create boundaries that clearly separate concerns. Efficient implementation of closed data structures is separated from the use of those data structures in application code.

The implementation of our closed data structures will almost certainly make use of open data structures such as list and dictionary. Choosing the most appropriate open data structure is clearly an important part of programming, but how do we make decisions about what is appropriate and what is efficient?

10.1 Data Structures

Python has sequences (lists and tuples) and dictionaries as built-in data structure types. It also has set, though we haven't introduced this type so far. (As the name suggests, set implements the idea of a mathematical set, it is a data structures that contains values but guarantees there will only ever be a single instance of a value held in the data structure.) Lists, tuples, and dictionaries are, however, not the only data structures that are useful, they are just the ones that the maintainers of the Python system deem are required to be built-in. If you hunt around in books and on the Web, you will undoubtedly find the following data structures as being important:

List	Associative Array (aka Dictionary)	Tree
Ordered List	Hash Table	Binary Tree
Queue	Open Hash Table	2-3 Tree
Ordered Queue	Chained Hash Table	Red–Black Tree
Priority Queue	Set	AVL Tree
Heap	Graph	B-Tree
Stack		

Whilst it is important to look at these different data structures in detail, it is material for the book that comes after this one. This book is an introduction, whereas studying these data structures in detail is material for a second course in programming. We are going to give a quick taster to show what the issues are, and to provide pointers to what you need to learn more about on the path to becoming a proficient programmer.

In the next few sections we are going to show how data structures and algorithms go hand in hand – certain data structures support different algorithms more easily. Conversely, using some data structures require specific algorithms. The aim here is to highlight the programming design and development issues rather than studying the data structures and algorithms in detail, to show you why studying the details is important.

10.2 Sequences

Sequence (list and tuple in Python) is the most basic open data structure. A sequence provides a way of collecting values into a single structure in which each value can be accessed by indexing. Accessing values by indexing is easy, but what do we do if we want to find whether a specific value is in the sequence. In Python, we can use the **in** operator:

```
>>> data = ( 'Bert' , 'James' , 'Brenda' , 'James' , 'Bert' , 'Jones' , 'Brenda' , 'Jones' )
>>> print 'Brenda' in data
True
>>> print 'Brian' in data
False
>>>
```

What if we need to know the index at which a specific value is stored? There is no Python operator for this, so we need to implement an algorithm to search the sequence.

10.2.1 Searching

There are two basic ways of searching a sequence: linear search and binary search.

Linear Search

Unless we know something about how values are stored in a sequence, there is only one way of searching a sequence: we start at the beginning and look through till we find the value we are looking for. This is called *Linear Search* and is the most basic of searching algorithms. Here is an implementation:

```
def linearByValue ( data , value , index = 0 ) :
    for i in range ( index , len ( data ) ) :
        if data[ i ] == value : return i
    return None
```

You may have spotted that our implementation does not require us to start searching from the beginning. The implemented algorithm is Linear Search, i.e. searching through the sequence until we find the sought value, or get to the end of the sequence and know that the sought value is not in the sequence, but our function has an 'extra' parameter that specifies the start point in the sequence of the search. This extra parameter has a default value of 0, which means the default is to start at the beginning of the sequence. So if we call our function thus:

```
linearByValue ( data , value )
```

the search starts at the beginning. However, if we call the function thus:

```
linearByValue ( data , value , index )
```

providing a value for the third parameter overriding the default, then the search starts at index index.

Why return None if the value is not found during the search? What is None anyway? The caller of the linearByValue function is expecting an integer to be returned that is the index of the item in the sequence. In general, all non-negative integers, including 0, are valid indexes. Moreover, in Python, all negative integers are valid indexes as well: they denote indexing from the end of the sequence (we covered this is Section 4.4.1, page 114). This means that there is no integer we can return to represent "Value not found" – unlike languages such as C, C++, Java, in which negative values are not valid indexes, so -1 can be used. Fortunately, Python is a dynamically typed language so we can return an object that is not an integer in the case when the sought value is not in the sequence. Python has the value None, which is of type NoneType, that is ideal for this purpose. Of course, even though this value is not an integer, the application code will try and use the value as an integer because it expected an integer value to be returned. If the application uses the value None as an index, a TypeError will be raised because NoneType is not int. So in Python returning a value that is not an integer is the right way of signaling that the value was not found in the sequence, even though the application expects an integer.

Binary Search

Think about trying to find the definition of a word in a dictionary by starting at 'a' and working forwards (Linear Search). Searching from the beginning does seem like an extraordinarily slow way of doing things. So why is looking up a word in a dictionary generally quick? Because the words are ordered alphabetically. This means that we can open the dictionary anywhere and decide whether the word we are looking for is before or after the place at which we opened the dictionary. This halves the size of the part of the dictionary we have to search. We can then open a page in the middle of the half where the word is known to be and decide which of the two halves of that part of the dictionary the word is in – we are halving the *search space*. Proceeding like this we very quickly find the page that contains our target word, and then it is a question of finding the word on the page. Having the definitions in the dictionary sorted enables us to create an algorithm for finding things that is far quicker that the general method we use if we cannot make assumptions about the ordering.

This technique of halving the search space to find something is called *Binary Search* or sometimes *Binary Chop*.

Following this line of thinking, if the data in a sequence is sorted and we are searching for a single item, we can use the Binary Search algorithm, which we can express as:

Binary Search is an example of a divide-and-conquer algorithm.

> Look at the value in the middle of the sequence
> if the value is the sought item, return the index
> If the value is greater than the sought item
>   Binary search the first half of the sequence
> If the value is less than the sought item
>   Binary search the second half of the sequence.

We can implement this directly as a recursive function:

The variables data and value that are parameters of the binarySearchByValueRecursive function are in scope in the nested _binarySearch function, so we can use them without them having to be parameters.

```
def binarySearchByValueRecursive ( data , value ) :
    def _binarySearch ( low , high ) :
        if low == high :
            if data[low] == value : return low
            else : return None
        else :
            mid = int ( ( low + high ) / 2 )
            if value < data[ mid ] : return _binarySearch ( low , mid - 1 )
            elif value > data[ mid ] : return _binarySearch ( mid + 1 , high )
            elif value == data[ mid ] : return mid
            else : return None
    return _binarySearch ( 0 , len ( data ) - 1 )
```

However, this is not the usual form of the implementation. Although the algorithm appears fundamentally recursive, it is easily expressed in iterative form and hence leads to an iterative function:

```
def binarySearchByValue ( data , value ) :
    low , high = 0 , len ( data ) - 1
    while low <= high :
        mid = int ( ( low + high ) / 2 )
        if value > data[ mid ] : low = mid + 1
        elif value < data[ mid ] : high = mid - 1
        else : return mid
    return None
```

which is more efficient than the recursive function.

Testing, Testing

We should always write the test code before we write the application code. In developing the above three search functions, we used the test code:

```
import unittest
import search

class search_Test ( unittest.TestCase ) :

    def test_linearByValue ( self ) :
        data = ( 'Bert' , 'James' , 'Brenda' , 'James' , 'Bert' , 'Jones' , 'Brenda' , 'Jones' )
        self.assertEquals ( 2 , search.linearByValue ( data , 'Brenda' ) )
        self.assertEquals ( 6 , search.linearByValue ( data , 'Brenda' , 4 ) )
        self.assertEquals ( None , search.linearByValue ( data , 'Bertrand' ) )

    def test_linearByComparator ( self ) :
        data = (
            ( 'Bert' , 'James' , ( 'CS 101' , 'CS 102' ) ) ,
            ( 'Brenda' , 'James' , ( 'CS 101' , 'CS 102' , 'CS 103' ) ) ,
            ( 'Bert' , 'Jones' , ( 'CS 101' , ) ) ,
            ( 'Brenda' , 'Jones' , ( 'CS 101' , 'CS 102' ) ) ,
            )
        self.assertEquals (1, search.linearByComparator(data, lambda x:'CS 103' in x[2]))
        self.assertEquals (2, search.linearByComparator(data, lambda x:'Jones'==x[1]))
        self.assertEquals (None, search.linearByComparator(data, lambda x:'Jenson'==x[1]))

    def test_binarySearchByValue ( self ) :
        data = ( 'Bert' , 'Bertrand' , 'Breeda' , 'Brenda' , 'James' , 'Jenson' , 'Jones' )
        self.assertEquals ( 3 , search.binarySearchByValue ( data , 'Brenda' ) )
        self.assertEquals ( None , search.binarySearchByValue ( data , 'Brian' ) )
        self.assertEquals ( 1 , search.binarySearchByValue ( data , 'Bertrand' ) )
        self.assertEquals ( 5 , search.binarySearchByValue ( data , 'Jenson' ) )
        self.assertEquals ( 6 , search.binarySearchByValue ( data , 'Jones' ) )

    def test_binarySearchByValueRecursive ( self ) :
        data = ( 'Bert' , 'Bertrand' , 'Breeda' , 'Brenda' , 'James' , 'Jenson' , 'Jones' )
        self.assertEquals ( 3 , search.binarySearchByValueRecursive ( data , 'Brenda' ) )
        self.assertEquals ( None , search.binarySearchByValueRecursive ( data , 'Brian' ) )
        self.assertEquals ( 1 , search.binarySearchByValueRecursive ( data , 'Bertrand' ) )
        self.assertEquals ( 5 , search.binarySearchByValueRecursive ( data , 'Jenson' ) )
        self.assertEquals ( 6 , search.binarySearchByValueRecursive ( data , 'Jones' ) )
```

linearByComparator is introduced in the next subsubsection.

```
if __name__ == '__main__' :
    unittest.main ()
```

which when executed results in:

```
....
-------------------------------------------------------------------
Ran 4 tests in 0.000s

OK
```

We have a Green. It is true that this is not a very extensive test of the functions. The tests can and should be improved, but even as they are they give us confidence that the functions are doing what they are supposed to do.

Comparing things

The linearByValue search function uses the equality operator (==) to test for equality. This assumes that there is a value that can be passed as a parameter to the function call that can be tested for equality with the values in the sequence using the == operator. What happens if we have a sequence of sequences to search and we want to find the sequence that has a specific value at a specific index? For example, what happens if we have the data:

> The data perhaps represents computing classes being taken by students.

```
data = (
    ('Bert' , 'James' , ('CS 101' , 'CS 102')) ,
    ('Brenda' , 'James' , ('CS 101' , 'CS 102' , 'CS 103')) ,
    ('Bert' , 'Jones' , ('CS 101' ,)) ,
    ('Brenda' , 'Jones' , ('CS 101' , 'CS 102')) ,
    )
```

and we want to search for the first sequence in the sequence that has as its second item the value 'Jones'? We cannot use linearByValue to perform this search, since it relies on testing for equality of the whole item and we want to do searching based on only part of the data.

To achieve our goal we need to be able to search the data using a Boolean function (predicate) of our own devising. This is quite a simple extension of linearByValue that we have called linearByComparator:

```
def linearByComparator ( data , comparator , index = 0 ) :
    for i in range ( index , len ( data )) :
        if comparator ( data[ i ]) : return i
    return None
```

Instead of passing a value to test for equality, we pass a *comparator*, a predicate that is used to test each value to determine which is the value we are seeking. The test code shows how this might be used:

```
def test_linearByComparator ( self ) :
    data = (
        ('Bert' , 'James' , ('CS 101' , 'CS 102')) ,
        ('Brenda' , 'James' , ('CS 101' , 'CS 102' , 'CS 103')) ,
        ('Bert' , 'Jones' , ('CS 101' ,)) ,
        ('Brenda' , 'Jones' , ('CS 101' , 'CS 102')) ,
        )
    self.assertEquals (1, search.linearByComparator(data, lambda x:'CS 103' in x[2]))
    self.assertEquals (2, search.linearByComparator(data, lambda x:'Jones'==x[1]))
    self.assertEquals (None, search.linearByComparator(data, lambda x:'Jenson'==x[1]))
```

Here we are using lambda functions to specify predicates, but we could equally well pass the name of a defined function. In this example, the first predicate realizes the search for the first person in the sequence who is taking the CS 103 course, while the following two are looking for students with particular surnames.

To Merge or Not To Merge...

A good question at this point is: "Should we have two separate functions for linear search (linearByValue and linearByComparator) or merge them into a single function?" The issue here is whether we should have two functions, the names of which determine whether the second parameter is a predicate or a value, or whether we should have a single function that is polymorphic in its second parameter, i.e. it can deal with either a predicate or value. Creating a single function is straightforward using the callable function:

```
def linear ( data , valueOrComparator , index = 0 ) :
    if callable ( valueOrComparator ) :
        for i in range ( index , len ( data ) ) :
            if valueOrComparator ( data[ i ] ) : return i
    else :
        for i in range ( index , len ( data ) ) :
            if data[ i ] == valueOrComparator : return i
    return None
```

The built-in function callable tests whether or not the object referred to by the parameter variable is something to which function call can be applied. Clearly if we pass a function, that is callable and it is assumed that it is a predicate. The penalty we pay with this implementation is that we can never search for a callable value as a data item, we would have to create a predicate to handle that situation.

There are many pros and cons for each of these two approaches (two functions or a single function). The issues are basically:

• A single function means it is easy to work with.

• Separate functions makes it clear what is and is not allowed as the second parameter.

The arguments one way or the other are not entirely clear cut.

We created a new function so, of course, we must previously have created tests for them. We added the methods:

```
def test_linear_ByValue ( self ) :
    data = ( 'Bert' , 'James' , 'Brenda' , 'James' , 'Bert' , 'Jones' , 'Brenda' , 'Jones' )
    self.assertEquals ( 2 , search.linear ( data , 'Brenda' ) )
    self.assertEquals ( 6 , search.linear ( data , 'Brenda' , 4 ) )
    self.assertEquals ( None , search.linear ( data , 'Bertrand' ) )

def test_linear_ByComparator ( self ) :
    data = (
        ( 'Bert' , 'James' , ( 'CS 101' , 'CS 102' ) ) ,
        ( 'Brenda' , 'James' , ( 'CS 101' , 'CS 102' , 'CS 103' ) ) ,
        ( 'Bert' , 'Jones' , ( 'CS 101' , ) ) ,
        ( 'Brenda' , 'Jones' , ( 'CS 101' , 'CS 102' ) ) ,
        )
    self.assertEquals ( 1 , search.linear ( data , lambda x : 'CS 103' in x[2] ) )
    self.assertEquals ( 2 , search.linear ( data , lambda x : 'Jones' == x[1] ) )
    self.assertEquals ( None , search.linear ( data , lambda x : 'Jenson' == x[1] ) )
```

to our test program before starting development of linear. Executing the updated tests after we implemented the new function gives us:

```
......
----------------------------------------------------------------------
Ran 6 tests in 0.001s

OK
```

so we have a Green.

Measuring Performance

We indicated in the introduction to this chapter that we were going to introduce a way of determining whether one algorithm is more efficient than another. The tool is called *Big O* notation and is a way of measuring the complexity of an algorithm and hence how long the algorithm will take to run. Proper consideration of Big O notation is a topic for a second course in programming. We are going to present a very basic introduction – just enough that we can talk about the complexity of algorithms in an informal way.

Taking linear search as an example: to find a value in a sequence of length n, we execute on average $n/2$ comparisons – it is $n/2$ because on average the item being searched for will be found half-way through the list of items being searched. Using Big O notation we have:

$$T(n) = O(n)$$

which says that the time complexity of the linear search algorithm is of order n, or, more colloquially: "Linear Search is an order n algorithm."

The complexity we are measuring here is the number of operations that must be executed to complete the algorithm. Each operation takes some amount of time, so we are measuring the time complexity of the algorithm. Hence $T(n)$. The T says we are considering time complexity and the n is the symbol that measures the size of the problem – usually this is the number of items in the data being worked on. If we wanted to measure the amount of memory used by an algorithm, we would be measuring the space complexity and would use $S(n)$.

Big O notation is only concerned with the comparison of algorithms in terms of the size of the problem – in this case n is the size of the problem. Constants do not matter in Big O notation so $O(n/2)$ is the same as $O(n)$: we simply ignore the constant 2.

Both the Linear Search and Binary Search algorithms used here require the data to be stored in memory. So, for both algorithms:

$$S(n) = O(n)$$

i.e. both algorithms have space complexity of order n. There is therefore no difference between the algorithms in terms of memory usage. The difference is clearly only in the time complexity. So what is the time complexity of Binary Search? Because we halve the search space with each operation, it turns out that:

$$T(n) = O(\log_2 n)$$

i.e. binary search is an order $\log_2 n$ algorithm. This means that binary search is a lot more efficient (i.e. has a smaller time complexity) than linear search. Not for small sequences, perhaps, but for large sequences it certainly does. To show this, let us consider the following numbers:

This is a very informal introduction to Big O notation and its use in comparing algorithms. To do the subject proper justice we would need a whole book.

n	$\log_2 n$
10	3.32192809489
100	6.64385618977
1,000	9.96578428466
10,000	13.2877123795
100,000	16.6096404744
1,000,000	19.9315685693
10,000,000	23.2534966642

For a list of 10,000,000 items, searching using linear search will, on average, take 5,000,000 comparisons, whereas binary search will take 24 comparisons. That is an enormous difference! Hopefully this convinces you that:

- Binary Search really is more efficient than linear search.

- Knowing the Big O complexity of an algorithm is worthwhile!

The moral of the story is that searching sorted data is just so much faster than searching unsorted data. This clearly begs the question: "How can we sort data so we can search it efficiently?"

10.2.2 Sorting

Sorting (as well as searching) is an activity that computers carry out regularly, for example Sorting addresses in a email client, sorting directory entries, etc. It will come as no surprise that sorting (as well as searching) has been analyzed extensively, and that there are a number of algorithms that are deemed 'best practice'.

You may be wondering then why we are looking at sorting algorithms and implementations when sorting is such a well investigated area – most particularly since there is a method for sorting lists (sort) in the standard Python library. There are a number of aspects to the answer:

> Sorting mutable sequences (lists) can be done in place. Immutable sequences (tuple, strings) cannot be sorted in place, a copy must be made to a mutable data structure.

- It is always good to understand the algorithms being used by standard library functions and methods to have a 'feel' for their performance characteristics. This is especially important if there are implementations of more than one algorithm, so that you can choose the right one for the task at hand.

- It is good to have knowledge of what possibilities there are other than those provided as standard, since it may sometimes be necessary to use customized algorithms rather than standard functions and methods. To put it another way, it may be that the best algorithm for your problem is not implemented as standard and using the one that is implemented would be the wrong thing to do.

- They are good examples of small but sophisticated Python functions.

Selection Sort

Selection Sort is probably the simplest sorting algorithm, and is very easily understood and implemented.

To sort our data, we search the list for the smallest item and move it to the first position in the list. Then we look for the next smallest item and move it to the second position, and so on until the list is sorted.

Here's an implementation:

```
def selectionSort ( data , comparator = _ltComparator ) :
    length = len ( data )
    for start in range ( length ) :
        location = start
        for compare in range ( start + 1 , length ) :
            if comparator ( data[compare] , data[location] ) : location = compare
        data[start] , data[location] = data[location] , data[start]
```

Yes, we do have unit test code, and we used it!

We have two nested loops: the outer loop increments the start variable, and represents the current start of the search for the smallest item. The inner loop is a linear search over the part of the list that is not yet sorted, looking for the next smallest value. The location variable stores the index in the list of the current smallest item. For each search of the list, this is first set to the beginning of the search area and then altered as we encounter smaller items.

We are doing the sorting 'in place', not creating a new data structure, so the data structure has to be mutable. This means that we can only sort lists, not strings or tuples.

We have used a comparator form for the function so that we can do more than just sort into a specific order. The default function _ltComparator is defined as:

```
def _ltComparator ( x , y ) : return x < y
```

Did you spot how we use the tuple assignment:

```
data[start] , data[location] = data[location] , data[start]
```

to swap items in the list? This is a classic way of doing things in Python (and Ruby) that is not possible in languages like C, C++, and Java. Those languages generally have to define a swap function, or do things with intermediate temporary variables, something like:

```
temporary = data[start]
data[start] = data[location]
data[location] = temporary
```

Python doesn't have to do this, it has tuple assignment. Python is far more elegant!

What about the Big O complexity? There are two nested loops: the algorithm is that for each element of the list, we check all the elements above it in the list. So for the first element, we check n-1 elements, for the second element we check n-2 elements, for the third element we check n-3 and so on till we get to the $(n$-1)th element, when we check 1 item. So the number of comparisons is:

$$(n-1) + (n-2) + (n-3) + \ldots 2 + 1$$

This is a simple arithmetic series:

$$\sum_{i=1}^{n-1} i = \frac{(n-1)(1+(n-1))}{2} = \frac{n(n-1)}{2}$$

As always in Big O notation, we ignore simple constants, so we ignore the divide by two. Also in Big O notation, we are only concerned with the highest power of n. So although the expression is:

$$n(n-1) = n^2 - n$$

we are only interested in the n^2. The time complexity of this sort is:

$$T(n) = O(n^2)$$

It is true that, at each iteration of the outer loop, we do not iterate over the whole of the list in the inner loop. So the number of comparisons is less than n^2, but the whole point of Big O notation is that it gives us an upper bound.

If the mathematics is a problem for you, don't worry. All that really matters is that Selection Sort is an order n^2 algorithm, which we can justify by noting that there are two nested loops, each of which iterates over the elements of the list.

Bubble Sort

Bubble Sort is a very different way of thinking about sorting. Instead of looking for the smallest value in the whole list and putting it in the right place, as we did with Selection Sort, we compare neighbors in the list to make sure they are in the right order, and swap them if they are not.

Iterating over a list, comparing neighbors and reordering as needed, means that we change the list so that it is 'more sorted' than it was before. It is not totally sorted on one pass of course, we need many passes. What we can say is that, if we are sorting into ascending order, at the end of the first pass the largest item will be in the last location of the list. But how can comparisons of neighbors ensure we get the largest item at the end? As we iterate over the list, we are always moving larger items up the list, thereby increasing the degree of order of parts of the list. In any particular comparison, we ensure the larger item is higher in the list. At some point, we 'pick up' the largest item in the list, and it will always cause swaps (since all other values in the list are smaller) until we get to the end of the list – therefore the largest item arrives at the end of the list.

On the next iteration over the list, we know that the largest item is already in the last location, so we do not need to check that. We also know that whatever other changes are made in the list, the second largest item will be placed in the second last location. Iterating again ensures that the third largest element is in the third to last location, whatever other changes may have happened. After n iterations, we can guarantee that the list is sorted.

This idea of values percolating up the list is where the name of the sort come from. Values 'bubble' up the list, hence Bubble Sort.

Here is an implementation:

```
def bubbleSortSimple ( data , comparator = _ltComparator ) :
    for i in range ( len ( data ) ) :
        for j in range ( len ( data ) - 1 ) :
            if not ( comparator ( data[j] , data[j+1] ) or ( data[j] == data[j+1] ) ) :
                data[j] , data[j+1] = data[j+1] , data[j]
```

Just as with Selection Sort, we have two nested loops, each of which iterates over the list. True, we don't iterate over the whole list in the inner loop, but despite this, just as with Selection Sort, we have an $O(n^2)$ algorithm. So the time complexity of Bubble Sort appears to be the same as Selection Sort. What is the benefit of Bubble Sort over Selection Sort? We can optimize the Bubble Sort algorithm so that it becomes an exceptionally useful sort, unlike Selection Sort.

The crucial difference between Selection Sort and Bubble Sort is that Bubble Sort acts locally, i.e. with adjacent pairs of values, whilst Selection Sort acts globally, i.e. with pairs of values anywhere in the list. Also Bubble Sort does far more work per iteration than Selection Sort. In each iteration, Selection Sort does some number of comparisons and one swap. Bubble Sort on the other hand does some number of comparisons and could do the same number of swaps. How can we make use of the fact that Bubble Sort is a harder working sort?

At any time it may be that the list is sorted. With Selection Sort we have no way of knowing this until the whole algorithm has completed. With Bubble Sort, however, we know the list is sorted if we do not have to make any swaps. Here we see the advantage of using only local comparisons. If we keep track of whether we actually undertook any swaps on a pass through the data, if we did not, we can terminate the sort early:

```
def bubbleSort ( data , comparator = _ltComparator ) :
    for i in range ( len ( data ) ) :
        swap = False
        for j in range ( len ( data ) - 1 ) :
            if not ( comparator ( data[j] , data[j+1] ) or ( data[j] == data[j+1] ) ) :
                data[j] , data[j+1] = data[j+1] , data[j]
                swap = True
        if not swap : break
```

Although the sort is still technically $T(n) = O(n^2)$, it has an early termination possibility, which means this is a superbly efficient sorting algorithm for 'almost sorted' data.

Divide and Sort

Can we create a sorting algorithm that is better than $O(n^2)$? The answer is "yes", and the observation that moves us forward here is directly related to the difference between Linear Search and Binary Search. In Binary Search we halve the search space at each stage, which leads to $O(log_2 n)$ complexity instead of the $O(n)$ complexity we have for Linear Search. The trick to finding a general sorting algorithm that is more efficient than Selection Sort and Bubble Sort is to apply the 'divide and conquer' approach. Instead of iterating over the list with a pair of nested loops (which results in a $O(n^2)$ algorithm), we need a way of partitioning the problem in two, in a way that allows us to apply the same approach to each half of the problem. So we need a sorting algorithm in which we partition the list into two and sort each half, where sorting is achieved by partitioning the sub-lists in two and then sorting each half, etc.

There are two 'divide and conquer' approach to sorting, and hence two different algorithms:

1. Sort the data during partitioning, which results in Quicksort.

2. Sort the data after partitioning, which results in Merge Sort.

Both algorithms are recursive algorithms and generally are implemented as recursive functions – there is no real advantage here in creating iterative versions, unlike with Binary Search.

Quicksort

Quicksort is a sorting algorithm that works by halving the list and ensuring that all the small items get put in one half and all the large items get put in the other half. Quicksort is then applied to the two halves separately. In more detail:

Quicksort was invented by C.A.R. Hoare and first published in 1961.

1. Pick an element in the list, call it *pivot*.

2. Partition the list so that all the values from the list that are smaller than *pivot* are at one end of the list – call this the *low* sub-list. The natural consequence of this is that all values bigger than or equal to the *pivot* are in the sub-list above low – call this the *high* sub-list – and that there is a clear split point separating low and high.

3. Sort the *high* and *low* sub-lists using Quicksort.

4. When the recursion terminates, the list is sorted.

Since we repeatedly divide the list, we eventually have single-element lists, which require no sorting. This provides the base case of the recursion, so we know there is a termination condition.

The hard part of Quicksort is clearly how to do the partitioning. The classic way is to work with two indexes into the list, one starting at 0 (call it *low*) and one starting at the top of the list, *n*-1 (call it *high*). We increment *low* till it indexes an item that is not smaller than *pivot*, then we decrement *high* till it indexes an item that is smaller than pivot. *high* and *low* index items that are in the wrong place, so we swap them to correct this. We then continue moving *high* and *low*, swapping items as needed until the two cross, i.e. until *high* is smaller than *low*. Having the indexes cross means that we have finished the partitioning, and we can guarantee that all items in the sub-list up to and including *high* comprise the low sub-list and the sub-list above *high* is the high sub-list.

Let's present a small example with diagrams to illustrate this algorithm. We start with the following example situation:

The *pivot* is the central item, so in this case 14. We move *low* up the list till it indexes an item that is not less than 14. For this example incrementing *low* to 1 gives us 23, which we have to move. We now move *high* down the list till it indexes an item that is smaller than the pivot. In fact it is already there: the 10 needs to be moved:

So we swap the items that *high* and *low* index and increment *low* and decrement *high*. This give us:

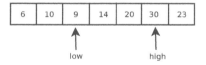

Now we increment *low* till we find an item not less than *pivot*, which means *low* is moved to index the 14. Now we decrement *high* till it indexes an item less than *pivot* (currently 14). In this example there is no such item until the indexes cross. So we end up with:

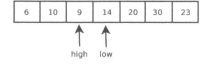

The low sub-list ends after *high* and the high sub-list is the rest of the list. The Quicksort algorithm now recursively sorts the two sub-lists. One recursive call operates on the low sub-list and a separate recursive call operates on the high sub-list. Hence we show two sets of indexes:

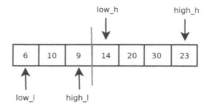

In the Quicksort working on the low sub-list, the pivot is 10, so we increment *low_l* till it indexes a value not smaller than the pivot. *high_l* already indexes an item less than the pivot, so we are ready to swap. Meanwhile in the Quicksort working on the high sub-list we have an even number of items, so there is no central item. We take the item just below the center as the pivot, i.e. 20. We increment *low_h* till it indexes an item whose value is not smaller than the pivot, and decrement *high_h* till it indexes an item smaller than the pivot. In this example there isn't one until the indexes cross:

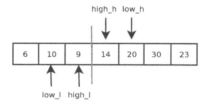

Now the 9 and the 10 get swapped in the Quicksort processing the low sub-list and the indexes are changed which leads to the high and low index variables crossing and so the next recursion. In the high sub-list we already have the crossing:

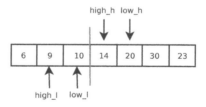

Now we can repeat the recursion so that we have four function calls active.

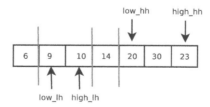

Two of the four partitions have only a single data item to work with (the 6 and the 14) so those calls terminate – there is no work to do. One function call is dealing with a two-item sub-list (9 , 10). We can sort this simply by comparing the two items and swapping if needed: there is no need for further recursion. In this case the items are already in order and so the function terminates. This leaves the top sub-list, which has (20, 30, 23) in it. We apply the partition function exactly as previously. The pivot is 30, so we move *low_hh* up till it indexes a value not less than the pivot (in this case the pivot value itself). *high_hh* already indexes a value that needs to be moved:

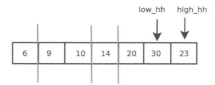

The swap is performed, the increments and decrements happen and we have index crossing:

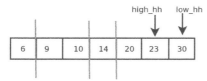

There is then more recursion, but both these calls result in quick computations: one because it is working on a pair (20, 23) which is already in the correct order, and the other because it is a single value (30). So all the recursive calls terminate and, voila, we have a sorted list.

So much for the algorithm, what about some code. Here is an implementation of Quicksort:

```
def quicksort ( data , comparator = _ltComparator ) :
    def _partition ( low , high ) :
        pivot = data[ int ( ( low + high + 1 ) / 2 ) ]
        while low < high :
            while comparator ( data[low] , pivot ) : low += 1
            while comparator ( pivot , data[high] ) : high -= 1
            if low < high :
                data[low] , data[high] = data[high] , data[low]
                low += 1
                high -= 1
        return high
    def _quicksort ( low , high ) :
        sliceLength = high - low + 1
        if sliceLength > 1 :
            if sliceLength == 2 :
                if not ( comparator ( data[low] , data[high] ) or ( data[low] == data[high] ) ) :
                    data[low] , data[high] = data[high] , data[low]
            else :
                splitIndex = _partition ( low , high )
                _quicksort ( low , splitIndex )
                _quicksort ( splitIndex + 1 , high )
    _quicksort ( 0 , len ( data ) - 1 )
```

An analysis of the number of compare and swap operations of Quicksort leads to the classification of this algorithm as $T(n) = O(n \log_2 n)$. We can justify this by observing:

- At each stage we have to access each entry in the list for comparison, so there are n operations per stage.

- Because we halve the problem space at each stage there are $\log_2 n$ stages. We can also justify this by analogy with Binary Search, which halves the search space in an analogous way leading to $O(\log_2 n)$ time complexity.

- Having $\log_2 n$ stages each of n operations leads to $O(n \log_2 n)$ time complexity.

Here is not the place to show the detailed analysis. If you are interested in this aspect of algorithms many books are available that present the proper analysis required to show that this Quicksort is indeed an $O(n \log_2 n)$ algorithm.

Looking at this table:

n	n^2	$n \log_2 n$
10	100	33.2192809489
100	10,000	664.385618977
1,000	1,000,000	9,965.78428466
10,000	100,000,000	132,877.123795
100,000	10,000,000,000	1,660,964.04744

it is fairly clear that $O(n \log_2 n)$ algorithms are a lot more efficient than $O(n^2)$ algorithms. Thus, Quicksort is far more efficient than Bubble Sort or Selection Sort.

However... in our Quicksort example, the pivot is chosen as the mid-point value from the list. This is not guaranteed to be the best choice – we may find that the partition leaves two lists of very different lengths. The worst-case scenario is that we have all but one value in one sub-list and one value in the other sub-list at each partitioning. In this case, which is termed a *pathological case*, the algorithm is $O(n^2)$, no more efficient than Selection Sort and *less* efficient than Bubble Sort! Applying Quicksort to already sorted data is just such a pathological case. This is exactly the case where Bubble Sort is very quick indeed.

The issue of pivot selection introduces one of the many complex issues associated with Quicksort. Another issue is the overhead associated with dividing and swapping elements, which means that while this algorithm can be extremely quick compared to Selection Sort or Bubble Sort on large inputs, it can be slower for short lists. One way to improve this is not to use Quicksort when the sub-lists are small, but instead switch to another sort algorithm. So for lists less that ten items we might use Bubble Sort for the sub-sort instead of Quicksort as part of the Quicksort implementation.

However, this book is not the place for the level of detail required to do the subject of Quicksort proper justice, we are only giving a cursory introduction here.

Merge sort

Is there a sorting algorithm as efficient or more efficient than Quicksort that does not have the pathological case? Yes, there is: Merge Sort. Again it is a 'divide and conquer' algorithm, but instead of doing all operations in situ, it makes copies of the data – though the final sorted data is placed into the original list. This means you have to have memory available to store the copies – if you have a lot of data, you have to have a lot of memory!

The Merge Sort algorithm is:

- Make a copy of the first and second halves of the list.

- Recursively sort the two sub-lists.

- At some point the sub-lists will be of length 1 and so not need sorting – this is the base case of the recursion.

- Merge the two (copied) sub-lists back into the list from which they were copied, ensuring that the new list is sorted. This is the actual sorting activity: items are selected from the two lists being merged so that the sorting order is imposed on the list.

So the 'divide' part of the Merge Sort algorithm is very simple, unlike Quicksort where partitioning is complicated – remember Quicksort is all about sorting during partitioning, whereas Merge Sort is all about sorting during merging. So the real core of the Merge Sort algorithm is the merging of the two sorted halves. There are a number of ways of doing this, but perhaps the most common one is:

1. Look at the first elements in each sub-list.

2. Whichever of the two values is smallest is removed from its sub-list and placed in the next empty position of the list being filled.

3. If both sub-lists still have elements, go to Step 1.

4. If one of the sub-lists has elements left (at this stage only one can have elements, the other sub-list must be exhausted) ,these are moved to the end of the new list – they must be greater than any of the values already in the original list, and they must already be sorted.

It is crucial to remember that the two sub-lists are already sorted when being merged.

Let us look through an example diagrammatically. We start out with an unsorted list:

| 6 | 23 | 9 | 14 | 20 | 30 | 10 |

We now 'split' the data in two by copying the lower half to one new list and the upper half to a separate list – where the list has an odd number of entries put the extra item in the upper half:

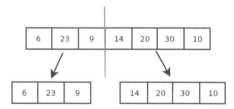

Not all the items are single item lists, so we recursively split the data:

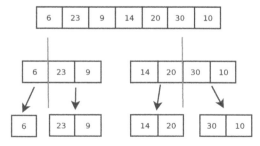

One of our sequences is of length one, but the others are not, so we must recursively split them:

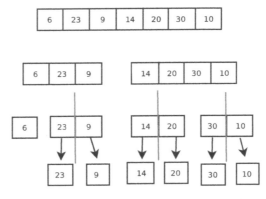

We now have all data held in lists of length one, so we can begin the merging. We merge the data back into the list it originally came from, but now sorting it. The first merge is easy, since all lists are of length one, so we just need to compare two items and insert the data in the right order:

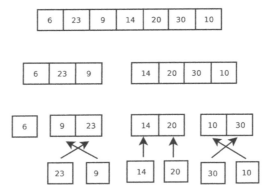

Now we are merging lists of length two, so we need to be more careful about doing the merging; the merge algorithm given above comes into play. In this example we get:

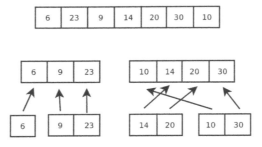

Doing another round of merging:

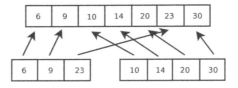

we end up with fully sorted data in the original list:

6	9	10	14	20	23	30

The whole Merge Sort algorithm is clearly a recursive one, and an implementation using a recursive function handles all the copying straightforwardly:

```
def mergeSort ( data , comparator = _ltComparator ) :
    length = len ( data )
    if length <= 1 : return
    mid = int ( length / 2 )
    d1 = data[ : mid ]
    d2 = data [ mid : ]
    mergeSort ( d1 , comparator )
    mergeSort ( d2 , comparator )
    data_i , d1_i , d2_i = 0 , 0 , 0
    while True :
        if d1_i >= len ( d1 ) : data [ data_i : ] = d2 [ d2_i : ] ; break
        if d2_i >= len ( d2 ) : data [ data_i : ] = d1 [ d1_i : ] ; break
        if comparator ( d1[ d1_i ] , d2[ d2_i ] ) :
            data[ data_i ] = d1[ d1_i ]
            d1_i += 1
        else :
            data[ data_i ] = d2[ d2_i ]
            d2_i += 1
        data_i += 1
```

Analyzing the number of operations required for Merge Sort, we find that it is an $O(n \log_2 n)$ algorithm, just as Quicksort is. The informal argument as to why this is the case is analogous to that for Quicksort:

- We split the list in half each time, so there are $\log_2 n$ levels to the decomposition.

- For each split we copy each of the n items.

- For each layer merge, we compare each of the n items.

So, ignoring constants, the algorithm has $O(n \log_2 n)$ time complexity. So in what way is Merge Sort better than Quicksort? Merge Sort does not have the pathological case that Quicksort has, it is guaranteed to have $O(n \log_2 n)$ time complexity. The penalty for this though is that Merge Sort has space requirement $O(n \log_2 n)$ whereas Quicksort has space requirement $O(n)$. Usually though the time complexity is the metric that matters most.

Testing, Testing

Yes, of course we have a unit test program for the sorting functions, and it was written prior to writing the sort functions:

```
import unittest
import sort

def _gtComparator ( x , y ) : return x > y
```

```
class Sort_Test ( unittest.TestCase ) :

    def setUp ( self ) :
        self.emptyData = [ ]
        self.emptyResult = [ ]
        self.singleData = [ 1 ]
        self.singleResult = [ 1 ]
        self.unsortedData = [ 3 , 5 , 3 , 2 , 4 , 9 , 8 , 7 , 3 , 1 , 6 , 2 ]
        self.sortedData = [ 1 , 2 , 2 , 3 , 3 , 3 , 4 , 5 , 6 , 7 , 8 , 9 ]
        self.sortedDataGT = [ 9 , 8 , 7 , 6 , 5 , 4 , 3 , 3 , 3 , 2 , 2 , 1 ]

    def test_selectionSort ( self ) :
        sort.selectionSort ( self.emptyData )
        self.assertEquals ( self.emptyResult , self.emptyData )
        sort.selectionSort ( self.singleData )
        self.assertEquals ( self.singleResult , self.singleData )
        sort.selectionSort ( self.unsortedData )
        self.assertEquals ( self.sortedData , self.unsortedData )

    def test_selectionSortGT ( self ) :
        sort.selectionSort ( self.emptyData , _gtComparator )
        self.assertEquals ( self.emptyResult , self.emptyData )
        sort.selectionSort ( self.singleData , _gtComparator )
        self.assertEquals ( self.singleResult , self.singleData )
        sort.selectionSort ( self.unsortedData , _gtComparator )
        self.assertEquals ( self.sortedDataGT , self.unsortedData )

    def test_bubbleSortSimple ( self ) :
        sort.bubbleSortSimple ( self.emptyData )
        self.assertEquals ( self.emptyResult , self.emptyData )
        sort.bubbleSortSimple ( self.singleData )
        self.assertEquals ( self.singleResult , self.singleData )
        sort.bubbleSortSimple ( self.unsortedData )
        self.assertEquals ( self.sortedData , self.unsortedData )

    def test_bubbleSortSimpleGT ( self ) :
        sort.bubbleSortSimple ( self.emptyData , _gtComparator )
        self.assertEquals ( self.emptyResult , self.emptyData )
        sort.bubbleSortSimple ( self.singleData , _gtComparator )
        self.assertEquals ( self.singleResult , self.singleData )
        sort.bubbleSortSimple ( self.unsortedData , _gtComparator )
        self.assertEquals ( self.sortedDataGT , self.unsortedData )

    def test_bubbleSort ( self ) :
        sort.bubbleSort ( self.emptyData )
        self.assertEquals ( self.emptyResult , self.emptyData )
        sort.bubbleSort ( self.singleData )
        self.assertEquals ( self.singleResult , self.singleData )
        sort.bubbleSort ( self.unsortedData )
        self.assertEquals ( self.sortedData , self.unsortedData )

    def test_bubbleSortGT ( self ) :
        sort.bubbleSort ( self.emptyData , _gtComparator )
        self.assertEquals ( self.emptyResult , self.emptyData )
        sort.bubbleSort ( self.singleData , _gtComparator )
        self.assertEquals ( self.singleResult , self.singleData )
```

```
            sort.bubbleSort ( self.unsortedData , _gtComparator)
            self.assertEquals ( self.sortedDataGT , self.unsortedData )

        def test_quicksort ( self ) :
            sort.quicksort ( self.emptyData )
            self.assertEquals ( self.emptyResult , self.emptyData )
            sort.quicksort ( self.singleData )
            self.assertEquals ( self.singleResult , self.singleData )
            sort.quicksort ( self.unsortedData )
            self.assertEquals ( self.sortedData , self.unsortedData )

        def test_quicksortGT ( self ) :
            sort.quicksort ( self.emptyData , _gtComparator )
            self.assertEquals ( self.emptyResult , self.emptyData )
            sort.quicksort ( self.singleData , _gtComparator )
            self.assertEquals ( self.singleResult , self.singleData )
            sort.quicksort ( self.unsortedData , _gtComparator )
            self.assertEquals ( self.sortedDataGT , self.unsortedData )

        def test_mergeSort ( self ) :
            sort.mergeSort ( self.emptyData )
            self.assertEquals ( self.emptyResult , self.emptyData )
            sort.mergeSort ( self.singleData )
            self.assertEquals ( self.singleResult , self.singleData )
            sort.mergeSort ( self.unsortedData )
            self.assertEquals ( self.sortedData , self.unsortedData )

        def test_mergeSortGT ( self ) :
            sort.mergeSort ( self.emptyData , _gtComparator )
            self.assertEquals ( self.emptyResult , self.emptyData )
            sort.mergeSort ( self.singleData , _gtComparator )
            self.assertEquals ( self.singleResult , self.singleData )
            sort.mergeSort ( self.unsortedData , _gtComparator )
            self.assertEquals ( self.sortedDataGT , self.unsortedData )

if __name__ == '__main__' :
    unittest.main ()
```

This test covers the data being an empty list, the data being a single item list, and the list having 12 items in the range [1 , 9], i.e. single digit integers. The sort functions should however work with a far wider range of data. The coverage of this unit test could be much larger. So we have this beginning of a good test for the functions.

Even though it is not a extensive test, it is critically important that it does not fail, since if that were the case we could have no confidence in our functions.

```
..........
----------------------------------------------------------------------
Ran 10 tests in 0.002s

OK
```

We have a Green. In fact, we feel confident that the sort functions are correct. We don't claim there are no bugs. If you think you spot a bug in any of the implementations, write a unit test that highlights the bug and send it to us. If the bug is real and we fix it for a revision or new edition of the book, then due acknowledgement to contributors will be given.

Searching the Unsorted

An interesting question is "If we have to search unsorted data, is it better to sort it first and then search it?"

For unsorted data we have to use Linear Search, which executes in $O(n)$ time. If, however, the data is sorted, we can use Binary Search, which executes in $O(\log_2 n)$ time. To use Binary Search on unsorted data, we must first sort it. So far, the best sorting algorithm we have executes in $O(n \log_2 n)$ time. In some specialist cases, there are sorting algorithms with better time complexity, i.e. $O(n)$, but in the general case there is not, so we must accept $T(n) = O(n \log_2 n)$ as the best sorting algorithm. Thus, to sort data and then to Binary Search we have an algorithm that executes in $O(n \log_2 n) + O(\log_2 n)$ time. With Big O notation we are only interested in the highest power of n, so the combination of sorting and Binary Search is a $T(n) = O(n \log_2 n)$ algorithm. Looking back at the table of n, n^2 and $n \log_2 n$ on page 328, it is fairly obvious that $O(n)$ is better than $O(n \log_2 n)$, so for searching unsorted data, Linear Search is better.

We can summarize thus:

- Sorting unsorted data is costly and should only be undertaken when really necessary.

- If data is stored unsorted and needs to be searched, use Linear Search.

- If data is to be searched it should ideally be stored in sorted form.

This begs the question: "How can we store data in sorted forms?" The study of data structures and appropriate representations of data for given problems and solutions is a very important one. It is a topic that deserves and requires a whole book. Even though can only give an initial brief introduction in this book, we must present something to give some pointers towards the detail.

10.3   Dictionaries

All the previous discussion of searching and sorting related to using sequences. We have already seen a data structure that makes searching very easy – dictionaries. The whole point about dictionaries is that they create an association between keys and values. In our code we write indexing expressions and all the implementation details of the association between keys and values is hidden away.

The standard Python system uses a data structure called an *open hash table* to implement dictionaries. Insertion into, deletion from, and access of data in a dictionaries are effectively $O(1)$ operations – $O(1)$ means is *constant time*, i.e. the algorithm has a constant time complexity no matter what size the data being manipulated is.

It is clear that if our program involves a lot of searching for specific keys, it is important to use dictionaries rather than sequences. $O(1)$ searching is clearly better than $O(n)$ or even $O(\log_2 n)$ searching, and so a dictionary is a better data structure for searching data than either a sorted or unsorted sequence.

What is a dictionary not good for? Any task where the order of items is important – this is the realm of sequence. Iterating over the values in a sequence is easy and fast. Iterating over the contents of a dictionary is certainly possible: we can iterate over the keys, we can iterate over the values, and we can iterate over the key–value pairs, but there is no ordering property so that items will appear in apparently random order.

If we have sequences and dictionaries, why is there a need for any other type of data structure? The algorithms we have looked at so far have either been iteration based requiring some form of sequence to be efficient, or searching based requiring some form of dictionary to be efficient. Other algorithms impose different requirements on data structures.

10.4   Sets

In mathematics, a set is a collection of things in which there is only one of each value in the set. For many algorithms knowing that a collection is a set can be very important. It therefore seems a good idea to create a set type that we can use in our programs. Can we do this using sequence and dictionary?

Thinking in terms of an abstract data type, a set is something with a way of storing values and a set of methods. The set operations will obviously be implemented as methods:

add – enter a new value (provided as a parameter) into the set if the value is not already in the set.

remove – remove a value (provided as a parameter) from the set.

contains – return **True** if the value provided as a parameter is in the set, **False** otherwise.

union – create a new set that contains all the values from self and the set that is the parameter.

intersection – creates a new set that contains only those values that are in both self and the set that is the parameter.

difference – creates a new set that contains the elements from self that are not in the set that is the parameter.

What about storing the values in the set? One way (the hard way) would be to use a sequence as the storage. This would require all the methods to ensure the uniqueness of each value in the set. So the add method would have to check that the value is not already in the set. This means using Linear Search which is an $O(n)$ operation.

A better way of storing the values is to use a dictionary. The observation we make is that a dictionary is a map (in the mathematical sense):

$$X \mapsto Y$$

in which the key from X maps to a value from Y, and a set is just a map in which the value a key maps to is the key itself. This means that we can implement sets efficiently with dictionaries. Of course, if we implement the set abstract data type correctly, people cannot tell whether a sequence or a dictionary is used for the implementation. Except for the performance: a set implemented using sequences would show $O(n)$ performance whereas implemented using dictionaries, it should be close to $O(1)$.

The $O(1)$ performance of a dictionary-based set stems from the fact that the uniqueness property is ensured because there is an open hash table underlying the dictionary. There is however an overhead in using a dictionary, it manages key–value pairs. Perhaps then we should write our own implementation of set using the same techniques used to implement dictionary? In fact there is no need. Sets are sufficiently important, that the standard Python system provides a built-in class set (that uses open hash tables) so we do not have to write our own.

The following is not a proper example of a program, but it does show that Python can carry out operations with sets:

```
s1 = set ( )
s1.add ( 1 )
s1.add ( 1 )
s1.add ( 1 )
print s1
s2 = set ( )
s2.add ( 1 )
s2.add ( 2 )
s2.add ( 3 )
s2.remove ( 3 )
print s2
s3 = s1.union ( s2 )
print s3
```

Which when executed results in the output:

```
set([1])
set([1, 2])
set([1, 2])
```

10.5   Trees

If you look back at the list of data structures we presented at the beginning of this chapter (page 314), you will see that 'trees' figure prominently. Why is this, and what is a tree? The answers lie in the boundary between sequences and dictionaries. Dictionaries are superb for lookup but the order of items in the collection is fairly random. Sequences are great for adding things in but they are awful for searching and dreadful for sorting. What is needed for many algorithms is a data structure that is sorted and efficient to search. The name gives the game away: search trees.

We introduced trees in Section 7.9 (page 235) under the heading 'non-linear data structures'. A tree is a hierarchical data structure in which each node has some number of children. There are tree structures that have many children per node, but the simplest case is binary trees which have up to two children per node.

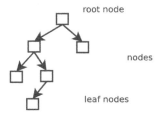

The top node of the tree is called the *root node*, or more usually the *root*. The nodes pointed to from a node are the children of that node. If a node has no children then it is called a *leaf node*.

Python doesn't have a built-in tree data structure but it is easy to construct one. Let us do so as an exercise in Test-Driven Development.

10.5.1   Implementing a Tree Type

Stage 1: The Groundwork

We start with a test program. Stage 1 is:

```
import unittest
from orderedBinaryTree_1 import OrderedBinaryTree

class OrderedBinaryTree_Test ( unittest.TestCase ) :

    def setUp ( self ) :
        self.tree = OrderedBinaryTree ( )

    def test_create ( self ) :
        self.assertEquals ( None , self.tree.root )

if __name__ == '__main__' :
    unittest.main ( )
```

Running the test, we get a Red because we don't have an OrderedBinaryTree class. So we implement something to ensure we have Green. In this case, we need to ensure that a valid object representing an empty tree is constructed:

```
class OrderedBinaryTree :

    def __init__ ( self ) :
        self.root = None
```

Now we get a Green:

```
.
----------------------------------------------------------------
Ran 1 test in 0.000s

OK
```

We call the class we are developing OrderedBinaryTree as the tree is binary, i.e. each node can have up to two children, and the data will always be stored such that it is in the correct ordered according to some rule of sorting.

Stage 2: Add Functionality

We need to be able to add items to the tree. This implies not only that there be an add method, but also that we need some way of outputting the values held in the tree so that we can test that the tree contains the objects we think it should. So we add the test methods:

```
    def test_stringifyEmpty ( self ) :
        self.assertEquals ( '{ }' , str ( self.tree ) )

    def test_addItem ( self ) :
        self.tree.add ( 1 )
        self.assertEquals ( '{ 1 }' , str ( self.tree ) )
```

to the test program. Running the tests we get Red, so we must fix this. We introduce the fact that a node in the tree is a thing with a datum and two children (left and right) – we create a trivial (nested) class to encode this. Implementing the 'add' operation is easy since we have an empty tree: we just need to put a node in with the data. We are also going to implement the __str__ method so that we can create a string representation of the tree. This will help us with testing and debugging. At this stage the __str__ method just has to print the node we put in if it is there. Putting all this together, we have:

```
class OrderedBinaryTree :

    class Node :
        def __init__ ( self , datum ) :
            self.datum = datum
            self.left = None
            self.right = None

    def __init__ ( self ) :
        self.root = None

    def add ( self , datum ) :
        if self.root == None : self.root = self.Node ( datum )
        else : pass

    def __str__ ( self ) :
        returnValue = '{ '
        if self.root != None : returnValue += str ( self.root.datum ) + ' '
        return returnValue + '}'
```

Each node in the tree holds a value, the datum, and has two pointers to other nodes, left and right. if there is no child, the value None is used.

Running the tests, we get Green:

```
...
-----------------------------------------------------------------------
Ran 3 tests in 0.000s

OK
```

Stage 3: Adding the Treeness

The next stage is to add new values into a non-empty tree, i.e. a tree that already has a node in it. Clearly in an ordered tree the items it contains must be held in order. This means that when we add a new item, we have to search the tree for the correct place to insert it. Because this is a binary search tree, we halve the search space at each comparison, so this is going to be an $O(\log_2 n)$ operation. We add the methods:

```
def _addFromSequence ( self , data ) :
    for datum in data : self.tree.add ( datum )

def test_addManyItems ( self ) :
    self._addFromSequence ( ( 2 , 1 , 5 , 1 , 8 ) )
    self.assertEquals ( '{ 1 1 2 5 8 }' , str ( self.tree ) )
```

to the test program (only one is a test method, the other is a support method that allows us to add a whole sequence of items easily and quickly) and execute it giving us Red. We must extend our implementation. 'Divide and conquer' approaches invariably make use of recursion and working with binary trees is no exception. We create some nested functions to manage the recursion:

```
class OrderedBinaryTree :

    class Node :
        def __init__ ( self , datum ) :
            self.datum = datum
            self.left = None
            self.right = None

    def __init__ ( self ) :
        self.root = None

    def add ( self , datum ) :
        def _add ( node ) :
            if datum < node.datum :
                if node.left == None : node.left = self.Node ( datum )
                else : _add ( node.left )
            elif datum >= node.datum :
                if node.right == None : node.right = self.Node ( datum )
                else : _add ( node.right )
        if self.root == None : self.root = self.Node ( datum )
        else : _add ( self.root )

    def __str__ ( self ) :
        def _stringify ( node ) :
            returnValue = ''
            if node.left != None : returnValue += _stringify ( node.left )
            returnValue += str ( node.datum ) + ' '
            if node.right != None : returnValue += _stringify ( node.right )
            return returnValue
        returnValue = '{ '
        if self.root != None : returnValue += _stringify ( self.root )
        return returnValue + '}'
```

We use the left sub-tree to hold values less than the datum of the current node, and the right sub-tree to hold values greater than or equal to the datum of the current node. This is how we introduce order into the tree.

Running the tests gives us Green:

```
...
----------------------------------------------------------------------
Ran 3 tests in 0.000s

OK
```

In this design we have totally passive nodes and all the activity is happening in the top-level methods using recursive support functions. Following the object-oriented approach, we should put the activity into the nodes themselves. We replace the recursive functions that pass nodes as parameters with method calls on objects. The idea is that the tree class is an interface to handle the root node and everything else should be dealt with by active nodes communicating amongst themselves.

Stage 4: Activating the Nodes

Changing from the procedural design to the object-oriented design is a refactoring: the test class stays exactly the same, but the implementation changes. Removing the recursive add and string representation creation methods from the tree class, and replacing them with the appropriate methods into the node class should not change the results of the tests. Having the tests ready made enables us to do this refactoring with confidence!

```python
class OrderedBinaryTree :

    class Node :
        def __init__ ( self , datum ) :
            self.datum = datum
            self.left = None
            self.right = None
        def __str__ ( self ) :
            returnValue = ''
            if self.left != None : returnValue += str ( self.left )
            returnValue += str ( self.datum ) + ' '
            if self.right != None : returnValue += str ( self.right )
            return returnValue
        def add ( self , datum ) :
            if datum < self.datum :
                if self.left == None : self.left = OrderedBinaryTree.Node ( datum )
                else : self.left.add ( datum )
            if datum >= self.datum :
                if self.right == None : self.right = OrderedBinaryTree.Node ( datum )
                else : self.right.add ( datum )

    def __init__ ( self ) :
        self.root = None

    def add ( self , datum ) :
        if self.root == None : self.root = self.Node ( datum )
        else : self.root.add ( datum )

    def __str__ ( self ) :
        returnValue = '{ '
        if self.root != None : returnValue += str ( self.root )
        return returnValue + '}'
```

Running the tests we get Green:

```
....
-------------------------------------------------------------------
Ran 4 tests in 0.001s

OK
```

Stage 5: Are You In There?

Now we have the ability to add things into the tree and we can create a string representation of the tree. Now we need to be able to determine whether an item is in the tree: we need to create a search function. As always, we create the test first, so we add the methods:

```python
def test_findEmpty ( self ) :
    self.assertEquals ( False , 1 in self.tree )

def test_findSingle ( self ) :
    self.tree.add ( 2 )
    self.assertEquals ( False , 1 in self.tree )
    self.assertEquals ( True , 2 in self.tree )
```

```
    def test_findManyItems ( self ) :
        self._addFromSequence ( ( 2 , 1 , 5 , 1 , 8 ) )
        self.assertEquals ( False , 9 in self.tree )
        self.assertEquals ( True , 2 in self.tree )
        self.assertEquals ( True , 1 in self.tree )
```

to the test program which gives us a Red. We therefore do some implementation to get a Green. In Python, one way of implementing the **in** and **not in** operations for a container type is to provide an implementation of the __contains__ method for the class. When an **in** or **not in** expression is executed, then, if there is a __contains__ method for the object, it is called. We therefore need our OrderedBinaryTree class to have a __contains__ method.

As we did for the the add method, we implement the __contains__ method by getting it to deal with the empty tree case, but otherwise pass the problem, via the root node, to the nodes so they can deal with the query. We have a method in the OrderedBinaryTree.Node class that does all the hard work of doing the search:

```
class OrderedBinaryTree :

    class Node :
        def __init__ ( self , datum ) :
            self.datum = datum
            self.left = None
            self.right = None
        def __str__ ( self ) :
            returnValue = ''
            if self.left != None : returnValue += str ( self.left )
            returnValue += str ( self.datum ) + ' '
            if self.right != None : returnValue += str ( self.right )
            return returnValue
        def add ( self , datum ) :
            if datum < self.datum :
                if self.left == None : self.left = OrderedBinaryTree.Node ( datum )
                else : self.left.add ( datum )
            if datum >= self.datum :
                if self.right == None : self.right = OrderedBinaryTree.Node ( datum )
                else : self.right.add ( datum )
        def contains ( self , item ) :
            if item == self.datum : return True
            elif item < self.datum :
                if self.left == None : return False
                else : return self.left.contains ( item )
            else :
                if self.right == None : return False
                else : return self.right.contains ( item )

    def __init__ ( self ) :
        self.root = None

    def add ( self , datum ) :
        if self.root == None : self.root = self.Node ( datum )
        else : self.root.add ( datum )

    def __str__ ( self ) :
        returnValue = '{ '
        if self.root != None : returnValue += str ( self.root )
        return returnValue + '}'
```

```
def __contains__ ( self , item ) :
    if self.root == None : return False
    else : return self.root.contains ( item )
```

Running the test, we get:

```
.......
-----------------------------------------------------------------
Ran 7 tests in 0.001s

OK
```

Green.

Stage 6: Traversing the Tree

It may not be obvious from the listing, but creating a string representation of the tree requires visiting every node and adding a string representation of the datum at that node to a string accumulator. This is a particular instance of a more general operation. What we are doing is to traverse the tree and apply a function at every node. Perhaps it is worth generalizing this action as a support function?

There are three ways of traversing a tree:

preorder – process the datum of the current node, then the left sub-tree, then the right sub-tree.

postorder – process the left sub-tree, then the right sub-tree, then the datum of the current node.

inorder – process the left sub-tree, then datum of the current node, then the right sub-tree.

The inorder traversal is the one that our 'stringify' function uses. Following the TDD approach, we first add the test cases to the test program:

```
def _appendToResultString ( self , x ) : self.resultString += str ( x ) + ' '

def test_preorderApplicator ( self ) :
    self._addFromSequence ( ( 2 , 1 , 5 , 1 , 8 ) )
    self.tree.preorderApplicator ( self._appendToResultString )
    self.assertEquals ( '2 1 1 5 8 ' , self.resultString )

def test_postorderApplicator ( self ) :
    self._addFromSequence ( ( 2 , 1 , 5 , 1 , 8 ) )
    self.tree.postorderApplicator ( self._appendToResultString )
    self.assertEquals ( '1 1 8 5 2 ' , self.resultString )

def test_inorderApplicator ( self ) :
    self._addFromSequence ( ( 2 , 1 , 5 , 1 , 8 ) )
    self.tree.inorderApplicator ( self._appendToResultString )
    self.assertEquals ( '1 1 2 5 8 ' , self.resultString )
```

resulting in a Red. To get to Green, we add methods to the OrderedBinaryTree class to process the empty tree case, but otherwise we pass the problem to the nodes. We add methods in OrderedBinaryTree.Node to actually do the traversal and the application of the function to each datum held in the tree.

```python
class OrderedBinaryTree :

    class Node :
        def __init__ ( self , datum ) :
            self.datum = datum
            self.left = None
            self.right = None
        def add ( self , datum ) :
            if datum < self.datum :
                if self.left == None : self.left = OrderedBinaryTree.Node ( datum )
                else : self.left.add ( datum )
            if datum >= self.datum :
                if self.right == None : self.right = OrderedBinaryTree.Node ( datum )
                else : self.right.add ( datum )
        def contains ( self , item ) :
            if item == self.datum : return True
            elif item < self.datum :
                if self.left == None : return False
                else : return self.left.contains ( item )
            else :
                if self.right == None : return False
                else : return self.right.contains ( item )
        def preorderApplicator ( self , action ) :
            action ( self.datum )
            if self.left != None : self.left.preorderApplicator ( action )
            if self.right != None : self.right.preorderApplicator ( action )
        def postorderApplicator ( self , action ) :
            if self.left != None : self.left.postorderApplicator ( action )
            if self.right != None : self.right.postorderApplicator ( action )
            action ( self.datum )
        def inorderApplicator ( self , action ) :
            if self.left != None : self.left.inorderApplicator ( action )
            action ( self.datum )
            if self.right != None : self.right.inorderApplicator ( action )

    def __init__ ( self ) :
        self.root = None

    def add ( self , datum ) :
        if self.root == None : self.root = self.Node ( datum )
        else : self.root.add ( datum )

    def __str__ ( self ) :
        # Python raises UnboundLocalVariable if we have returnValue as a local
        # variable rather than an instance variable.
        self.returnValue = '{ '
        if self.root != None :
            def accumulateString ( datum ) : self.returnValue += str ( datum ) + ' '
            self.inorderApplicator ( accumulateString )
        return self.returnValue + '}'

    def __contains__ ( self , item ) :
        if self.root == None : return False
        else : return self.root.contains ( item )
```

```
def preorderApplicator ( self , action ) :
    if self.root != None : self.root.preorderApplicator ( action )

def postorderApplicator ( self , action ) :
    if self.root != None : self.root.postorderApplicator ( action )

def inorderApplicator ( self , action ) :
    if self.root != None : self.root.inorderApplicator ( action )
```

Executing the test program, we get:

```
..........
--------------------------------------------------------------------
Ran 10 tests in 0.001s

OK
```

giving us Green.

What we have now in this implementation of OrderedBinaryTree is enough to make it useful as a way of storing data in a sorted way that can be searched relatively quickly. Inserting an item into the tree is an $O(\log_2 n)$ operation, since we have to do a search through the tree to find the right place to insert the new node. Searching for an item is also an $O(\log_2 n)$ operation, since the same search of the tree is required to find an item.

How does this performance compare with sequences and dictionaries?

	insertion	search
unsorted sequence	$O(1)$	$O(n)$
sorted sequence	$O(n)$???	$O(\log_2 n)$
ordered binary tree	$O(\log_2 n)$	$O(\log_2 n)$
dictionary	$O(1)$	$O(1)$

Why the ??? for inserting into a sorted sequence? The algorithm is either "find the insertion point, move values to create a space, and insert the value", or "append the value to the list and re-sort.". The former is a $O(n)$ algorithm since although we can use Binary Search to find the insertion point ($O(\log_2 n)$), moving data in $O(n)$. If we use the second algorithm then we need to choose a sorting algorithm. Merge Sort ($O(n \log_2 n)$) is probably the best choice, which would make inserting to a sorted sequence $O(n \log_2 n)$ – not as good as 'search and insert'. However, we observe that a sorted list with an item appended is almost totally sorted already. This looks like a job for Bubble Sort. Although classified as an $O(n^2)$ algorithm, the early exit of Bubble Sort means that it is far more efficient than $O(n^2)$ on almost sorted data. In this case, the resort using Bubble Sort will complete on a single pass – Bubble Sort completes in $O(n)$ time in this situation.

Looking at the last line of the table above, you may be thinking "No contest. Use a sequence or a dictionary." There is a lot to this viewpoint. Clearly the Python developers agree – there is no tree implementation as standard whereas there are sequence and dictionary implementations. However, things are not quite so clear cut. In languages such as C++ and Java, trees have an important place, as important as sequences and dictionaries. The reason is to do with the flexibility of trees compared to the lack of flexibility of the hash tables used to implement dictionaries. Here is not however, the right place to delve into this issue. Suffice it to say that trees are important, but Python favors the use of dictionaries even where you would use trees in other programming languages.

Going on

There are many things we could do to extend this tree class, the most obvious of which is to add a method to remove a node from the tree. However, this turns out to be extraordinarily complicated in comparison to what we have done so far. Another thing we should perhaps do is provide iterators over the tree – currently we have applicators and whilst useful, iterators do tend to be even more useful. Creating iterators over a tree turns out also to be non-trivial, but not particularly difficult, it just requires us to add some complexity to the tree. This is all material for a second course in programming.

Chapter Summary

In this chapter we have found that:

- There are many different data structures that have different properties and performances with various algorithms.
- There are two searching algorithms on sequences: Linear Search and Binary Search.
- Big O notation is an important tool for describing the complexity of algorithms.
- Linear Search in an $O(n)$ algorithm and Binary Search is an $O(\log_2 n)$ algorithm.
- There are a number of algorithms for sorting a list:

    Selection Sort – an $O(n^2)$ algorithm.

    Bubble Sort – an $O(n^2)$ algorithm.

    Quicksort – an $O(n \log_2 n)$ algorithm.

    Merge Sort – an $O(n \log_2 n)$ algorithm.

- Dictionaries have $O(1)$ performance for searching.
- Sets are an important data structure, and that the standard Python distribution has set type already implemented.
- Non-linear data structures such as binary trees can be constructed in Python even though there is no built-in implementation.
- There are multiple ways of traversing a binary tree: preorder, postorder and inorder.

Self-Review Questions

Self-review 10.1 Why are data structures other than sequence and dictionary useful?

Self-review 10.2 Why is Binary Search better than Linear Search?

Self-review 10.3 Why is it not always possible to use Binary Search for all searches in sequences?

Self-review 10.4 What alternatives to sequence are there for storing data to be searched?

Self-review 10.5 What is a comparator?

Self-review 10.6 Why is Big O notation useful?

Self-review 10.7 Why might we want to sort a list?

Self-review 10.8 Why are 'divide and conquer' algorithms important?

Self-review 10.9 Why investigate tree data structures at all when we have sequences and dictionaries?

Self-review 10.10 What is output when the following code is executed?

```
a = [ 1 , 2 , 3 , 4 ]
b = a
b[0] = 100
print a
```

What is output when the following code is executed?

```
a = [ 1 , 2 , 3 , 4 ]
b = a
b = a + [ 5 , 6 , 7 ]
b[0] = 100
print a
```

Explain why in the first code sequence there is a change to the list referred to by a when there is a change to b, but in the second code sequence there is not.

Self-review 10.11 Is an algorithm that has time complexity $O(n)$ faster or slower that one that has time complexity $O(\log_2 n)$? How does a time complexity of $O(n \log_2 n)$ compare to them?

Self-review 10.12 In the recursive version of Quicksort, what are the base cases and recursive cases of the algorithm?

Self-review 10.13 When is it better to use Bubble Sort rather than Quicksort?

Self-review 10.14 The following class represents a tree structure in Python.

```
class MyTree :
    def __init__ ( self , value , left , right ) :
        self.value = value
        self.left = left
        self.right = right
```

Which of the figures below correctly represents trees constructed with this class?

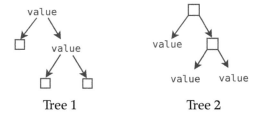

Tree 1   Tree 2

Self-review 10.15 What is the *root node* of a tree data structure?

Programming Exercises

Exercise 10.1 Extend the unit test program for testing the search functions so that its coverage is far better.

Exercise 10.2 Extend the unit test program for testing the sort functions so that its coverage is far better.

Exercise 10.3 Create a quicker Quicksort by extending the implementation in this chapter so that Bubble Sort is used instead of a recursive call of Quicksort when the parameter is a sequence with less than 10 items.

Exercise 10.4 Create an improved Quicksort implementation by changing the algorithm for selecting the pivot so that the two sub-sequences created by the partition are approximately the same length.

Exercise 10.5 This exercise is about using the ideas from the binary search algorithm to play a simple "20 Questions" type game. The (human!) player thinks of a number between 0 and 100. The program asks the player a series of yes/no questions. The first question will be "Is the number between 0 and 50?", the rest follows the binary chop approach.

What is the maximum number of questions the program will have to ask the player in order to obtain the correct answer?

Exercise 10.6 Different comparators can be used to sort different kinds of data. Write comparators implementing the following comparisons and test them by using them to sort some appropriate data:

1. A lexicographical comparator – i.e. one that compares two strings based on their alphabetic ordering.

2. An ASCII comparator that can be used to sort characters based on their ASCII value. *Hint: remember the ord function!*

3. A comparator that can be used to sort names based on their surname. This comparator should use strings of the form 'Sarah Mount', 'James Shuttleworth', 'Russel Winder', and 'James T Kirk' and compare them alphabetically on the *last* word in the string.

Exercise 10.7 When deciding what sorting algorithm to use on a list, it is useful to find out whether a list is nearly sorted. There are several ways to do this. Write functions which implement the following measures – if any of the functions return 0 the list is already sorted. Make sure that you compare the different functions on a range of sorted and unsorted data:

1. Return 1 if the list is unsorted.

2. Consider every adjacent pair of list elements. Add one to the 'unsortedness' score for every pair which is unsorted.

3. Find the longest sorted sub-sequence of elements in the list. Return the length of the list minus this number. For example, if the list is [2, 9, 3, 5, 6, 7, 1, 4], the longest sorted sub-sequence is 3, 5, 6, 7, which is of length 4. So your function should return 8-4 which is 4.

Exercise 10.8 In Section 10.4 we introduced the built-in class set which efficiently implements sets (using hash tables). This class contains many useful set operations such as intersection, union and difference, but it does not have a Cartesian product (aka cross product) operation. The Cartesian product of two sets is the set of all pairs created by taking an item from the first set and an item from the second set. For example if we have the set { 1 , 2 } and the set { 'a' , 'b' } then the Cartesian product is the set { (1 , 'a') , (1 , 'b') , (2 , 'a') , (2 , 'b') }.

For this exercise write a subclass of set that provides a method for calculating Cartesian products.

Exercise 10.9 Subclass the OrderedBinaryTree class from Section 10.5.1 to create a class that has a method reflect which exchanges the left and right subtrees of each branch, like this:

Exercise 10.10 The timeit module can be used to time the execution of code. For example, the following interpreter session shows that the built-in sort method for Python lists takes 1 s to sort the list [1 , 2 , 3 , 4 , 5] one million times on the machine we tried it on:

```
>>> import timeit
>>> t = timeit.Timer ( stmt = '[ 1 , 2 , 3 , 4 , 5 ].sort ( )' )
>>> t.timeit ( 1000000 )    # Run the statement 1000000 times.
0.99292302131652832
>>>
```

Use timeit to compare how long the various sorting algorithms covered in this chapter take to sort a given list.

Challenges

Challenge 10.1 Create a type that has the same methods as a dictionary but which uses an ordered binary tree to store the data.

Challenge 10.2 Other well-known sorting algorithms are:

> Insertion Sort
> Shell Sort
> Heapsort
> Radix Sort

Research these algorithms, extend the unit test program to test implementations of these algorithms, then add implementations of these algorithms.

Threading the Code

Learning Outcomes

At the end of this chapter you will be able to:

- Explain how Python programs can perform multiple actions concurrently even when they are run on a single-processor machine.

- Explain why concurrency is a vital part of interactive applications.

- Write multi-threaded programs using the threading.Thread class.

- Explain in summary, but not necessarily in detail, common bugs in concurrent programs, such as *deadlock* and *livelock*.

- Use locking to avoid deadlock.

- Implement simple concurrent programs with a graphical user interface using the Tkinter package.

Computers are generally idle things. That is, computers spend most of their time doing nothing. Except for those computers being used for games involving lots of high-quality, interactive graphics. These computers are doing a lot of work, are under great stress, and it is of no surprise that they get very hot and bothered. Why are most computers idle most of the time? Generally it is because they are waiting for input from users. Whilst humans are very fast at visual pattern recognition, visual perception, and cognition, they are very slow at typing and hence very slow at entering things into a computer – and that includes the people who can type accurately at 100 words per minute.

User interfaces, disks, memory and processors all work on totally different time scales. User interface input devices have to process events every few seconds or tenths of a second, disks process events every few thousandths of a second, memory processes events every few millionths of a second, and processors just keep getting faster – until 2007 anyway. It is certain that processor manufacturers could make faster and faster processors but they would run very hot and require cooling mechanisms other that fans and air flow. People don't want computers that have to use liquid cooling and be 'plumbed in', so processor manufacturers are putting multiple, cool-running processors into computers in order to provide the processor power required in modern computer systems. All new computers now have multiple processors and so can compute more than one thing at once – whereas computers with a single processor can only give the appearance of computing more than one thing at once.

Why does this matter? Our programs so far have only ever needed to do one thing at a time: our programs have started at the beginning of the code and progressed via some route through the code to arrive at the end. This is, however, a restriction that limits the programs we can write. It is extremely useful in a number of situations to be able to do more than one thing at a time.

As an example, think of a multi-user game. There is a central server that manages the total game state and interacts with multiple users:

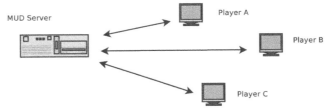

The server needs to be able to monitor each of the players and perform time-dependent changes to the state of the game, all at the same time. Each player's machine needs to interact with the server and the user at the same time. Trying to implement such a server or player client using code that does only one thing at a time is possible but hard. Having the ability to do more than one thing at a time, makes this sort of program much easier to implement.

Clearly, to be able to do more than one thing at the same time in the same program, we need a new programming language feature: *threads*.

11.1   Introducing Threads

Let's write a program that does a lot of waiting, well ten lots of waiting for of 2 s anyway:

```
import time

class WaitingClass :
    def __init__ ( self , x ) :
        self.x = x
    def waitAndPrint ( self ) :
        time.sleep ( 2 )
        print self.x , 'finished.'


if __name__ == '__main__' :
    for i in range ( 10 ) :
        WaitingClass ( i ).waitAndPrint ()
```

The time.sleep method causes the computer (with operating system support) to pause execution of our program for the number of seconds that is the parameter.

This program loops ten times. In each loop an object that is an instance of WaitingClass is created, and the waitAndPrint method called on that object. When this program is executed the following is displayed:

```
0 finished.
1 finished.
2 finished.
3 finished.
4 finished.
5 finished.
6 finished.
7 finished.
8 finished.
9 finished.
```

with overall execution taking around 20 s. Exactly as expected, ten 2 s waits should take 20 s.

In the above program, the objects are created and their waitAndPrint method called *sequentially*. What we want to do now is to have all the objects created and do their waiting at the same time, i.e. *concurrently*. To do this we need to have our program be able to do more than one thing at a time: we want our program to have more than one *thread of execution*. All our programs until now have used threads but there was only one of them. When we start the programs, a thread is created that runs the script. Now we want to be able to create multiple threads so that we can create concurrent activity. To introduce multiple threads into our program, we use inheritance: the WaitingClass is made a subclass of threading.Thread. Each instance of WaitingClass can then be executed concurrently because it is a threaded object. The new code is:

```
import time
import threading

class WaitingClass ( threading.Thread ) :
    def __init__ ( self , x ) :
        threading.Thread.__init__ ( self )
        self.x = x
    def run ( self ) :
        time.sleep ( 2 )
        print self.x , 'finished.'


if __name__ == '__main__' :
    for i in range ( 10 ) :
        WaitingClass ( i ).start ()
```

A 'thread of execution' or *thread* is an independent active execution of the code. If a program has many threads, they share the same code and state.

The most obvious differences between this and the previous program are that the waitAndPrint method has been renamed run and that we call start on the object instead of waitAndPrint in the main loop. The run method of a threaded object is the method that is executed when a thread is started: it is never called explicitly. The start method is what we call – it has the responsibility of ensuring that the threaded object is properly set up and initialized, and that the run method gets called correctly. We need this two-stage approach because the Python system has to do lots of background work for multiple threads to work.

What happens when we execute this threaded version of the program? We get:

```
0 finished.
1 finished.
2 finished.
3 finished.
4 finished.
5 finished.
6 finished.
7 finished.
8 finished.
9 finished.
```

but it only takes just over 2 s! Instead of each of the waits happening one after the other, the threaded version causes all the waits to happen at the same time. So we do 20 s of waiting in 2 s because they all happen in parallel.

In the threaded version we use the Thread class from the package threading. The Thread class is the workhorse part of the threading package. An instance of Thread is

---

*Package **thread** and Package **threading***

If you look at the Python documentation you will find that there is a package called thread and one called threading. The thread package provides the ability to work with threads but it is low level, requiring all the control activity to be handled manually – and if we do it wrong it can lead to truly nasty situations. The threading package is a higher-level package that abstracts all the detail, allowing us to focus on how we use threads as part of our algorithm rather than worrying about how to control threads. As you might expect the threading package makes use of the thread package.

---

a thread – no surprise there. Instantiation of a subclass of Thread creates a thread, but the new thread doesn't do anything until the start method is called – then and only then does the new thread start executing. What does the new thread do when it is told to start? It executes the run method of the thread object. When the run method finishes, the thread terminates.

When creating new threads in a program, people often talk about 'spawning a thread'. This emphasizes that the thread doing the creation is the parent, and the thread being created is the child.

In the program we have a for loop that loops ten times. On the first iteration we instantiate WaitingClass (a subclass of Thread) with parameter 0. This creates a new thread object, and ensures that the instance variable x is associated with the value 0. The object is a new thread, but it doesn't do anything at this stage. Having instantiated the thread object we call the start method, which is a method inherited from Thread. This causes the new thread to begin execution, which it does by executing the run method. Now we have two threads, the new one that we just started and the original one – let's call the original thread the 'main' thread.

The main thread now executes the next iteration of the loop. It instantiates a new thread object initialized with the parameter 1 and starts it. So the new thread runs its run method and immediately waits for 2 s, just like the thread we spawned earlier. Now we have three threads: the main thread executes the next iteration of the loop and we have two uniquely identified threads that are waiting.

After ten times around the loop, the main thread has spawned ten threads that are all waiting for 2 s: we therefore have eleven threads all executing concurrently.

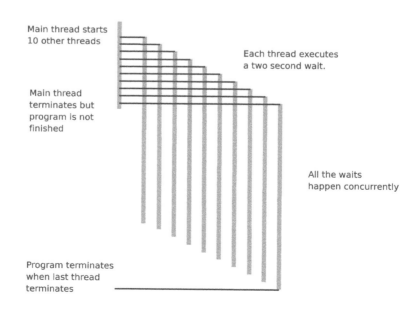

Figure 11.1

The threads and events of the multi-threaded waiting program. The vertical lines represent running threads. The horizontal lines represent events. The first ten events are the creation and starting of threads. The final event is the last thread terminating, which terminates the program.

Main thread starts
10 other threads

Each thread executes
a two second wait.

Main thread
terminates but
program is not
finished

All the waits
happen concurrently

Program terminates
when last thread
terminates

The main thread now terminates since there is no more code for it to execute. But the program doesn't terminate because there are ten threads still executing – they may all be just sleeping, but they have not terminated. A program only terminates when all its threads have terminated.

Each of the sleeping threads wakes up after 2 s, executes the print statement and then terminates because its run method has completed. When the last of the ten spawned threads terminates, the program terminates as all its threads have terminated. We describe this behavior diagrammatically in Figure 11.1.

An executing program is the code and all threads spawned by the main thread.

So this is how we can wait ten times for 2 s and it only takes 2 s instead of 20 s. All the waiting happens concurrently because all ten threads are executing (or rather waiting) concurrently.

The point of using threads is that they allow us to do computation concurrently. This is not always to make overall execution time shorter: sometimes it is because using multiple threads is the only way of implementing an algorithm. A particularly pertinent example is graphics, and especially graphical user interfaces (GUIs). It can be very difficult to make GUIs work without using multiple threads.

Unfortunately, multi-threaded programs can be hard to make work correctly. In particular, *deadlock* and *livelock* are two critical problems in multi-threaded systems:

Deadlock This is where the state of the program is such that no thread can continue executing. Deadlock happens when threads are waiting for a change of state that cannot happen because the thread that would change the state is itself waiting for a change of state in order to execute. Deadlock is usually caused because a program is not sufficiently careful about managing state shared by multiple threads.

Livelock This is where threads continually change shared state so as to create a form of 'infinite loop': the changes of state mean that no progress is made.

Detailed discussion of these topics is outside the scope of this book – it is a topic for specialist books on concurrency and parallelism in programming. Having said this let us investigate using threads a little further to show the sort of things that can be done.

11.2 Guessing Games

11.2.1 Turn and Turn Again

Guessing games are often turn based: one player decides on an answer and another player has a turn at guessing the answer. We can create a (trivial) turn-based guessing game. In the game, the program decides on a letter (a , b , c, or d, in this game) and the player has to enter a guess at the keyboard. After each guess (turn), the program chooses a new answer. This seems like an ideal situation for a generator – the generator creates an infinite list of guesses that we can use a loop to process:

```python
import random

def letterGenerator ( ) :
    data = [ 'a' , 'b' , 'c' , 'd' ]
    while True :
        yield data [ random.randint ( 0 , len ( data ) - 1 ) ]
```

Deadlock

The classic example of deadlock is exemplified by the following diagram:

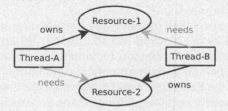

There are two threads, A and B, and two resources, 1 and 2. The resources can only be owned by one thread at any time. If Thread-A has acquired Resource-1 but needs Resource-2 to continue, and Thread-B has acquired Resource-2 but needs Resource-1 to continue, then we have deadlock. Neither thread can continue, because the resources needed are not, and can never become, available.

Deadlock avoidance is where a check is made for each resource claim to see whether deadlock would occur. So in the above examples, when a thread tries to own a resource, a check is made to see if a deadlock state would be entered and if it would then the resource claim is refused. *Deadlock prevention* is writing the algorithm and program so that deadlock can never occur. *Deadlock detection* is where a program monitors itself to detect whether deadlock has occurred, and, if it has, apply some remedy – the usual remedy is to restart the whole program.

```
if __name__ == '__main__' :
    for expected in letterGenerator () :
        try :
            guess = raw_input ( 'What is the next character? ' )
            if guess == expected : print 'You got it right, well done.'
            else : print 'Sorry, no, it was' , expected
        except :
            print
            break
```

letterGenerator is a generator that provides an infinite list of answers. The program loops posing the question, collecting the answer, and providing a response. The input code is in a try/except block so that the user can type Ctrl+d or Ctrl+c to exit the infinite loop.

```
|> python guessingGame_turnbased.py
What is the next character? d
Sorry, no, it was c
What is the next character? d
Sorry, no, it was a
What is the next character? s
Sorry, no, it was c
What is the next character? d
You got it right, well done.
What is the next character? a
Sorry, no, it was b
What is the next character?
|>
```

Perhaps we should extend the game by keeping count of the correct and incorrect guesses, so that there is a score and potentially a winner. Did you spot that the player tried s, which is a useless guess. Perhaps we should extend the code to make some comment about not guessing a possible answer. If we were developing this for actual use we would extend it along those lines. However, we are really interested in threads, and there is no obvious reason for using threads in turn-based systems. This implies changing the rules...

11.2.2 Playing Out of Turn

Turn-based games are everywhere: most card games are turn based. It seems though that we only ever need a single thread for processing such games. So what feature of a game would lead us to need multiple threads? It is where multiple things happen concurrently. As a simple variation on the letter guessing game from the previous subsection, let's say that the period of time for which an answer is valid is between 1 s and 5 s. This is no longer turn based – the answer is not known until the player actually makes a guess: the answer could have changed many times before the guess is made. This change of rules means we have to do two things at once: we must be ready to accept the player's guess at any time, and the program must change the answer at random intervals. Definitely a job for a main thread and a spawned thread.

So we create a program in which the main thread handles the user input and a separate thread manages the current answer. As a start we might come up with something like:

```python
import random
import threading
import time

class Generator ( threading.Thread ) :
    def __init__ ( self ) :
        threading.Thread.__init__ ( self )
        self.data = [ 'a' , 'b' , 'c' , 'd' ]
        self.currentIndex = 0
    def run ( self ) :
        while True :
            self.currentIndex = random.randint ( 0 , len ( self.data ) -1 )
            time.sleep ( random.randint ( 2 , 5 ) )
            print '#'
    def getValue ( self ) :
        return self.data [ self.currentIndex ]

if __name__ == '__main__':
    generator = Generator ()
    generator.start ()
    while True :
        try :
            guess = raw_input ()
            expected = generator.getValue ()
            if guess == expected : print 'You got it right, well done.'
            else : print 'Sorry, no, it was' , expected
        except :
            print
            break
```

The Generator class is a thread so we have to ensure that the threading.Thread constructor is called and that we have a run method. We have to call the threading.Thread constructor explicitly (this is usually the first statement of a constructor), then we initialize the state: we set self.data to list of possible answers, and self.currentIndex to 0, which is the index of the first current answer. The run method is an infinite loop that causes the current answer to change at randomly determined times – the # is output to show when the answer changes. We have the getter getValue so we can discover the current answer value.

The main code creates an instance of the Generator class and starts it running, so we have a thread that changes the answer at random intervals of between 2 s and 5 s. It then continues into an infinite loop, processing the player's input. We have two threads, one acting for the player and one being the answer changer. To program this without threads would be hard.

11.2.3 Fixing the Obvious Bug

The program in the previous subsection has one rather serious bug. Have you spotted it? The object that is an instance of Generator never terminates. When the user terminates the main thread by typing Ctrl+d, the generator thread just keeps on going and the program never terminates. We need to amend our Generator class so that the main thread can inform any instances of the class that it is time to quit. We add a new variable keepGoing that controls the behavior:

```
import random
import threading
import time

class Generator ( threading.Thread ) :
    def __init__ ( self ) :
        threading.Thread.__init__ ( self )
        self.data = [ 'a' , 'b' , 'c' , 'd' ]
        self.currentIndex = 0
        self.keepGoing = True
    def run ( self ) :
        while self.keepGoing :
            self.currentIndex = random.randint ( 0 , len ( self.data ) -1 )
            time.sleep ( random.randint ( 2 , 5 ))
            print '#'
    def getValue ( self ) :
        return self.data [ self.currentIndex ]
    def terminate ( self ) :
        self.keepGoing = False

if __name__ == '__main__':
    generator = Generator ()
    generator.start ()
    while True :
        try :
            guess = raw_input ()
            expected = generator.getValue ()
            if guess == expected : print 'You got it right, well done.'
            else : print 'Sorry, no, it was' , expected
        except :
            generator.terminate ()
            break
```

*self.keepGoing = **True** added*

***while** self.keepGoing : instead of **while True** :*

Added new method terminate

*generator.terminate () instead of **print***

The terminate method gives the main thread a way of setting the control variable that determines whether the generator thread keeps going or not. The threads communicate with each other by using shared data. We try and protect access to the data to avoid deadlock or livelock. One thread asking another thread to change its behavior by calling a method is an idiomatic technique well worth remembering.

11.3 Controlling Traffic Lights

We said at the end of Section 7.9.3 (page 242) that we would revisit the traffic light example when we knew about threads. Well, now we have introduced threads, so we should make good on the promise and revisit the traffic light code.

The problem we had is that, having set up the traffic light, we had no way of animating it. We need to be able to do more than one thing at once to get the graphics to do anything. In this case we need to create and start a new thread to process the changing of the light color whenever the 'go' button is pressed – a thread that is separate from the thread that is managing the graphics. We do this by encapsulating the color changing behavior in a class Sequencer (which is a subclass of Thread) and having a method (sequence) that creates and starts a new Sequence thread as required:

```python
import time
import Tkinter
import threading

class TrafficLight ( Tkinter.Frame ) :
    '''A standard three-light traffic light.'''

    class Light ( Tkinter.Canvas ) :
        '''An individual light to be part of a traffic light.'''
        def __init__ ( self , master , color ) :
            size = 30
            halfPadding = 2
            Tkinter.Canvas.__init__ (
                self , master ,
                width = size + 2 * halfPadding , height = size + 2 * halfPadding )
            self.id = self.create_oval (
                halfPadding , halfPadding ,
                size + halfPadding , size + halfPadding ,
                fill = 'black' )
            self.color = color
        def on ( self ) : self.itemconfigure ( self.id , fill = self.color )
        def off ( self ) : self.itemconfigure ( self.id , fill = 'black' )

    class Sequencer ( threading.Thread ) :
        '''A thread to sequence a traffic light.'''
        def __init__ ( self , lightSet ) :
            threading.Thread.__init__ ( self )
            self.lightSet = lightSet
        def run ( self ) :
            for i in range ( len ( self.lightSet.timings ) ) :
                time.sleep ( self.lightSet.timings[self.lightSet.current] )
                self.lightSet.current = ( self.lightSet.current + 1 ) % len ( self.lightSet.states )
                for i in range ( len ( self.lightSet.lights ) ) :
                    if self.lightSet.states[self.lightSet.current][i] : self.lightSet.lights[i].on ()
                    else : self.lightSet.lights[i].off ()

    states = ( ( True , False , False ) , ( False , False , True ) , ( False , True , False ) )
```

```
def __init__ ( self , master , timings ) :
    Tkinter.Frame.__init__ ( self , master )
    if len ( timings ) != len ( self.states ) :
        raise ValueError , "Incorrect number of timing values."
    self.timings = timings
    self.current = 0
    self.lights = (
        TrafficLight.Light ( self , 'red' ) ,
        TrafficLight.Light ( self , 'yellow' ) ,
        TrafficLight.Light ( self , 'green' )
        )
    self.lights[0].on ( )
    for l in self.lights : l.pack ( )
    self.button = Tkinter.Button ( self , text = 'go' , command = self.sequence )
    self.button.pack ( )
    self.pack ( )

def sequence ( self ) :
    TrafficLight.Sequencer ( self ).start ( )

if __name__ == '__main__' :
    root = Tkinter.Tk ( )
    eastWestLight = TrafficLight ( root , ( 5 , 5 , 2 ) )
    root.mainloop ( )
```

We cannot show that this program works as required in this book because it is the dynamic nature of the code that is the important thing, and it is impossible to show anything other than static behavior in a book. Try executing the program for yourself to see what happens – there is nothing quite as good as experimental data for proving a point.

It really is worth trying this program out for yourself – it has a bug!

11.4 So What's Hard?

We have seen three programs now that have been multi-threaded, and none of them seemed hard or tricky. This seems to belie our comment that multi-threaded programs can be hard to get correct.

Try the experiment of clicking the 'go' button six or seven times in quick succession. The light starts changing as expected, then goes into a manic phase of changing totally out of timing.

What is happening here? Let's 'walk through' the code. Every time we click the 'go' button, we create a new thread and start it running, and it sequences the change of light color. While there is only a single sequencer thread in action at any one time (i.e. we click 'go' only when the light is in its red waiting state) there is no problem. If though we have multiple sequencer threads active concurrently, we have a problem, because they are all working with the same light object – all the sequencer threads are sharing data. Resources shared between multiple active threads are at the heart of most problems in multi-threaded programming. Clearly we need tools to control access to shared resource among multiple active threads. The problem we have in this case is that we can create many threads, all of which work with the same traffic light. We can change the user interface slightly, thereby removing the need to worry about the problem. If we ignore all button clicks that occur during a sequencing, then the only time a button click starts a new thread is when the traffic light is in the 'red' state awaiting a button click to start sequencing.

Critical Sections

In a multi-threaded context, any sequence of code that manipulates resources that are shared by multiple threads should only be executed by one thread at a time. Such a sequence of code is called a *critical section*. Programming languages that support multi-threaded programming have tools and techniques for creating critical sections, and managing thread execution.

Looking at the documentation for the threading package, we find that there are *condition variables*, *locks* and *semaphores*, all of which are about controlling access to resources. These three mechanisms are all different ways of temporarily stopping the execution of threads – this is called *blocking*. Condition variables, locks and semaphores are tools for allowing threads to communicate with each other. They allow threads to block and unblock, so that any one shared resource can only ever be used by one thread at any one time, i.e. in critical sections.

This means we can never have more than one sequencing thread at any one time, which means we cannot have a problem and don't need to worry about critical sections.

So, in the sequence method, we need to ask the question "Are we in the wait state?" and, only if the answer is yes, action the sequence; if we are currently sequencing, we should not create and start a new sequencing thread. This implies we need a Boolean variable that is set when a new sequencing thread is created and started, and unset when that thread terminates. This means we need a Boolean variable that is accessible in the sequence method and the sequencer.run method. This is straightforward since the Sequencer instance knows which TrafficLight instance it is associated with, so we can have an instance variable in TrafficLight as a shared variable. We amend the Sequencer.run method by adding a statement at the end:

> Avoiding the need for critical sections is always a better solution than managing them!

```
def run ( self ) :
    for i in range ( len ( self.lightSet.timings ) ) :
        time.sleep ( self.lightSet.timings[self.lightSet.current] )
        self.lightSet.current = ( self.lightSet.current + 1 ) % len ( self.lightSet.states )
        for i in range ( len ( self.lightSet.lights ) ) :
            if self.lightSet.states[self.lightSet.current][i] : self.lightSet.lights[i].on ( )
            else : self.lightSet.lights[i].off ( )
    self.lightSet.isSequencing = False
```

and we amend the constructor to ensure that the instance variable isSequencing is created and initialized at the time the TrafficLight instance is created:

```
def __init__ ( self , master , timings ) :
    Tkinter.Frame.__init__ ( self , master )
    if len ( timings ) != len ( self.states ) :
        raise ValueError , "Incorrect number of timing values."
    self.timings = timings
    self.current = 0
    self.isSequencing = False
    self.lights = (
        TrafficLight.Light ( self , 'red' ) ,
        TrafficLight.Light ( self , 'yellow' ) ,
        TrafficLight.Light ( self , 'green' )
        )
    self.lights[0].on ( )
    for l in self.lights : l.pack ( )
    self.button = Tkinter.Button ( self , text = 'go' , command = self.sequence )
    self.button.pack ( )
    self.pack ( )
```

Finally, and most crucially, we extend the sequence method so that it checks the current state (i.e. the isSequencing variable) to see whether the button press should be ignored or a new sequencing thread started:

```
def sequence ( self ) :
    if not self.isSequencing :
        self.isSequencing = True
        TrafficLight.Sequencer ( self ).start ()
```

The traffic light now starts sequencing when the 'go' button is clicked and the sequence is not disrupted by any excessive clicking of the button. We have managed to sort this problem out without using any of the technology of critical sections (locks, semaphores, condition variables). It is an example of *lock-free programming*, which is the multi-threaded programming style of choice. Locks take a lot of computing resource, and can severely compromise performance. Where there are ways to make multi-threaded programs safe against deadlock, livelock, and incorrect behavior without using locks, they are to be preferred.

In this particular example there is one potential danger. The test of the self. isSequencing variable and the amending of it to show that a thread is about to be created are separate actions. This means that there is a period in which a decision has been made to create a new thread but the variable that signals that no other thread should be created has not been amended. There is therefore the possibility of creating more than one thread. The problem is that the testing and setting of the control variable is not an *atomic operation*, i.e. an operation that happens with no possibility of anything else happening during its execution. To really be truly safe we would need to use an atomic *test and set* operation, but Python does not have such an operation. How else can we deal with this? We could declare it to be a critical section, created using locks from the threading package, and thereby guarantee that there can be no problems. If we add the line:

```
self.isSequencing = False
```

into the constructor (so as to create a lock object associated with the traffic light object), and then replace the sequence method above with:

```
def sequence ( self ) :
    self.lock.acquire ()
    if not self.isSequencing :
        self.isSequencing = True
        TrafficLight.Sequencer ( self ).start ()
    self.lock.release ()
```

then we make the body of sequence a critical section. The call of self.lock.acquire means that the lock must be obtained by the thread before it can proceed. If the lock is available (i.e. the lock is in the state 'unlocked') then it is acquired (i.e. the state of the lock becomes 'locked'), the critical section is executed, and then the lock is released (i.e. the state of the lock becomes 'unlocked') by calling self.lock.release. If the lock is not available (i.e. the lock is in state 'locked') when the self.lock.acquire method is executed, then the thread is blocked (i.e. execution is suspended) until such time as the thread can acquire the lock. When the self.lock.acquire method returns, it is guaranteed that the thread has acquired the lock and that no other thread is executing or can execute the critical section. Even though the testing and setting of self.isSequencing are not atomic, we can guarantee that it doesn't matter because the code is in a critical section: no other thread can interfere with correct execution of the non-atomic code.

This is a very heavy-handed solution to a potential problem, but it acts as an example of using locks to create critical sections in code. Whether the cost of using locks here is worthwhile is a complex question, but one we are not going to address in this book. Even though concurrency, concurrent programming, and parallel programming are important – and becoming more and more so daily as computer technology changes – we are going to leave things with the two points:

1. Programming user interfaces requires a little knowledge of threads and concurrency.

2. Concurrency and parallelism are very important areas of programming and you should learn more about them by going to the specialist books on these subjects.

Chapter Summary

In this chapter we have found that:

- Concurrency is an important factor in many algorithms.
- Threads are a way of providing concurrency in a program.
- threading.Thread is the class used for creating threads.
- Shared resources are a problem in concurrent programming.
- concurrency is a huge area with a specialist literature. Pointers to issues, tools and techniques for further investigation, include: critical sections, locks, semaphores, mutexes, monitors, condition variables.

Self-Review Questions

Self-review 11.1 What is a 'thread' and what is a 'process'? What is the difference between the two?

Self-review 11.2 What does the 'scheduler' in an operating system take responsibility for?

Self-review 11.3 What does the following line of code do?

```
time.wait ( 5 )
```

Self-review 11.4 Threading is used extensively in interactive programming in applications such as games, GUIs, Web browsers, and so on. Why is threading so important for programs that need to interact with humans?

Self-review 11.5 What is happening in the following code?

```
import threading , time

class Foobar ( threading.Thread ) :
    def __init__ ( self ) :
        threading.Thread.__init__ ( self )
    def run ( self ) :
        time.sleep ( 1 )
        print self.getName ( )
```

```
if __name__ == '__main__' :
    pool = [ Foobar () for i in range ( 10 ) ]
    map ( lambda t : t.start () , pool )
```

Self-review 11.6 On one occasion when we ran the code above, we got the following output:

```
Thread-1
Thread-2
Thread-7
Thread-3
Thread-9
Thread-8
Thread-6
Thread-10
Thread-4
Thread-5
```

Why don't the numbers appear sequentially?

Self-review 11.7 To the nearest second, how long will the code in Self-review 11.5 take to execute?

Self-review 11.8 The second threaded guessing game program can take up to 5 s to terminate after the user has entered Ctlr+d. Why is this?

Self-review 11.9 'Livelock' and 'deadlock' are two problems that are commonly associated with multi-threaded programs. Define 'deadlock' and 'livelock'.

Self-review 11.10 What are 'critical sections' in programs?

Self-review 11.11 What does it mean for a piece of code to be 'atomic'?

Self-review 11.12 What does the threading.Thread.start method do?

Self-review 11.13 Why must the run method be overridden in subclasses of threading.Thread?

Self-review 11.14 What does the following code do?

```
print threading.currentThread ()
```

What output would it give if used outside a thread object, like this:

```
if __name__ == '__main__':
    print threading.currentThread()
```

Self-review 11.15 Imagine you are writing a multi-player game. Your game will have some interesting graphics that need to be generated quickly to provide a smooth animation. There will be a sound track to the game-play and several players will be interacting at once. Inside the game there will be both player and non-player characters. What parts of this program would you want to separate out into their own threads?

Programming Exercises

Exercise 11.1 Write a program that creates two threads, each of which should sleep for a random number of seconds, then print out a message which includes its thread ID.

Exercise 11.2 Starting with your code from the previous exercise, add a counter to your program. Each thread should include the value of the counter in the message it prints to the screen and should increment the counter every time it wakes up. So, the counter will hold the total number of messages printed to the screen by all the running threads.

You will need to use some form of concurrency control to ensure that the value of the counter is always correct. Several of these are available in Python. One simple solution is to use locks. The idea here is that if a variable is locked, it cannot be changed by code in another thread until it has been unlocked. In this way we can use locks to create critical sections in our code.

Here's a code fragment to get you started:

```
import threading

foobar = 10 # Shared data!
foobar_l = threading.Lock ()
. . .
# Start critical section
foobar_l.acquire () # Acquire lock on foobar
foobar = . . .
foobar_l.release () # Let other threads alter foobar
# End critical section
. . .
```

Locking isn't everyone's favorite method of concurrency control. Acquiring and releasing locks is relatively very slow – remember concurrency is often used in time-critical applications such as games.

Exercise 11.3 Python provides a special data structure in a class called Queue.Queue that is specifically for use in multi-threaded programs. You have already learned about queue types in Sections 6.6 (page 202) and 6.6.4 (page 204). In Python's queues, data can be added to a queue using a method called put and removed from it using the method get. Here's an example:

```
>>> import Queue
>>> q = Queue.Queue ()
>>> q.put ( 5 )
>>> q.put ( 4 )
>>> q.get ()
5
>>> q.get ()
4
>>> q.get ()
```

Here we have added the objects 5 and 4 to a queue we have created, then retrieved those two values. Note that we have called q.get a third time, even though the queue is now empty. You might have expected Python to raise an exception here, because we tried to access a value that doesn't exist. In fact, what is happening here is that Python is waiting (blocking) on the queue to provide a value. Because queues are expected to be used in concurrent programs, the authors of the Queue.Queue class knew that other threads might be placing data on the queue even when one thread is waiting to fetch data from it.

For this exercise, write a small program in which several threads access a single queue at the same time. Each thread should randomly either place some random data on the queue, or take data off it. Make sure you print out lots of useful information about what each thread is doing to the queue so you can watch how the program proceeds!

Challenges

Challenge 11.1 Tkinter provides a number of methods to control concurrency and scheduling in GUIs, including:

- widget.after
- widget.update
- widget.wait_visibility

Read the Tkinter documentation to find out what these methods do.

Start out by creating a simple GUI that implements an alarm. To help with this, Tkinter buttons have methods called bell and flash that 'beep' and make the button flash, respectively. Use the after method to schedule an alarm to sound after a given number of milliseconds. Make sure the user has a way of turning the alarm off!

When you have a basic alarm program working, implement the following improvements:

- Allow the user to schedule the alarm to go off at a particular time.
- Allow the user to schedule the alarm to go off at given intervals (for example, every half hour).
- Allow the user to schedule several alarms to go off at various times during the day.

Challenge 11.2 The classic problem in the area of concurrent programming, was proposed by Edsgar Dijkstra in 1971, and recast by Tony Hoare as the The Dining Philosophers Problem.

Five philosophers are sitting at a round table. Philosophers are quite eccentric, all they do all day is think and eat, but they can't do both at once. Between each pair of philosophers is a fork and each philosopher needs two forks to eat. What would happen if all the philosophers organize themselves to pick up their left fork and then their right fork whenever they stop thinking? Can you think of a better way for philosophers to eat?

Research this problem and write a program that uses threads to represent each philosopher to explore how to avoid deadlock.

The Life of the Game

In Section 5.1 (page 151), we created a program to play Conway's Game of Life. However, simply printing the state of the game universe to the terminal didn't really provide a good user experience. We said then that we needed a graphical user interface for the game to truly come to life. In this chapter we are going enliven the Game of Life by constructing an interactive version of the game using Tkinter. The move from console output to GUI will be done in a number of small steps. There are two reasons for this:

1. It makes it easier to follow the transformation.

2. It is a good way of working – always evolve a working program in small steps, ensuring that it works as required after each step.

We have already produced the game model, so it is now time to develop the interface by adding user interaction elements.

12.1   Stage 0: Groundwork

When we last saw the Game of Life code, it consisted of a set of functions that output the state of the game universe as text on the terminal:

```
import random

def createGrid ( x , y ) :
    global grid
    grid = [ [ False for j in range ( y ) ] for i in range ( x ) ]
```

```
def applyToEachCellOfGrid ( function ) :
    for i in range ( len ( grid ) ) :
        for j in range ( len ( grid[i] ) ) :
            function ( i , j )

def populateGridRandomly ( x ) :
    random.seed ()
    def setRandomly ( i , j ) :
        if random.random () < x : grid[i][j] = True
    applyToEachCellOfGrid ( setRandomly )

def calculateNextGeneration () :
    global grid
    newGrid = [ [ False for j in range ( len ( grid[i] ) ) ] for i in range ( len ( grid ) ) ]
    def calculateLiveness ( x , y ) :
        count = 0
        for i in range ( x - 1 , x + 2 ) :
            if 0 <= i < len ( grid ) :
                for j in range ( y - 1 , y + 2 ) :
                    if 0 <= j < len ( grid[i] ) :
                        if ( ( i != x ) or ( j != y ) ) and grid[i][j] : count += 1
        if grid[x][y] : return 2 <= count <= 3
        else : return count == 3
    def setNewGrid ( x , y ) :
        newGrid[x][y] = calculateLiveness ( x , y )
    applyToEachCellOfGrid ( setNewGrid )
    grid = newGrid

def printGrid () :
    def printIt ( i , j ) :
        if grid[i][j] : print '#' ,
        else : print '_' ,
        if j == len ( grid[i] ) - 1 : print
    applyToEachCellOfGrid ( printIt )

def printSeparator () :
    print '\n--------------------------------------\n'

if __name__ == '__main__' :
    createGrid ( 10 , 8 )
    populateGridRandomly ( 0.4 )
    printGrid ()
    for i in range ( 3 ) :
        calculateNextGeneration ()
        printSeparator ()
        printGrid ()
```

We stopped development then because we wanted to change to using a GUI to provide a better user experience, but at that time we did not have the right programming tools. In particular, to program GUIs in Python we need to work with classes, objects and threads. Now that we have the necessary information, we can proceed with GUI Life.

First though, we undertake some groundwork. Since the generally accepted best way of structuring applications that have GUIs is to use classes and objects we need to 'classify' and 'objectify' the program. We don't try to extend it in any way, we just change the structure. This makes it easier to deal with any problems and bugs: by changing only one thing at a time about the program it is easier to reason about the changes that are happening.

This groundwork transformation of this program is relatively straightforward and leads us to:

```python
import random

class Life :
    def __init__ ( self , x , y ) :
        self.grid = [ [ False for j in range ( y ) ] for i in range ( x ) ]

    def _applyToEachCellOfGrid ( self , function ) :
        for i in range ( len ( self.grid ) ) :
            for j in range ( len ( self.grid[i] ) ) :
                function ( i , j )

    def populateGridRandomly ( self , x ) :
        random.seed ( )
        def setRandomly ( i , j ) :
            if random.random ( ) < x : self.grid[i][j] = True
        self._applyToEachCellOfGrid ( setRandomly )

    def calculateNextGeneration ( self ) :
        newGrid = [ [ False for j in range ( len ( self.grid[i] ) ) ] for i in range ( len ( self.grid ) ) ]
        def calculateLiveness ( x , y ) :
            count = 0
            for i in range ( x - 1 , x + 2 ) :
                if 0 <= i < len ( self.grid ) :
                    for j in range ( y - 1 , y + 2 ) :
                        if 0 <= j < len ( self.grid[i] ) :
                            if ( ( i != x ) or ( j != y ) ) and self.grid[i][j] : count += 1
            if self.grid[x][y] : return 2 <= count <= 3
            else : return count == 3
        def setNewGrid ( x , y ) :
            newGrid[x][y] = calculateLiveness ( x , y )
        self._applyToEachCellOfGrid ( setNewGrid )
        self.grid = newGrid

    def printGrid ( self ) :
        def printIt ( i , j ) :
            if self.grid[i][j] : print '#' ,
            else : print '_' ,
            if j == len ( self.grid[i] ) - 1 : print
        self._applyToEachCellOfGrid ( printIt )

    def printSeparator ( self ) :
        print '\n----------------------------------------\n'

if __name__ == '__main__' :
    game = Life ( 10 , 8 )
    game.populateGridRandomly ( 0.4 )
    game.printGrid ( )
    for i in range ( 3 ) :
        game.calculateNextGeneration ( )
        game.printSeparator ( )
        game.printGrid ( )
```

The constructor replaces the createGrid function.

The attribute self.grid replaces the global variable grid.

The functions applyToEachCellOfGrid, populateGridRandomly, calculateNextGeneration, printGrid, and printSeparator become methods of the class.

The only changes to the function bodies are to use the self. syntax to work with attributes of an object.

The main block now instantiates an object and then calls methods on that object.

The behavior of this program is the same as the earlier version, it just uses classes and objects instead of functions. On a test run, we got:

```
# # _ # _ _ _ #
# # _ _ # _ _ _
_ _ # _ _ _ _ _
_ _ _ _ # # _ #
_ # # _ # _ # #
_ _ _ # _ _ _ _
_ _ _ # _ _ # #
_ # _ _ # _ _ _
_ _ _ _ _ # _ _
_ # _ _ _ _ _ _
---------------------------------------
# # # _ _ _ _ _
# _ _ # _ _ _ _
_ # _ # # # _ _
_ # # _ # # _ #
_ _ # _ # _ # #
_ _ _ # # # _ _
_ _ # # # _ _ _
_ _ _ _ # # # _
_ _ _ _ _ _ _ _
_ _ _ _ _ _ _ _
---------------------------------------
# # # _ _ _ _ _
# _ _ # _ _ _ _
# # _ _ _ # # _
_ # _ _ _ _ _ #
_ # # _ _ _ _ #
_ _ _ _ _ _ # _
_ _ # _ _ _ # _
_ _ _ _ # # _ _
_ _ _ _ _ # _ _
_ _ _ _ _ _ _ _
---------------------------------------
# # # _ _ _ _ _
_ _ _ _ _ _ _ _
# # # _ _ _ # _
_ _ _ _ _ _ _ #
_ # # _ _ _ # #
_ # # _ _ _ # #
_ _ _ _ _ _ # _
_ _ _ _ # # # _
_ _ _ _ # # _ _
_ _ _ _ _ _ _ _
```

What about a unit test? Since we last saw the Game of Life we have introduced unit testing, and to do proper development, we must have appropriate unit tests. So what can we test and how can we test it? The following points spring to mind:

- We should test that creating a new game creates a square array of cells each initialized to **False**.

- We should test the correct calculation of the next generation. There are a few obvious tests and these are the known static and dynamic stable shapes – for example Block, Boat, Blinker.

Stable Societies in the Game of Life

The Game of Life has very simple rules and yet it turns out to be very complex. One of the really interesting properties of the 'game' is that there are some stable shapes – stable in the sense they the can preserve life potentially for all time. There are three types of stable shapes:

Still Lifes These are static, unchanging shapes in which each live cell is immortal. The group is immortal only if isolated from all other life.

Oscillators These are shapes that switch between a few configurations. If isolated from any other life, the shape remains active for ever even though individual cells may live and die.

Spaceships These are shapes that travel through the universe. Like Oscillators, Spaceships are dynamic – cells die and live – but the live group is not stationary, it moves. As with the other two shapes, stability requires no interaction with other life.

Perhaps the three simplest stable shapes are:

Block Four live cells in a square is a Still Life – it just exists until other life interacts with it:

Boat These four five-cell shapes are also Still Lifes – they are all the same shape, but just rotated:

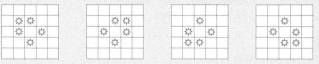

Blinker A row of three live cells in isolation will blink between a vertical and a horizontal triplet – it is an Oscillator that flips between the two states:

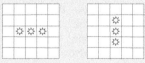

- We should test that an empty universe stays empty – life cannot spring from the void, at least not in The Game of Life.

Based on this thinking, we can construct the following test code:

```python
import unittest
import life

class Life_Test ( unittest.TestCase ) :
    """Test the implementation of the Game of Life."""

    def test_newGame ( self ) :
        game = life.Life ( 10 , 8 )
        assert len ( game.grid ) == 10
        assert len ( game.grid[0] ) == 8
        for i in range ( len ( game.grid ) ) :
            assert len ( game.grid[i] ) == len ( game.grid[i] )
            for j in range ( len ( game.grid[i] ) ) :
                assert not game.grid[i][j]
```

```python
def doStillLifeTest ( self , datum ) :
    """Run a test for a static, stable shape."""
    #### We instantiate a 0x0 universe and then replace the universe with the one
    #### passed as a parameter. We should perhaps check that the parameter is
    #### a rectagular array of Boolean values.
    game = life.Life ( 0 , 0 )
    game.grid = datum
    game.calculateNextGeneration ()
    assert game.grid == datum
    game.calculateNextGeneration ()
    assert game.grid == datum

def test_empty ( self ) :
    """Ensure that an empty world stays empty."""
    self.doStillLifeTest ( [ [ False for j in range ( 10 ) ] for i in range ( 10 ) ] )

def test_block ( self ) :
    """Test that Block is a static, stable shape."""
    self.doStillLifeTest ( [
        [ False , False , False , False ] ,
        [ False , True , True , False ] ,
        [ False , True , True , False ] ,
        [ False , False , False , False ]
        ] )

def test_boat ( self ) :
    """Test that Boat is a static stable shape."""
    self.doStillLifeTest ( [
        [ False , False , False , False , False ] ,
        [ False , True , True , False , False ] ,
        [ False , True , False , True , False ] ,
        [ False , False , True , False , False ] ,
        [ False , False , False , False , False ]
        ] )
    self.doStillLifeTest ( [
        [ False , False , False , False , False ] ,
        [ False , False , True , True , False ] ,
        [ False , True , False , True , False ] ,
        [ False , False , True , False , False ] ,
        [ False , False , False , False , False ]
        ] )
    self.doStillLifeTest ( [
        [ False , False , False , False ] ,
        [ False , False , True , False , False ] ,
        [ False , True , False , True , False ] ,
        [ False , False , True , True , False ] ,
        [ False , False , False , False , False ]
        ] )
    self.doStillLifeTest ( [
        [ False , False , False , False , False ] ,
        [ False , False , True , False , False ] ,
        [ False , True , False , True , False ] ,
        [ False , True , True , False , False ] ,
        [ False , False , False , False , False ]
        ] )
```

```
def test_blinker ( self ) :
    """Test that Blinker is a dynamic, stable shape alternating between the two states."""
    even = [
        [ False , False , False , False , False ] ,
        [ False , False , True , False , False ] ,
        [ False , False , True , False , False ] ,
        [ False , False , True , False , False ] ,
        [ False , False , False , False , False ]
        ]
    odd = [
        [ False , False , False , False , False ] ,
        [ False , False , False , False , False ] ,
        [ False , True , True , True , False ] ,
        [ False , False , False , False , False ] ,
        [ False , False , False , False , False ]
        ]
    game = life.Life ( 0 , 0 )
    game.grid = even
    game.calculateNextGeneration ()
    assert game.grid == odd
    game.calculateNextGeneration ()
    assert game.grid == even
    game.calculateNextGeneration ()
    assert game.grid == odd
    game.calculateNextGeneration ()
    assert game.grid == even

if __name__ == '__main__' :
    unittest.main ()
```

Obviously there are many more tests we could add. For now though this test will give us some confidence that the program is doing what we think it should. Executing the test we get Green:

```
| > python life_Test.py
.....
--------------------------------------------------------------------
Ran 5 tests in 0.009s

OK
| >
```

12.2   Stage 1: A Bit of a GUI Situation

We are now in a position to replace the textual output with a GUI. The core question is: how do we represent the two-dimensional grid of cells in the GUI? To decide this, we really need to have some conception of the 'game play', i.e. how the user is going to interact with the game. It is always right to start programming an interactive system by designing the user experience. So let us describe how we see the game being played:

1. Player starts the game, which comes up as a dead universe.

2. Player selects which cells should be made alive – probably by clicking with the mouse.

3. Player initiates the game, which causes the generations to be calculated and displayed.

This implies that the cells need to be clickable in some way. There are two basic ways this could be achieved:

1. Use a simple drawing area (a *canvas* in Tkinter terminology), draw the cells on the canvas, and work out how to convert mouse clicks on the canvas into cell identifications. This is a very flexible approach, but is hard work – everything from drawing to responding to the mouse has to be coded explicitly in our program.

2. Use buttons to represent the cells, using all the ready-made button clicking capability.

Clearly for a first prototype, using buttons seems like a very good idea – buttons already have all the infrastructure for processing mouse clicks, so they are very easy to work with. If we find working with buttons becomes awkward or worse, impossible, then we can change our mind and work out how to use a canvas.

We can add a few other items of functionality to the design before starting on the evolution of the code:

1. The player should be able to quit the game.

2. The player should be able to change the period between generations.

3. The player should be able to pause and restart the generation calculation.

Putting all this together, we get the idea that we can:

- Use an array of buttons to represent the cells.

- Have buttons for:

  - Quitting the system.
  - Running the calculation and display of the generations.
  - Pausing the system.

- Use a widget that allows changing of the time between generations. Generally there are a number of different sorts of widget for doing this, but Tkinter documentation seems to indicate that the use of a Scale widget is preferred. The Scale widget is a *slider* type widget: a slider is a thing we can move left and right, or up and down, depending on the orientation of the slider, and the position determines the value of a float or integer value. For an initial implementation let us assume that the period between generations will be in the range [1, 10] seconds. If we don't like the look of the result, we can always investigate alternatives.

We are leading towards something that looks as shown if Figure 12.1.

The code for this turns out to be a relatively straightforward evolution of the previous code. First we remove the printGrid and printSeparator methods – there is no point in having console printing functions that will never be used. We keep the method populateGridRandomly as that may still prove useful. Also the method _applyToEachCellOfGrid remains because it is still used in many places, and it makes programing the iteration over the cells of the grid so much easier. The constructor needs to be changed a lot, to create the GUI, and we have to add a trio of methods (pause, run, and setPeriod) because these are actions the user will need to be able to execute. The complete code is:

```python
import random
import Tkinter

class Life ( Tkinter.Frame ) :

    def __init__ ( self , x , y ) :
        Tkinter.Frame.__init__ ( self )
        self.master.title ( "The Game of Life" )
        self.grid = [ [ False for j in range ( y ) ] for i in range ( x ) ]
        universe = Tkinter.Frame ( self )
        def createButton ( i , j ) :
            bitmap = None
            if self.grid[i][j] : bitmap = 'gray75'
            gridEntry = Tkinter.Button ( universe , bitmap = bitmap )
            gridEntry.grid ( row = i , column = j )
        self._applyToEachCellOfGrid ( createButton )
        universe.pack ( side = 'top' )
        scale = Tkinter.Scale ( self , orient = Tkinter.HORIZONTAL , from_ = 1 , to = 10 ,
                               command = self.setPeriod )
        scale.pack ( side = 'top' )
        quit = Tkinter.Button ( self , text = 'Quit' , command = self.quit )
        quit.pack ( side = 'left' )
        run = Tkinter.Button ( self , text = 'Run' , command = self.run )
        run.pack ( side = 'right' )
        pause = Tkinter.Button ( self , text = 'Pause' , command = self.pause )
        pause.pack ( side = 'right' )
        self.pack ( )

    def _applyToEachCellOfGrid ( self , function ) :
        for i in range ( len ( self.grid ) ) :
            for j in range ( len ( self.grid[i] ) ) :
                function ( i , j )
```

A bitmap is an image (usually rectangular) that is displayed on the button. Here we use a predefined bitmap called gray75.

The third parameter to the Scale constructor is called from_ because **from** is a keyword and cannot be used as a parameter name.

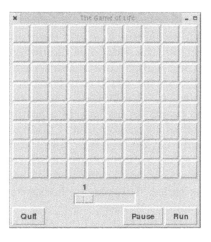

Figure 12.1

The Game of Life frame, Stage 1.

```
        def populateGridRandomly ( self , x ) :
            random.seed ()
            def setRandomly ( i , j ) :
                if random.random () < x : self.grid[i][j] = True
            self._applyToEachCellOfGrid ( setRandomly )

        def calculateNextGeneration ( self ) :
            newGrid = [ [ False for j in range ( len ( self.grid[i] ) ) ] for i in range ( len ( self.grid ) ) ]
            def calculateLiveness ( x , y ) :
                count = 0
                for i in range ( x - 1 , x + 2 ) :
                    if 0 <= i < len ( self.grid ) :
                        for j in range ( y - 1 , y + 2 ) :
                            if 0 <= j < len ( self.grid[i] ) :
                                if ( ( i != x ) or ( j != y ) ) and self.grid[i][j] : count += 1
                if self.grid[x][y] : return 2 <= count <= 3
                else : return count == 3
            def setNewGrid ( x , y ) :
                newGrid[x][y] = calculateLiveness ( x , y )
            self._applyToEachCellOfGrid ( setNewGrid )
            self.grid = newGrid

        def pause ( self ) :
            print 'pause called.'

        def run ( self ) :
            print 'run called'

        def setPeriod ( self , value ) :
            print 'setPeriod called with value' , value

if __name__ == '__main__' :
    game = Life ( 8 , 10 )
    game.mainloop ()
```

The complex part is clearly in the constructor (__init__). The first part of the constructor creates the universe of cells: all the buttons representing cells of the universe are packed into their own Frame widget. There are two reasons for this: it
gives a single widget that can be manipulated as the universe in the GUI, and it
provides a widget in which to create the array needed to pack the buttons that
represent cells. Having packed the universe into the main frame, the rest of the
constructor adds the widgets for the slider and the three buttons. Note that, via
the command parameter of the widget constructors, each of the widgets has an
association with a method from the Life class. These 'command' functions are
called *event handlers* or *callbacks*. A callback is a function that is executed when
a widget receives an action event. In the case of a button, when the user clicks
the button, its associated callback gets executed. Clicking the Quit button causes
the self.quit method to execute, clicking the Run button causes the self.run method
to execute and clicking the Pause button causes the self.pause method to execute.
The slider, i.e. the Scale widget, also has a callback that is called whenever the user
changes the position of the slider. This means that our program is informed of
every change to the slider made by the user.

At this stage of development, the Quit button works as a quit button, but the
other callbacks just print something on the terminal to show that the GUI widgets

are working as they should. This is a fairly standard way of progressing an application such as this: it enables us to try out the GUI to ensure that things behave as expected. We have created *stubs* to enable testing: we have the right methods but we do not put real content in. Using stubs supports our evolutionary approach to development. We don't try to implement everything all at once. Instead we create the GUI, test it as much as we can, and then implement the game behind the GUI.

If we execute the code and try clicking the Run button and the Pause button a couple of times each, and also try moving the slider up and down, we get:

```
|> python life.py
setPeriod called with value 1
run called
run called
pause called.
pause called.
setPeriod called with value 2
setPeriod called with value 4
setPeriod called with value 7
setPeriod called with value 8
setPeriod called with value 9
setPeriod called with value 10
setPeriod called with value 9
setPeriod called with value 8
setPeriod called with value 7
setPeriod called with value 5
setPeriod called with value 3
setPeriod called with value 2
setPeriod called with value 1
|>
```

So it seems that things are working as we expect.

What about unit tests? We can run the unit test we already have with this code. Trying this, we get a Green:

```
|> python life_Test.py
.....
-----------------------------------------------------------------------
Ran 5 tests in 6.379s

OK
|>
```

In changing the code from a console-based interface to a GUI, we have not caused any of the tests to fail. This should not be a surprise as we have not actually changed anything to do with the calculation of the generations, we have just changed the presentation: we have created a GUI, but we have not made the game playable. This provides a good lead into the next stage of development...

It might be wise to try the program as it is now and make sure you understand it before progressing to Stage 2.

12.3 Stage 2: Getting Very Animated

The previous version of the code clearly needs further development – the game does not do anything once started. Clearly, we need to amend the pause and run callbacks to actually do something. What is it they should do? Thinking about the run method, it should cause a new generation to be calculated every period, where the period is given by the number of seconds specified by the slider (which is a number in the range 1 to 10). We might, perhaps, think of having a while loop in the run method that continuously calculates the next generation, then waits the requisite time. However, this is not the right solution. Why? If the callback executes the calculation and waiting loop, how will the user interface continue working? If it is calculating the generations, the thread that drives the GUI is busy doing things other than managing the GUI, so the GUI will not be responsive to user actions. Not a good state of affairs.

Here we have a very important observation: to be responsive, GUIs must involve more than one thread. Callbacks must execute and complete quickly in order for a GUI to work correctly. If there is work to be done as part of a callback then a new thread should be created to do that work so that the callback may complete quickly. This means that the run callback should start a separate thread to execute the calculation of the generations. Consequently, the pause callback simply needs to cause the generation calculation thread to cease activity.

To create a new thread we need a class, we'll call it GenerationIncrementer, that is a subclass of threading.Thread. The run method of GenerationIncrementer loops performing the appropriate wait and call of calculateNextGeneration. The Life.run callback can then instantiate GenerationIncrementer and set the thread running, while the Life.pause method stops it. Looking at the threading.Thread class, there is no terminate method – there are very good reasons for this. We leave explaining the details to a specialist book on concurrency and parallelism, but the key point is that a thread must control its own termination so that it can ensure that any resources it has claimed can be freed – this is all part of avoiding *livelock* and *deadlock*. This means that we have to program the thread termination in the GenerationIncrementer class. The usual technique is to add a **terminate** method which alters the state variable that determines whether the run method terminates.

Putting all this together, we come up with the following class and new versions of the callback methods:

Asking a thread to terminate itself, rather than having a mechanism to forcibly terminate a thread from outside the thread, is an extremely important idiom to help avoid livelock and deadlock.

```
class GenerationIncrementer ( threading.Thread ) :
    def __init__ ( self , universe ) :
        threading.Thread.__init__ ( self )
        self.carryOn = True
        self.universe = universe
    def run ( self ) :
        while self.carryOn :
            time.sleep ( float ( self.universe.period ) )
            self.universe.calculateNextGeneration ( )
    def terminate ( self ) :
        self.carryOn = False

def pause ( self ) :
    if self.runThread != None :
        self.runThread.terminate ( )
        self.runThread = None

def run ( self ) :
    if self.runThread == None :
        self.runThread = self.GenerationIncrementer ( self )
        self.runThread.start ( )

def setPeriod ( self , value ) :
    self.period = value
```

Note that it is very important to look at the indentation correctly: __init__, run and terminate are methods of GenerationIncrementer, whereas pause, run, and setPeriod are not.

Of course we also have to add:

```
import threading
import time
```

at the beginning of the file because we are using the threading.Thread class and the time.sleep method – if we don't include these import statements our amended program will not compile.

Now all we are left with is trying to set the state of each cell, and deciding what the calculateNextGeneration actually has to do to change the state of the buttons.

Reading through various Tkinter manuals (there are many available online), we find that Tkinter supports updateable text on buttons. A button can be set up to be associated with a Tkinter.StringVar variable and the button will automatically display whatever the variable refers to. This sounds very useful indeed – all the hard work is done for us!

This situation, of a widget being associated with a variable is, called an *observer*: the button is an observer of the variable. This sounds like a fundamentally ideal thing for us: we create the array of buttons as observers of an array of StringVars and then we use the StringVars to hold the state of the game. So instead of using an array of Booleans to represent the state of the universe, we use an array of StringVars. This means we have to change the code we already have since we are changing the representation of the state of the game.

What do we change to achieve the goal? We add a couple of class variables to specify the strings that we will write to the button:

> No part of any program should be deemed sacrosanct, all code is open to change, as long as the change improves things and doesn't introduce bugs.

```
live = '#'
dead = ' '
```

and we change the constructor to incorporate that change to the grid, i.e. we use a StringVar instead of a Boolean:

```
def __init__ ( self , x , y ) :
    Tkinter.Frame.__init__ ( self )
    self.master.title ( "The Game of Life" )
    self.period = 1
    self.runThread = None
    self.grid = [ [ None for j in range ( y ) ] for i in range ( x ) ]
    universe = Tkinter.Frame ( self )
    def createButton ( i , j ) :
        def flipState ( ) :
            if self.grid[i][j].get ( ) == self.live : self.grid[i][j].set ( self.dead )
            else : self.grid[i][j].set ( self.live )
        gridVariable = Tkinter.StringVar ( )
        gridVariable.set ( self.dead )
        self.grid[i][j] = gridVariable
        gridEntry = Tkinter.Button ( universe , textvariable = gridVariable ,
                                     command = flipState )
        gridEntry.grid ( row = i , column = j )
    self._applyToEachCellOfGrid ( createButton )
    universe.pack ( side = 'top' )
    scale = Tkinter.Scale ( self , orient = Tkinter.HORIZONTAL , from_ = 1 , to = 10 ,
                            command = self.setPeriod )
    scale.pack ( side = 'top' )
    quit = Tkinter.Button ( self , text = 'Quit' , command = self.quit )
    quit.pack ( side = 'left' )
    run = Tkinter.Button ( self , text = 'Run' , command = self.run )
```

> We have to use the get method to get the value of, and the set method to set the value of, any StringVar variable.

```
run.pack ( side = 'right' )
pause = Tkinter.Button ( self , text = 'Pause' , command = self.pause )
pause.pack ( side = 'right' )
pause = Tkinter.Button ( self , text = 'Fill Randomly' ,
                                    command = self.populateGridRandomly )
pause.pack ( side = 'right' )
self.pack ()
```

and there are some consequential changes to calculateNextGeneration:

```
def calculateNextGeneration ( self ) :
    newGrid = [ [ False for j in range ( len ( self.grid[i] ) ) ] for i in range ( len ( self.grid ) ) ]
    def calculateLiveness ( x , y ) :
        count = 0
        for i in range ( x - 1 , x + 2 ) :
            if 0 <= i < len ( self.grid ) :
                for j in range ( y - 1 , y + 2 ) :
                    if 0 <= j < len ( self.grid[i] ) :
                        if ( ( i != x ) or ( j != y ) ) and self.grid[i][j].get () == self.live :
                            count += 1
        if self.grid[x][y].get () == self.live : return 2 <= count <= 3
        else : return count == 3
    def setNewGrid ( x , y ) :
        newGrid[x][y] = calculateLiveness ( x , y )
    self._applyToEachCellOfGrid ( setNewGrid )
    def setGrid ( x , y ) :
        if newGrid[x][y] : self.grid[x][y].set ( self.live )
        else : self.grid[x][y].set ( self.dead )
    self._applyToEachCellOfGrid ( setGrid )
```

We have changed the way we update the grid. Instead of replacing the whole array of arrays, we iterate over newGrid and update the values of the corresponding observed variables in self.grid.

With these changes in place we have an animated game. When the game is started, all the cells are 'dead' as shown in Figure 12.2. By clicking on a cell, we change its state – a dead cell comes to life, a live cell dies. Or if we want we can use the 'random fill' button (which has the method self.populateGridRandomly as its callback) to randomly bring to life some of the cells leaving the others dead. When we are satisfied with the initial condition, we can set the animation running and the second thread does all the hard work. Figure 12.3 shows an example filled state. If we pause the game, we can change the state of the universe arbitrarily and then set things running again.

We do have a unit test. It is a little different to the previous one due to the change of representation of the universe:

Figure 12.2

The Game of Life starting state in Stage 2.

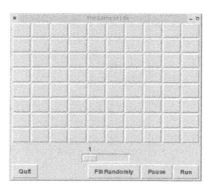

```
import unittest
import life

class Life_Test ( unittest.TestCase ) :
    """Test the implementation of the Game of Life."""

    def initializeGame ( self , grid ) :
        """Create a Game of Life using the parameter as information on which cells to set to live."""
        game = life.Life ( len ( grid[0]) , len ( grid ) )
        for i in range ( len ( grid ) ) :
            for j in range ( len ( grid[0] ) ) :
                if grid[j][i] : game.grid[j][i].set ( game.live )
        return game

    def assertEqual ( self , game , grid ) :
        """Assert all that is needed to check that the cell's state is as the parameter specifies."""
        assert len ( game.grid ) == len ( grid )
        assert len ( game.grid[0] ) == len ( grid[0] )
        for i in range ( len ( grid ) ) :
            for j in range ( len ( grid[0] ) ) :
                state = game.grid[j][i].get ()
                if grid[j][i] : assert state == game.live
                else : assert state == game.dead

    def test_newGame ( self ) :
        game = life.Life ( 10 , 8 )
        assert len ( game.grid ) == 10
        assert len ( game.grid[0] ) == 8
        for i in range ( len ( game.grid ) ) :
            assert len ( game.grid[i] ) == len ( game.grid[i] )
            for j in range ( len ( game.grid[i] ) ) :
                assert game.grid[i][j].get () == game.dead

    def doStillLifeTest ( self , datum ) :
        """Run a test for a static, stable shape."""
        game = self.initializeGame ( datum )
        game.calculateNextGeneration ()
        self.assertEqual ( game , datum )
        game.calculateNextGeneration ()
        self.assertEqual ( game , datum )
```

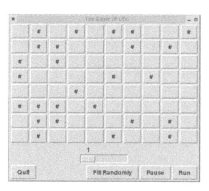

Figure 12.3

The Game of Life
a state in Stage 2.

```python
    def test_empty ( self ) :
        """Ensure that an empty world stays empty."""
        self.doStillLifeTest ( [ [ False for j in range ( 10 ) ] for i in range ( 10 ) ] )

    def test_block ( self ) :
        """Test that Block is a static, stable shape."""
        self.doStillLifeTest ( [
            [ False , False , False , False ] ,
            [ False , True , True , False ] ,
            [ False , True , True , False ] ,
            [ False , False , False , False ]
            ] )

    def test_boat ( self ) :
        """Test that Boat is a static stable shape."""
        self.doStillLifeTest ( [
            [ False , False , False , False , False ] ,
            [ False , True , True , False , False ] ,
            [ False , True , False , True , False ] ,
            [ False , False , True , False , False ] ,
            [ False , False , False , False , False ]
            ] )
        self.doStillLifeTest ( [
            [ False , False , False , False , False ] ,
            [ False , False , True , True , False ] ,
            [ False , True , False , True , False ] ,
            [ False , False , True , False , False ] ,
            [ False , False , False , False , False ]
            ] )
        self.doStillLifeTest ( [
            [ False , False , False , False , False ] ,
            [ False , False , True , False , False ] ,
            [ False , True , False , True , False ] ,
            [ False , False , True , True , False ] ,
            [ False , False , False , False , False ]
            ] )
        self.doStillLifeTest ( [
            [ False , False , False , False , False ] ,
            [ False , False , True , False , False ] ,
            [ False , True , False , True , False ] ,
            [ False , True , True , False , False ] ,
            [ False , False , False , False , False ]
            ] )

    def test_blinker ( self ) :
        """Test that Blinker is a dynamic stable shape alternating between the two states."""
        even = [
            [ False , False , False , False , False ] ,
            [ False , False , True , False , False ] ,
            [ False , False , True , False , False ] ,
            [ False , False , True , False , False ] ,
            [ False , False , False , False , False ]
            ]
        odd = [
            [ False , False , False , False , False ] ,
```

```
                [ False , False , False , False , False ] ,
                [ False , True , True , True , False ] ,
                [ False , False , False , False , False ] ,
                [ False , False , False , False , False ]
                ]
        game = self.initializeGame ( even )
        game.calculateNextGeneration ( )
        self.assertEqual ( game , odd )
        game.calculateNextGeneration ( )
        self.assertEqual ( game , even )
        game.calculateNextGeneration ( )
        self.assertEqual ( game , odd )
        game.calculateNextGeneration ( )
        self.assertEqual ( game , even )

if __name__ == '__main__' :
    unittest.main ( )
```

We choose to continue to specify the input states and expected results as two-dimensional arrays of Booleans, but we have to deal with the fact that this is not actually the data structure used in the representation of the game universe. The new methods initializeGame and assertEqual have been introduced to make the change easy to handle.

12.4   Stage 3: Avoiding the RuntimeError

If you set the game running and click the quit button before clicking the pause button, you get the output:

```
Exception in thread Thread-1:
Traceback (most recent call last):
  File "threading.py", line 442, in __bootstrap
    self.run()
  File "life.py", line 79, in run
    self.universe.calculateNextGeneration ( )
  File "life.py", line 65, in calculateNextGeneration
    self._applyToEachCellOfGrid ( setNewGrid )
  File "life.py", line 44, in _applyToEachCellOfGrid
    function ( i , j )
  File "life.py", line 64, in setNewGrid
    newGrid[x][y] = calculateLiveness ( x , y )
  File "life.py", line 60, in calculateLiveness
    if ( ( i != x ) or ( j != y ) ) and self.grid[i][j].get ( ) == self.live : count += 1
  File "lib-tk/Tkinter.py", line 235, in get
    value = self._tk.globalgetvar(self._name)
RuntimeError: main thread is not in main loop
```

Given that the program is terminating, errors like this might seem trivial and not to be worried about, but that would be a mistake. This raising of RuntimeError really needs to be investigated and solved, just in case it indicates a more important problem with either our program or our understanding of the Python system.

The message seems to indicate that there is a problem with the threads. So what happens when the Quit button is pressed? The method self.quit is called – this method is inherited from the Thread class. Clearly the self.quit method is being called before we have properly cleared up the state. In particular, we have a problem when the generation calculating thread is still running. We failed to terminate it before quiting. This is easily fixed. First we change the callback function in the button creation:

```
quit = Tkinter.Button ( self , text = 'Quit' , command = self.terminate )
```

Then we add the code for the callback:

```
def terminate ( self ) :
    if self.runThread != None :
        self.runThread.terminate ( )
        self.runThread.join ( )
    self.quit ( )
```

What we are doing here is ensuring that, if the generation calculating thread is running, that it gets terminated before we make the call to self.quit. The terminate method is called on the thread, then the join method is called. This causes the user interface thread to wait for the generation calculating thread to terminate – we say that the user interface thread *blocks* on termination of the generation calculating thread. Then and only then is the quit method called. This should guarantee that the application is in the right state to terminate gracefully instead of raising a RuntimeError.

Bizarrely though, it seems that doing this makes matters worse. If we now try to press the Quit button whilst the generation calculating thread is running, the whole application just 'freezes' and nothing happens – you have to use the operating system program control features to forcibly terminate the program. This is deadlock.

Where is the problem? Clearly the generation calculating thread is not terminating as it should, so the problem must be in the GenerationIncrementer.run method. This means that the loop is not terminating. By inserting print methods between each statement in the loop:

Putting print statements between each statement in the block means that, when the program is executed, we are sure which statements are executed, and hence can find when the deadlock happens.

```
def run ( self ) :
    while self.carryOn :
        print 'A'
        time.sleep ( float ( self.universe.period ) )
        print 'B'
        self.universe.calculateNextGeneration ( )
        print 'C'
```

we find that when the Quit button is pressed everything freezes after a call to calculateNextGeneration – we see output like:

```
A
B
C
A
B
```

So we know the calculateNextGeneration was called but did not return. So we put some print statements in that function, on the suspicion that there is a problem with the get method call – nothing else seems at all problematic. The rest of the function used to work fine and the get method associated with the StringVar variables is new. So we have the function:

```
def calculateNextGeneration ( self ) :
    print 'calculateNextGeneration -- A'
    newGrid = [ [ False for j in range ( len ( self.grid[i] ) ) ] for i in range ( len ( self.grid ) ) ]
    print 'calculateNextGeneration -- B'
    def calculateLiveness ( x , y ) :
        count = 0
        for i in range ( x - 1 , x + 2 ) :
            if 0 <= i < len ( self.grid ) :
                for j in range ( y - 1 , y + 2 ) :
                    if 0 <= j < len ( self.grid[i] ) :
                        print 'calculateLiveness -- A'
                        if ( ( i != x ) or ( j != y ) ) and self.grid[i][j].get ( ) == self.live :
                            count += 1
                        print 'calculateLiveness -- B'
        if self.grid[x][y].get ( ) == self.live : return 2 <= count <= 3
        else : return count == 3
    print 'calculateNextGeneration -- C'
    def setNewGrid ( x , y ) :
        newGrid[x][y] = calculateLiveness ( x , y )
    self._applyToEachCellOfGrid ( setNewGrid )
    print 'calculateNextGeneration -- D'
    def setGrid ( x , y ) :
        if newGrid[x][y] : self.grid[x][y].set ( self.live )
        else : self.grid[x][y].set ( self.dead )
    self._applyToEachCellOfGrid ( setGrid )
    print 'calculateNextGeneration -- E'
```

We place print statements in places that tell us useful things about which statements get executed. We create a hypothesis about our program, then place print statements and execute the program to test the hypothesis. In this case the hypothesis is that the call of the get method is causing the deadlock.

Now we get the output:

```
A
B
calculateNextGeneration -- A
calculateNextGeneration -- B
calculateNextGeneration -- C
calculateLiveness -- A
calculateLiveness -- B
calculateLiveness -- A
```

Remember to remove the print statements afterwards!

This appears to confirm our hypothesis that there is an issue with the get method call. It seems that once the user interface thread has called the join method, any call to the get method on a StringVar causes deadlock. If you delve into the details of what Tkinter does, this makes sense, but that level of detail is not for this book. A solution to the problem is very easy – don't call the get after the thread is supposed to have terminated. How do we do this? Not in the calculateNextGeneration function, it is fine (once we have removed all the print statements anyway). The problem is that we call the calculateNextGeneration function when we shouldn't – in this case, we are executing calculateNextGeneration even when self.carryOn is **False** because the thread was asleep when the variable changed value. This problem is solved by a relatively trivial change to the GenerationIncrementer.run method:

```
def run ( self ) :
    while self.carryOn :
        time.sleep ( float ( self.universe.period ) )
        if self.carryOn :
            self.universe.calculateNextGeneration ( )
```

Although execution of the loop is already controlled by the carryOn variable, we check it explicitly after the sleep and before we call calculateNextGeneration, as well as after the generation is calculated. Although this might seem slightly bizarre, it is a classic idiom in user interface programming: check the state carefully after any waiting period.

It seems appropriate to show the whole program as it is now, since it has changed dramatically since we last showed the whole program:

```python
import random
import Tkinter
import threading
import time

class Life ( Tkinter.Frame ) :

    live = '#'
    dead = ' '

    def __init__ ( self , x , y ) :
        Tkinter.Frame.__init__ ( self )
        self.master.title ( "The Game of Life" )
        self.period = 1
        self.runThread = None
        self.grid = [ [ None for j in range ( y ) ] for i in range ( x ) ]
        universe = Tkinter.Frame ( self )
        def createButton ( i , j ) :
            def flipState ( ) :
                if self.grid[i][j].get ( ) == self.live : self.grid[i][j].set ( self.dead )
                else : self.grid[i][j].set ( self.live )
            gridVariable = Tkinter.StringVar ( )
            gridVariable.set ( self.dead )
            self.grid[i][j] = gridVariable
            gridEntry = Tkinter.Button ( universe , textvariable = gridVariable ,
                                         command = flipState )
            gridEntry.grid ( row = i , column = j )
        self._applyToEachCellOfGrid ( createButton )
        universe.pack ( side = 'top' )
        scale = Tkinter.Scale ( self , orient = Tkinter.HORIZONTAL , from_ = 1 , to = 10 ,
                                command = self.setPeriod )
        scale.pack ( side = 'top' )
        quit = Tkinter.Button ( self , text = 'Quit' , command = self.terminate )
        quit.pack ( side = 'left' )
        run = Tkinter.Button ( self , text = 'Run' , command = self.run )
        run.pack ( side = 'right' )
        pause = Tkinter.Button ( self , text = 'Pause' , command = self.pause )
        pause.pack ( side = 'right' )
        pause = Tkinter.Button ( self , text = 'Fill Randomly' ,
                                 command = self.populateGridRandomly )
        pause.pack ( side = 'right' )
        self.pack ( )

    def _applyToEachCellOfGrid ( self , function ) :
        for i in range ( len ( self.grid ) ) :
            for j in range ( len ( self.grid[i] ) ) :
                function ( i , j )
```

```python
    def populateGridRandomly ( self ) :
        random.seed ()
        def setRandomly ( i , j ) :
            if random.random () < 0.4 : self.grid[i][j].set ( self.live )
        self._applyToEachCellOfGrid ( setRandomly )

    def calculateNextGeneration ( self ) :
        newGrid = [ [ False for j in range ( len ( self.grid[i] ) ) ] for i in range ( len ( self.grid ) ) ]
        def calculateLiveness ( x , y ) :
            count = 0
            for i in range ( x - 1 , x + 2 ) :
                if 0 <= i < len ( self.grid ) :
                    for j in range ( y - 1 , y + 2 ) :
                        if 0 <= j < len ( self.grid[i] ) :
                            if ( ( i != x ) or ( j != y ) ) and self.grid[i][j].get () == self.live :
                                count += 1
            if self.grid[x][y].get () == self.live : return 2 <= count <= 3
            else : return count == 3
        def setNewGrid ( x , y ) :
            newGrid[x][y] = calculateLiveness ( x , y )
        self._applyToEachCellOfGrid ( setNewGrid )
        def setGrid ( x , y ) :
            if newGrid[x][y] : self.grid[x][y].set ( self.live )
            else : self.grid[x][y].set ( self.dead )
        self._applyToEachCellOfGrid ( setGrid )

class GenerationIncrementer ( threading.Thread ) :
    def __init__ ( self , universe ) :
        threading.Thread.__init__ ( self )
        self.carryOn = True
        self.universe = universe
    def run ( self ) :
        while self.carryOn :
            time.sleep ( float ( self.universe.period ) )
            if self.carryOn :
                self.universe.calculateNextGeneration ()
    def terminate ( self ) :
        self.carryOn = False

def pause ( self ) :
    if self.runThread != None :
        self.runThread.terminate ()
        self.runThread = None

def run ( self ) :
    if self.runThread == None :
        self.runThread = self.GenerationIncrementer ( self )
        self.runThread.start ()

def setPeriod ( self , value ) :
    self.period = value

def terminate ( self ) :
    if self.runThread != None :
        self.runThread.terminate ()
        self.runThread.join ()
    self.quit ()
```

```
if __name__ == '__main__' :
    game = Life ( 8 , 10 )
    game.mainloop ( )
```

Here we have a program that behaves as desired and which terminates gracefully in all situations. By carefully checking the state at all appropriate moments, we avoid deadlock situations. But how do we know it behaves as expected? We run our unit tests:

```
|> python life_Test.py
.....
-----------------------------------------------------------------
Ran 5 tests in 0.308s

OK
|> ||
```

We have a Green, so we haven't broken anything. However, we have something of a problem...

12.5   Testing, Testing

The unit tests that we have ensure that the code that calculates the generations behaves as it should. However this is only part of the program: we have lots of code that implements the user interface. It seems sensible to ask the question: "Is there a way of testing the user interface?" The answer is "Yes, but..."

We have so far been using PyUnit (module name unittest) for our testing, and this is well suited to testing code that does not implement a user interface. It does not, however, have facilities for testing user interfaces. A quick search of the Web using a search engine (2007-10-06) gives us information about:

guitest a GUI testing framework for testing PyGTK applications.

PyGUIUnitTest a GUI testing framework for testing PyQt applications.

wxStubmaker a GUI testing framework for testing wxPython applications.

Dogtail a GUI testing framework written in Python for testing GUI applications running under the Gnome windowing system.

No mention of Tkinter. It seems there is no GUI testing framework for Tkinter applications generally, though we can try Dogtail if we are running with Gnome. So it seems that we must test by exhaustive manual testing, i.e. we have to play the game and try all the user interface features manually.

12.6   Stage 4: Separating the Concerns

Now that we have a program that appears to work, it is appropriate to review what we have achieved and ask ourselves the questions: "Is the structure and presentation of the program OK?" and "Can I improve the code?". This stage in the development of this program is exactly the right time to ask these questions, before we do any further work.

12.6.1   Reviewing the Code

Looking at the code, the biggest thing that springs to mind is that everything is mixed in together: the code dealing with the GUI is mixed in with the code managing the game state and game play. Many will argue that this program is small enough for this mixing not to be an issue, but the question arises: "What happens when the program grows as new functionality or features are added?" With the current structure of the code the answer is almost certainly: "Everything becomes incomprehensible and unmaintainable." We need to impose a better structure on the code so that we have a modularity that makes the code easier to work with. In particular, it is better to restructure code early on to enhance testability and avoid mess, even if it seems a little like effort for no gain just now. The benefit will come later.

12.6.2   Refactoring for the Future

How can we separate the GUI and non-GUI parts of the code? The obvious direction appears to be to separate code into two distinct classes, one dedicated to GUI issues and one dealing with the game play – separation of concerns in action!

So we introduce a class LifeState to represent the state of the game and put all state-related code into this class. The Life class is then solely responsible for the GUI. Imposing this separation, we get:

```python
import random
import Tkinter
import threading
import time

class LifeState :

    live = '#'
    dead = ' '

    def __init__ ( self , x , y ) :
        self.period = 1
        self.runThread = None
        self.grid = [ [ Tkinter.StringVar ( ) for j in range ( y ) ] for i in range ( x ) ]
        def initialize ( i , j ) :
            self.grid[i][j].set ( self.dead )
        self._applyToEachCellOfGrid ( initialize )

    def _applyToEachCellOfGrid ( self , function ) :
        for i in range ( len ( self.grid ) ) :
            for j in range ( len ( self.grid[i] ) ) :
                function ( i , j )

    def populateGridRandomly ( self ) :
        random.seed ( )
        def setRandomly ( i , j ) :
            if random.random ( ) < 0.4 : self.grid[i][j].set ( self.live )
        self._applyToEachCellOfGrid ( setRandomly )

    def calculateNextGeneration ( self ) :
        newGrid = [ [ False for j in range ( len ( self.grid[i] ) ) ] for i in range ( len ( self.grid ) ) ]
```

```python
        def calculateLiveness ( x , y ) :
            count = 0
            for i in range ( x - 1 , x + 2 ) :
                if 0 <= i < len ( self.grid ) :
                    for j in range ( y - 1 , y + 2 ) :
                        if 0 <= j < len ( self.grid[i] ) :
                            if ( ( i != x ) or ( j != y ) ) and self.grid[i][j].get ( ) == self.live :
                                count += 1
            if self.grid[x][y].get ( ) == self.live : return 2 <= count <= 3
            else : return count == 3
        def setNewGrid ( x , y ) :
            newGrid[x][y] = calculateLiveness ( x , y )
        self._applyToEachCellOfGrid ( setNewGrid )
        def setGrid ( x , y ) :
            if newGrid[x][y] : self.grid[x][y].set ( self.live )
            else : self.grid[x][y].set ( self.dead )
        self._applyToEachCellOfGrid ( setGrid )


    class GenerationIncrementer ( threading.Thread ) :
        def __init__ ( self , universe ) :
            threading.Thread.__init__ ( self )
            self.carryOn = True
            self.universe = universe
        def run ( self ) :
            while self.carryOn :
                time.sleep ( float ( self.universe.period ) )
                if self.carryOn :
                    self.universe.calculateNextGeneration ( )
        def terminate ( self ) :
            self.carryOn = False


    def pause ( self ) :
        if self.runThread != None :
            self.runThread.terminate ( )
            self.runThread = None


    def run ( self ) :
        if self.runThread == None :
            self.runThread = self.GenerationIncrementer ( self )
            self.runThread.start ( )


    def setPeriod ( self , value ) :
        self.period = value


    def terminate ( self ) :
        if self.runThread != None :
            self.runThread.terminate ( )
            self.runThread.join ( )


class Life ( Tkinter.Frame ) :

    def __init__ ( self , x , y ) :
        Tkinter.Frame.__init__ ( self )
        self.master.title ( "The Game of Life" )
        self.state = LifeState ( x , y )
```

```
                universe = Tkinter.Frame ( self )
                def createButton ( i , j ) :
                    def flipState ( ) :
                        if self.state.grid[i][j].get ( ) == self.state.live :
                            self.state.grid[i][j].set ( self.state.dead )
                        else :
                            self.state.grid[i][j].set ( self.state.live )
                    gridEntry = Tkinter.Button ( universe , textvariable = self.state.grid[i][j] ,
                                                 command = flipState )
                    gridEntry.grid ( row = i , column = j )
                self.state._applyToEachCellOfGrid ( createButton )
                universe.pack ( side = 'top' )
                scale = Tkinter.Scale ( self , orient = Tkinter.HORIZONTAL , from_ = 1 , to = 10 ,
                                        command = self.state.setPeriod )
                scale.pack ( side = 'top' )
                quit = Tkinter.Button ( self , text = 'Quit' , command = self.terminate )
                quit.pack ( side = 'left' )
                run = Tkinter.Button ( self , text = 'Run' , command = self.state.run )
                run.pack ( side = 'right' )
                pause = Tkinter.Button ( self , text = 'Pause' , command = self.state.pause )
                pause.pack ( side = 'right' )
                pause = Tkinter.Button ( self , text = 'Fill Randomly' ,
                                         command = self.state.populateGridRandomly )
                pause.pack ( side = 'right' )
                self.pack ( )

        def terminate ( self ) :
            self.state.terminate ( )
            self.quit ( )


    if __name__ == '__main__' :
        game = Life ( 8 , 10 )
        game.mainloop ( )
```

Clearly we have to introduce an extra variable in the Life class (self.state) to connect to the instance of LifeState that holds the state of the universe. The Life class is responsible only for representing the current state and sending events to the LifeState instance for processing.

Why does this help? The separation means we don't have to look at LifeState if we are changing the GUI and we don't have to look at Life if we are working with the state. The separation of concerns is focused on modularizing the code and so helping to make it comprehensible and easy to maintain. Furthermore, it makes testing easier. It is now clear that we can test the LifeState class without worrying about any aspect of the GUI. The separation of concerns also enhances testability.

Ironically, the test code we have been using to date is exactly the code we need to be the unit test for LifeState – except that a few trivial changes are needed to deal with the change of class name (we just change life.Life to life.LifeState) and the fact that we have to instantiate Tkinter.Tk so there is a context in which the StringVar can be instantiated. Rather than show the whole program, we use the 'diff' tool to show the difference between the earlier code and the code we need for this stage:

```
|> diff Stage_3/life_Test.py Stage_4/lifeState_Test.py
0a1
> import Tkinter
4,5c5,11
< class Life_Test ( unittest.TestCase ) :
```

```
<    """Test the implementation of the Game of Life."""
---
> class LifeState_Test ( unittest.TestCase ) :
>     """Test the implementation of the state of the Game of Life."""
>
>     # There has to be a Tkinter root window for the StringVar variables to be instantiable.
>     # Create one as a class variable so that only one is created and it is created early.
>
>     tk = Tkinter.Tk ( )
8,9c14,15
<     """Create a Game of Life using the parameter as information on which cells to set to live."""
<     game = life.Life ( len ( grid[0]) , len ( grid ) )
---
>     """Create a Game of Life state using the parameter as information on which cells to set to live."""
>     game = life.LifeState ( len ( grid[0]) , len ( grid ) )
26c32
<     game = life.Life ( 10 , 8 )
---
>     game = life.LifeState ( 10 , 8 )
|>
```

When the test is executed we get a Green:

```
|> python lifeState_Test.py
......
----------------------------------------------------------------------
Ran 5 tests in 0.045s

OK
|>
```

We really ought to put more test methods in to test more cases and thus increase our confidence that the code does what it is supposed to. It is now clear that we are only testing the state aspects of the program, we are not testing the GUI aspects.

Chapter Summary

In this chapter we have found that:

- This version of the Game of Life is an example of a Tkinter GUI.
- Developing a GUI application is an iterative process.
- A GUI is structure of widgets.
- GUI widgets are instances created by repeatedly calling a function.
- Event handlers (aka callbacks) are associated with widgets to provide actions for GUIs.
- We need to use multi-threaded programming when working with GUIs.
- Both threading and timing are important issues in an interactive GUI-based program.
- Aspects of this version of the Game of Life can be tested with unit testing techniques and frameworks such as PyUnit.
- Bug fixing is an integral part of iterative code development.

Self-Review Questions

Self-review 12.1 Why did we create a class for this application rather than just leave it as a set of functions in a module? Is this actually needed?

Self-review 12.2 What do the terms *event, event handler* and *event loop* mean.

Self-review 12.3 Which are the event handler/callback methods in the Life class?

Self-review 12.4 Why have we used multiple threads in this program?

Self-review 12.5 What is the reason for changing from using a list of list of Booleans as the representation of the state of the universe?

Self-review 12.6 Why have buttons been used to present the cells of the game universe?

Self-review 12.7 What have the test programs tested?

Self-review 12.8 What have the test programs not tested?

Self-review 12.9 What was the run-time error that had to be avoided in Section 12.4? Why did it need to be avoided?

Self-review 12.10 Why is 'separation of concerns' a good approach to program design?

Self-review 12.11 The Game of Life has many stable patterns. In the text, we mentioned Block, Boat and Blinker. Other stable shapes are *Toad, Glider* and *Lightweight Spaceship* (*LWSS*). What are these shapes and why are they stable?

> *Hint: The answer to the question isn't in this book. You will need to research another sources.*

Self-review 12.12 What are *observer variables* and how are they used in GUIs?

Self-review 12.13 What is the Tkinter 'scale' widget used for?

Self-review 12.14 What does the join method (in the Thread class) do?

Self-review 12.15 We've said that the universe which starts off with no life is stable. What would happen if we started the game with every cell being live?

Programming Exercises

Exercise 12.1 Extend the test program for the Game of Life code to include *Toad, Glider* and *LWSS* as part of the test.

Exercise 12.2 Extend the test program for the Game of Life code to include *Gosper's Gliding Gun* as part of the test.

Exercise 12.3 Amend the Game of Life program to use an icon rather than # as the displayed symbol.

Exercise 12.4 HighLife is a variation on Conway's Game of Life. Instead of the 23/3 rule (a live cell stays alive only if it has two or three neighbors otherwise it dies, and dead cell is made live if it has exactly three live neighbors), HighLife uses the 23/36 rule (a live cell stays alive only if it has two or three neighbors otherwise it dies, and dead cells become alive if they have either three or six live neighbors). Create a version of the Game of Life program that uses the HighLife rules.

Exercise 12.5 As presented in this chapter, the user can use the Game of Life GUI to populate the universe randomly. Add a list box which gives the user options to try out the Block, Boat and Blinker societies.

Hint: Storing these societies as lists in the program should make things straightforward.

Exercise 12.6 In the exercise above, you allowed the user to try out some pre-selected societies. Storing the societies as data structures in the code makes it difficult to extend the range of possibilities. For this exercise extend the program so that the societies are stored in files that are read in when the program starts. The list box of possible societies for the user to try should be calculated from the files that were read in and not predefined.

Exercise 12.7 Add the functionality to the Game of Life program of allowing users to store the *current* game state in a file, and to reload it when they next start the program.

Exercise 12.8 The Game of Life program in this chapter is an example of a program which can have multiple user interfaces – in this case, one on the console and a GUI. This exercise is to write a program that implement the Caesar Cipher from Section 4.6.2 (page 131) but which has multiple user interfaces. The program should have two interfaces to the cipher – one using the console and one which is a GUI.

Hint: Make sure that the GUI classes, the classes to control console interaction and the actual cipher are all separate. This will mean that you should be able to swap between the two interfaces and add new ones without changing the Caesar Cipher.

Challenges

Challenge 12.1 Investigate the technique of using mock objects to help test the user interface.

Challenge 12.2 Create a class called LifeCell that removes the need for dealing directly with StringVars and button construction (for the grid, anyway). That is, something that can be used to set state (cella.makeAlive, or cella.setState(**True**), perhaps) and expose an associated button for adding to the GUI (cella.getButton might be appropriate).

Challenge 12.3 Exercise 12.4 introduces the HighLife rules and a simple notation for rules for this kind of cellular automata. The standard Game of Life is described in this notation as 23/3, whilst HighLife is described as 23/36. Modify the program so that the rule is set by the user by entering two sequences of numbers into two text boxes.

When your new version of the game is working, enter the rule in the image above. Try it on a single live cell.

Challenge 12.4 Sudoku is a popular single-player puzzle game played on a 9×9 grid (see the example below). The object of the game is to fill every square with a digit from 1–9 such that each row and column contains exactly one instance of each digit, as does every 3×3 square.

5	3			7				
6			1	9	5			
	9	8					6	
8				6				3
4			8		3			1
7				2				6
	6					2	8	
			4	1	9			5
				8			7	9

For this challenge you should implement a stand-alone GUI-based Sudoku. Sudoku puzzles are quite hard to generate so it might be sensible to download a set of puzzles and solutions from a free online source rather than making your own in the first instance. Doing random creation of puzzles is a natural evolution of the program. From a usability point of view being able to pause a game and restart it later part solved is a good idea so storing puzzles and solutions in a sensible format that you can easily parse is an important part of the solution.

Wikipedia has a good article on Sudoku at http://en.wikipedia.org/Sudoku.

PyGames

One of the really nice things about the Python programming language is that many powerful libraries have been written for it. In this chapter we'll be looking at one of the most entertaining ones, PyGame, which we think will give you a good idea of the scope of Python's capabilities. Hopefully, it will encourage you to go out and find more libraries to use. And possibly write a few games!

PyGame is for creating games of all sorts using Python. We think there is enough in the two examples we present to give you a strong introduction to what this library can do, and also give you some idea of how professional programmers might use it.

We recommend that you read the documentation for the PyGame library in conjunction with this chapter. We don't have the space here to cover all the details of PyGame and it is not the right thing to do since it is important to learn to read and use documentation.

13.1 A Quick Introduction to PyGame

Perhaps the most important thing to say about PyGame is that its website is at:

http://www.pygame.org

This is an extensive resource and well worth browsing.

What are the important things we need to know before we can look at how to program using PyGame? First and foremost, PyGame programs are interactive programs. So like GUIs, they are multi-threaded and event driven. A program that uses PyGame sets up all its data and then passes control to the event management system that is part of PyGame. Our program is the code that handles the events that we listen for.

Peter Shinners is the original author of PyGame.

The second most important thing is to note that PyGame is actually a lightweight wrapper around Simple Directmedia Layer (SDL). To quote from the SDL website (http://www.libsdl.org/):

> Simple Directmedia Layer is a cross-platform multimedia library designed to provide low level access to audio, keyboard, mouse, joystick, 3D hardware via OpenGL, and 2D video framebuffer. It is used by MPEG playback software, emulators, and many popular games, including the award winning Linux port of "Civilization: Call To Power."

Cross-platform means that the SDL library works on a large number of platforms. All the major workstation and laptop operating systems are included: Linux, Unix, Solaris, Mac OS X, and Windows. SDL is also available on an increasing number of other platforms such as mobile phones. So an SDL program originally written on a Linux machine should run on a Windows, Mac OS X machine or supported mobile phone without any changes to the source code.

The SDL library is written in C. Python has mechanisms for making use of C and C++ libraries, but programming at this level requires knowing all the low-level details and writing Python code that works in a C/C++ style. The PyGame library provides an adapter to the SDL using these mechanisms that allows games programmers to work entirely in Python using Python idioms rather than having to deal with all the Python↔C issues: PyGame provides a Pythonic way of working with SDL.

There are some concepts that are core to the way SDL and hence PyGame work:

Surface a representation of an image.

Sprite a representation of a game object.

Rect a representation of a rectangular region of an image.

Event loop the code block that waits for and then processes events.

The best way of understanding these concepts is to see them being used in context...

13.2 Bouncing A Ball Around – With Sound

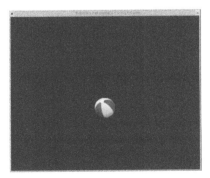

A ball bouncing around a screen seems to have become the traditional first example in any presentation on animation programming. Since it is actually a very good first introduction to programming with PyGame, we will not buck the trend. The best way of introducing PyGame and its features is to present a whole program and then 'deconstruct' it:

```
import pygame
import sys

if __name__ == '__main__':
    ballImage = 'BouncingBall/beachball.png'
    bounceSound = 'BouncingBall/bong.wav'
    caption = 'Bouncing ball animation using PyGame.'
    width , height = 600 , 500
    backgroundColor = 0 , 0 , 0
    velocity = [ 1.0 , 1.0 ]
    pygame.init ()
    frame = pygame.display.set_mode ( ( width , height ) )
    pygame.display.set_caption ( caption )
    ball = pygame.image.load ( ballImage ).convert ()
    ballBoundary = ball.get_rect ()
    sound = pygame.mixer.Sound ( bounceSound )
    while True:
        for event in pygame.event.get () :
            if event.type == pygame.QUIT : sys.exit ( 0 )
        if ballBoundary.left < 0 or ballBoundary.right > width :
            sound.play ()
            velocity[0] = -velocity[0]
        if ballBoundary.top < 0 or ballBoundary.bottom > height :
            sound.play ()
            velocity[1] = -velocity[1]
        ballBoundary = ballBoundary.move ( velocity )
        frame.fill ( backgroundColor )
        frame.blit ( ball , ballBoundary )
        pygame.display.flip ()
```

This example is an amended and extended version of a program from Pete Shinners' Python PyGame Introduction. See http://www.pygame.org/docs/tut/intro/intro.html.

To see the animation and hear the sounds, you need to execute the code.

To start with, we initialize some variables:

ballImage – the file path of an image of the ball to be displayed.

bounceSound – the file path of the sound to play when the ball hits a boundary.

caption – the caption to display on the frame of the animation.

width – the width of the frame for the ball to bounce in.

height – the height of the frame for the ball to bounce in.

backgroubdColor – a tuple specifying the background color for the frame. (0, 0, 0) is black.

velocity – a two-item list containing the current x and y components of the velocity of the ball. We use a list as we want the value to be mutable. Velocity is measured here in pixels per frame refresh.

Specifying Color

Specifying colors is a complex business, but we do not have the space here to do the subject proper justice. Fortunately, for computer displays things are relatively straightforward: computer displays invariably use the red–green–blue (RGB) color space. With RGB, a color is specified by giving the value of the red, green and blue component of the color. Most modern hardware uses 24-bit color, so each component is an 8-bit number, i.e. in the range [0, 255]: a color is a triplet of values, for example (25, 123, 76). (0, 0, 0) is black and (255, 255, 255) is white.

> *Velocity*
>
> Velocity measures both the speed and direction of travel. In a two-dimensional world we have to specify two values to specify a velocity. It is usually the case that the x and y components of velocity are specified, but this is by no means the only way. Using an (v_x, v_y) notation, (4, 3) specifies a velocity with x component 4 and y component 3, which means a speed 5 in a known direction. Speed is calculated using:
>
> $$speed = \sqrt{v_x^2 + v_y^2}$$

It is worth noting the two assignments involving tuples:

```
width , height = 600 , 500
backgroundColor = 0 , 0 , 0
```

The first assignment is a standard tuple assignment – there is a tuple of equal length on either side of the assignment operator, so the statement is simultaneous assignment of two variables. The second statement is assigning a single tuple of three items to a variable – in an assignment statement comma separated values denote a tuple whether or not there are parentheses.

Having set the values of all the variables, we execute:

```
pygame.init ( )
```

The PyGame system needs to be initialized so we have to call the **pygame.init** function before we can do any work with the PyGame system. Once things are initialized, we can tell the PyGame system what size the frame will be, and what frame title to display:

```
frame = pygame.display.set_mode ( ( width , height ) )
pygame.display.set_caption ( caption )
```

PyGame automatically works out all the graphics mode details for the platform (operating systems and hardware) on which the program is running, so we don't have to worry about any platform-specific issues. **pygame.display.set_mode** returns an object of type **pygame.Surface** that represents the graphics that will be displayed on the screen when the program is executed. Any drawing done on this surface will be visible on the screen, and any graphics that should be visible on the screen must be written on a **pygame.Surface**.

The next two statements set up the image of the ball so that it can be displayed and so that we can calculate when the frame boundaries are reached, at which point the velocity has to be changed:

```
ball = pygame.image.load ( ballImage ).convert ( )
ballBoundary = ball.get_rect ( )
```

The first statement loads the image that represents the ball. It is extremely important that we call the function **convert** after the image is loaded: this method converts an image from whatever format is stored on disk into the format that is used internally within PyGame. If we do not call **convert**, the PyGame system would have to work with the original format, and this would mean converting to the internal format for every operation – in this case, conversion would have to happen for each drawing action, which would slow the program down dramatically. It is imperative therefore to do the format conversion once at the beginning to let PyGame work with its own internal format during the animation. The second of these statements is preparing the ground for collision. The ball is asked to return

You might want to try removing the call to convert and running the program to see what happens.

the *rect* that is the smallest rectangle that completely surrounds the image – this is the image's bounding box. A rect in PyGame is an object that gives the coordinates of the bounding box of an object on the screen. Rects are used a lot for calculating position and hence collision of items in an animation.

It is not entirely clear why the load function doesn't just always call convert.

The line:

```
sound = pygame.mixer.Sound ( bounceSound )
```

creates the sound object for the sound to be played during the animation.

The rest of the program is an infinite loop:

```
while True :
    . . .
```

This is the event loop for the program, which is an infinite loop as we want the ball to bounce forever. Obviously though the user might interact, by pressing a key or a mouse button, or by moving the mouse or joystick, and the program must process the *events* generated by such actions. The function **pygame.event.get** delivers a list of all pending events – i.e. all the events that have occurred since we last checked. For a responsive program, it is important to process the event list often and quickly – this is especially true for real-time games. For this program, in its current state of development, the only event we are interested in is a 'Quit' event. All events other than this are simply ignored. So the loop:

```
for event in pygame.event.get () :
    if event.type == pygame.QUIT : sys.exit ( 0 )
```

is the event processing loop, and it ignores all events other than **pygame.Quit**. There are at least two ways of creating a 'Quit' event: clicking on the ✗ button on the frame, and pressing the key combination Alt+F4. There may be other, platform-specific ways as well. Thankfully, we don't have to check for each of these events individually. PyGame does all such low-level processing for us: all we have to do is to process events it has labeled with **pygame.QUIT**.

The rest of the code in the infinite loop is about moving and displaying the ball. The two if statements deal with checking to see whether the ball has collided with the sides of the frame.

```
if ballBoundary.left < 0 or ballBoundary.right > width :
    sound.play ()
    velocity[0] = -velocity[0]
if ballBoundary.top < 0 or ballBoundary.bottom > height :
    sound.play ()
    velocity[1] = -velocity[1]
```

Instead of expecting the ball to exactly collide with the frame edge, we check to see if any part of the ball has moved beyond the edge of the frame – defensive programming in case the ball moves in way that does not lead to an exact collision with the frame edge. We do the checking by examining the attributes of the rect that represents the ball's position in the frame. If the ball has 'hit' the edge of the frame, we do two things: play the sound (by calling the play method on the sound object), and change the direction in which the ball is moving. In this simple example, we just reverse the component of velocity at right angles to the frame edge against which the ball is bouncing – so if we 'hit' the top or bottom of the frame we reverse the *y* component, if we 'hit' the left or right of the frame we reverse the *x* component. This is *specular reflection*. Specular reflection is perfect bouncing with no loss of energy. This is clearly not a realistic model of the physics of a bouncing ball, but it suffices for a first version of the code. If we take this example further, we need to introduce some more sophisticated physics to model the bouncing more realistically.

The next statement:

```
ballBoundary = ballBoundary.move ( velocity )
```

calculates the next position of the ball relative to its current position. The move function calculates the next rect given the rect for which the method was called and a velocity tuple parameter. It returns a new rect, but does not change the value of the rect for which it was called. Hence we have to assign the new rect to ballBoundary explicitly. Just to amplify this, we can move the ball by one pixel left with:

```
ballBoundary = ballBoundary.move ( [ -1 , 0 ] )
```

and down one pixel like this:

```
ballBoundary = ballBoundary.move ( [ 0 , 1 ] )
```

We can use lists or tuples to specify the movement amount.

Finally in the infinite loop we have:

```
frame.fill ( backgroundColor )
frame.blit ( ball , ballBoundary )
pygame.display.flip ()
```

The fill function fills the frame with a color, black in this case, removing whatever was there before. This erases the previous image of the ball. Once the old ball image has been removed we need to draw the ball in its new position. Remember that we already know that the ball should be placed in the position represented by the ballBoundary object. To draw the ball, we need to copy this data onto the background, which in computer graphics is called *blitting*. So, to blit the ball to the screen, we call the blit method on the frame object, passing the ball (containing the ball's pixel data) and the ballBoundary (which specifies where to do the blitting) – this draws the ball image at the location specified by ballBoundary. This blitting does not actually display anything on the screen, it simply prepares the data structures ready for display. The pygame.display.flip function is what causes the PyGame system to actually do the redraw and hence make the newly drawn frame visible. The name of the function, flip, is derived from the underlying technique for displaying surfaces.

Computer animation works by drawing a series of images in sequence, fast enough that humans watching the animation are fooled into seeing continuous motion. This is the same principle on which films are based: showing 24 or more frames per second allows human perception to see continuous movement.

In this program, we animate the ball by redrawing the whole frame each time. This is not an efficient animation technique, though it works fine here. A more sophisticated (and much faster) technique is *dirty rect animation*, which we use in the next example.

13.3   Some Extra (Abstracting) Bits

PyGame is a low-level games library. This is appropriate as it is a library for supporting any type of game. This means that PyGame cannot make any assumptions about the high-level abstractions that might be useful. If we are writing a set of games that have major similarities, then it is desirable to create some higher-level support functions. Say we are going to write a series of 'retro' arcade games (1970s and 1980s computer games, Pong, Space Invaders, Pacman, for example), it makes a great deal of sense to define a set of functions that we can use in more that one of these games – which share a lot of similar features despite their differences. We've put a collection of functions that are used in all the games in a module called game_functions.

The documentation for the module, as generated by pydoc, is:

Help on module game_functions:

NAME
   game_functions - Functions common to many games built with PyGame.

FILE
   game_functions.py

FUNCTIONS
   display_score(screen, score, fgcol=(255, 255, 255), bgcol=(0, 0, 0))
     Displays the current score.

   load_png(filename)
     Load a PNG image and return an image object and its rect.

   loading(screen, fgcol=(255, 255, 255))
     Tells the user that the game is loading.

   lose(screen, fgcol=(255, 255, 255), credits=None, fade=1500)
     Called when the player loses the game. Fades out any music that might be
     playing and (optionally) displays author credits.

   start(screen, game='', fgcol=(255, 255, 255), bgcol=(0, 0, 0))
     Asks the user to start the game.

DATA

   . . .

VERSION
   1.1

DATE
   2007-06-08

AUTHOR
   Sarah Mount <s.mount@wlv.ac.uk>
   Amendments by Russel Winder <russel.winder@concertant.com>

We are not going to look into the details of these functions, we are just going to use them in the following example. We have provided the source code in Appendix C (page 441). Exercise 13.9 asks you to add a function to this module which implements a high score table. That will be a good opportunity to look through the game_functions code and make sure that you understand it.

13.4 Snake, A Retro Arcade Game

As a more complex example of a PyGame-based game, we present the game Snake. We are not going to show the development of the Snake program: we are treating this as a presentation of a program that uses PyGame. We will though present material in an order that highlights the thinking and development activity rather than the order of code in the file.

Snake has a rectangular 'universe' in which a snake continuously moves. Food appears at random intervals at random locations in the universe. In order to grow, the snake must 'eat' the food, which it does when the head of the snake passes through the location in the universe where the food is. The goal of the game is to create the longest snake possible. If the head of the snake impacts the frame or crosses its own body then the game is over.

A sprite is an object that represents a feature in the game.

Given the way things work in PyGame, it is a sensible design decision that the snake will be comprised of sprites, with the head being a special type of snake-part sprite. This definitely leads to inheritance: there will be snake parts and special snake parts, the special snake parts will be subclasses of snake parts. The food will also be represented by sprites. The universe will be a PyGame frame of some specified size.

Figure 13.1

Snake: The loading frame and the opening frame.

Figure 13.2

Snake: The game over frame.

Even with these simple rules, the game is too complicated to code in a single step, so we work to a sequence of intermediate goals to give us a base for each evolution. In the version we present here, we do not have the food, but instead lengthen the snake after a given period of time. We will get you to evolve the code we present into the complete game as an exercise – see Exercise 13.8.

> *The PyGame Documentation*
>
> Whilst you're reading this material it would be sensible to have a copy of the PyGame documentation to refer to, so that you can look up methods and classes in the PyGame API. Reading API documentation is an important skill for any programmer to master. You can find the PyGame documentation at http://www.pygame.org/docs/.

13.4.1   Game Variables

The structure of the Snake code is carefully constructed and is similar to many PyGame programs, particularly arcade games. At the top of the file, after the module documentation and the import statements, we put all the global variables comprising the game state that has to be shared by all classes and functions. So, the size of the window we want the game to run in, colors we'll need later, file names of images and sounds, text for various purposes, and so on:

```
fgcol = pygame.color.Color ( 'white' ) # Foreground color
bgcol = pygame.color.Color ( 'black' ) # Background color
screen_size = ( 500 , 500 )
head_img = 'Snake/snake-head.png'
body_img = 'Snake/snake-body.png'
soundtrack = 'Snake/ATT.ogg'
caption = 'Snake built with PyGame'
credits = [ 'Sarah Mount (code)' , 'James Shuttleworth (music)' ]
fps = 30 # Frames per second
```

The music we're using here is a piece by James, "All The Trips", which can be downloaded from his website http://dis-dot-dat. net/content/music/ ATT.ogg.

13.4.2   Overall Structure

After the global variables, we have all the classes that are used for instantiating the objects used in the game – in this case parts of the snake. Following the classes we have the function which describes how the game is animated and played. This function, which we have called main, will handle events like user input, manage drawing of the game objects on the screen, and so on. Lastly, we'll have the usual main block **if** __name__ == '__main__': which will be true if the program is run from the command line, or by double-clicking on an icon.

The overall structure of Snake is:

```
### Global variables
. . .
### Game classes
class SnakePart ( pygame.sprite.Sprite ) :
    . . .
class SnakeHead ( SnakePart ) :
    . . .
class SnakeBody ( SnakePart ) :
    . . .
```

```
### Game logic
def main ( ) :
    . . .
    # Event loop
    clock.tick ( fps )
    frame += 1
    # Handle events
    for event in pygame.event.get ( ) :
        . . .
    . . .
# Run the game if appropriate.
if __name__ == '__main__':
    main ( )
```

There are many ways of structuring the Snake program, some simpler than others. The separation of classes and functions we're using here is probably slightly more complex than it needs to be, but it should give you a good idea of how to structure a more complex arcade game. Most importantly, we're keeping related code together. All the event handling goes in one place, all the drawing goes in one place, the sprites are kept together and so on. This should make the code easy to read and maintain.

13.4.3   Game Classes

The three game classes we have for Snake will be:

SnakePart – the superclass containing information common to any part of a snake.

SnakeHead – represents the first segment of the snake that can be moved around the screen by the user.

SnakeBody – represents the parts of the snake that follow the head. These are not controllable by the user. In the game animation they just follow the path of the head as it moves around the screen.

The SnakePart class inherits from PyGame's class **pygame.sprite.Sprite**. In games and animation a sprite is just a two-dimensional, pre-rendered (drawn) image that is used as part of a larger scene. You can read more about PyGame's **Sprite** class on the PyGame documentation pages: http://www.pygame.org/docs/ref/sprite.html.

In our case, our SnakePart class only really needs to hold its location on the screen and the rectangle in which is it drawn. Like the previous PyGame program, we can make use of PyGame's Rect class here. Lastly, we want a way of representing the current direction in which the snake is moving. Only the SnakeHead needs to move, but here we want to create some values to represent the four direction of motion: up, down, left and right. In this case we're using the following line of code:

UP, DOWN, LEFT, RIGHT = [0 , -1] , [0 , 1] , [-1 , 0] , [1 , 0]

The tuple assignment is in a class but outside any method: the variables are not instance variables, they are class variables. To refer to these class variables we can say SnakePart.UP, SnakePart.DOWN, and so on.

Remembering that the top left-hand corner of the screen is the origin, our four values representing direction tell us something about movement relative to the x and y axes. Think of each of the four two-item lists as being an x, y pair. So, [0, -1] means *zero motion in the x direction and negative motion in the y direction*

UP, DOWN, LEFT, and RIGHT represent the different directions and hence we can use them as base vectors for specifying velocity. We only really need two of these four, since UP = -DOWN and LEFT = -RIGHT, but it seems natural to have all four.

– so that pair represents upwards motion. There are other ways of representing movement, but later we'll see how this makes some of our algorithms extremely simple. Here's the full listing for the SnakePart class:

```
class SnakePart ( pygame.sprite.Sprite ) :
    """Segment of a snake."""
    UP, DOWN, LEFT, RIGHT = [ 0 , -1 ] , [ 0 , 1 ] , [ -1 , 0 ] , [ 1 , 0 ]
    def __init__( self , position ) :
        pygame.sprite.Sprite.__init__ ( self )
        self.rect.center = position
        self.area = pygame.display.get_surface ( ).get_rect ( )
```

Next we'll look at the SnakeBodyPart class, which represents a segment of the snake that follows the head. This is a very simple class – all we need to do is to be able to draw a body part in a particular place on the screen. To keep things really simple we won't move the SnakeBodyPart sprites. Instead, each time the snake moves we'll destroy the old body and create a new one.

Notice that we're using a PNG image to represent each body part on the screen. We use different images for the head and the body parts. Here's the code:

Portable Network Graphics (PNG) is a file format for efficiently storing bitmap images without any loss of information.

```
class SnakeBodyPart ( SnakePart ) :
    """Body part of a snake. Body parts are not expected to be updated."""
    def __init__ ( self , position ) :
        self.image , self.rect = game.load_png ( body_img )
        super ( SnakeBodyPart , self ).__init__ ( position )
```

Next we need to write the SnakeHead class. This is more complicated because we need to make sure that a head can move around the screen. Instead of creating a new head each time a new frame is drawn, we'll move the existing head along. This will mean we need a little more logic in our class to tell Python how that should happen.

First of all, though, we need a constructor method for SnakeHead. This needs to hold:

- The current position of the head on the screen.

- The current direction in which the head is moving.

- The current size of the body (so we know how many SnakeBodyParts to draw).

- A list of the positions the SnakeHead has been drawn in (so we know where to draw all the sprites in the body).

Here's the code:

```
class SnakeHead ( SnakePart ) :
    """Snake head. The head of a snake can change direction and update its position."""
    def __init__ ( self , screen ) :
        self.image, self.rect = game.load_png ( head_img )
        self.screen = screen
        start_pos = ( 10 , 10 )
        super ( SnakeHead , self ).__init__ ( start_pos )
        self.direction = SnakePart.DOWN
        self.trail = [self.rect.center] # Keep track of previous positions.
        self.bodysize = 0 # Length of the body behind the snake head.
```

Next, we want the SnakeHead to be able to change direction when the user presses a key. We've already said that event handling will go in a method called main and not in this class, so all the SnakeHead has to do is set its self.direction attribute. The code for this couldn't be simpler:

```
def change_direction ( self , dir ) :
    """Change the direction in which the snake head is moving."""
    self.direction = dir
```

Before we write the update method, which is the last one for this class, we need one helper method. This helper method multiplies the contents of two lists together, returning a new list. For example, if we wanted to perform this multiplication:

$$[1 , 2 , 3 , 4] * [5 , 6 , 7 , 8]$$

we would expect the answer:

$$[1 * 5 , 2 * 6 , 3 *7 , 4 * 8]$$

which evaluates to:

$$[5 , 12 , 21 , 32]$$

The code to do this is straightforward: we create an empty list, write a loop to populate it with the right values and return it:

```
def __dotproduct ( self , l1 , l2 ) :
    """Vector dot product."""
    product = [ ]
    for i in range ( len ( l1 ) ) : product.append ( l1[i] * l2[i] )
    return product
```

There are a couple of brief comments regarding the name of this method:

1. It starts with a double underscore (__), which tells the Python system that this is a private method that can only be used by code inside the same class.

2. It comes from the 'dot product' concept in mathematics – vectors and matrices have the dot product operator and this is what we are modeling here with lists.

Now we are in a position to add the last method to this class, update. This method is responsible for:

- Updating the position of the head on the screen.

- Managing the list of positions that the head has occupied.

- Checking whether the head has hit the sides of the screen – in which case the game is over and the lose function from the game_functions module is called.

To move the head, we need to decide where the new position of the head should be, then tell PyGame to change which rectangle the head is drawn in. To make moving the snake simple we'll move the head by its own length or height, depending on whether it's moving horizontally or vertically, and ensure that the head and the body parts are all the same size. As long as the head and the body parts are the same size then to determine where the body parts should be drawn, we only need to store the centers of each rectangle the head has occupied. So, if we want to move the head up, we need to move it by 0 in the x direction and -height in the y direction, where height is the height of the head:

```
self.__dotproduct ( SnakePart.UP , self.rect.size )
```

SnakePart.UP is [0, -1] and self.rect.size is a list containing the width and height of the rectangle in which the head is drawn. So, to calculate the new position of the head in our program, we just need this line of code:

```
movepos = self.__dotproduct ( self.direction , self.rect.size )
```

Unlike the bouncing ball animation, we won't use the move from the Rect class to move the head, instead we'll use a similar method called move_ip. From the PyGame website, the documentation for move_ip says:

```
Rect.move_ip
    moves the rectangle, in place
    Rect.move_ip(x, y): return None

    Same as the Rect.move - moves the rectangle method, but operates in place.
```

So, instead of destroying the old Rect object and creating a new one at the new location, move_ip just changes the coordinates of the original Rect. This should be faster. Speed and responsiveness are an important part of making software such as games usable and useful, so ensuring this program runs quickly is important. This gives us the first half of the update method as:

```
def update ( self ) :
    """Update the position of the snake head."""
    movepos = self.__dotproduct ( self.direction , self.rect.size )
    self.rect.move_ip ( movepos )
```

To manage the list of positions in which the head has been drawn, we need to first append the new position to the list self.trail. Also, we want to make sure that if the size of the snake's body is small, we don't keep an enormous list of positions that we don't really need. So we check the length of the self.trail list against the size of the snake body – held in self.bodysize – and delete an element in the trail if the list is bigger than it needs to be. We need the following as the next part of the update method:

```
self.trail.append ( self.rect.center )
if len ( self.trail ) > ( self.bodysize + 1 ) : del self.trail[0] # Keep the list small.
```

In the bouncing ball animation we checked for collisions of the ball with the frame by comparing the coordinates of the rectangle containing the ball with the height and width of the frame. In this snake game we have taken a slightly different approach. The SnakePart class has an instance variable self.area that is the rectangle of the game universe. We can use one of the methods in PyGame's Rect class (contains) to check if the self.area rectangle still contains the rectangle used to draw the head. If the head is not in the universe then it has gone outside the universe and the game is over. So the last line of the update method is:

```
if not self.area.contains ( self.rect ) : game.lose ( self.screen , credits=credits )
```

13.4.4   Game Functions

The main method contains all the code to animate the game and handle events. As with the bouncing ball example, or any other PyGame program, we need to initialize PyGame's internal variables, and while we're setting things up, we can display a caption on the title bar of the application window:

```
def main ( ) :
    """Play Snake."""
    pygame.init ( )
    screen = pygame.display.set_mode ( screen_size ) # Blit buffer.
    pygame.display.set_caption ( caption )
```

Next we'll fill the screen with black pixels and call the loading function in the game_functions module to tell the user that the game is currently busy. We'll be loading some large files, which will take time, and without giving the user any feedback it might look as if the program has crashed.

As before, to fill the screen we'll ask PyGame for a surface on which to draw that is the same size as the application window (we've called that **background**). Then we'll fill that surface with the background color, blit the surface onto the screen, and call **pygame.display.flip** to actually complete the update of the screen. Remember that this is a time-consuming process because we're updating every single pixel in the application window. When we draw the game animation, we'll be a bit more sophisticated about how we manage drawing.

```
background = ( pygame.Surface ( screen.get_size ( ) ) ).convert ( )
background.fill ( bgcol )
screen.blit ( background , ( 0 , 0 ) )
pygame.display.flip ( )
game.loading ( screen )
```

We next initialize all our game objects. In this program, we have to instantiate the SnakeHead class, and although we won't start off with any SnakeBodyPart objects, we create a group of sprites for the body. One of the advantages of using sprites is that they can be stored in groups, which means that you can render all the sprites at once rather than having to write loops to do this. Also we use PyGame's facilities for detecting collisions between sprites.

Lastly, we load the soundtrack for the game, create a clock that will automatically manage the frame rate of the game's animation for us, and start a counter to tell us how many frames have been drawn. Note that you can find the **Clock** class listed in the documentation for the **pygame.time** module.

```
head = SnakeHead ( screen )
headsprite = pygame.sprite.RenderPlain ( head )
body = pygame.sprite.Group ( )
bodysprite = pygame.sprite.RenderPlain ( body )
music = pygame.mixer.Sound ( soundtrack )
clock = pygame.time.Clock ( )
```

Once we've loaded our game objects, we can start the game. First we start playing the soundtrack. The play method in the pygame.mixer.Sound class will play the music. Passing -1 to the method ensures that the music loops indefinitely.

We also need to redraw the background to cover up the message that told the player that the game was loading. Then we call the start function from the game_functions module which will tell the player to "Press any key to start playing Snake".

```
music.play ( -1 )
screen.blit ( background , ( 0 , 0 ) )
pygame.display.flip ( )
pygame.event.clear ( )
game.start ( screen , game='Snake' )
```

The event loop is a little different that the one in the bouncing ball animation. In that example we looped the animation as fast as possible. In this game we want to be able to control the speed of the animation so that we can choose the most playable speed for the player. The fps variable at the top of the file controls the number of frames per second that are displayed and hence the speed of progress of the snake.

In PyGame, animation speed is controlled by a clock that we've already instantiated from the pygame.time.Clock class. We can ask the clock to "tick" at the right time and update our frame counter like this:

```
while True :
    clock.tick ( fps )
    frame += 1
```

Next we need to handle user events. Like the bounce animation, we need to check whether the user has asked the application to quit, in which case our main function can return. We also need to enable the user to move the head. Events of type KEYDOWN are posted whenever the user presses a key. The pygame.locals module contains constants representing (among other things) keys on the keyboard that the user can press. Look through the help for that module and note that the constants whose names begin with K_ are keyboard keys, those starting with JOY represent joystick movements, and so on. For this game we'll use the arrow keys to control the snake, although if you play games regularly you may be used to other key combinations, such as A, S, W and D.

When the user requests a change of direction, we need to make a note of the new vector and instruct the head to redirect its motion. Here's the code:

```
for event in pygame.event.get ( ) :
    if event.type == QUIT : return
    elif event.type == KEYDOWN :
        if event.key == K_UP : dir = SnakePart.UP
        elif event.key == K_DOWN : dir = SnakePart.DOWN
        elif event.key == K_LEFT : dir = SnakePart.LEFT
        elif event.key == K_RIGHT : dir = SnakePart.RIGHT
        head.change_direction ( dir )
```

Next, we can check whether the head has collided with any of the sprites in the snake body, in which case the player has lost the game. Since we've used sprites, we can make use of PyGame's spritecollideany function (in the pygame.sprite module) which detects whether one sprite has collided with a group of sprites:

```
if pygame.sprite.spritecollideany ( head , body ) : game.lose ( screen , credits=credits )
```

Before we deal with the details of the animation, we need to increment the bodysize field in the head object. This is the number that tells us how many sprites should be in the body of the snake. We decided earlier that we would increase the size of the snake every so often. Here is where we specify how much bigger the snake gets and how often. We choose to increase the size of the snake every 2 s:

```
if frame % ( 2 * fps ) == 0 : head.bodysize += 1
```

13.4.5 Dirty Rect Animation

In the bouncing ball animation we created the illusion of a moving object by drawing the ball on the screen, then creating a new image with the ball slightly moved, filling the screen with black pixels, then blitting the updated image onto the screen. This is particularly inefficient – every pixel on the screen has to be updated every time something moves! Better, surely, to simply update those rectangles of the screen that change between each frame. This technique is known as *dirty rect animation*. It's very simple to implement – we just need to keep a list of all the rectangles (the *dirty rectangles*) that need to be updated then blit the updates for those rectangles straight onto the screen, leaving the remaining pixels unchanged.

So, first of all, we need to keep a list of all dirty rects:

```
dirty = [ ] # Dirty rects.
```

Next we can add to the list all the rectangles containing parts of the snake, the head and all the body parts. We can also fill those rectangles with background color to blank them out.

It's important to remember when you read the following code that we have two variables: screen and pygame.display. screen is just an image in memory that we write to (the *blit buffer*), whereas pygame.display is the actual image the user will see on the screen.

```
dirty.append ( copy.copy ( head.rect ) )
screen.fill ( bgcol , head.rect )
for b in body.sprites ( ) :
    dirty.append ( b.rect )
    screen.fill ( bgcol , b.rect )
```

Now we've got a list of all the old positions of the snake parts, and we've drawn over them, we can move the head and draw all the new body parts. Again, we only draw in the blit buffer, and we make sure these rectangles also appear in the dirty rect list, so that we know to update them on the display. First, we'll deal with the head:

```
head.update ( )
dirty.append ( head.rect )
```

… and now the body. Remember, the head was moved 'in place', whereas we decided to destroy all the body parts on every frame. So, here we need to create new SnakeBodyPart objects and place them in the body sprite group. The head.trail list holds all the locations on the screen where we ought to be drawing body parts. As with everything else, these rectangles need to go in the dirty rect list, so that we remember to update them on the display:

```
body.empty ( )
for i in range ( head.bodysize ) :
    new_part = SnakeBodyPart ( head.trail[i] )
    body.add ( new_part )
    dirty.append ( new_part.rect )
```

Now, we're almost there. We have a list of every rectangle that needs to be updated on the display and we've created all the sprites that have been drawn in the blit buffer. As with the first frame of the animation, we need to make sure the sprites are rendered correctly by calling the RenderPlain and draw methods for each sprite (or sprite group). We'll also want to update the score:

```
game.display_score ( screen , head.bodysize )
headsprite = pygame.sprite.RenderPlain ( head )
bodysprite = pygame.sprite.RenderPlain ( body )
headsprite.draw ( screen )
bodysprite.draw ( screen )
```

Last of all, we need to blit all our dirty rects to the display:

```
pygame.display.update ( dirty )
```

And that's it. Well, for this round of development any way!

13.4.6   The Complete Listing

```
"""
Snake built with PyGame.
"""


__author__ = 'Sarah Mount <s.mount@wlv.ac.uk>'
__date__ = '2007-05-30'
__version__ = '1.0'
__copyright__ = 'Copyright (c) 2007 Sarah Mount'
__licence__ = 'GNU General Public Licence (GPL)'


import copy , math , pygame
from pygame.locals import *
import game_functions as game


if not pygame.font : print 'Warning, fonts disabled'
if not pygame.mixer : print 'Warning, sound disabled'


### Global variables
fgcol = pygame.color.Color ( 'white' ) # Foreground color
bgcol = pygame.color.Color ( 'black' ) # Background color
screen_size = ( 500 , 500 )
head_img = 'Snake/snake-head.png'
body_img = 'Snake/snake-body.png'
soundtrack = 'Snake/ATT.ogg'
caption = 'Snake built with PyGame'
credits = [ 'Sarah Mount (code)' , 'James Shuttleworth (music)' ]
fps = 30 # Frames per second


### Game classes.
class SnakePart ( pygame.sprite.Sprite ) :
    """Segment of a snake."""
    UP, DOWN, LEFT, RIGHT = [ 0 , -1 ] , [ 0 , 1 ] , [ -1 , 0 ] , [ 1 , 0 ]
    def __init__( self , position ) :
        pygame.sprite.Sprite.__init__ ( self )
        self.rect.center = position
        self.area = pygame.display.get_surface ( ).get_rect ( )
```

```python
class SnakeHead ( SnakePart ) :
    """Snake head. The head of a snake can change direction and update its position."""
    def __init__ ( self , screen ) :
        self.image, self.rect = game.load_png ( head_img )
        self.screen = screen
        start_pos = ( 10 , 10 )
        super ( SnakeHead , self ).__init__ ( start_pos )
        self.direction = SnakePart.DOWN
        self.trail = [self.rect.center] # Keep track of previous positions.
        self.bodysize = 0 # Length of the body behind the snake head.

    def update ( self ) :
        """Update the position of the snake head."""
        movepos = self.__dotproduct ( self.direction , self.rect.size )
        self.rect.move_ip ( movepos )
        self.trail.append ( self.rect.center )
        if len ( self.trail ) > ( self.bodysize + 1 ) : del self.trail[0] # Keep the list small.
        # Check if head has collided with the side of the screen.
        if not self.area.contains ( self.rect ) : game.lose ( self.screen , credits=credits )

    def change_direction ( self , dir ) :
        """Change the direction in which the snake head is moving."""
        self.direction = dir

    def __dotproduct ( self , l1 , l2 ) :
        """Vector dot product."""
        product = [ ]
        for i in range ( len ( l1 ) ) : product.append ( l1[i] * l2[i] )
        return product

class SnakeBodyPart ( SnakePart ) :
    """Body part of a snake. Body parts are not expected to be updated."""
    def __init__ ( self , position ) :
        self.image , self.rect = game.load_png ( body_img )
        super ( SnakeBodyPart , self ).__init__ ( position )

def main ( ) :
    """Play Snake."""
    pygame.init ( )
    screen = pygame.display.set_mode ( screen_size ) # Blit buffer.
    pygame.display.set_caption ( caption )
    # Draw the game background.
    background = ( pygame.Surface ( screen.get_size ( ) ) ).convert ( )
    background.fill ( bgcol )
    screen.blit ( background , ( 0 , 0 ) )
    pygame.display.flip ( )
    game.loading ( screen )
    # Initialise the snake.
    head = SnakeHead ( screen )
    headsprite = pygame.sprite.RenderPlain ( head )
    body = pygame.sprite.Group ( )
    bodysprite = pygame.sprite.RenderPlain ( body )
    music = pygame.mixer.Sound ( soundtrack )
    clock = pygame.time.Clock ( )
```

```
        frame = 0 # Number of frames we have drawn so far.
        # Ask the player to start the game.
        music.play ( -1 )
        screen.blit ( background , ( 0 , 0 ) )
        pygame.display.flip ( )
        pygame.event.clear ( )
        game.start ( screen , game='Snake' )
        # Event loop
        while True :
            clock.tick ( fps )
            frame += 1
            # Handle events.
            for event in pygame.event.get ( ) :
                if event.type == QUIT : return
                elif event.type == KEYDOWN :
                    if event.key == K_UP : dir = SnakePart.UP
                    elif event.key == K_DOWN : dir = SnakePart.DOWN
                    elif event.key == K_LEFT : dir = SnakePart.LEFT
                    elif event.key == K_RIGHT : dir = SnakePart.RIGHT
                    head.change_direction ( dir )
            # Check if the head has collided with the body.
            if pygame.sprite.spritecollideany ( head , body ) : game.lose ( screen , credits=credits )
            # Add a new SnakePart object every 2 s.
            if frame % ( 2 * fps ) == 0 : head.bodysize += 1
            dirty = [ ] # Dirty rects.
            # Draw over the old snake.
            dirty.append ( copy.copy ( head.rect ) )
            screen.fill ( bgcol , head.rect )
            for b in body.sprites ( ) :
                dirty.append ( b.rect )
                screen.fill ( bgcol , b.rect )
            # Move the snake head.
            head.update ( )
            dirty.append ( head.rect )
            # Delete old sprites and create new snake body.
            body.empty ( )
            for i in range ( head.bodysize ) :
                new_part = SnakeBodyPart ( head.trail[i] )
                body.add ( new_part )
                dirty.append ( new_part.rect )
            # Render the current score and the snake.
            game.display_score ( screen , head.bodysize )
            headsprite = pygame.sprite.RenderPlain ( head )
            bodysprite = pygame.sprite.RenderPlain ( body )
            headsprite.draw ( screen )
            bodysprite.draw ( screen )
            # Update dirty rects.
            pygame.display.update ( dirty )

if __name__ == '__main__':
        main ( )
```

In this chapter we have found that:

- Animation is a technique for displaying still images sufficiently quickly for humans to perceive continuous motion.
- Rects are bounding boxes and that calculating using bounding boxes can make animation easy.
- Animation often requires specialist techniques such as blitting and dirty rect animation to provide good performance.
- PyGame is an excellent package for creating games written in Python.

Self-Review Questions

Self-review 13.1 Define the term *API*.

Self-review 13.2 What is 'blitting'? Why is it important for animation?

Self-review 13.3 What is a Rect object in PyGame? What does it represent?

Self-review 13.4 What is the difference between the Rect.move and Rect.move_ip methods in the pygame.Rect class? Give two examples of how these methods can be used in a line of code.

Self-review 13.5 Most programs that manipulate images and animations put the origin, (0, 0), of the screen at the top-left hand corner of the application window. Why is this?

Self-review 13.6 What does the pygame.init function do?

Self-review 13.7 In the Snake game, what did the following names represent and what are they used for:

　　clock　　frame　　SnakePart.UP　　fps　　dirty　　body　　bodysprite

Self-review 13.8 What does the pygame.Surface.convert do? Why did we use it in our code?

Self-review 13.9 What does the following code do?

```
for event in pygame.event.get () :
    if event.type == pygame.locals.QUIT :
        sys.exit ()
```

Self-review 13.10 What is the difference between a KEYDOWN and a KEYUP event?

Self-review 13.11 What names in pygame.locals are used to represent the following keys on the keyboard:

　　q　　Enter　　Shift　　Tab　　Space

Self-review 13.12 How can we find the current position of the mouse when using PyGame?

Self-review 13.13 What is a 'sprite' and what is a 'sprite group'?

Self-review 13.14 What does it mean to 'render' a sprite?

Self-review 13.15 What does the pygame.Sprite.update method do? Why is it usually overridden in subclasses?

Self-review 13.16 Briefly describe the technique of 'dirty rect animation'. Why is it more efficient than other methods?

Self-review 13.17 What is a 'blit buffer'? What name did we give the blit buffer in the Snake code in Section 13.4.5?

Programming Exercises

Exercise 13.1 Change the bouncing ball animation so that the animation begins with the ball in a random position on the screen.

Exercise 13.2 The speed at which the ball travels will make a big difference to how *smooth* the animation looks. Allow the user to vary the speed of the animation by using the 'up' and 'down' arrow keys on the keyboard. Experiment with different speeds – which looks best?

Exercise 13.3 Add another ball to the bouncing ball animation and have them both begin in random positions.

Exercise 13.4 Having completed the previous exercise, make sure that the two balls bounce off each other whenever they collide.

Exercise 13.5 Write a simple demonstration program to show how PyGame allocates numbers (*scancodes*) to different keys on the keyboard. You should start with a blank screen, and whenever the user presses a key, display its scancode (which you can get from event.key).

Hint: *Have a look at pygame.time.wait, which might be useful to you!*

Exercise 13.6 Write a PyGame program to simulate an Etch A Sketch. The user should be able to use the arrow keys on the keyboard to draw a continuous line on a blank screen.

Hint: *Wikipedia has a short article on Etch A Sketch at http://en.wikipedia.org/wiki/Etch_A_Sketch.*

Hint: *Look in the pygame.draw module. What does the aa mean in the name pygame.draw.aaline?*

Exercise 13.7 The Bouncing Ball animation has almost everything necessary to create a game of single-player Pong, except a bat. Add a new subclass of Sprite to represent the bat, and make sure that the ball collides correctly with it. Use the display_score function in the game_functions module to display the score (which should increment every time the ball hits the bat).

Hint: *You might want to make the ball a Sprite too, to make collision detection easier.*

Exercise 13.8 Change the Snake program so that the snake only grows in length when the head collides with randomly placed sprites (snake food), which should be the same size as a SnakePart. Make sure that after a random period, new food is made available to the snake.

Exercise 13.9 Augment the game_functions module with a high score table. Use either the shelve or pickle module to store the scores.

Exercise 13.10 Add a second snake to the Snake game that is controlled by the computer. This second snake should move in random directions around the screen. If the player's snake collides with the computer's, the player loses the game. Allow the computer's snake to eat food too – preventing the player's snake from gaining valuable points!

Exercise 13.11 Add 'lives' to the Snake game. The player should lose a life if the snake collides with itself or the sides of the screen, but only lose the game when all the player's lives are exhausted. Make sure that the player is always aware of how many lives they have left.

Hint: Think about which parts of your code should go in the snake.py file and which should go in the game_functions module.

Challenges

Challenge 13.1 Implement a single-player Space Invaders arcade game (see Space Invaders on Wikipedia for a description: http://en.wikipedia.org/wiki/Space_Invaders).

Hint: You should start by creating a game with a single level. Then you can evolve this to a multi-level game, for which you will probably want to write code to use configuration files to describe what should happen on each level.

You should create any images and sounds you need to use in the game. We recommend GIMP (http://www.gimp.org/) or Inkscape (http://www.inkscape.org) for graphics.

Challenge 13.2 Python can run on a variety of devices apart from PCs. These include PDAs, embedded computers and mobile phones. Any Linux or Symbian based phone should be able to run Python: the phone manufacturer's support site should have details. We used a Nokia Series 60 phone for our solution to this challenge, having downloaded a port of the Python interpreter from the Nokia website. This port of Python comes with some good documentation which should be read before trying to load the Python system and run Python programs on your phone.

For this challenge, write a single-player Pong game for your phone. Make sure you read the documentation carefully. In particular, you will need to know about the canvas (in appuifw.Canvas), the Keyboard class, the Image class and (of course!) rects. You will also want to read about the e32.ao_yield function which provides a very simple form of concurrency control.

Appendix A

Glossary

Abstract data type A type whose internal data structures are hidden behind a set of access functions or methods. Instances of the type may only be created and inspected by calls to methods. This allows the implementation of the type to be changed without changing any code that instantiates that type.

ADT *Abstract data type.*

Aggregation A class has an aggregation relationship with another when the former class has a data structure in its state comprising instances of the latter class. Aggregation is a special form of *association*.

Algorithm A sequence of instructions carried out to perform a specific task.

and The logical operator that is true when both its operands are true.

API *Application programming interface.*

Application A program that is solving a problem for a user.

Application programming interface The set of functions or methods that is made available for use in programs.

Argument A value provided as a parameter in a function call. Also know as *parameter value.*

Assignment The act of associating a *variable* with a *value.* After an assignment *statement,* a variable refers to the value specified in the assignment.

Association A relationship between two classes: there is an association between two classes when an instance of one class can call methods on an instance of the other class.

Atomic operation An indivisible operation. An atomic operation is a sequence of operations during which no other operation can happen.

Attribute A name in the state of an object. A name–value pair that describes some property of an object. Attributes are accessed using the '.' operator. So in the expression x.a, a is an attribute of the object referred to by x.

Base The value that is to be raised to some power in an exponentiation operation: in the expression x^y, x is the base (y is the *exponent*).

Base case The terminating case in *recursion*.

Bazaar A distributed *version control system*. See http://bazaar-vcs.org/.

Big O notation A tool for specifying the *time complexity* or *space complexity* of an *algorithm*.

Binary Search A search method that requires ordered data in a random access *sequence* and executes in $O(\log_2 n)$ time for n items.

Binary operator An *operator* that requires two operands.

Binary tree A tree with *branching factor* 2, i.e. each parent can have 0, 1 or 2 children.

Binding The process of associating an *event* (such as a key press or mouse movement) with a *callback* or *event handler*. For example, we might bind the key accelerator Ctrl-S with the callback onSave.

Blitting The action of copying pixel data into memory so that it becomes visible on the screen.

bool A built-in Python function that returns a Boolean value calculated from the value of the argument. For example with lists, bool returns **True** if the list argument is non-empty (equivalent to the expression **not** len (mylist) == 0), or **False** for empty lists.

Block There are two meanings for this term, depending on context:

1. A block is a sequence of code that is part of a compound *statement* or the body of a function.
2. To block is when a thread suspends its execution pending a specific event. Once the event occurs, the thread continues execution.

Bounding box A rectangular area around an image or part of an image. In the Python Imaging Library (PIL) bounding boxes are represented using a four-tuple containing an x-coordinate, a y-coordinate, a width and a height. The x and y coordinates represent the top left-hand corner of the bounding box.

Branching factor The number of children a node can have in a tree or graph.

break *Statement* used to jump out of the innermost enclosing loop.

Bubble Sort The sorting algorithm in which high values 'bubble' to one end of the sequence. The algorithm is covered in Section 10.2.2 (page 323).

Buffer A space for temporary storage, used to collect data and perform block operations instead of many small operations.

Bug A mistake or error in a program.

Cache A temporary store used to speed up processing. See *buffer*.

Callback An alternative name for an *event handler*.

Class A construct that groups *variables* and *methods* and gives it a name. Classes are *instantiated* to create *objects*. In Python, a class is defined by a *compound statement*, which has the following syntax:

```
class <name> ( <superclass-name-list> ) :
    <statements>
```

Class invariant A Boolean expression that should remain true throughout the lifetime of an *object*.

Class method A *method* defined in a class but which needs no *object* in order to be called, it can be called by reference to the class name.

Command A command used to perform a task. Commands tell the Python system to do something for you – **print** prints something to the screen, **import** imports a module. Unlike *functions* (for example turtle.reset) commands are not followed by parentheses when used in code.

Command-line argument The switches, options, data, etc., passed to a program when executed.

Compiler A program that transforms a program written in one language into a program expressed in another language. Python programs (in files with a .py extension) are compiled into an internal form (files with a .pyc or .pyo extension).

Compound statement A statement that collects more than one statement into a block.

Compound type A type that contains more than one piece of data.

Condition variable A special variable used for synchronization in multi-threaded code.

Container widget A widget that may have other widgets embedded within it. For example, a top-level container for an application may contain a menu, status bar, toolbar and so on.

continue A *statement* that skips back to the top of the innermost enclosing loop.

Constructor A special *method* that is called immediately after an *object* has been created in order to initialize the state of the newly created *instance*. Constructors are always called __init__.

Control flow The order in which statements are executed. Choice statements such as if statements, loop statements such as if and while statements, and function call are the statements that affect the flow of control.

Counter A variable which holds a count value that is used as part of an algorithm. Counters can be used in association with loops to control the number of time the body of a loop is executed – counted *iteration*.

Critical section A section of code that must only be executed by one thread at any one time – usually because it manipulates resources shared by multiple threads.

Deadlock The state in a multi-threaded program in which no thread can execute because all are blocked on a shared resource whose state cannot be changed because that would require one of the threads to execute.

Debug To fix the mistakes in a program.

Declarative programming A style of programming that emphasizes specifying the result of a computation rather than how a computation is undertaken. *Functional programming* and *logic programming* are examples of declarative programming.

Deep copy A copy of a data structure in what all the items in the data structure are also copied. The copy and the original share no references to objects.

del The *command* for deleting something from a data structure.

De Morgan's laws From mathematics:

$$\neg(p \land q) \Leftrightarrow \neg p \lor \neg q$$

$$\neg(p \lor q) \Leftrightarrow \neg p \land \neg q$$

In programming, these equivalences can be used to rearrange Boolean expressions.

Design by Contract Using preconditions, postconditions and class invariants to describe how a new type should behave.

Destructor A special *method* that is called just before an *object* is about to be destroyed.

Dictionary A store for data in which each entry is a pair with a key and a value. Other names for this data structure are associative array, and map.

Dirty rect animation A technique in which only the rectangles that need to be drawn for each frame are *blitted* to the screen. Using this technique improves the speed and efficiency of animations, as the whole screen isn't redrawn for each new frame.

Divide and conquer A strategy for subdividing a problem until it becomes a series of much simpler sub-problems.

elif Can follow an **if** block to add another, mutually exclusive, conditional block.

else Is used to provide a 'default' behavior. Code in this block will execute if none of the other associated blocks (**if** or **elif**) have been executed.

EAFP "It is **E**asier to **A**sk for **F**orgiveness than to ask for **P**ermission". A style of programming (common when programming using Python) in which the code tries something that ought to work and deals with the error when it doesn't. This style is especially useful when deviation from the expected case is rare.

Encapsulation Containing a series of *statements* within a *namespace* so that the statements can be executed anywhere and cannot be altered by client code.

Exponent The power to which a value (the *base*) is to be raised in an exponentiation operation: in the exponentiation expression x^y, y is the exponent.

Expression Part of a *statement* that can be evaluated to give a value.

Event A message to a program from an outside agent. In GUIs, an event is usually some form of input or interaction by the user. Examples include keyboard key presses, mouse movements and button presses, drag'n'drop, and so on. Most events will be uninteresting (e.g. mouse movements) but some require a response from the GUI (such as button presses and key accelerators).

Event handler A *function* or *method* which is executed when an event occurs. For example, the function onQuit may be executed when the key Alt-F4 is pressed by the user. Note that event handlers are written by the GUI programmer but scheduled for execution by the GUI toolkit via the *event loop*.

Event Loop A loop which is used to dispatch *event handlers* in response to *events*. The event loop for a GUI is usually provided by the GUI toolkit and doesn't need to be written by the programmer of an application.

Factorial The product of all integers from the given integer down to 1.

Fibonacci Sequence The sequence of numbers defined by the recurrence relation:

$$F_n = \begin{cases} 1 & n = 0 \\ 1 & n = 1 \\ F_{n-1} + F_{n-2} & n > 1 \end{cases}$$

So the nth item in the sequence is the sum of the two previous ones – except for the first two, which are both 1. So the sequence starts:

1, 1, 2, 3, 5, 8, 13, 21, 34, 55, 89, . . .

File A device for storing data. Files are generally on permanent storage such as disks, but operating systems may provide other forms of file.

File handle An object that gives us access to a specific *file*.

filter The function that applies a *predicate* to every value in a list and returns a list of all those values for which the predicate returned **True**.

Finite state automaton Another name for a *finite state machine*.

Finite state machine A theoretical machine which transitions between *states* in its *state space*.

Imperative programming language A programming language that provides facilities for managing state (such as assignment). Python, C, C++, and Java are examples of imperative programming languages.

Float A floating point number.

Floating point number A number with an integer part and a fractional part.

for Introduces a for statement that performs *iteration*. A for statement implements bounded iteration in that the iteration occurs for each item in a sequence.

```
for < variable> in < sequence> :
  <body>
else :
  <statements>
```

Fractal curve A curve exhibiting self-similarity – no matter at what scale you look at the curve it shows the same structure.

from Import particular names from a module so that they can be used without using the module name. For example:

```
from turtle import forward , left
forward ( 100 )
left ( 90 )
```

Function A construct that associates a block of code with a name. Functions the simplest way of encapsulating reusable code. Functions can return values using return statements.

```
def <name> ( <parameter-list> ) :
    <statements>
```

For example, turtle.reset resets the turtle window. Unlike *commands*, functions always require parentheses. Some functions can be given extra information (*arguments*) by placing values inside the parentheses. For example, calling turtle.circle (100 , 270) causes the turtle to draw 270° of a circle with radius 100 pixels.

Functional programming A programming style in which all functions are *referentially transparent* – i.e. programming without *side effects*. Haskell, Objective Caml and Erlang are (probably) the most used functional programming languages at the time of going to press.

Generator function A function that uses the yield statement. A generator function behaves differently to a function, instead of starting execution at the beginning of the function body on each call, generator functions start execution where they were when the last yield statement was executed. Generator functions can be used to implement *lazily evaluated* sequences.

global Used inside functions to tell Python that a particular name is declared at module level, not in local scope.

Graph A non-linear data structure in which each node can have many children and many parents. A tree is a graph with the restriction that each node can have only one parent.

Green Term used in *unit testing* to indicate that all unit tests pass.

if Introduces an if statements that allows the conditional execution of a code block.

Immutable Fixed, unchangeable. Tuples are immutable sequences.

import Command that causes the Python system to find and load a module. All the names in the module are imported. For example:

```
import turtle
turtle.forward ( 100 )
turtle.left ( 90 )
```

Inconsistent state A state in which the relationship between the values violates the consistency criteria.

Index A variable used to hold a position in a sequence; the value of the position in a sequence of an item of data; or the act of retrieving a data item by its position in the sequence.

Infinite loop Iteration without a termination condition.

Infinite recursion Recursion without a termination condition.

Inheritance The situation in which a *subclass* has one (*single inheritance*) or more (*multiple inheritance*) *superclasses*.

Instance A value of a particular type. Usually an object that has been created from a class by *instantiation*. For example, 1 is an instance of int and the object returned by Die() is an instance of the class Die.

Instance method A function defined as part of a class that is not a *static method* or a *class method*. Instance methods must always be called on an object.

Instance variable A variable forming part of the state of an object. Created by being assigned in the constructor of a class.

Instantiate To create a new object which is an *instance* of some class. In the example below we instantiate the class Foobar:

```
>>> class Foobar :
...    def __str__ ( self ) :
...         return 'foobar'
...
>>> obj = Foobar ()
>>> print obj
foobar
>>>
```

Integer A number with no fractional part. The data type for representing integers in Python is called int.

Interpreter A program that reads and executes a program. The Python system does not interpret the statements of a Python program directly. The *source code* is first *compiled* into an intermediate form. It is the intermediate form that is interpreted.

isinstance A function to determine whether a value is an instance of a particular type. For example:

```
>>> isinstance(1, int)
True
>>> isinstance(1.0, int)
False
>>> isinstance(set(), set)
True
>>>
```

Iterate To use iteration.

Iteration To perform some action repeatedly. The *for statement* (bounded iteration) and the *while statement* (unbounded iteration) are the tools for creating iteration in Python.

JPEG Acronym for Joint Photographic Experts Group but used as a label for the image file format that this group created. Hence " a JPEG file". The JPEG file format is a lossy format that is good for photographic images but poor for display screen dumps – lossy formats are not good for images with sharp lines as screen dumps generally have.

Key Data identifying a value in a *dictionary*.

lambda Introduces an anonymous function definition, e.g. **lambda** x: x+1

Lazy evaluation Evaluating the result of an expression only when it is needed.

Lazy list A *list* in which the items in the list are only created as they are needed. This technique allows the use of infinite lists in programs since only those values from the list that are used in the computation are calculated. *Generator functions* can be used to implement infinite sequences and hence infinite lists.

LBYL "Look Before You Leap". A description of the programming approach where a check of the state is made before executing an algorithm to ensure that the algorithm will execute successfully.

Leaf node A node in a tree or graph that has no children.

Lexer A state machine that takes a string as input and outputs a series of *tokens* that represent the words and symbols in the original string. For example, if the input to a lexer is:

```
foo = bar + 100
```

the resulting tokens might be:

```
NAME "foo"
EQUALS
NAME "bar"
PLUS
INT 100
```

Lexical token Another name for a *token*.

LEGB rule The rule determining the order of look up of names during program execution: local scope, enclosing scopes, global scope, built-ins.

Linear search A search algorithm that checks each element in turn. Works on any form of data that can be treated as a *sequence*. Required $O(n)$ time to search n items.

List A type that stores a mutable sequence of objects.

Literal A representation of a value used in source code. For example, the integer literal 220 represents the integer value 220.

Livelock In a multi-threaded program, livelock is where all threads can execute but no action by any thread causes the system to progress constructively.

Lock A mechanism for creating *critical sections*. Required in multi-threaded programs.

Logic programming A style of programming based on mathematical logic. The classic example of a logic programming language is Prolog.

Lookup table A data structure containing pre-computed values from a function. Lookup tables are usually used when it is faster to access a value in a data structure than to call a function to calculate the value. In image processing a lookup table is often called a LUT.

Loop an iteration *statement* in a programming language.

LUT *Lookup table.*

map A function that creates a new list by applying a function to every value in a list.

Marshaling Create a representation of a data value that can be stored on disc or transported across a network. See *Serialization.*

Merge Sort An efficient *divide and conquer* sorting algorithm. The algorithm is covered in Section 10.2.2 (page 328).

Method A *function* in the *namespace* of an *object.* Placing functions inside objects means that all the code needed to handle a particular sort of data can be placed in the class where that data is defined. This means that related code is kept together which makes programs easier to read and maintain. To call a method, the syntax <object>.<method>(<args>) is used. Here's an example:

```
>>> class Foo:
...     def my_method ( self ) :
...         print 'Foobar!'
...
>>> f = Foo ()
>>> f.my_method ()
Foobar!
>>>
```

Note that a critical difference between a method and any other variety of function is that methods always have at least one parameter. This first parameter is a reference to the *instance* the method was called on and is conventionally called *self.*

Module A file containing Python source code. Modules are the basic unit of code reuse in Python. A module is used by a Python program by loading it. The **import** command and the **from** command are the mechanisms for loading modules. To run functions from a module after it has been loaded using **import**, you need to specify the name of the module followed by a dot followed by the name of the function and parentheses (with any arguments). For example turtle.circle(100).

Monitor A code structuring technique for multi-threaded code. Monitors define *critical sections* at the programming language level rather than having to explicitly program mutual exclusion using *locks* or *semaphores.*

Multiple inheritance Where a *subclass* has more than one *superclass.* In Python multiple superclasses can be listed as comma-separated names in class definitions, like this:

```
class <name> ( <superclass1> , <superclass2> , ... ) :
    <statements>
```

Mutable Changeable. Lists are mutable sequences.

Named parameter The use of assignment in function calls to provide parameter values to specific parameter variables.

Namespace See *scope*.

Nested loop A loop inside another loop.

Node An element in a *tree* or *graph* that can have children and parents.

None A special object that is generally used to signify the absence of a value. For example, if a function or method does not explicitly return a value, the Python system will use the value None as the return value. The type of None is NoneType.

not The logical operator that is true when its operand is false and false when its operand is true.

Object An *instance* of a *class*. In the following example, obj is an instance of Foobar:

```
>>> class Foobar:
...    def __str__ ( self ) :
...          return 'foobar'
...
>>> obj = Foobar ( )
>>> print obj
foobar
>>>
```

Object-oriented programming Programming with objects, classes and inheritance.

OOP *Object-oriented programming.*

Operand An operand is an item on which an operation is performed.

Operating system The software that makes computer hardware usable by *applications.*

Operator An operator is a symbol representing some action to be performed.

or The logical operator that is true when one or more of its *operands* are true.

Overload Defines how an existing function or operator should behave when applied to a new type. In Python this is done by providing some special methods in a new class, for example:

```
>>> class Foobar:
...    def __init__ ( self ) :
...          self.foo = 'foobar'
...    def __add__ ( self , other ) :
...          return self.foo + other.foo
...
>>> f = Foobar ( )
```

```
>>> g = Foobar ( )
>>> f + g
'foobarfoobar'
>>>
```

Override To re-implement a method that has already been defined in a superclass.

Parameter A value passed from the caller of a function to the code of the function.

Parameter value The value of a parameter in the function call. Also known as *argument*.

Parameter variable The variable in the function definition that is a parameter.

Persistent Data that is preserved between different executions of a program. Opposite of *volatile*.

Pickle To serialize data. This term is specific to Python and derives from the name of the package – Pickle.

Pixel Truncation of picture element. A pixel is the smallest possible displayable part of an image. Each pixel has its own brightness and color. On most displays, pixels are sufficiently small that they appear to merge into a smooth image.

PNG *Portable network graphics.*

Polymorphism The situation in which *objects* of different types respond to *method* calls in their own, type-specific way.

Polymorphic function A function that works correctly for all types of parameter value.

Portable Network Graphics This is a lossless image file format that is very good for display screen dumps. See http://www.libpng.org/pub/png/.

Positional parameter A parameter value in a function call that is associated with a parameter variable in the function by its position in the parameter list.

Postcondition A *predicate* which a function is committed to meeting when it returns.

Precondition A *predicate* which should be True when a function is called. The precondition should be met by the code calling the function.

Predicate A function which returns a Boolean value.

Prime number A number that can be divided exactly only by itself and 1.

print Commands Python to print something.

PyUnit Python's *unit testing* framework. The *module* that implements the framework is called unittest. Documentation for PyUnit can be found at http://docs.python.org/lib/module-unittest.html

Quicksort A *divide and conquer* sorting algorithm that can perform very efficiently.The algorithm is covered in Section 10.2.2 (page 324).

Recursion An operation that is defined in terms of itself. A classic joke is that the dictionary definition should be:

> **recursion** *n.* see recursion.

Recursion depth The number of times a *recursive function* calls itself.

Recursive case The self-referential case in *recursion*.

Recursive function A function which calls itself. A recursive function should have a *base case* and an *recursive case* and should ensure its *termination condition* is achievable.

Red Term used in *unit testing* to indicate that some tests are failing.

Refactor The process of amending code that passes all its tests to improve the code but so that it continues to pass all its tests. The definitive definition is a quote from Martin Fowler:

> "Refactoring is a disciplined technique for restructuring an existing body of code, altering its internal structure without changing its external behavior. Its heart is a series of small behavior preserving transformations. Each transformation (called a 'refactoring') does little, but a sequence of transformations can produce a significant restructuring."

Referentially transparent A function is referentially transparent if it always returns the same value when called with the same arguments.

Regression When a feature that used to work stops working due to a change in the system.

Regression testing Testing that seeks to uncover regression bugs.

Regular expression A pattern for matching text.

reload Re-import a module which has already been imported:

```
import turtle
turtle.forward ( 100 )
turtle.left ( 90 )
reload ( turtle )
turtle.forward ( 100 )
turtle.left ( 90 )
```

Revision control system See *version control system*.

RGB Red–Green–Blue. This is a color model in which each pixel is represented by a three-tuple containing its red value, green value and blue value. For most computer systems, the RGB value is a 24-bit integer value comprised of three 8-bit values, one each for the red, green and blue value. Thus each of the red, green and blue values are in the range 0–255. This scheme allows 256^3 (16,777,216) different colors to be described.

Root node The *node* in a *tree* or *graph* that has no parent.

Scope The area of a program in which a particular variable can be referred to and modified.

Search Select one (single search) or all (exhaustive search) items from a sequence that match given criteria.

Selection Sort Simple sorting algorithm that repeatedly searches for the next lowest item to put into the correct sorted position. The algorithm is covered in Section 10.2.2 (page 321).

self The name conventionally used as the first *parameter* in all *methods*, it refers to the *object* the method is called on. When writing classes, self can be used to access data and methods. For example:

```
>>> class Num :
...    def __init__ ( self , num ) :
...          self.num = num
...    def __str__ ( self ) : return str ( self.num )
...
>>> n1 = Num ( 1 )
>>> n2 = Num ( 2 )
>>> print n1
1
>>> print n2
2
>>>
```

Semaphore A mechanism for managing shared resources using a variable to hold the state of the lock.

Semantic error A mistake in the meaning of a program.

Separation of concerns Structuring code into functions, modules or classes that do not overlap in responsibilities and actions.

Sequence An ordered data structure. Each item in the data structure has a position (*index*). In Python, *lists* are *mutable* sequences, while *tuples* and strings are *immutable* sequences.

Serialize To convert complex structures into representations that are simple to save, transmit, etc. See *marshaling* and *pickle*.

Set An unordered collection of items in which no item appears more than once. For example:

```
{1, 2, 3, 4}
{"Alice", "Bob", "Charlie"}
{True, False}
```

Shallow copy A copy of a data structure where only the storage for the structure itself is copied all the objects in the structure are shared with the original.

Shell An interface to the functions of an operating system, application or language.

Shelve To serialize and store items. This is a term specific to Python that stems from the name of a package.

Side effect A function has side effects if it alters the *state* outside its *scope*.

Signature The signature of a function comprises the name of the function and the number and type of the parameters of the function.

Simultaneous assignment Alternative name for *tuple assignment*.

Single inheritance The form of *inheritance* in which a *subclass* has exactly one *superclass*.

```
class <name> ( <superclass> ) :
    <statements>
```

Sort To take a *sequence* of items and arrange them in order.

Source code A program that is compiled to an intermediate form for execution or interpretation, or is interpreted directly.

Space complexity A measure of the amount of memory an algorithm will require to complete execution.

Specular reflection Perfect reflection from a surface – reflection where there is no loss of energy by the moving, reflected body.

Sprite A two-dimensional, usually pre-rendered, image that is used as part of a larger animation or game.

State The state of a program is the set of values of all the variables in that program. As statements execute the values are changed and so the state changes.

State space The set of all possible states that a program or machine can be in.

State transition The transition of a program or machine from one state to another. In programming this usually happens by making an assignment to a variable.

Statement A statement is the smallest complete program instruction.

String A *sequence* of characters.

Stub An incomplete 'placeholder' class or function that is completed later.

Subclass A subclass inherits all the data and *methods* of its *superclasses*. It may override some (by declaring new data and methods with the same names or signatures) and it may add new data and methods.

Substitution Replacing a variable name with its value, as part of a *walk-through*. This is usually written $[x \backslash 1]$ meaning "substitute 1 for 'x".

Subversion A centralized *version control system*. See http://subversion.tigris.org/.

Superclass A *class* from which *subclasses* are derived.

Syntax The rules governing the construction of *statements*.

Tail recursion A special case of *recursion* in which the recursive call is the last action of the body of the function. Some programming languages specially support tail recursion making it efficient for iteration as well as tail recursive algorithms.

Termination condition In *iteration* the *state* needed for iteration to stop. For *while statements* this means the condition needed for the Boolean expression to become false. In *recursion* the condition needed for the base case to apply and hence for the recursion to be complete.

TDD *Test-driven development.*

Test-driven development An approach to software development where every change to the system is preceded by creating a test. The new test creates a Red state, which leads to development of the system to achieve Green state.

Thread A thread of execution. An independent flow of control executing code. A program may have many threads all of which share the same code and data.

Time complexity A measure of how long an algorithm will take to complete execution.

Token The output of a lexer.

Top-down design A design approach that begins with a general, abstract plan and moves towards details.

Tree A non-linear data structure in which each *node* in the tree has some number of child nodes. In a tree a child can only have a single parent. A structure where the child can have multiple parents is a *graph*.

Truth table An enumeration of all possible inputs and all consequential outputs for Boolean-valued operators.

Tuple A type that stores an immutable ordered list of objects.

Tuple assignment Assigning values to two or more variables at once. For example:

```
x , y , z = 1 , 2 , 2 ** 3
```

Type The type of something describes the nature of that thing – the range of values it may have and the operations that may be performed on it.

Unary operator A unary operator is one that has a single *operand*.

Unit testing A method of testing in which each part of a program (often each *class* in a program) is tested separately. Usually, testing is implemented before the program is written and test cases are run every time the program is modified. In Python, unit testing can be implemented with the unittest module – known as PyUnit.

Variable A name that can refer to a value.

Version control system A store for directories and files that maintains a history of all the files. Examples of version control systems are Subversion and Bazaar.

Volatile Remaining only while the program is running. Opposite of *persistent*.

Walk-through The activity of looking through a program and determining what each line of code means without the help of a computer. This is often done by teams of programmers to check the quality of code and find bugs.

while Introduces a while statement that performs *iteration*. A while statement performs unbounded iteration in that there is no constraint on the condition.

> while *<condition>* :
>   *<body>*
> else :
>   *<statements>*

Whitespace Characters that are printable but do not leave a mark. Usually space, tab and newline.

Widget An element in a graphical user interface such as a button, menu item, text field, scroll bar, etc.

Xor Exclusive or. The logical operator that is true when either of its operands are true, but not both.

yield Statement used to return a value in a *generator function*.

__add__ The method to overload the + operator.

__and__ The method to overload the & operator.

__author__ The special variable in a module to hold details of the author.

__contains__ The method to overload the **in** operator.

__copyright__ The special variable in a module to hold details of the copyright holder(s) of the code.

__credits__ The special variable in a module to hold details of anyone who has contributed to developing a module.

__date__ The special variable in a module to hold the date that it was last modified.

__del__ The *destructor* method is called just as an object is about to be destroyed.

__div__ The method to overload the / operator.

__eq__ The method to overload the == operator.

__ge__ The method to overload the >= operator.

__gt__ The method to overload the > operator.

__init__ The *constructor* method is executed automatically when a new *object* is created.

__le__ The method to overload the <= operator.

__len__ The method to overload the len function.

__license__ The special variable in a module to hold details of which license the code is issued under. Example licences are GNU General Public License (GPL), Apache Software License (ASL), but there are many to choose from – see http://www.opensource.org/licenses

__lt__ The method to overload the < operator.

__mul__ The method to overload the * operator.

__name__ The special variable in a module which is automatically assigned either the name of the module which imported it or __main__ if the module has been run from the command line.

__ne__ The method to overload the != operator.

__or__ The method to overload the | operator.

__repr__ The method to tell Python how to represent an object as a string. This is a special, special method since there are conventions about what form the string should take. In effect, this method should write a string that can be parsed by the Python system to recreate the value.

__revision__ The special variable in a module to hold details of which revision of the software this is. See __version__.

__str__ The method to tell Python how to represent an object as a string. This method is called whenever a print *statement* or str function call occurs.

__sub__ The method to overload the - operator.

__xor__ The method to overload the ^ operator.

__version__ The special variable in a module to hold details of which version of the software this is.

Boolean Algebra

Operators in programming languages are generally founded on operations from algebras in mathematics – the arithmetic operators $+$, $-$, $\times$ and $\div$, for example, have, as their foundation, the mathematical algebras of integers and real numbers. As we mentioned in the aside on page 36, Boolean Algebra is the algebra of systems that have only two values. Boolean Algebra is the foundation for the Python **and**, **or**, and **not** operators.

The 'Laws'

Boolean Algebra differs from Algebra as we learnt in school. Boolean Algebra doesn't involve the arithmetic operators $+$, $-$, $\times$, and $\div$, instead it has the operators $\wedge$, $\vee$, and $\neg$: $\wedge$ and $\vee$ are binary operators (there are two operands) and $\neg$ is a unary operator (there is only one operand). The two values are represented as 0 (false) and 1 (true). It is usual to define what the operators do by enumerating all possibilities:

$$0 \wedge 0 = 0 \qquad 0 \vee 0 = 0$$
$$1 \wedge 0 = 0 \qquad 1 \vee 0 = 1 \qquad \neg 0 = 1$$
$$0 \wedge 1 = 0 \qquad 0 \vee 1 = 1 \qquad \neg 1 = 0$$
$$1 \wedge 1 = 1 \qquad 1 \vee 1 = 1$$

and then to present all the equations and 'laws':

Associativity	$a \vee (b \vee c) = (a \vee b) \vee c$	$a \wedge (b \wedge c) = (a \wedge b) \wedge c$
Commutativity	$a \vee b = b \vee a$	$a \wedge b = b \wedge a$
Absorption	$a \vee (a \wedge b) = a$	$a \wedge (a \vee b) = a$
Distributivity	$a \vee (b \wedge c) = (a \vee b) \wedge (a \vee c)$	$a \wedge (b \vee c) = (a \wedge b) \vee (a \wedge c)$
Complements	$a \vee \neg a = 1$	$a \wedge \neg a = 0$
Idempotency	$a \vee a = a$	$a \wedge a = a$
Boundedness	$a \vee 0 = a$	$a \wedge 0 = 0$
	$a \vee 1 = 1$	$a \wedge 1 = a$
De Morgan's Law	$\neg (a \vee b) = \neg a \wedge \neg b$	$\neg (a \wedge b) = \neg a \vee \neg b$
Involution	$\neg \neg a = a$	

where a, b, and c are mathematical variables that can have either the value 0 or 1, i.e. they are Boolean variables (of a mathematical rather than a Python nature).

Having the equations is all very well, but how can we think of the operators? What do they mean?

- The $\wedge$ operator is applied to two Boolean values as an infix, binary operator, and evaluates to true if both of the operands are true, otherwise it evaluates to false: both operands must be true for the result to be true, hence the name *and*.

- The $\vee$ operator is applied to two Boolean values as an infix, binary, operator, and evaluates to true if either of its operands are true: the result is true if either operand is true, hence the name *or*.

- The $\neg$ operator is applied to one Boolean value as a prefix, unary operator, and evaluates to true if the value is false and false if the value is true – it returns the opposite of the value it is applied to, hence the name *not*.

The Python operator **and** behaves like $\wedge$, **or** like $\vee$, and **not** like $\neg$.

Alternative Notations

Some of you (particularly those interested in digital electronics) may well be saying: "But that isn't the way Boolean Algebra is expressed." In fact there are many notations for representing Boolean Algebra. The one presented in the previous section is the most usual. However, many people, particularly people in the electronics field, prefer the notation where $\cdot$ is used for *and*, $+$ for *or* and $^-$ (a line over) for *not*. Using this notation, Boolean Algebra is expressed as:

$$
\begin{array}{lll}
0 \cdot 0 = 0 & 0 + 0 = 0 & \\
1 \cdot 0 = 0 & 1 + 0 = 1 & \bar{0} = 1 \\
0 \cdot 1 = 0 & 0 + 1 = 1 & \bar{1} = 0 \\
1 \cdot 1 = 1 & 1 + 1 = 1 &
\end{array}
$$

Associativity	$a + (b + c) = (a + b) + c$	$a \cdot (b \cdot c) = (a \cdot b) \cdot c$
Commutativity	$a + b = b + a$	$a \cdot b = b \cdot a$
Absorption	$a + (a \cdot b) = a$	$a \cdot (a + b) = a$
Distributivity	$a + (b \cdot c) = (a + b) \cdot (a + c)$	$a \cdot (b + c) = (a \cdot b) + (a \cdot c)$
Complements	$a + \bar{a} = 1$	$a \cdot \bar{a} = 0$
Idempotency	$a + a = a$	$a \cdot a = a$
Boundedness	$a + 0 = a$	$a \cdot 0 = 0$
	$a + 1 = 1$	$a \cdot 1 = a$
De Morgan's Law	$\overline{a + b} = \bar{a} \cdot \bar{b}$	$\overline{a \cdot b} = \bar{a} + \bar{b}$
Involution	$\bar{\bar{a}} = a$	

Another variant on the notation is to use a prime (′) after the variable instead of an overbar (¯) over the variable to represent *not*. Of course, the mathematics is exactly the same, it is just the way things are written that is different.

Expressions and Sub-expressions

Just as we can combine arithmetic expressions to create more complex expressions, we can combine Boolean expressions. So, for example, if we have Boolean expressions A and B (these are expressions involving variables, not just variables) then we can write an expression that evaluates to true if either A or B are true, but not both:

$$(A \lor B) \land (\neg(A \land B))$$

We have used parentheses to ensure that the evaluation order is totally unambiguous. It is normal to use parentheses in this sort of mathematics; although $\neg$ has a higher precedence that either $\land$ or $\lor$, it is normally assumed that $\land$ and $\lor$ have the same precedence, and so parenthesizing sub-expressions is necessary. With this in mind, one pair of the parentheses is not needed – we could have written:

$$(A \lor B) \land \neg(A \land B)$$

and the expression is still unambiguous. Removing any more parentheses though could lead to ambiguity.

This expression is the definition of *exclusive or* (often written *xor*) which is used a lot in digital electronics. Arguably even more used is the right-hand sub-expression:

$$\neg(A \land B)$$

This is the definition of *nand* (not-and), which is an important operation for computer hardware: many of the logic circuits making up computers are made from 'nand gates'.

Python and Boolean Algebra

So Boolean Algebra is the mathematics behind the Boolean expressions of Python. Why have the symbols **and**, **or**, and **not** for the Boolean operations in Python? It is very simple: the symbols $\land$, $\lor$ and $\neg$ don't appear on the keyboard ($\neg$ does in fact appear on some keyboards) so Python uses the words **and**, **or**, and **not**.

As we have shown, the values in Boolean Algebra are generally 0 and 1. We have shown that Python uses **False** and **True**. In fact, Python also allows the literals 0 and 1 to be used for **False** and **True** respectively. However, it is perhaps best always to use **False** and **True**, since they are clear and obvious to readers of the programs, whereas 0 and 1 could be taken for integers.

The Game Functions Module

Here is the source of the game_functions module:

```
"""
Functions common to many games built with PyGame.
"""

__author__ = '''Sarah Mount <s.mount@wlv.ac.uk>
Amendments by Russel Winder <russel.winder@concertant.com>'''
__date__ = '2007-06-08'
__version__ = '1.1'
__copyright__ = 'Copyright (c) 2005, 2007 Sarah Mount'
__licence__ = 'GNU General Public Licence (GPL)'

import pygame , sys
from pygame.locals import *

def load_png ( filename ) :
    """ Load a PNG image and return an image object and its rect."""
    try:
        image = pygame.image.load ( filename )
        if image.get_alpha ( ) is None : image = image.convert ( )
        else : image = image.convert_alpha ( )
    except pygame.error, message :
        print 'Cannot load image:' , filename
        raise SystemExit , message
    return image , image.get_rect ( )

def loading ( screen , fgcol = ( 255 , 255 , 255 ) ) :
    """Tells the user that the game is loading."""
    font = pygame.font.Font ( None , 36 )
    msg = 'Game loading ...'
    text = font.render ( msg , 1 , fgcol )
    textpos = text.get_rect ( )
    textpos.center = screen.get_rect ( ).center
    screen.blit ( text , textpos )
    pygame.display.update ( textpos )
```

```python
def start ( screen , game = '' , fgcol = ( 255 , 255 , 255 ) , bgcol = ( 0 , 0 , 0 ) ) :
    """Asks the user to start the game."""
    font = pygame.font.Font ( None , 36 )
    msg = 'Press any key to start playing ' + game + '...'
    text = font.render ( msg , 1 , fgcol )
    textpos = text.get_rect ()
    textpos.center = screen.get_rect ().center
    screen.blit ( text , textpos )
    pygame.display.update ( textpos )
    pygame.event.pump ()
    event = pygame.event.wait ()
    while not event.type == KEYDOWN : event = pygame.event.wait ()
    screen.fill ( bgcol , textpos )
    pygame.display.update ( textpos )

def display_score ( screen , score , fgcol = ( 255 , 255 , 255 ) , bgcol = ( 0 , 0 , 0 ) ) :
    """Displays the current score."""
    font = pygame.font.Font ( None , 36 )
    text = font.render ( 'Score: '+str ( score ) , 1 , fgcol )
    textpos = text.get_rect ()
    textpos.center = ( screen.get_size ()[0] / 2 , 20)
    screen.fill ( bgcol , textpos )
    screen.blit ( text , textpos )
    pygame.display.update ( textpos )

def lose ( screen , fgcol = ( 255 , 255 , 255 ) , credits = None , fade = 1500 ) :
    """Called when the player loses the game. Fades out any music that might be
    playing and (optionally) displays author credits."""
    font = pygame.font.Font ( None , 36 )
    text = font.render ( 'Game Over!' , 1 , fgcol )
    scr = screen.get_rect ().center
    textpos = text.get_rect ()
    textpos.center = scr
    screen.blit ( text , textpos )
    pygame.display.update ( textpos )
    if ( not credits == None ) and ( len ( credits ) > 0 ) :
        text = font.render ( 'Credits:' , 1 , fgcol )
        textpos = text.get_rect ()
        textpos.center = ( scr[0] , scr[1] + ( 36 * 2 ) )
        screen.blit ( text , textpos )
        pygame.display.update ( textpos )
        for i in range ( len ( credits ) ) :
            text = font.render ( credits[i] , 1 , fgcol )
            textpos = text.get_rect ()
            textpos.center = ( scr[0] , scr[1] + ( 36 * ( i + 3 ) ) )
            screen.blit ( text , textpos )
            pygame.display.update ( textpos )
    pygame.mixer.fadeout ( fade )
    event = pygame.event.wait ()
    while not event.type == QUIT :
        event = pygame.event.wait ()
    sys.exit ()
```

Index

Milton Keynes UK
Ingram Content Group UK Ltd.
UKHW052101141024
449526UK00001B/3

9 781844 807017